HONDA

XL/XR250-600 SINGLES · 1978-1983
SERVICE · REPAIR · PERFORMANCE

By
ED SCOTT

SYDNIE A. WAUSON
Editor

JEFF ROBINSON
Publisher

CLYMER PUBLICATIONS

*World's largest publisher of books devoted exclusively to
automobiles and motorcycles.*

12860 MUSCATINE STREET · P.O. BOX 20 · ARLETA, CALIFORNIA 91331

FIRST EDITION
First Printing March, 1980
Second Printing May, 1980

SECOND EDITION
First Printing February, 1981

THIRD EDITION
Revised by Ed Scott to include 1981 models
First Printing July, 1982

FOURTH EDITION
Revised by Ed Scott to include 1982-1983 models
First Printing December, 1983

Printed in U.S.A.

ISBN: 0-89287-310-8

MOTORCYCLE INDUSTRY COUNCIL

Production Coordinator, Victor Williams

*COVER: Photographed by Michael Brown Photographic Productions, Los Angeles, California. Ridden by Brad
Zimmerman. Helmet courtesy of Simpson Helmets, Torrance, California. Boots courtesy of Scott U.S.A., Sun
Valley, Idaho.*

CONTENTS

QUICK REFERENCE DATA

TUNE-UP SPECIFICATIONS

Valve clearance	
Intake	
XR250	0.003 in. (0.08 mm)
All other models	0.002 in. (0.05 mm)
Exhaust	
XR350R	0.003 in. (0.08 mm)
All other models	0.004 in. (0.10 mm)
Compression pressure	
XR250, XR250R	192 psi (13.5 kg/cm^2)
All other models	175 psi (12.5 kg/cm^2)
Spark plug type (standard)	
1978-1981	ND X24ES-U or NGK D8EA
1982	ND X24ESR-U or NGK DR8ES-L
1983	ND X24EPR-U9 or NGK DPR8EA-9
Spark plug gap	
1978-1982	0.6-0.7 mm (0.024-0.028 in.)
1983	0.8-0.9 mm (0.032-0.036 in.)
Ignition timing	"F" mark @ 1,200 ±100 rpm
Idle speed	1,200 ±100 rpm

TIRE INFLATION PRESSURE*

| Tire size | Air pressure | |
	psi	kg/cm^2
Front tire		
3.00-21 6PR	14	1.0
3.00-21 4PR	21	1.5
3.00-23 4 PR	21	1.5
90/80-21 6PR	15	1.03
Rear tire		
5.10-17 6PR	15	1.03
5.10-17 4PR	21	1.5
4.60-18 4PR	21	1.5
4.60-18 6PR	17	1.2
130/80-17 6PR	15	1.0

* Tire inflation pressure for factory equipped tires. Aftermarket tire inflation pressure may vary according to manufacturer's instructions.

ENGINE OIL CAPACITY

| Engine size | Oil drain | | Rebuild | |
	U.S. qt.	Liter	U.S. qt.	Liter
250 cc	1.6	1.5	2.1	2.0
350 cc	1.9	1.8	2.1	2.0
500 cc (1979-1982)	1.6	1.5	2.1	2.0
500, 600 cc (1983)	2.1	2.0	2.6	2.5

FRONT FORK AIR PRESSURE

Model	psi	kg/cm^2
1982 XL250R	0-2.8	0-0.2
1982 XL500R		
XL600R, XR350R	0	0
1983 XR500R	0-14	0.98

FRONT FORK OIL CAPACITY*

Model	Standard Capacity		Standard distance from top of fork	
	cc	fl. oz.	mm	in.
XL250S	190	6.4	–	–
XL250R	300	10.14	173	6.81
XR250R				
1981	368	12.4	152	6
1982	395	13.4	156	6.125
XR250	202	6.8	–	–
XR350R	553	18.7	132	5.2
XR500	202	6.8	–	–
XL500S	190	6.4	–	–
XL500R	379	12.75	163	6.42
XR500R				
1981-1982	345	11.7	181	7.1
1983	651	22	141	5.5
XL600R	455	15.4	150	5.9

* Capacity for each fork leg.

REPLACEMENT BULBS*

Model	Headlight	Taillight/ brakelight	Turn signal
XL250S	6V 35/36.5W	6V/32W	6V/18W
XL250R	12V 35/36.5W	12V/32W	12V/23W
XR250	6V 25/25W	6V/6/3	–
XR250R	6V 25/25W	6V/3W	–
XR350R			
Standard	6V/35W	6V/3W	–
Optional	12V/55W	12V/3.4W	–
XL500S	6V 35/36.5W	6V/32W	6V/17W
XL500R	12V 35/36.5W	12V/32W	12V/23W
XR500	6V 25/25W	6V/6/3	–
XR500R			
1981-1982	6V 25/25W	6V/3W	–
1983	12V 25/25W	12V/3W	–
XL600R	H4JA 12V/60/55W	12V/32W	12V/23

*All indicator and illumination bulbs 6V or 12V and 1.7W or 3W.

DRIVE CHAIN REPLACEMENT NUMBERS

Model	Standard
XL250S	102L
XL250R	520VC-102L
XR250	102L
XR250R	520DS-106RJ
XR350R	520MS-104FJ
XL500S	520KD-96
XL500R	520VS-100LE
XR500	DID520KD-100L or DID520KD-102L
XR500R	520KO-104FJ
XL600R	520VS-104CE or 520SO-104LE

HONDA

XL/XR250-600 SINGLES · 1978-1983
SERVICE · REPAIR · PERFORMANCE

CHAPTER ONE

GENERAL INFORMATION

This detailed, comprehensive manual covers the Honda XL250S, XL250R, XR250, XR250R, XR350R, XL500S, XL500R, XR500, XR500R and XL600R. The XL series is street-legal but is also suited for the dirt. It has a quiet exhaust system, small carburetor(s) (some models have an accelerator pump) and conservative ignition timing. It has a heavier alternator flywheel than the XR models, which allows it to idle smoothly. The XL models have a battery and all the necessary lighting equipment for use on the street.

The XR series is strictly for off-road use. Being a competition-oriented machine, it has a noisier, less restrictive muffler, larger carburetor(s), tighter gearing and hotter ignition timing than the XL models. For better throttle response it has a lighter alternator flywheel.

The expert text gives complete information on maintenance, tune-up, repair, overhaul and performance improvement. Hundreds of photos and drawings guide you through every step. The book includes all you need to know to keep your Honda running right. Throughout this book where differences occur among the models, they are clearly identified.

A shop manual is a reference. You want to be able to find information fast. As in all Clymer books, this one is designed with you in mind. All chapters are thumb tabbed. Important items are extensively indexed at the rear of this book. All most frequently used specifications and capacities are summarized on the blue *Quick Reference Data* pages at the front of the book.

Keep the book handy in your tool box. It will help you to better understand your Honda, lower repair and maintenance costs, keep your fuel efficiency up to where it belongs and generally improve your satisfaction with your bike.

Refer to **Figures 1A** and **1B** for locations of major controls and components.

MANUAL ORGANIZATION

All dimensions and capacities are expressed in English units familiar to U.S. mechanics as well as in metric units.

This chapter provides general information and discusses equipment and tools useful both for preventive maintenance and troubleshooting. **Table 1**, at the end of the chapter, contains model designation information.

Chapter Two provides methods and suggestions for quick and accurate diagnosis and repair of problems. Troubleshooting procedures discuss typical symptoms and logical methods to pinpoint the trouble.

Chapter Three explains all periodic lubrication and routine maintenance necessary to keep your bike running well. Chapter Three also includes recommended tune-up procedures, eliminating the need to constantly consult chapters on the various assemblies.

Subsequent chapters describe specific systems such as the engine, transmission and electrical system. Each chapter provides disassembly, repair and assembly procedures in simple step-by-step form. If a repair is impractical for a home

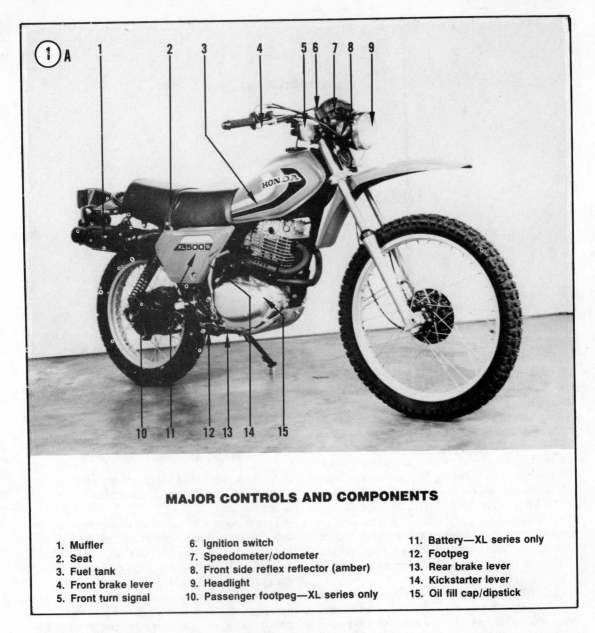

MAJOR CONTROLS AND COMPONENTS

1. Muffler
2. Seat
3. Fuel tank
4. Front brake lever
5. Front turn signal

6. Ignition switch
7. Speedometer/odometer
8. Front side reflex reflector (amber)
9. Headlight
10. Passenger footpeg—XL series only

11. Battery—XL series only
12. Footpeg
13. Rear brake lever
14. Kickstarter lever
15. Oil fill cap/dipstick

mechanic, it is so indicated. It is usually faster and less expensive to take such repairs to a dealer or competent machine shop. Specifications concerning a particular system are included at the end of the appropriate chapter.

Some of the procedures in this manual specify special tools. In all cases, the tool is illustrated either in actual use or alone. A well-equipped mechanic may find he can substitute similar tools already on hand or can fabricate his own.

The terms NOTE, CAUTION and WARNING have specific meanings in this manual. A NOTE provides additional information to make a step or procedure easier or clearer. Disregarding a NOTE could cause inconvenience, but would not cause damage or personal injury.

A CAUTION emphasizes areas where equipment damage could result. Disregarding a CAUTION could cause permanent mechanical damage; however, personal injury is unlikely.

A WARNING emphsizes areas where personal injury or even death could result from negligence. Mechanical damage may also occur. WARNINGS *are to be taken seriously.* In some cases, serious injury or death has resulted from disregarding similar warnings.

MAJOR CONTROLS AND COMPONENTS

16. Clutch lever
17. Headlight dimmer, turn signal
18. Choke knob
19. Fuel fill cap
20. Engine kill switch
21. Throttle grip/control
22. Shock absorber adjustment

23. Rear turn signal—XL series only
24. Tail/brakelight and rear reflex
     reflector (red)—XL series only;
     taillight only—XR series
25. Speedometer drive housing
26. Fuel shut-off valve
27. Ignition timing inspection hole

28. Gear shift lever
29. Side stand
30. Air cleaner element
31. Helmet lock
32. Tool box—XL series only
     (XR series located on rear
     fender)

Throughout this manual, keep in mind two conventions. "Front" refers to the front of the bike. The front of any component, such as the engine, is the end which faces toward the front of the bike. The "left" and "right" sides refer to a person sitting on the bike facing forward. For example, the shift lever is on the left side. These rules are simple, but even experienced mechanics occasionally become disoriented.

SERVICE HINTS

Most of the service procedures covered are straightforward and can be performed by anyone reasonably handy with tools. It is suggested, however, that you consider your own capabilities carefully before attempting any operation involving major disassembly of the engine.

Some operations, for example, require the use of a press. It would be wiser to have these performed by a shop equipped for such work than to try to do the job yourself with makeshift equipment. Other procedures require precise measurements. Unless you have the skills and equipment required, it would be better to have a qualified repair shop make the measurements for you.

Repairs go much faster and easier if your machine is clean before you begin work. There are special cleaners, such as Gunk Cycle Degreaser, for washing the engine and related parts. Just brush or spray on the cleaning solution, let it stand, then rinse it away with a garden hose. Clean all oily or greasy parts with cleaning solvent as you remove them.

WARNING
Never use gasoline as a cleaning agent. It presents an extreme fire hazard. Be sure to work in a well-ventilated area when using cleaning solvent. Keep a fire extinguisher, rated for gasoline fires, handy in any case.

Special tools are required for some repair procedures. These may be purchased at a dealer, rented from a tool rental dealer or fabricated by a mechanic or machinist, often at considerable savings.

Much of the labor charge for repairs made by dealers is for removal and disassembly of other parts to reach the defective unit. Is is frequently possible to perform preliminary operations yourself and then take the defective unit to the dealer for repair at considerable savings.

Once you have decided to tackle the job yourself, read the entire section in this manual which pertains to it, making sure you have identified the proper one. Study the illustrations and text until you have a good idea of what is involved in completing the job satisfactorily. If special tools are required, make the arrangements to get them before you start. It is frustrating and time-consuming to get partly into a job and then be unable to complete it.

Simple wiring checks can be easily made at home, but knowledge of electronics is almost a necessity for performing tests with complicated electronic testing gear.

During disassembly of parts, keep a few general cautions in mind. Force is rarely needed to get things apart. If parts are a tight fit, such as a bearing in a case, there is usually a tool designed to separate them. Never use a screwdriver to pry apart parts with machined surfaces such as

crankcase halves and cam cover. You will mar the surfaces and end up with leaks.

Make diagrams wherever similar-appearing parts are found. For instance, case cover screws are often not the same length. You may think you can remember where everything came from—but mistakes are costly. There is also the possibility you may be sidetracked and not return to work for days or even weeks, in which interval, carefully laid out parts may have become disturbed.

Tag all similar parts for location and mark all mating parts for position. Record number and thickness of any shims as they are removed. Small parts, such as bolts, can be identified by placing them in plastic sandwich bags. Seal and label the bags with masking tape.

Wiring should be tagged with masking tape and marked as each wire is removed. Again, do not rely on memory alone.

Protect finished surfaces from physical damage or corrosion. Keep gasoline off painted surfaces.

Frozen or very tight bolts and screws can often be loosened by soaking with penetrating oil, such as WD-40 or Liquid Wrench, then sharply striking the bolt head a few times with a hammer and punch (or screwdriver for screws). Avoid heat unless absolutely necessary, since it may melt, warp or remover the temper from many parts.

Avoid flames or sparks when working near a charging battery or flammable liquids such as gasoline.

No parts, except those assembled with a press fit, require unusual force during assembly. If a part is hard to remove or install, find out why before proceeding.

Cover all openings after removing parts to keep dirt, small tools, etc., from falling in.

When assembling two parts, start all fasteners, then tighten evenly.

Clutch plates, wiring connections and brake shoes and drums should be kept clean and free of grease and oil.

When assembling parts, be sure all shims and washers are installed exactly as they came out.

Whenever a rotating part butts against the stationary part, look for a shim or washer. Use new gaskets if there is any doubt about the condition of old ones. Generally, you should apply gaskets cement to one mating surface only so the parts may be easily disassembled in the future. A thin coat of oil on gaskets helps them seal effectively.

Heavy grease can be used to hold small parts in place if they tend to fall out during assembly. However, keep grease and oil away from electrical components or brake shoes and drums.

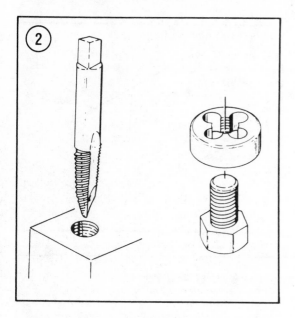

High spots may be sanded off a piston with sandpaper, but emery cloth and oil do a much more professional job.

Carburetors are best cleaned by disassembling them and soaking the parts in a commercial carburetor cleaner. Never soak gaskets and rubber parts in these cleaners. Never use wire to clean out jets and air passages; they are easily damaged. Use compressed air to blow out the carburetor only if the float has been removed first.

A baby bottle makes a good measuring device for adding oil to forks and engines. Get one that is graduated in ounces and cubic centimeters.

Take your time and do the job right. Do not forget that a newly rebuilt motorcycle engine must be broken in the same as a new one. Keep rpm within the limits given in your owner's manual.

TORQUE SPECIFICATIONS

Torque specifications throughout this manual are given in foot-pounds (ft.-lb.) and Newton meters (N•m). Newton meters are being adopted in place of meter-kilograms (mkg) in accordance with the *International Modernized Metric System*. Tool manufacturers are producing torque wrenches calibrated in Newton meters and Sears has a complete line calibrated in both of these values.

Existing torque wrenches, calibrated in meter-kilograms, can be used by performing a simple conversion. All you have to do is move the decimal point one place to the right; for example, 4.7 mkg = 47 N•m. This conversion is sufficient for use in this manual even though the exact mathematical conversion is 3.5 mkg=34.3 N•m.

SAFETY FIRST

Professional motorcycle mechanics can work for years and never sustain a serious injury. If you observe a few rules of common sense and safety, you can enjoy many hours of servicing your own machine. You could hurt yourself or damage the bike if you ignore these rules.

1. Never use gasoline as a cleaning solvent.
2. Never smoke or use a torch in the vicinity of flammable liquids such as cleaning solvent in open containers.
3. Never smoke or use a torch in an area where batteries are being charged. Highly explosive hydrogen gas is formed during the charging process.
4. If welding or brazing is required on the machine, remove the fuel tank to a safe distance, at least 50 feet away. Welding on gas tanks requires special safety procedures and must be performed by someone skilled in the process.
5. Use the proper sized wrenches to avoid damage to nuts and injury to yourself.
6. When loosening a tight or stuck nut, be guided by what would happen if the wrench should slip. Protect yourself accordingly.
7. Keep your work area clean and uncluttered.
8. Wear safety goggles during all operations involving drilling, grinding or use of a cold chisel.
9. Never use worn tools.
10. Keep a fire extinguisher handy and be sure it is rated for gasoline and electrical fires.

MECHANIC'S TIPS

Removing Frozen Nuts and Screws

When a fastener rusts and cannot be removed, several methods may be used to loosen it. First, apply penetrating oil such as Liquid Wrench or WD-40 (available at any hardware or auto supply store). Apply it liberally. Rap the fastener several times with a small hammer; do not hit it hard enough to cause damage.

For frozen screws, apply penetrating oil as described, then insert a screwdriver in the slot and rap the top of the screwdriver with a hammer. This loosens the rust so the screw can be removed in the normal way. If the screw head is too chewed up to use a screwdriver, grip the head with Vise Grip pliers and twist screw out.

Remedying Stripped Threads

Occasionally, threads are stripped through carelessness or impact damage. Often the threads can be cleaned up by running a tap (for internal threads on nuts) or die (for external threads on bolts through threads. See **Figure 2**.

Removing Broken Screws or Bolts

When the head breaks off a screw or bolt, several methods are available for removing the remaining portion.

If a large portion of the remainder projects out, try gripping it with Vise Grips. If the projecting portion is too small, try filing it to fit a wrench or cut a slot in it to fit a screwdriver. See **Figure 3**.

If the head breaks off flush, try using a screw extractor. To do this, centerpunch the exact center of the remaining portion of the screw or bolt. Drill a small hole in the screw and tap the extractor into the hole. Back the screw out with a wrench on the extractor. See **Figure 4**.

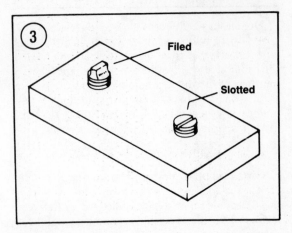

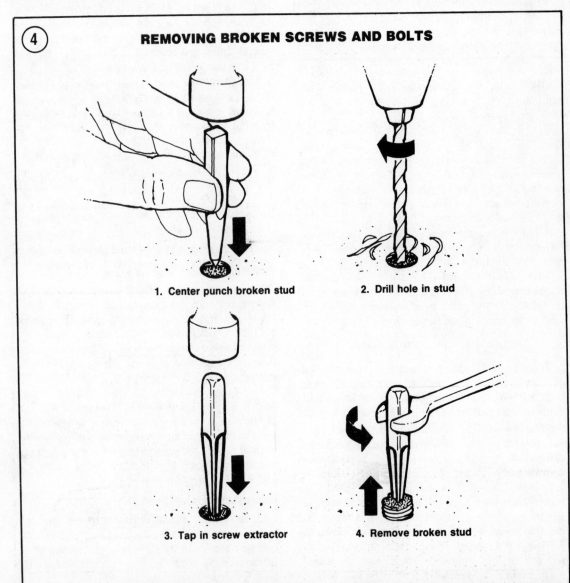

REMOVING BROKEN SCREWS AND BOLTS

1. Center punch broken stud

2. Drill hole in stud

3. Tap in screw extractor

4. Remove broken stud

PARTS REPLACEMENT

Honda makes frequent changes during a model year—some minor, some relatively major. When you order parts from the dealer or other parts distributor, always order by engine and chassis number. Write the numbers down and carry them with you. Compare new parts to old before purchasing them. If they are not alike, have the parts manager explain the difference to you.

EXPENDABLE SUPPLIES

Certain expendable supplies are also required. These include grease, oil, gasket cement, wiping rags, cleaning solvent and distilled water. Ask your dealer for the special compounds, silicone lubricants and commercial chain lube products which make motorcycle maintenance simpler and easier (**Figure 5**). Solvent is available at most service stations and distilled water for the battery is available at most supermarkets.

TOOLS

To properly service your motorcycle, you will need an assortment of ordinary hand tools. As a minimum, these include:

a. Combination wrench.
b. Socket wrenches.
c. Plastic mallet.
d. Small hammer.
e. Snap ring pliers.
f. Phillips screwdrivers.
g. Slot screwdrivers.
h. Impact driver.
i. Pliers.
j. Feeler gauges.
k. Spark plug gauge.
l. Spark plug wrench.
m. Drift.
n. Torque wrench.
o. Allen wrenches.

Engine tune-up and troubleshooting procedures require a few more tools, described in the following sections.

Hydrometer

This instrument measures state of charge of the battery and tells much about battery conditions. Such an instrument is available at any auto parts store and thorough most larger mail order outlets. See **Figure 6**.

Multimeter or VOM

This instrument (**Figure 7**) is invaluable for electrical system troubleshooting and service. A few of its functions may be duplicated by locally fabricated substitutes, but for the serious hobbyist, it is a must. Its uses are described in the applicable sections of this book. Multimeters are available at electronic hobby stores and mail order outlets.

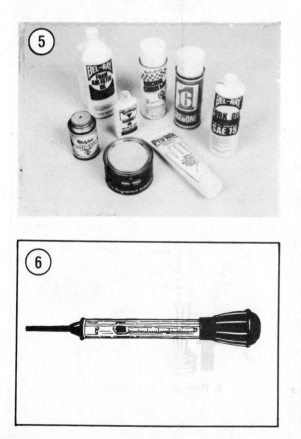

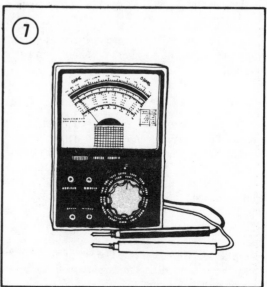

Compression Gauge

An engine with low compression cannot be properly tuned and will not develop full power. A compression gauge measures engine compression. The one shown in **Figure 8** is the press-in type suitable for this Honda. These are available at auto accessory stores or by mail order from large catalog order firms.

Impact Driver

This tool makes removal of engine components easy and eliminates damage to bolt and Phillips screw heads. Good ones are available at larger hardware stores. See **Figure 9**.

Ignition Gauge

This tool has round wire gauges for measuring spark plug gap. See **Figure 10**.

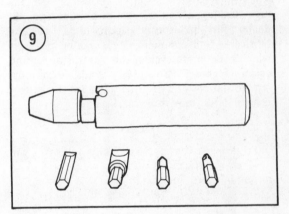

Strobe Timing Light

This instrument is necessary for tuning. By flashing a light at the precise instant the cylinder fires, the position of the timing advancer at that instant can be seen. Marks on the timing advancer are lined up with the timing mark while the engine is running.

Suitable lights range from inexpensive neon bulb types to powerful xenon strobe lights. See **Figure 11**. Neon timing lights lights are difficult to see and must be use in dimly lit areas. Xenon strobe timing lights can be use outside in bright sunlight. Both types work on this motorcycle; use according to the manufacturer's instructions.

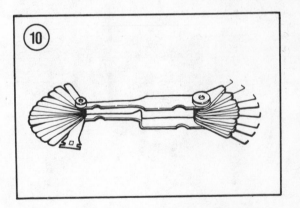

Other Special Tools

A few other special tools may be required for major service. These are described in the appropriate chapters and are available from Honda dealers.

SERIAL NUMBERS

You must know the bike's serial numbers for registration purposes and when ordering parts.

The frame serial number is stamped on the right-hand side of the steering head (**Figure 12**). The engine serial number is stamped on the lower left-hand side (**Figure 13**) of the crankcase adjacent to the shift lever on 1983 XR350R, XR500R and XL600R models. On all other models, the engine serial number is located on the top surface of the crankcase (**Figure 14**). The carburetor serial number is located on the carburetor body next to the float bowl (**Figure 15**).

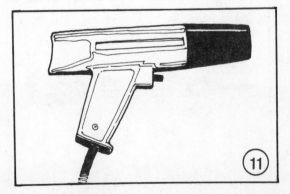

1

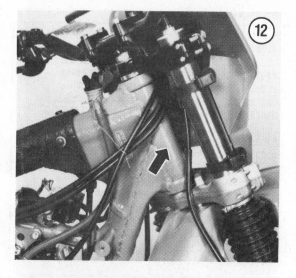

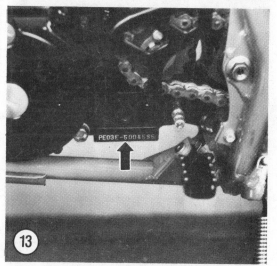

Table 1 MODEL, YEAR AND FRAME NUMBER

Model	Year	Engine begining serial number	Frame begining serial number
XL250S	1978 1979 1980 1981	L250SE-5000094-on L250SE-5100007-on MD01E-5200001-on MD01E-5300001-on	L250S-500071-on L250S-510007-on MD01-5200001-on MD010-BM300001-on
XL250R	1982 1983	MD03E-5000005-on MD03E-5100001-on	MD030-CM000002-on MD030-DM100001-on
XR250	1979 1980	ME01E-5000040-on ME01E-5100001-on	MD01-5000032-on MD01-5100001-on
XR250R	1981 1982	ME01E-5200010-on ME01E-5300001-on	MD010-BM200010-on MD010-CM300001-on
XR350R	1983	NE01E-5000033-on	NE010-DM000023-on
XL500S	1979 1980 1981	PD01E-5000057-on PD01E-5100001-on PD01E-5200001-on	PD01-5000054-on PD01-5100001-on PD01-BM200001-on
XL500R	1982	PD02E-5000006-on	PD020-CM500006-on
XR500	1979 1980	PE01E-5000001-on PE01E-5100001-on	PE01-5000001-on PE01-5100001-on
XR500R	1981 1982 1983	PE01E-5200014-on PE01E-5300001-on PE03E-5000034-on	PE010-BM200009-on PE010-CM300001-on PE030-DM000022-on
XL600R	1983	PD03E-5000053-on	PD030-DM000027-on

CHAPTER TWO

TROUBLESHOOTING

Diagnosing mechanical problems is relatively simple if you use orderly procedures and keep a few basic principles in mind.

The troubleshooting procedures in this chapter analyze typical symptoms and show logical methods of isolating causes. These are not the only methods. There may be several ways to solve a problem, but only a systematic, methodical approach can guarantee success.

Never assume anything. Do not overlook the obvious. If you are riding along and the bike suddenly quits, check the easiest, most accessible problem spots first. Is there gasoline in the tank? Is the shutoff in the ON or RESERVE position? Has a spark plug wire fallen off? Check the ignition switch. Sometimes the weight of keys on a key ring may turn the ignition off suddenly.

If nothing obvious turns up in a cursory check, look a little further. Learning to recognize and describe symptoms will make repairs easier for you or a mechanic at the shop. Describe problems accurately and fully. Saying that "it won't run" isn't the same as saying "it quit on the highway at high speed and wouldn't start" or that "it sat in my garage for three months and then wouldn't start."

Gather as many symptoms together as possible to aid in diagnosis. Note whether the engine lost power gradually or all at once, what color smoke (if any) came from exhaust, and so on. Remember that the more complicated a machine is, the easier it is to troubleshoot because symptoms point to specific problems.

After the symptoms are defined, areas which could cause the problems are tested and analyzed. Guessing at the cause of a problem may provide the solution, but it can also lead to frustration, wasted time and a series of expensive, unnecessary parts replacement.

You do not need fancy equipment or complicated test gear to determine whether repairs can be attempted at home. A few simple checks could save a large repair bill and time lost while the bike sits in a dealer's service department. On the other hand, be realistic and do not attempt repairs beyond your abilities. Service departments tend to charge heavily for putting together a disassembled engine that may have been abused. Some won't even take on such a job, so use common sense; don't get in over your head.

OPERATING REQUIREMENTS

An engine needs three basics to run properly: correct fuel-air mixture, compression and a spark at the right time. If one or more are missing, the engine won't run. The electrical system is the weakest link of the three basics. More problems result from electrical breakdowns than from any other source. Keep that in mind before you begin tampering with carburetor adjustments and the like.

If a bike has been sitting for any length of time and refuses to start, install a fresh spark plug and then look to the gasoline delivery system. This includes the tank, fuel shut-off valve, lines and the carburetor. Rust may have formed in the tank, obstructing fuel flow. Gasoline deposits may have gummed up carburetor jets and air passages. Gasoline tends to lose its potency after standing for long periods. Condensation may contaminate it with water. Drain old gas and try starting with a fresh tankful.

TROUBLESHOOTING INSTRUMENTS

Chapter One lists many of the instruments needed.

EMERGENCY TROUBLESHOOTING

When the bike is difficult to start or won't start at all, it does not help to wear out your leg on the kickstarter. Check for obvious problems even before getting out your tools. Go down the following list step-by-step. Do each one; you may be embarrassed to find your kill switch off, but that is better than wearing out your leg. If the bike still will not start, refer to the appropriate troubleshooting procedures which follow in this chapter.

1. Is there fuel in the tank? Remove the filler cap and rock the bike; listen for fuel sloshing around.

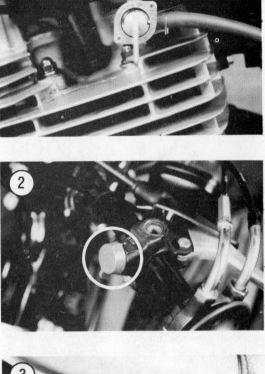

> *WARNING*
> *Do not use an open flame to check in the tank. A serious explosion is certain to result.*

2. Is the fuel shutoff valve in the ON position (**Figure 1**)? Turn to RES to be sure that you get the last remaining gas.
3. Is the engine kill switch in the RUN position (**Figure 2**)?
4. Is the spark plug wire on tight (**Figure 3**)? Push on it and slightly rotate it to clean the electrical connection between the plug and the connector.

Pull off a spark plug cap, remove the spark plug and reconnect the cap. Lay the plug against the cylinder head so its base makes a good connection and turn the engine over with the kickstarter. A fat, blue spark should jump across the electrodes. If there is no spark or only a weak one, there is electrical system trouble. Check for a defective plug by replacing it with a known good one. Don't assume a plug is good just because it is new.

5. Is the choke in the right position? On 1983 XR350R, XR500R and XL600R models, the choke lever should be in the raised position for a cold engine. On all other models, the choke knob should be pulled up (**Figure 4**) for a cold engine. On a warm engine the lever should be lowered or the knob pushed down.

> *NOTE*
> *Do not run a warm engine with the choke lever or knob in the half-way or the fully open position. This will result in excessive exhaust emissions and will give poor performance and gas mileage.*

6. Is the vent tube (**Figure 5**) from the fuel fill cap blocked?
7. On XL models, has the main fuse blown (**Figure 6**)? Replace it with a good one.

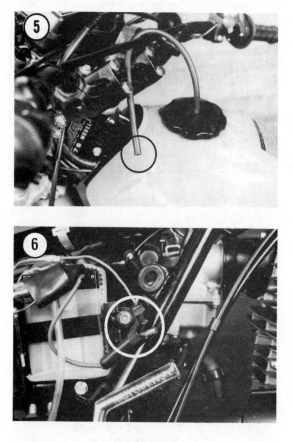

ENGINE

These procedures assume the kickstarter cranks the engine over normally.

Poor Performance

1. *Engine misses erratically at all speeds*—Intermittent trouble like this can be difficult to find. The fault could be in the ignition system, exhaust system (exhaust restriction) or fuel system. Follow troubleshooting procedures for these systems carefully to isolate the trouble.
2. *Engine misses at idle only*—Trouble could exist anywhere in ignition system. Refer to *Ignition System* in Chapter Eight. Trouble could exist in the carburetor idle circuits.
3. *Engine misses at high speed only*—Trouble could exist in the fuel system or ignition system. Check the fuel lines, etc., as described under *Fuel System Troubleshooting*. Also check spark plugs and wires. Refer to *Ignition System* in Chapter Eight.
4. *Poor performance at all speeds, lack of acceleration*—Trouble usually exists in ignition or fuel system. Check each with the appropriate troubleshooting procedure.

5. *Excessive fuel consumption*—This can be cause by a wide variety of seemingly unrelated factors. Check for clutch slippage, brake drag and defective wheel bearings. Check ignition and fuel systems.

Engine Noises

1. *Valve clatter*—This is a light to heavy tapping sound from under the cam cover. It is usually caused by excessive valve clearance. Adjust clearance as described under *Valve Clearance Adjustment* in Chapter Three.
2. *Knocking or pinging during acceleration*—Caused by using a lower octane fuel than recommended. May also be caused by poor fuel available at some "discount" gasoline stations. Pinging can also be caused by spark plugs of the wrong heat range. Refer to *Spark Plug Heat Range* in Chapter Three.
3. *Slapping or rattling noises at low speed or during acceleration*—May be caused by piston slap, i.e., excessive piston-cylinder wall clearance.
4. *Knocking or rapping while decelerating*—Usually caused by excessive rod bearing clearance.
5. *Persistent knocking and vibration*—Usually caused by excessive main bearing clearance.
6. *Rapid on-off squeal*—Compression leak around cylinder head gasket or spark plugs.

EXCESSIVE VIBRATION

This can be difficult to find without disassembling the engine. Usually this is caused by loose engine mounting hardware or worn engine or transmission bearings.

LUBRICATION TROUBLES

Excessive oil consumption—May be caused by worn rings and bores. Overhaul is necessary to correct this; see Chapter Four or Five. This may also be caused by worn valve guides or defective valve guide seals. Also check for exterior leaks.

FUEL SYSTEM

Fuel system troubles must be isolated to the carburetor, fuel tank, fuel shutoff valve or fuel lines. These procedures assume that the ignition system has been checked and properly adjusted.
1. *Engine will not start*—First determine that the fuel is being delivered to the carburetor. Turn the fuel shutoff valve to the OFF position; remove the flexible fuel line to the carburetor. Place the loose end onto a small container and turn the shutoff valve to the ON or RESERVE position. Fuel should run out of the tube. If it does not, remove

the shutoff valve and check for restrictions within it or the fuel tank. Refer to Chapter Seven.

2. *Rough idle or engine miss with frequent stalling*—Check carburetor adjustment. See Chapter Three.

3. *Stumbling when accelerating from idle*—check idle speed adjustment. See Chapter Three.

4. *Engine misses at high speed or lacks power*—This indicates possible fuel starvation. Clean main jets and float needle valves.

5. *Black exhaust smoke*—Black exhaust smoke means a badly overrich mixture. Check that manual choke disengages. Check idle speed. Check for leaky floats or worn float needle valves. Also check that jets are proper size.

CLUTCH

All clutch troubles, except adjustments, require partial engine disassembly to identify and cure the problem. Refer to Chapter Six for procedures.

1. *Slippage*—This is most noticeable when accelerating in a high gear at relatively low speed. To check slippage, shift to second gear and release the clutch as if riding off. If the clutch is good, the engine will slow and stall. If the clutch slips, continued engine speed will give it away. Slippage results from insufficient clutch lever free play, worn discs or pressure plate or weak springs.

2. *Drag or failure to release*—This trouble usually causes difficult shifting and gear clash, especially when downshifting. The cause may be excessive clutch lever free play, warped or bent pressure plate or clutch disc or broken or loose linings.

3. *Chatter or grabbing*—A number of things can cause the trouble. Check tightness of engine mounting bolts. Also check lever free play.

TRANSMISSION

Transmission problems are usually indicated by one or more of the following symptoms:

   a. Difficulty in shifting gears.
   b. Gear clash when downshifting.
   c. Slipping out of gear.
   d. Excessive noise in NEUTRAL.
   e. Excessive noise in gear.

Transmission symptoms are sometimes hard to distinguish from clutch symptoms. Be sure that the clutch is not causing the trouble before working on the transmission. Refer to Chapter Six.

BRAKES

1. *Brake lever or pedal goes all the way to its stop*—This may be caused by excessively worn linings, stretched cable or improper cable or rod adjustment.

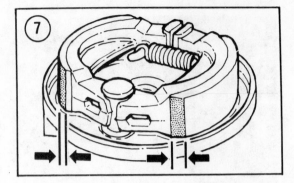

2. *Dragging brakes*—Check for wear or broken return springs or contaminated linings.

3. *Brakes grab*—There is probably oil or grease on the linings. Also, the drums may be out-of-round, there may be glazed brake shoes or shoes with no "lead angle" on the leading edges of the brake linings (**Figure 7**).

4. *Hard lever or pedal*—Check brake linings for contamination. Also check the brake lever or pedal pivot point for lack of lubrication.

5. *High speed fade*—Check for glazed or contaminated brake linings.

6. *Pulsating lever or pedal*—Check for out-of-round brake drums. Undetected accident damage is also a frequent cause of this.

FRONT SUSPENSION AND STEERING

1. *Too stiff or too soft*—Make sure forks have not been leaking and oil is correct. If in doubt, drain and refill as described under *Front Fork Oil Change* in Chapter Three.

2. *Leakage around seals*—There should be a light film of oil on fork tubes. However, large amounts of oil on tubes means the seals are leaking. Replace seals as described under *Front Fork Oil Disassembly* in Chapter Nine.

3. *Fork action is rough*—Check for bent tube.

4. *Steering wobbles*—Check for correct steering head bearing tightness as described under *Steering Head Adjustment* in Chapter Nine.

ELECTRICAL PROBLEMS

Bulbs which continuously burn out may be caused by excessive vibration, loose connections that permit sudden current surges or the installation of the wrong type bulb.

A majority of light and horn or other electrical accessory problems are caused by loose or corroded ground connections. Check those first and then substitute known good units for easier troubleshooting.

LUBRICATION, MAINTENANCE AND TUNE-UP

Regular maintenance is the best guarantee of a trouble-free, long lasting motorcycle. An afternoon spent now, cleaning and adjusting, can prevent costly mechanical problems in the future and unexpected breakdowns.

The procedures presented in this chapter can be easily carried out by anyone with average mechanical skills. The operations are presented step-by-step; if they are followed, it is difficult to go wrong.

Tables 1-12 are at the end of the chapter.

ROUTINE CHECKS

The following simple checks should be performed at each stop at a service station for gas.

Engine Oil Level

Refer to *Checking Engine Oil Level* under *Periodic Lubrication* in this chapter.

General Inspection

1. Quickly examine the engine for signs of oil or fuel leakage.
2. Check the tires for imbedded stones. Pry them out with your ignition key.
3. Make sure all lights work.

> *NOTE*
> *At least check the brakelight. It can burn out anytime. Motorists cannot stop as quickly as you and need all the warning you can give.*

Tire Pressure

Tire pressure must be checked with the tires cold. Correct tire pressure depends a lot on the load you are carrying. See **Table 1**.

Wheel Spoke Tension

1. Tap each spoke with a wrench. The higher the pitch of sound it makes, the tighter the spoke. The lower the sound frequency, the looser the spoke. A "ping" is good; a "klunk" says the spoke is too loose.
2. If one or more spokes are loose, tighten them as described under *Wheels* in Chapter Nine.

Crankcase Breather Hose

Inspect the hoses for cracks and deterioration and make sure that all hose clamps are tight **(Figure 1)**.

Lights and Horn

With the engine running, check the following:

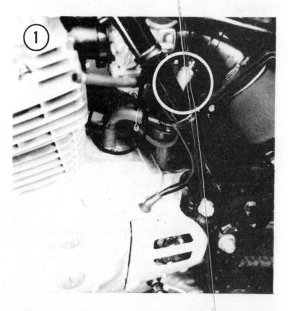

NOTE
XR series bikes are equipped only with a headlight and taillight. The headlight is controlled by a dimmer switch.

1. Pull the front brake lever and check that the brakelight comes on.
2. Push the rear brake pedal and check that the brakelight comes on soon after you have begun depressing the pedal.
3. Turn the headlight switch to the ON position. Check to see that headlight and taillight are on.
4. Move the dimmer switch up and down between the high and low positions and check to see that both headlight elements are working.
5. Push the turn signal switch to the left position and the right position and check that all 4 turn signal lights are working.
6. Push the horn button and note that the horn blows loudly.
7. If, during the tests, the rear brake pedal traveled too far before the brakelight came on, adjust the rear brakelight switch (see the *Rear Brakelight Switch Adjustment* procedure in Chapter Eight). If the horn or any light failed to work properly, refer to Chapter Eight.

SERVICE INTERVALS

The services and intervals shown in **Table 2** are recommended by the factory. Strict adherence to these recommendations will go a long way toward insuring long service from your Honda.

Service intervals differ between the XL and XR series because the XR will most likely be ridden harder and in dirtier areas. If your bike is an XL but is used off-road frequently you should follow the service recommended for the XR.

If you are riding your bike in competition events, refer to **Table 3** for suggested pre-race inspection areas and items.

For convenience in maintaining your motorcycle, most of the services shown in **Table 2** are described in this chapter. However, some procedures which require more than minor disassembly or adjustment are covered elsewhere in the appropriate chapter.

TIRES

Pressure

Tire pressure should be checked and adjusted frequently. A simple, accurate gauge (**Figure 2**) can be purchased for a few dollars and should be carried in your motorcycle tool kit. The appropriate tire pressures are shown in **Table 1**.

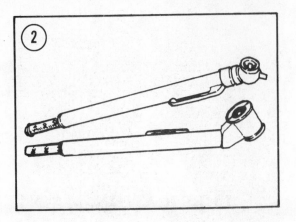

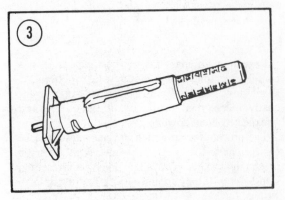

Inspection

Check tread for excessive wear, deep cuts or imbedded objects such as stones, nails, etc. If you find a nail in a tire, mark its location with a light crayon before pulling it out. This will help locate the hole in the inner tube. Refer to *Tire Changing* in Chapter Nine.

Check local traffic regulations concerning minimum tread depth. Measure with a tread depth gauge (**Figure 3**) or small ruler. Honda recommends replacement when the depth is 0.30 in. (8 mm) or less.

BATTERY
(XL SERIES ONLY)

Checking Electrolyte Level

The battery is the heart of the electrical system. It should be checked and serviced as indicated. The majority of electrical system troubles can be attributed to neglect of this vital component.

The electrolyte level may be checked with the battery installed. However, it is necessary to remove the right-hand side panel and battery bracket. The electrolyte level should be maintained between the two marks on the battery case (**Figure 4**). If the electrolyte level is low, it's a good idea to

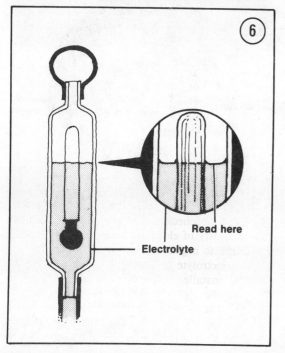

Read here
Electrolyte

remove the battery so that it can be thoroughly serviced and checked.

1. Remove the right-hand side cover.
2. Pull the main fuse holder (A, **Figure 5**) out of the battery bracket.
3. Remove the bolt (B, **Figure 5**) securing the bracket and hinge it out.
4. On 1978-1982 models, pull the battery partially out of the compartment. On all models, first disconnect the negative and then the positive electrical cables from the terminals.
5. Remove the battery from the compartment.

CAUTION
Be careful not to spill battery electrolyte on painted or polished surfaces. The liquid is highly corrosive and will damage the finish. If it is spilled, wash it off immediately with soapy water and thoroughly rinse with clean water.

6. Remove the caps from the battery cells and add distilled water to correct the level. Never add electrolyte (acid) to correct the level.
7. After the level has been corrected and the battery allowed to stand for a few minutes, check the specific gravity of the electrolyte in each cell with a hydrometer (**Figure 6**) as described in this chapter.

Testing

Hydrometer testing is the best way to check battery condition. Use a hydrometer with numbered graduations from 1.100 to 1.300 rather than one with color-coded bands. To use the hydrometer, squeeze the rubber ball, insert the tip into the cell and release the ball. Draw enough electrolyte to float the weighted float inside the hydrometer. Note the number in line with surface of the electrolyte; this is the specific gravity for this cell. Return the electrolyte to the cell from which it came.

The specific gravity of the electrolyte in each battery cell is an excellent indication of that cell's condition. A fully charged cell will read 1.275-1.280, while a cell in good condition reads from 1.225-1.250 and anything below 1.225 is practically dead.

Specific gravity varies with temperature. For each 10° that electrolyte temperature exceeds 80°F, add 0.004 to reading indicated on hydrometer. Subtract 0.004 for each 10° below 80°F.

If the cells test in the poor range, the battery requires recharging. The hydrometer is useful for checking the progress of the charging operation. **Table 4** shows approximate state of charge.

Charging

> *CAUTION*
> *Always remove the battery from the motorcycle before connecting charging equipment.*

> *WARNING*
> *During charging, highly explosive hydrogen gas is released from the battery. The battery should be charged only in a well-ventilated area and open flames and cigarettes should be kept away. Never check the charge of the battery by igniting the terminals; the resulting spark can ignite the hydrogen gas.*

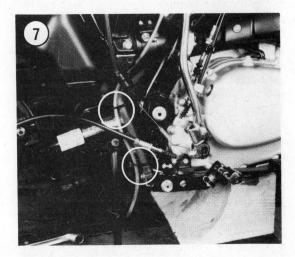

LUBRICATION POINTS

1. Front brake cam
2. Steering head bearings
3. Control cables
4. Throttle grip
5. Rear swing arm
6. Air cleaner element
7. Rear brake cam
8. Front wheel bearings
9. Speedometer housing
10. Front forks
11. Engine oil
12. Rear brake pedal
13. Side stand pivot point
14. Drive chain
15. Rear wheel bearings

1. Connect the positive (+) charger lead to the positive battery terminal and the negative (-) charger lead to the negative battery terminal.

2. Remove all vent caps from the battery, set the charger at the proper voltage and switch it on. If the output of the charger is variable, it is best to select a low setting—1 1/2 to 2 amps.

3. After the battery has been charged for about 8 hours, turn the charger off, disconnect the leads and check the specified gravity. It should be within the limits specified in **Table 4**. If it is, and remains stable for one hour, the battery is charged.

4. Clean the battery terminals, case and plastic cover and reinstall them in the bike, reversing the removal steps. Coat the terminals with Vaseline or silicone spray to retard decomposition of the terminals. Be sure to reinstall the vent tube and route it correctly through the frame (**Figure 7**). Failure to do so will cause damage to any components that battery vapor and acid come in contact with.

New Battery Installation

When replacing the old battery with a new one, be sure to charge it completely (specific gravity 1.260-1.280) before installing it on the bike.

Failure to do so, or using the battery with a low electrolyte level, will permanently damage the battery.

PERIODIC LUBRICATION

Refer to **Figure 8** for lubrication points.

Engine Oil Level Check (Dry-sump Models)

The 1983 XR500R and XL600R have a dry-sump type engine. The major portion of the engine oil is stored in a closed-off section of the bike's frame while some of the oil is carried in the crankcase.

Engine oil level is checked in 2 places—the dipstick on the frame and the oil level check bolt on the crankcase.

1. Place wood blocks under the frame to support the bike securely in a vertical position.

2. Start the engine and allow it to run for a couple of minutes.

3. Shut off the engine and allow the oil to settle.

4. Unscrew the dipstick (**Figure 9**) from the frame between the steering head and the fuel tank.

5. Wipe the dipstick clean and reinsert it into the hole. *Do not screw it in*, just rest it on the threads of the hole in the frame.

6. Remove the dipstick and check the oil level. The bike must be level for a correct reading. The level should be between the 2 lines but not above the upper one. If necessary, add the recommended type and quantity of engine oil (**Figure 10**) to correct the level.

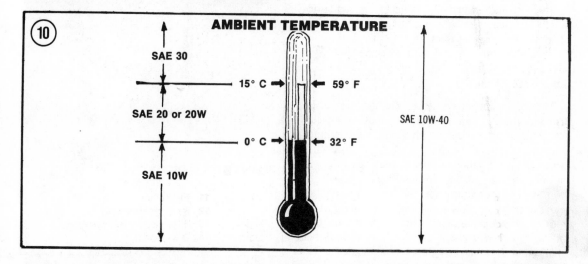

AMBIENT TEMPERATURE

SAE 30

SAE 20 or 20W

SAE 10W

15° C → ← 59° F

0° C → ← 32° F

SAE 10W-40

7. Install the dipstick and tighten securely.

8. Restart the engine and allow it to run for a couple of minutes.

9. Shut off the engine and allow the oil to settle.

10. Remove the crankcase oil level check bolt (**Figure 11**).

11. The crankcase oil level is correct if the oil is up to the bottom surface of the threads in the hole.

12. If the oil level is correct on the dipstick but the crankcase oil level is incorrect, some part of the oil system is not operating properly. Do not operate the bike until you have found and fixed the problem. Perform the following:

   a. Reckeck the oil level on the dipstick.

   b. Inspect the oil lines and fittings from the engine to the bike's frame.

   c. Inspect the oil pump; refer to Chapter Five.

13. Reinstall the oil level check bolt and tighten securely.

Engine Oil Level Check (Wet-sump Models)

All models other than the 1983 XR500R and XL600R have a wet-sump engine; all the engine oil is kept in the crankcase.

1. Place wood blocks under the frame to support the bike securely in a vertical position.

2. Start the engine and allow it to run for a couple of minutes.

3. Shut off the engine and allow the oil to settle.

4. Unscrew the dipstick (**Figure 12**) from the right-hand crankcase cover.

5. Wipe the dipstick clean and reinsert it into the hole. *Do not screw it in,* just rest it on the threads of the hole in the crankcase cover.

6. Remove the dipstick and check the oil level. The bike must be level for a correct reading. The level should be between the 2 lines but not above the upper one (**Figure 13**). If necessary, add the recommended type and quantity of engine oil (**Figure 10**) to correct the level.

7. Install the dipstick and tighten securely.

Engine Oil Change

The factory-recommended oil change interval is listed in **Table 2**. This assumes that the motorcycle is operated in moderate climates. In extreme climates, oil should be changed every 30 days. The time interval is more important than the mileage interval because acids formed by combustion blow-by will contaminate the oil even if the motorcycle is not run for several months. If the motorcycle is operated under dusty conditions, the oil will get dirty more quickly and should be changed more frequently than recommended.

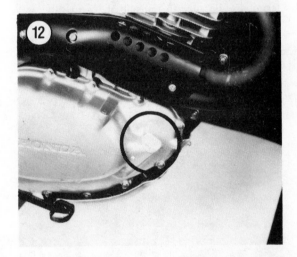

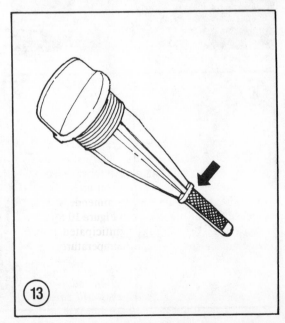

Use only a high-quality detergent motor oil with an API rating of SE or SF. The quality rating is stamped or printed on top of the can (**Figure 14**). Try to use the same brand of oil at each change. Use of oil additives is not recommended as it may cause clutch slippage. Refer to **Figure 10** for correct oil viscosity to use under anticipated ambient temperatures (not engine oil temperature).

CAUTION
Do not add any friction-reducing additives to the oil as they will cause clutch slippage. Also do not use an

engine oil with graphite added. The use of graphite oil will void any applicable Honda warranty. It is not established at this time if graphite will build up on the clutch friction plates and cause clutch problems. Until further testing is done by the oil and motorcycle industries, do not use this type of oil.

To change the engine oil and filter you will need the following:
   a. Drain pan.
   b. Funnel.
   c. Can opener or pour spout.
   d. 17 mm wrench (drain plug).
   e. 2 quarts of oil.

There are a number of ways to discard the old oil safely. Some service stations and oil retailers will accept your used oil for recycling; some may even give you money for it. Never drain the oil onto the ground.

1. Start the engine and let it reach operating temperature; 15-20 minutes of stop-and-go riding is usually sufficient.

2. Turn the engine off and place the bike on the side stand.

3. Place a drain pan under the left-hand crankcase cover and remove the drain plug and washer (**Figure 15**).

4. On 1983 XR500R and XL600R models, remove the bolts securing the skid plate and remove the skid plate.

5A. On dry-sump models, remove the dipstick (**Figure 9**) on the frame; this will speed up the flow of oil.

5B. On wet-sump models, remove the dipstick (**Figure 12**) from the crankcase cover; this will speed up the flow of oil.

CAUTION
Make sure the ignition switch is OFF.

6. Let the oil drain for at least 15-20 minutes. During this time, kick the kickstarter a couple of times to help drain any remaining oil.

7. Inspect the sealing washer on the drain plug. Replace if its condition is in doubt. Install the drain plug.

8. On dry-sump models, perform the following:
   a. Move the drain pan under the frame down-tube and remove the drain plug (**Figure 16**) from the frame.
   b. Let the oil drain for at least 15-20 minutes.
   c. Inspect the sealing washer on the drain plug; replace if necessary.
   d. Install the drain plug and tighten to 25-33 ft.-lb. (35-45 N•m).

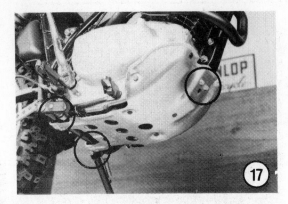

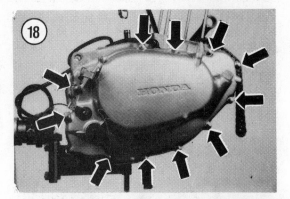

9. If the oil filter screen is to be cleaned, perform *Oil Filter Screen Cleaning* as described in this chapter.

10. On 1983 350-600 cc models, if the oil filter is going to be replaced, peform *Oil Filter Replacement (1983 350-600 cc Models)* as described in this chapter.

11. On dry-sump models, remove and clean the oil strainer nut as described in this chapter.

10. Install the drain plug and tighten to 22-29 ft.-lb. (30-39 N•m).

12. Insert a funnel into the oil dipstick hole (on the frame or crankcase cover) and fill the engine with the correct viscosity and quantity of engine oil. Refer to **Table 5** for the correct capacity.

> *NOTE*
> *On dry-sump models, pour in only about 2 U.S. qts. (2 liters) of oil at first. Since only a portion of the engine oil is stored in the frame the engine must be started and then additional oil added to correct the level.*

13. Install the dipstick/oil filler cap.

14. On XR500R and XL600R models, install the skid plate.

15. Start the engine and let it idle for 2-3 minutes; check for leaks.

16. Turn the engine off and check for correct oil level; adjust as necessary. This step is especially important on dry-sump models.

Oil Filter Screen Cleaning

1. Drain the engine oil as described in this chapter.

2. Remove the bolts (**Figure 17**) securing the skid plate and remove the skid plate.

3. Remove the kickstarter arm.

4. Disconnect the clutch and compression release cables from the right-hand crankcase cover.

5. Remove the front right-hand footpeg.

6. Remove the rear brake pedal.

7. Remove the bolts (**Figure 18**) securing the right-hand crankcase cover and remove the cover and gasket.

8. On XR500R and XL600R models, remove the bolt securing the filter to the crankcase.

9. Pull out the filter (**Figure 19**) and clean it in solvent with a medium soft toothbrush. Carefully dry with compressed air.

10. Inspect the screen; replace it if there are any breaks or holes in it. Install the screen with the thick end facing toward the outside.

> *NOTE*
> *On models with a chain-driven balancer system, it is a good idea to adjust the balancer chain while the crankcase cover is removed. Refer to* **Balancer Chain Adjustment** *in this chapter.*

11. On XR500R and XL600R models, install the bolt securing the filter screen.

12. Install the crankcase cover with a new gasket. Hold the compression release follower lever in the raised position.

13. Install the following items:

    a. Rear brake pedal.

    b. Front right-hand footpeg.

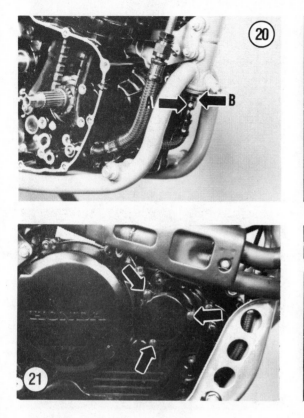

c. Clutch and compression release cables.
d. Kickstarter arm.
e. Skid plate.

14. Refill the crankcase with the recommended type and quantity of engine oil as described in this chapter.

15. Adjust the clutch, compression release and rear brake as described in this chapter.

Oil Strainer Nut
(XR500R and XL600R)

1. Drain the engine oil as described in this chapter.
2. Loosen the oil hose nut (A, **Figure 20**) and disconnect the oil line from the oil strainer nut.
3. Remove the oil strainer nut and O-ring (B, **Figure 21**) from the frame down-tube.
4. Clean the oil strainer in solvent with a medium soft toothbrush and carefully dry with compressed air.
5. Inspect the screen; replace it if there are any breaks or holes in it.
6. Inspect the O-ring seal; replace if damaged or deteriorated.
7. Install the oil strainer nut and O-ring. Tighten the nut to 25-32 ft.-lb. (35-45 N•m).
8. Install the oil hose. Hold the oil strainer nut with a wrench and tighten the oil hose to 25-32

ft.-lb. (35-45 N•m). Make sure the oil hose curves naturally from the frame down-tube to the engine and is not kinked.

Oil Filter Replacement
(1983 350-600 cc models)

1. Drain the engine oil as described in this chapter.
2. Place the drain pan under the right-hand crankcase cover.
3. Remove the bolts (**Figure 21**) securing the oil filter cover and remove the cover.
4. Remove the oil filter and spring. Discard the filter.
5. Wipe out the oil filter cavity with a shop rag and cleaning solvent. Remove any sludge.
6. Install the spring (**Figure 22**) and the filter element (**Figure 23**).
7. Inspect the O-ring seal on the cover and replace if necessary.
8. Install the cover and tighten the bolts securely.

Front Fork Oil Change
(Without Air-assist)

It is a good practice to change the front fork oil at the interval indicated in **Table 2** or once a year. If it becomes contaminated with dirt or water, change it immediately.

1. Remove the upper plastic protective cap and remove the upper fork cap bolt (use the 17 mm male socket provided in the factory tool kit or a 17 mm bolt head held with Vise-Grip pliers). See **Figure 24**.

2. Place a drip pan under the fork and remove the drain screw (**Figure 25**). Allow the oil to drain for at least 5 minutes. *Never reuse the oil.*

> *CAUTION*
> *Do not allow the fork oil to come in contact with any of the brake components.*

3. With both of the bike's wheels on the ground and the front brake applied, push down on the handlebar grips to work the forks up and down. Continue until all oil is expelled.

4. Install the drain screw.

5. Repeat for the other fork.

6. Fill each fork with automatic transmission fluid. The correct amount is listed in **Table 6**.

> *NOTE*
> *In order to measure the correct amount of oil, use a plastic baby bottle. These have measured increments in fluid ounces (oz.) and cubic centimeters (cc) on the side.*

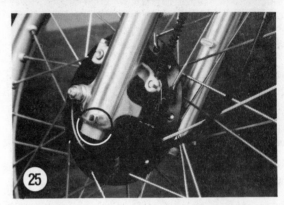

7. After filling each fork tube, slowly pump the forks several times to expel air from the upper and lower fork chambers.

8. Install the fork cap bolts and tighten to the torque specifications listed in **Table 7**.

9. Road test the bike and check for leaks.

Front Fork Oil Change
(With Air-assist)

It is a good practice to change the oil at the interval indicated in **Table 2** or once a year. If it becomes contaminated with dirt or water, change it immediately.

1. Unscrew the dust cap (**Figure 26**) and *bleed off all air pressure* by depressing the valve stem.

> *NOTE*
> *Release air pressure gradually. If it is released too fast, oil will spurt out with the air. Protect your eyes and clothing accordingly.*

2. Slowly unscrew the fork cap bolt/air valve assembly (**Figure 27**); it is under spring pressure from the fork spring.

3. Place a drain pan under the drain screw (**Figure 28**) and remove the drain screw. Allow the oil to drain for at least 5 minutes. *Never reuse the oil.*

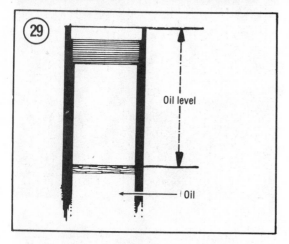

Oil level

Oil

CAUTION
Do not allow the fork oil to come in contact with any of the brake components.

4. Inspect the gasket on the drain screw; replace it if necessary. Install the drain screw.
5. Repeat for the other fork.
6. Withdraw the fork spring from each fork tube.
7. Refill each fork leg with DEXRON automatic transmission fluid or fork oil. Refer to **Table 6** for fork oil capacity.

NOTE
In order to measure the correct amount of fluid, use a plastic baby bottle. These have measurements in fluid ounces (oz.) and cubic centimeters (cc) on the side.

8. After filling each fork tube, slowly pump the fork tubes several times to expel air from the upper and lower fork chambers and to distribute the oil.
9. Apply the front brake and push down on the handlebar. Hold the handlebar in this position with the forks totally compressed. Have an assistant measure the distance from the top of the fork tube to the top of the fork oil (**Figure 29**). Different fork damping characteristics will result from varying the amount of fork oil in the fork tube (using the standard air inflation pressure). Refer to **Table 6**.
10. Inspect the O-ring seal on the fork cap bolt; replace if necessary. Install the fork cap bolt while pushing down on the spring. Start the bolt slowly; don't cross thread it. Tighten the fork cap bolt to the torque specification listed in **Table 7**.
11. Inflate the forks to the recommended air pressure listed in **Table 8**. Do not use compressed air; only use a small hand-operated air pump like the one shown in **Figure 30**.

WARNING
*Never use any type of compressed gas as an explosion may be lethal. Never heat the fork assembly with a torch or place it near an open flame or extreme heat as this will also result in an explosion. **Never** exceed the maximum air pressure of 14.0 psi (1.0 kg/cm²).*

12. Road test the bike and check for leaks.

Swing Arm Bearing Lubrication

Lubricate the swing arm bushings at the interval indicated in **Table 2**. Apply the lubricant with a small hand-held grease gun. On dual-shock models, use a good grade multipurpose grease. On Pro-Link models, use molybdenum disulfide grease (NLGI No. 2).
1. Wipe the grease fitting clean of all road dirt and grease residue. Force the grease into the fitting until the grease runs out of both ends of the swing arm.
2. Clean off excess grease.
3. If the grease will not run out of the ends of the swing arm, unscrew the grease fitting from the swing arm. Clean it out with solvent; make sure the ball check valve is free. Reinstall the fitting or replace with a new one.

4. Apply the grease gun again. If grease still does not run out of both ends of the swing arm, remove the swing arm as described in Chapter Ten. Disassemble the swing arm and thoroughly clean and regrease.

Pro-Link Suspension Lubrication

Lubricate the Pro-Link suspension every 1,000 miles (1,600 km). Apply molybdenum disulfide grease (NLGI No. 2) with a small hand-held grease gun.

1. Wipe the grease fittings clean of all road dirt and grease residue. Force the grease into the fitting until the grease runs out past the dust seals on each of the links. There is one fitting where the shock arm is attached to the swing arm (**Figure 31**) and one where the shock arm is attached to the shock link (A, **Figure 32**). One additional fitting is on the shock link where it attaches to the lower portion of the frame (B, **Figure 32**).

2. Clean off excess grease.

3. If the grease will not run out of the ends of the joints, unscrew the grease fitting from the arm or link. Clean it out with solvent; make sure the ball check valve is free. Reinstall the fitting or replace with a new one.

4. Apply the grease gun again. If grease still does not run out of both ends, remove the suspension components as described in Chapter Ten.

Control Cables

Every 2,500 miles (4,000 km) the control cables should be lubricated. They should also be inspected at this time for fraying and the cable sheath be checked for chafing. The cables are relatively inexpensive and should be replaced when found to be faulty.

The control cables can be lubricated either with oil or with any of the popular cable lubricants and a cable lubricator. The first method requires more time and the complete lubricated of the entire cable is less certain.

Oil method

1. Disconnect the cables from the clutch lever and the throttle grip assembly.

2. Make a cone of stiff paper and tape it to the end of the cable sheath (**Figure 33**).

3. Hold the cable upright and pour a small amount of light oil (SAE 10W/30) into the cone. Work the cable in and out of the sheath for several minutes to help the oil work its way down to the end of the cable.

4. Remove the cone, reconnect the cable and adjust the cable as described in this chapter.

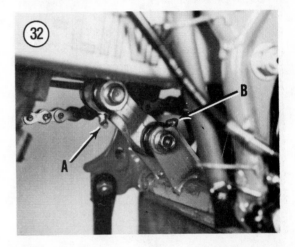

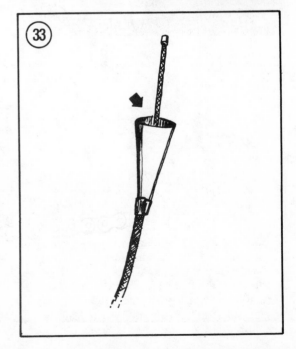

Lubricator method

1. Disconnect the cables from the clutch lever and the throttle grip assembly.
2. Attach the lubricator following the manufacturer's instructions.
3. Insert the nozzle of the lubricant can in the lubricator, press the button on the can and hold down until the lubricant begins to flow out of the other end of the cable.
4. Remove the lubricator, reconnect the cable and adjust the cable as described in thes chapter.

Miscellaneous Lubrication Points

Lubricate the clutch lever, front brake lever, side stand pivot points and footpeg pivot points. Use SAE 10W-30 motor oil.

PERIODIC MAINTENANCE

Drive Chain Adjustment (Dual-shock Models)

The drive chain should be checked, lubricated and adjusted every 300 miles (500 km) or more often if ridden in wet or dusty conditions. It should be removed, cleaned and lubricated every 2,000 miles (3,200 km).

1. Place the transmission in NEUTRAL.
2. Remove the rear axle cotter pin. Loosen the axle nut (A, **Figure 34**) and the axle adjuster locknuts (B, **Figure 34**).
3. On XL250S and XL500S models:
   a. Place the motorcycle on a support block.
   b. Measure the free play of the chain when it is pushed up midway between the sprockets (**Figure 35**). Specifications for free play are listed in **Table 9**.
   c. Rotate the rear wheel to move the chain to another position and recheck the free play; chains rarely wear or stretch evenly and, as a result, the free play will not remain constant over the entire chain.
   d. To adjust free play, turn the adjuster bolts (C, **Figure 34**) either in or out, as required, in equal amounts.
   e. If the chain cannot be adjusted within the limits is **Table 9**, it is excessively worn and stretched and should be replaced.
   f. After adjustment, tighten the axle adjuster locknuts (B, **Figure 34**).
4. On Models XR250 and XR500, inspect the drive chain tensioner slider (**Figure 36**). If it is worn to the wear line, remove the screw and replace it before adjusting the chain.

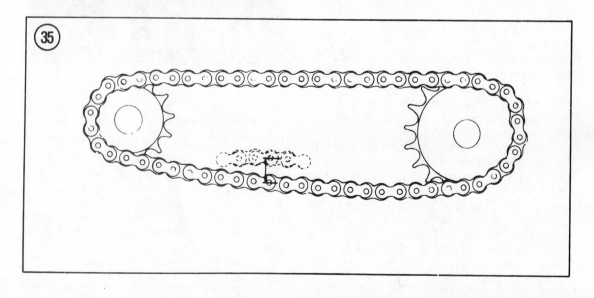

5. On XR250 and XR500 models, measure the distance between the bottom of the swing arm and the top of the chain (**Figure 37**). Adjust if the distance is 3/4 in. (20 mm) or less. Turn the adjuster bolt (C, **Figure 34**) until the distance shown in **Figure 37** is the same as that listed in **Table 9**. Tighten the axle adjuster locknuts.

6. On all models, make sure the index marks on the rear swing arm align with the same reference mark on both the right- and left-hand side (**Figure 38**).

> *NOTE*
> *Sight along the top of the chain from the rear sprocket to see that it is correctly aligned. It should leave the top of the rear sprocket in a straight line (A, Figure 39). If it is cocked to one side or the other (B or C, Figure 39) the wheel is incorrectly aligned and must be corrected.*

7. Tighten the rear axle nut to the torque specification in **Table 7**. Install a new cotter pin.

8. After the drive chain has been adjusted, the rear brake pedal free play has to be adjusted as described in this chapter.

Drive Chain Adjustment (Pro-Link Models)

The drive chain should be checked and adjusted at the intervals indicated in **Table 2**. The correct amount of chain free play (when pushed up midway between the sprockets on the upper chain run) is listed in **Table 9**. See A, **Figure 40**. If adjustment is necessary, perform the following.

1. Place wood block(s) under the engine to support the bike securely with the rear wheel off of the ground.

2. Shift the transmission into NEUTRAL.

3. Loosen the axle nut (A, **Figure 41**).

4. Turn both axle snail adjusters (B, **Figure 41**) in equal amounts to either increase or decrease chain tension. After adjustment is complete, make sure that the same adjustment mark number on the snail adjuster aligns with the stopper pin on both sides of the swing arm (**Figure 42**).

5. Rotate the rear wheel to move the chain to another position and recheck the adjustment; chains rarely wear or stretch evenly and, as a result, the free play will not remain constant over the entire chain. If the chain cannot be adjusted within these limits, it is excessively worn and stretched and should be replaced. Always replace both sprockets when replacing the drive chain; never install a new chain over worn sprockets. The replacement chain is listed in **Table 10**.

> *WARNING*
> *Excessive free play can result in chain breakage which could cause a serious accident.*

6. Sight along the top of the drive chain from the rear sprocket to see that it is correctly aligned. It should leave the top of the rear sprocket in a straight line (A, **Figure 39**). If it is cocked to one side or the other (B or C, **Figure 39**), the wheel is incorrectly aligned and must be corrected. Refer to Step 4.

7. Tighten the self-locking rear axle nut to the torque specification listed in **Table 7**.

3

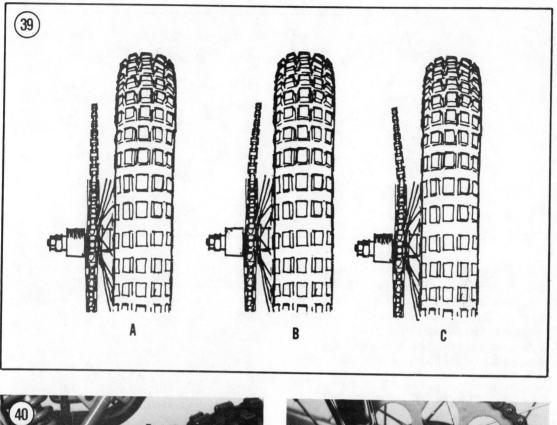

A   B   C

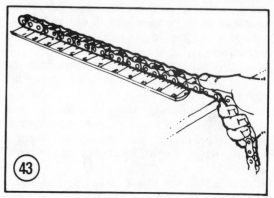

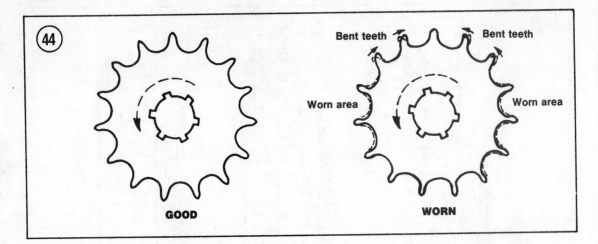

8. After the drive chain has been adjusted to the correct amount of free play, drill a small hole in the drive chain guard (B, **Figure 40**) directly above the top of the chain. This can be used as a reference point for further checking.

9. After the drive chain has been adjusted, the rear brake pedal free play must be adjusted as described in this chapter.

**Drive Chain Cleaning,
Inspection, and Lubrication
(Except XR500R and XL600R Pro-Link)**

Every 2,000 miles (3,200 km), or more frequently if ridden in dusty or muddy terrain, remove, thoroughly clean and lubricate the chain.

Failure to clean the chain regularly will result in premature chain wear.

1. Remove the drive chain as described under *Rear Wheel Removal/Installation* in Chapter Ten.
2. Immerse the chain in a pan of cleaning solvent and allow it to soak for about a half hour. Move it around and flex it during this period so that dirt between the pins and rollers may work its way out.
3. Scrub the rollers and side plates with a stiff brush and rinse away loosened grit. Rinse it a couple of times to make sure all dirt and grit is washed out. Hang up the chain and allow it to thoroughly dry.
4. After cleaning the chain, examine it carefully for wear or damage. If any signs are visible, replace the chain.
5. Lay the chain alongside a ruler (**Figure 43**) and compress the links together. Then stretch them apart. If more than 1/4 in. (6 mm) of movement is possible, replace the chain; it is too worn to be used again.
6. One additional check is to lay the chain alongside a ruler with the links stretched apart

completely. Measure the distance between the number of pins indicated in **Table 11**. Replace the chain if it has stretched to the service limit listed in **Table 11**.

> *CAUTION*
> *Always check both sprockets (Figure 44) every time the chain is removed. If any wear is visible on the teeth, replace the sprocket. Never install a new chain over worn sprockets or a worn chain over new sprockets.*

7. Check the inner faces of the inner plates (**Figure 45**). They should be lightly polished on both sides. If they show considerable wear on both sides, the sprockets are not aligned. Adjust alignment as described in *Drive Chain Adjustment* in this chapter.
8. Lubricate the chain with a good grade of chain lubricant carefully following the manufacturer's instruactions.
9. Reinstall the chain as described under *Rear Wheel Removal/Installation* in Chapter Ten.
10. Adjust chain free play as described under *Drive Chain Adjusment* in this chapter.

**Drive Chain Cleaning,
Inspection and Lubrication
(XR500R and XL600R Pro-Link)**

> *NOTE*
> *These 2 models have an O-ring type drive chain.*

1. Remove the drive sprocket cover.
2. Carefully remove the drive chain master link retaining clip and remove the master link. Don't lose the O-rings when removing the retaining clip and master link.

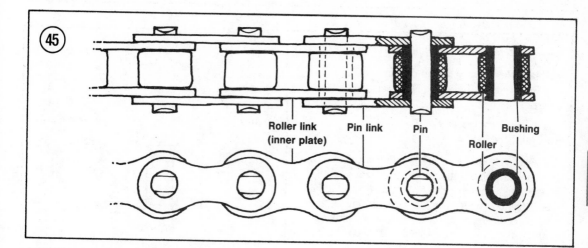

Roller link (inner plate)　　Pin link　　Pin　　Bushing
Roller

3

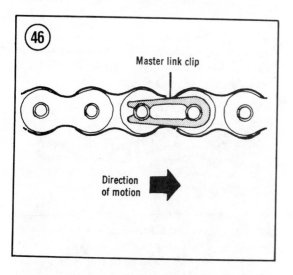

Master link clip

Direction of motion

8. Check the inner faces of the inner plates. They should be lightly polished on both sides. If they show considerable wear on both sides, the sprockets are not aligned. Adjust alignment as described under *Drive Chain Adjustment* in this chapter.

9. Lubricate the drive chain with SAE 80 or 90 gear oil or a good grade of chain lubricant (formulated for O-ring chains) carefully following the manufacturer's instructions.

10. Reinstall the drive chain onto both sprockets.
11. Make sure the O-rings are in place on the master link. Install the master link from the backside of the chain.
12. Install the O-rings onto the pins and install the master link plate. Install a new master link retaining clip with the closed end of the clip facing the direction of travel (**Figure 46**).

3. Remove the drive chain from the front and rear sprockets.
4. Immerse the chain in a pan of kerosene (or other suitable solvent that will not destroy the rubber O-rings) and allow it to soak for about 10-15 minutes. Move it around and flex it during this period so that dirt may work its way out.
5. Scrub the rollers and side plates with a soft brush and rinse away loosened grit. Rinse it a couple of times to make sure all dirt is washed out. Wipe the drive chain dry with a shop cloth; hang up the chain and allow it to thoroughly dry.
6. After cleaning the chain, examine it carefully for wear or damage. If any signs are visible, replace the chain.
7. Lay the chain alongside a ruler and pull the chain taut. Measure the distance between the span of pins listed in **Table 11**. If the chain has stretched to the service limit it must be replaced. The replacement chain is listed in **Table 10**.

*retaining clip (**Figure 47**). If a space does exist the O-rings are not installed. Disassemble and assemble correctly.*

13. Install the drive sprocket cover.

14. Adjust chain free play as described in this chapter.

Drive Chain Tensioners (Pro-Link Models)

On Pro-Link models there is either a roller or a slider on the chain tensioner arm (**Figure 48**). There is also a chain guide (A, **Figure 49**) and a flat slider attached to the front left-hand side of the swing arm (B, **Figure 49**) near the pivot point.

There are no factory-specified wear limit dimensions for the rollers. If they are worn unevenly or worn close to the attachment bolt, they should be replaced. Remove the bolt and nut securing the roller and replace with a new roller.

Check the slider attached to the swing arm. If a groove is worn more than 3/4 of the way through the slider it must be replaced. If worn through the drive chain will rub on the swing arm and wear prematurely. Remove the screws securing the slider to the swing arm and replace with a new one.

Drum Brake Lining

Check the front and rear brake linings for wear. If the arrow on the brake arm aligns with the raised index mark on the brake backing plate (**Figure 50**) when the brake pedal is appled the brake linings require replacement.

If replacement is necessary, refer to Chapter Eleven.

Disc Brake Fluid Level

The hydraulic fluid in the disc brake master cylinder should be checked as listed in **Table 2** or whenever the level drops, whichever comes first. The fluid level for the front brake in the reservoir should be up to the upper mark within the reservoir. This upper level mark is only visible when the master cylinder top cover is removed. If the brake fluid level reaches the lower level mark visible through the viewing port on the side of the master cylinder reservoir, the fluid level must be corrected by adding fresh brake fluid.

1. To add fluid to the front brake master cylinder, place the bike on level ground and position the handlebars so the master cylinder reservoir is level.

2. Clean any dirt from the area around the top cover prior to removing the cover.

3. Remove the top cover (**Figure 51**) and the diaphragm. Add fresh DOT 4 brake fluid from a sealed brake fluid container.

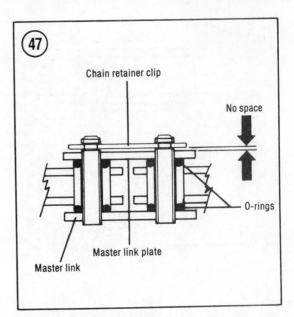

3

Disc Brake Line

Check the brake line between the master cylinder and the brake caliper. If there is any leakage, tighten the connections and bleed the brakes as described in Chapter Eleven. If this does not stop the leak or if a brake line is obviously damaged, cracked or chafed, replace the brake line and bleed the system.

Disc Brake Pad Wear

Inspect the brake pads for excessive or uneven wear, scoring and oil or grease on the friction surface. Look up at the bottom of the caliper assembly and check the wear lines on the brake pads. If the pads are worn to the wear line, they must be replaced. Refer to Chapter Eleven.

CAUTION
Always replace both pads at the same time.

Disc Brake Fluid Change

Every time the reservoir cap is removed, a small amount of dirt and moisture enters the brake fluid. The same thing happens if a leak occurs or any part of the hydraulic system is loosened or disconnected. Dirt can clog the system and cause unnecessary wear. Water in the brake fluid vaporizes at high temperature, impairing the hydraulic action and reducing the brake's stopping ability.

To maintain peak performance, change the brake fluid as indicated in **Table 2**. To change brake fluid, follow the *Bleeding the Brake System* procedure in Chapter Eleven. Continue adding new fluid to the master cylinder and bleeding out at the caliper until the fluid leaving the caliper is clean and free of contaminants.

WARNING
Use brake fluid clearly marked DOT 4 only. Others may vaporize and cause brake failure.

Front Drum Brake Lever Adjustment

The front brake cable should be adjusted so there is 1-1 1/4 in. (25-30 mm) of brake lever movement required to actuate the brake, but it must not be adjusted so closely that the brake shoes contact the drum with the lever relaxed. The primary adjustment should be made with the control lever adjuster.

1. Loosen the locknut (A, **Figure 52**) and turn the adjusting barrel (B, **Figure 52**) to achieve the correct amount of free play. Tighten the locknut (A).

WARNING
Use brake fluid clearly marked DOT 4 only and specified for disc brakes. Others may vaporize and cause brake failure. Do not intermix different brands of brake fluid as they may not be compatible.

CAUTION
Be careful when handling brake fluid. Do not spill it on painted or plated surfaces as it will destroy the surface. Wash the area immediately with soapy water and thoroughly rinse it off.

4. Reinstall the diaphragm and the top cover and tighten the screws securely.

2. Because of normal brake wear, this adjustment will eventually be "used up." It is then necessary to loosen the locknut (A) and screw the adjusting barrel (B) all the way in toward the hand grip. Tighten the locknut (A).

3. At the lower adjustment on the fork leg, loosen the locknut (C, **Figure 53**) and adjust the adjuster nut (D, **Figure 53**) until the brake lever can be used once again for fine adjustment. Be sure to tighten the locknut (C).

4. When the 2 arrows on the brake arm and brake plate align (**Figure 50**), the brake shoes must be replaced. Refer to Chapter Eleven.

Front Disc Brake
Lever Free Play

The front disc brake lever has 2 free play positions.

1. Slide back the rubber protective boot from the brake lever pivot point area.

2. To increase free play, use a flat-bladed screwdriver to rotate the eccentric screw (**Figure 54**) until the single dot on the screw aligns with the index mark on the brake lever.

3. To decrease free play, use a flat bladed screwdriver and rotate the adjust eccentric screw (**Figure 54**) so the double dot on the screw aligns with the index mark on the brake lever.

> *CAUTION*
> *Do not leave the eccentric screw between the 2 positions. It must always be aligned with one of the marks or the brake lever will not operate properly.*

Rear Brake Pedal
Height Adjustment

The rear brake pedal should be adjusted as indicated in **Table 2**.

1. Check that the brake pedal is in the at-rest position.

2A. Cable-operated brake: To change height position, loosen the locknut (A, **Figure 55**) and turn the adjuster bolt (B, **Figure 55**). Tighten the locknut.

2B. Rod-operated brake: To change height position, loosen the locknut (A, **Figure 56**) and turn the adjuster bolt (B, **Figure 56**). Tighten the locknut.

3. Adjust the brake pedal free play as described in this chapter.

Rear Brake Pedal Free Play Adjustment

Adjust the brake pedal to the correct height. Turn the adjustment nut on the end of the brake

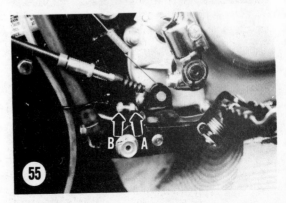

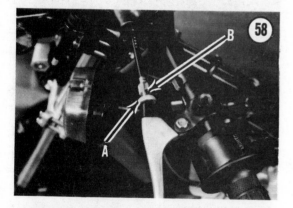

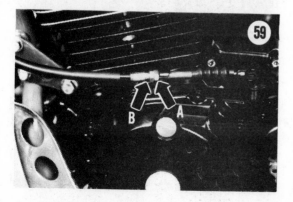

rod (**Figure 57**) until the brake pedal has 3/8-5/8 in. (10-15 mm) free play. Free play is the distance the pedal travels from the at-rest position to the applied position when the pedal is depressed lightly by hand.

Rotate the rear wheel and check for brake drag. Also operate the pedal several times to make sure it returns to the at-rest position immediately after release.

Adjust the rear brakelight switch as described in Chapter Eight (XL models only).

Clutch Adjustment

Adjust the clutch at the interval indicated in **Table 2**. For the clutch to fully engage and disengage there must be the following amount of free play:

   a. 1983 XR350R, XR500R, XL600R: 3/8-3/4 in. (10-20 mm).

   b. All other models: 5/8-1 in. (15-25 mm).

If the proper amount of clutch free play cannot be achieved by using this procedure, the clutch cable has stretched to the point that it needs to be replaced. Refer to *Clutch Cable Replacement* in Chapter Six.

1. Minor adjustments can be made at the upper adjuster at the hand lever as follows:

   a. Pull back the rubber protective boot.

   b. Loosen the locknut (A, **Figure 58**) and turn the adjuster barrel (B, **Figure 58**) in or out to obtain the correct amount of free play. Tighten the locknut.

NOTE
If the proper amount of free play cannot be achieved at the hand lever, additional adjustment can be made at the clutch actuating lever on the engine as described in Step 2 and Step 3.

2. At the hand lever, loosen the locknut and turn the adjuster barrel all the way in toward the hand lever. Tighten the locknut.

3A. XR350R, XR500R and XL600R: On the left-hand crankcase cover, loosen the locknut (A, **Figure 59**) and turn the adjuster (B, **Figure 59**) until the correct amount of free play can be achieved. Tighten the locknut.

3B. All other models: Near the right-hand crankcase cover, loosen the locknut (A, **Figure 60**) and turn the adjuster (B, **Figure 60**) until the correct amount of free play can be achieved. Tighten the locknut.

4. If necessary, repeat Step 1 for fine adjustment.

5. After adjustment is complete, check that the locknuts are tight both at the hand lever and at the clutch actuating lever on the crankcase.

3

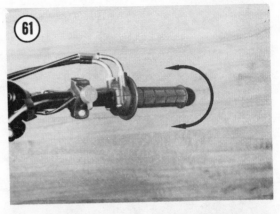

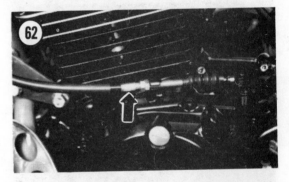

6. Test ride the bike and make sure the clutch is operating correctly.

Throttle Adjustment and Operation

The throttle grip should have 1/8-1/4 in. (2-6 mm) rotational free play (**Figure 61**). Minor adjustments should be made at the throttle grip; major adjustments can be made where the cable attaches to the carburetor assembly.

NOTE
There are 2 throttle cables, but only the "pull" cable is adjustable.

1A. XR350R, XR500R and XL600R: If adjustment is necessary, perform the following:
  a. SLide back the rubber protective boot.
  b. Loosen the locknut and turn the adjuster (**Figure 62**) on the lower throttle cable at the throttle grip in or out to achieve proper free play rotation. Tighten the locknut.
  c. If additional adjustment is necessary, remove the fuel tank as described in Chapter Seven.
  d. Loosen the locknut and turn the adjuster (**Figure 63**) on the lower throttle cable at the carburetor assembly in or out to achieve proper free play rotation. Tighten the locknut.

1B. All other models: If adjustment is necessary, perform the following:
  a. Loosen the locknut and turn the adjuster (**Figure 64**) on the rear throttle cable at the throttle grip in or out to achieve proper free play rotation. Tighten the locknut.
  b. If additional adjustment is necessary, remove the fuel tank as described in Chapter Seven.
  c. Loosen the locknut and turn the adjuster (**Figure 65**) on the upper throttle cable at the carburetor assembly in or out to achieve proper free play rotation. Tighten the locknut.

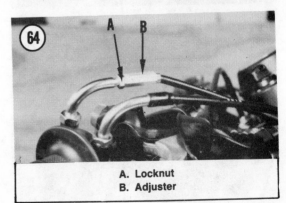

A. Locknut
B. Adjuster

2. Check the throttle cables from grip to carburetor. Make sure they are not kinked or chafed. To replace the cables, refer to *Throttle Cable Replacement* in Chapter Seven.

3. Make sure the throttle grip rotates freely from a fully closed to fully open position. Check with the handlebar at center, at full right and at full left. If necessary, remove the throttle grip and apply a lithium base grease to it.

Camshaft Chain Tensioner Adjustment (1983 350-600 cc Models)

There is no provision for cam chain tensioner adjustment on these models. Chain tension is maintained automatically.

Camshaft Chain Tensioner Adjustment (All Other Models)

The cam chain tensioner should be adjusted at the interval indicated in **Table 2**.

In time, the camshaft chain and guide will wear and develop slack. This will cause engine noise and, if neglected too long, will cause engine damage.

1. Start the engine and let it reach normal operating temperature.

2. Let the engine idle. Loosen the upper tensioner bolt (A, **Figure 66**) and the lower locknut (B, **Figure 66**) 1 1/2-2 turns.

> *CAUTION*
> *Do not loosen the upper tensioner bolt or lower locknut any more than 2 turns or the tensioner assembly within the engine may work loose and cause severe engine damage.*

3. When the tensioner bolt and locknut are loosened as described in Step 2, the tensioner will automatically move to create the correct chain tension.

4. Tighten the tensioner bolt and the locknut securely.

Starter Decompressor Adjustment (Single-cable Models)

> *NOTE*
> *Valve clearance must be correctly adjusted prior to adjusting the decompressor. Refer to **Valve Clearance Adjustment** in this chapter.*

1. Remove the 2 inspection covers on the left-hand crankcase cover (**Figure 67**).

2. Remove the spark plug.

3. Rotate the crankshaft with the nut on the alternator rotor. Turn it *counterclockwise* until the piston is at top dead center (TDC) on the compression stroke.

> *NOTE*
> *A cylinder at TDC will have both its rocker arms loose, indicating that the exhaust and intake valves are closed. Remove the valve adjusting covers and make this test.*

4. Make sure the "T" mark on the alternator rotor aligns with the fixed notch in the case (**Figure 68**).

5. Measure the free play at the top of the decompressor valve lifter (A, **Figure 69**). The correct amount of free play is as follows:

a. 250 cc models—0.04-0.12 in. (1-3 mm).

b. 500 cc models—0.04-0.08 in. (1-2 mm).

6. To adjust the free play, loosen the locknut (B, **Figure 69**) and turn the adjusting nut (C, **Figure 69**) until the correct amount of free play is achieved.

7. Tighten the locknut, install the valve adjusting covers and install the 2 inspection covers (**Figure 67**).

Starter Decompressor Adjustment (Dual-cable Models)

These models have a manual starter decompressor (on the left-hand handlebar) and a decompressor that works directly with the kickstarter lever. Both the manual and kickstarter decompressor cables must be adjusted correctly or neither will work.

> *NOTE*
> *Valve clearance must be correctly adjusted prior to adjusting the decompressor. Refer to **Valve Clearance Adjustment** in this chapter.*

1. Place the bike on the side stand.

2. Remove the fuel tank as described in Chapter Seven.

3. Remove the 2 inspection hole covers (**Figure 70**) on the left-hand crankcase cover.

4. Remove the spark plug. This will make it easier to rotate the engine by hand.

5. Rotate the crankshaft with the nut on the alternator rotor. Turn the nut *counterclockwise* until the piston is at top dead center (TDC) on the compression stroke.

> *NOTE*
> *A cylinder at TDC will have both of its rocker arms loose, indicating that both the exhaust and the intake valves are closed. Remove the valve adjustment covers and make this test.*

6. Make sure the "T" mark on the alternator rotor aligns with the fixed notch in the case (**Figure 68**).

7A. On XR350R models, the correct amount of free play at the tip of the kickstarter decompressor lever cable is 1/32-1/16 in. (1-2 mm). The correct amount of free play at the tip of the manual decompressor lever is 3/16-5/16 in. (5-8 mm). If adjustment is necessary at either location, perform the following:

    a. Loosen the locknut and adjust nut and disconnect the manual decompressor cable from the actuating lever.

    b. If adjustment is necessary at the kickstarter, loosen the locknut and turn the adjust nut

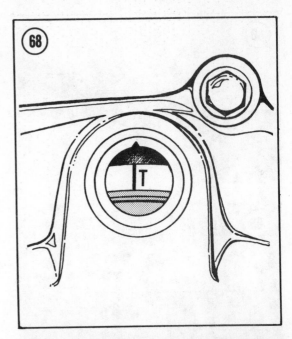

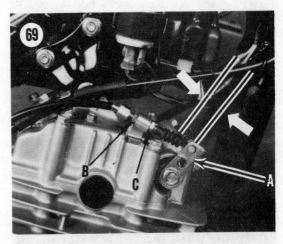

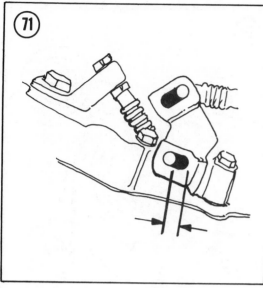

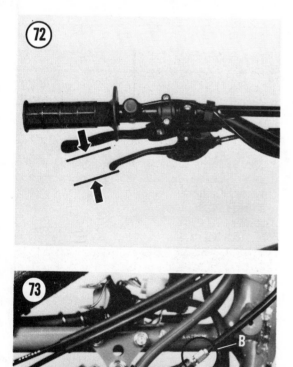

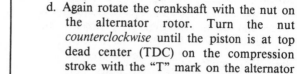

until the correct amount of free play is achieved.

c. Tighten the locknut and operate the kickstarter several times; recheck free play. Adjust if necessary.

d. Again rotate the crankshaft with the nut on the alternator rotor. Turn the nut *counterclockwise* until the piston is at top dead center (TDC) on the compression stroke with the "T" mark on the alternator rotor aligned with the fixed notch in the case (**Figure 68**).

e. Connect the manual starter decompressor cable to the lever.

f. If adjustment is necessary at the manual lever, loosen the locknut and turn the adjusting nut until the correct amount of free play is achieved. Tighten the locknut.

CAUTION
Excessive free play will result in hard starting. Insufficient free play will cause erratic engine idle and a burned exhaust valve(s).

7B. On 1983 XR500R models, the correct amount of free play at the tip of the kickstarter decompressor lever cable is 1/32-1/8 in. (1-3 mm) as shown in **Figure 71**. The correct amount of free play measured at the tip of the manual decompressor lever (**Figure 72**) is 3/16-5/16 in. (5-8 mm). If adjustment is necessary at either location, perform the following:

a. Loosen the kickstarter cable locknut and turn the adjusting nut (A, **Figure 73**) until the correct amount of free play is achieved (**Figure 71**). Tighten the locknut.

b. Operate the kickstarter and check the operation of the kickstarter decompressor mechanism. Recheck the free play and readjust if necessary.

c. Loosen the manual cable locknut and turn the adjusting nut (B, **Figure 73**) until the correct amount of free play is achieved (**Figure 72**). Tighten the locknut.

d. Operate the manual decompressor lever. Recheck the free play and readjust if necessary.

CAUTION
Excessive free play will result in hard starting. Insufficient free play will cause erratic engine idle and a burned exhaust valve(s).

7C. On XL600R models, the correct amount of free play at the tip of the kickstarter decompressor lever cable is 1/32-1/8 in. (1-3 mm) as shown in

Figure 71. The correct amount of free play measured at the tip of the manual decompressor lever (**Figure 72**) is 1/32-1/16 in. (1-2 mm). If adjustment is necessary at either location, perform the following:

a. Loosen the manual cable locknut and turn the adjusting nut until the correct amount of free play is achieved. Tighten the locknut.

b. Operate the manual decompressor lever. Recheck the free play and readjust if necessary.

c. At the back of the cylinder head, loosen the kickstarter cable locknut and turn the adjusting nut until the correct amount of free play is achieved. Tighten the locknut.

d. Operate the kickstarter and check the operation of the kickstarter decompressor mechanism. Recheck the free play and readjust if necessary.

> *CAUTION*
> *Excessive free play will result in hard starting. Insufficient free play will cause erratic engine idle and a burned exhaust valve(s).*

7D. On all other models, the correct amount of free play at the tip of the kickstarter decompressor lever cable is 1/32-1/16 in. (1-2 mm) as shown in **Figure 74**. The correct amount of free play measured at the tip of the manual decompressor lever (**Figure 72**) is 3/16-5/16 in. (5-8 mm). If adjustment is necessary at either location, perform the following:

a. Loosen the manual cable locknut and the adjusting nut to gain cable slack.

b. Disconnect the manual cable from the decompressor starter valve lifter lever on the cylinder head cover.

c. Loosen the locknut on the kickstarter cable and turn the adjusting nut until the correct amount of free play is achieved. Tighten the locknut.

d. Operate the kickstarter and check the operation of the decompressor mechanism.

e. Reconnect the manual cable to the lever.

f. Loosen the locknut on the manual cable and turn the adjusting nut until the correct amount of free play is achieved. Tighten the locknut.

> *CAUTION*
> *Excessive free play will result in hard starting. Insufficient free play will cause erratic engine idle and a burned exhaust valve(s).*

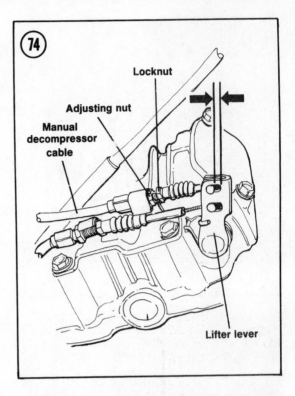

8. Install the valve adjusting covers, the spark plug, the 2 inspection hole covers and the fuel tank.

Balancer Chain Adjustment

The balancer chain should be adjusted at the interval listed in **Table 2**. This procedure applied only to the following models:

a. 1981 XL250R.

b. 1981 XL250S.

c. 1981 XL500S.

d. 1981-1982 XR500R.

e. 1982 XL500R.

All other models have a gear-driven balancer system that does not require periodic adjustment.

1. Drain the engine oil as described under *Changing Engine Oil* in this chapter.

2. Remove the bolts securing the skid plate and remove it.

3. Remove the kickstarter arm.

4. Disconnect the clutch and compression release cables from the right-hand crankcase cover.

5. Remove the right-hand footpeg.

6. Remove the brake pedal.

7. Remove the bolts securing the right-hand crankcase cover and remove it.

8. Loosen the bolt (A, **Figure 75**) securing the balancer holder flange.

9. When the bolt is loosened, the spring (B, **Figure 75**) will pull the holder flange counterclockwise.

NOTE
If the holder flange bottoms out on the bolt, it will have to be repositioned. Refer to Steps 12-18.

10. Move the holder flange *clockwise* one graduation from where it stops (C, **Figure 75**).

NOTE
Align the graduations on the holder flange with the arrow on the crankcase.

11. Tighten the bolt (A, **Figure 75**) to 16-22 ft.-lb. (22-30 N•m).
12. To reposition the holder flange, remove the small circlip (D, **Figure 75**) and slide off the balancer weight and thrust washer (E, **Figure 75**).

13. Remove the spring (A, **Figure 76**) and bolt (B, **Figure 76**).
14. On 250 cc models, remove the large (38 mm) circlip.
15. Note the original position of the holder flange on the shaft. On 500 cc models, remove the circlip and washer (C, **Figure 76**). On all models, slide the holder flange off the shaft spline and reposition it one graduation to the left of the original position.
16. On 250 cc models, install the large circlip.
17. Install the thrust washer, balancer weight and circlip.

CAUTION
The index mark on the balancer weight must align with the punch mark on the end of the shaft (E, Figure 75).

18. Install the spring (B, **Figure 75**) and bolt—do not tighten the bolt at this time.
19. Repeat Steps 10 and 11.
20. Complete by reversing Steps 1-7.
21. Fill the crankcase with the recommended type and quantity of engine oil; refer to *Changing Engine Oil* in this chapter.

Air Filter Element Cleaning (1983 350-600 cc Models)

The air filter element should be removed and cleaned at the interval listed in **Table 2**.

The air filter element removes dust and abrasive particles before the air enters the carburetors and the engine. Without the air filter element, very fine particles could enter into the engine and cause rapid wear of the piston rings, cylinder and bearings. They also might clog small passages in the carburetors. Never run the bike without the air filter element installed.

Proper air filter servicing can ensure long service from your engine.
1. Place the bike on the side stand.
2. Remove the left-hand side cover.
3A. On 600 cc models, perform the following:
   a. Remove the screws securing the air filter cover and remove the cover.
   b. Withdraw the element holder and element from the air box.
3B. On 350 and 500 cc models, perform the following:
   a. Unhook the element retaining strap (**Figure 77**).
   b. Withdraw the element and element holder from the air box.
4. Separate the element from the element holder (**Figure 78**).

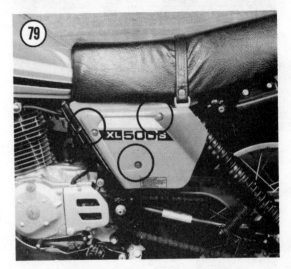

5. Wipe out the interior of the air box with a shop cloth and cleaning solvent. Remove any foreign matter that may have passed through a broken filter element.

6. Clean the element gently in cleaning solvent until all dirt is removed. Throughly dry in a clean shop cloth until all solvent residue is removed. Let it dry for about one hour.

7. Inspect the element; if it is torn or broken in any area it should be replaced. Do not run the bike with a damaged element as it may allow dirt to enter the engine.

8. Pour a small amount of SAE 80-90 gear oil or foam air filter oil onto the element and work it into the porous material. Do not oversaturate the element as too much oil will restrict the air flow. The element will be discolored by the oil and should have an even color indicated that the oil is distributed evenly.

9. If foam air filter oil is used, let the element dry for another hour prior to installation. If installed too soon, the chemical carrier in the oil will be drawn into the engine and may cause damage.

10. Install the air filter element onto the element holder.

11. Install the air filter element and holder into the air box. Make sure that the element is properly seated against the air box.

CAUTION
An improperly installed air filter element will allow dirt and grit to enter the carburetor and engine, causing expensive engine damage.

12A. On 350 and 500 cc models, hook the element retaining strap onto the element.

12B. On 600 cc models, install the air filter cover and tighten the screws securely.

13. Install the left-hand side cover.

Air Filter Element Cleaning
(All Other Models)

The air filter element should be removed and cleaned at the interval listed in **Table 2**.

The air filter element removes dust and abrasive particles before the air enters the carburetors and the engine. Without the air filter element, very fine particles could enter into the engine and cause rapid wear of the piston rings, cylinder and bearings. They also might clog small passages in the carburetor. Never run the bike without the air filter element installed.

Proper air filter servicing can ensure long service from your engine.

1. Place the bike on the side stand.

2. Remove the screws (**Figure 79**) securing the left-hand side cover and remove the cover.

80

7. Inspect the element; if it is torn or broken in any area it should be replaced. Do not run the bike with a damaged element as it may allow dirt to enter the engine.

8. Pour a small amount of SAE 80-90 gear oil or foam air filter oil onto the element and work it into the porous material. Do not oversaturate the element as too much oil will restrict the air flow. The element will be discolored by the oil and should have an even color indicated that the oil is distributed evenly.

9. If the foam air filter oil is used, let the element dry for another hour prior to installation. If installed too soon, the chemical carrier will be drawn into the engine and may cause damage.

10. Install the air filter element onto the element holder.

11. Install the air filter element and holder into the air box. Make sure that the element is properly seated against the air box.

NOTE
An improperly installed air filter element will allow dirt and grit to enter the carburetor and engine, causing expensive engine damage.

12. Inspect the raised sealing ridge that fits into the perimeter gasket of the air box. If the ridge is cracked or broken, the side cover must be replaced.

13A. On 500 cc models, install the wing nut and tigthen securely.

13B. On 250 cc models, attach the retainer to the element.

14. Install the left-hand side cover.

Fuel Shutoff Valve/Filter Removal/Cleaning/Installation

The integral fuel filter in the fuel shutoff valve removes particles in the fuel which might otherwise enter the carburetor. This could cause the float needle to stay in the open position or clog one of the jets.

1. Turn the fuel shutoff valve to the OFF position and remove the fuel line from the valve.

NOTE
The fuel tank can either be removed or left in place; drain all fuel from it in either case.

2. Install a longer piece of clean fuel line to the valve and place the loose end into a clean, sealable metal container. If the fuel is kept clean, it can be reused.

3. Turn the fuel shutoff valve to the RES position and open the fuel filler cap. This will speed up the flow of fuel. Drain the tank completely.

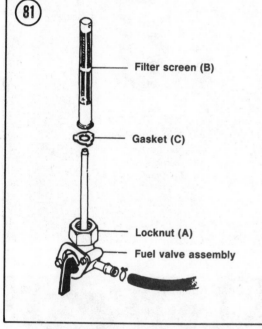

81

Filter screen (B)

Gasket (C)

Locknut (A)

Fuel valve assembly

3A. On 500 cc models, remove the wing nut (**Figure 80**) and withdraw the element holder and element from the air box.

3B. On 250 cc models, pull back on the retainer and withdraw the element and element holder from the air box.

4. Separate the element from the element holder.

5. Wipe out the interior of the air box with a shop cloth and cleaning solvent. Remove any foreign matter that may have passed through a broken filter element.

6. Clean the element gently in cleaning solvent until all dirt is removed. Throughly dry in a clean shop cloth until all solvent residue is removed. Let it dry for about one hour.

4A. On metal fuel tanks, unscrew the locknut (A, **Figure 81**) securing the valve to the tank. Remove the valve.

4B. On plastic fuel tanks, unscrew the screws securing the fuel shutoff valve to the fuel tank. Remove the small collars that surround the screws and remove the valve.

5. After removing the valve, insert a corner of a clean shop rag into the opening in the tank to stop the dribbling of fuel onto the engine and frame.

6. Remove the fuel filter (B, **Figure 81**) from the shutoff valve. Clean it with a medium soft toothbrush and blow out with compressed air. Replace if it is defective.

7. Install by reversing these removal steps, noting the following.

8A. On metal fuel tanks, be sure to install the gasket (C, **Figure 81**) between the valve and the tank. Tighten the locknut.

8B. On plastic fuel tanks, be sure to install the O-ring seal onto the valve. Do not forget to install the small collars that surround the screws.

9. Check for fuel leakage after installation is completed.

Fuel Strainer (XL600R)

1. Turn the fuel shutoff valve to the OFF position.
2. Remove the fuel cup, O-ring seal and filter screen from the bottom of the fuel shutoff valve. Dispose of fuel remaining in the fuel cup properly.
3. Clean the filter screen with a medium soft toothbrush and blow out with compressed air. Replace the filter screen if it is broken in any area.
4. Wash the fuel cup in solvent to remove any residue or foreign matter. Thoroughly dry with compressed air.
5. Align the index marks on the filter screen and the fuel shutoff valve body (**Figure 82**).
6. Install the O-ring seal and screw on the fuel cup.
7. Hand-tighten the fuel cup and then tighten to a final torque of 2-4 ft.-lb. (3-5 N•m). Do not overtighten the fuel cup as it may be damaged.
8. Turn the fuel shutoff valve to the ON position and check for leaks.

Fuel Line Inspection

Inspect the fuel line for cracks or deterioration; replace if necessary. Make sure the hose clamps are in place and holding securely.

Crankcase Breather (U.S.A. Only)

Every 4,000 miles (6,400 km), or sooner if a considerable amount of riding is done at full throttle or in the rain, remove the drain plug (**Figure 83**) and drain out all residue. Install the cap.

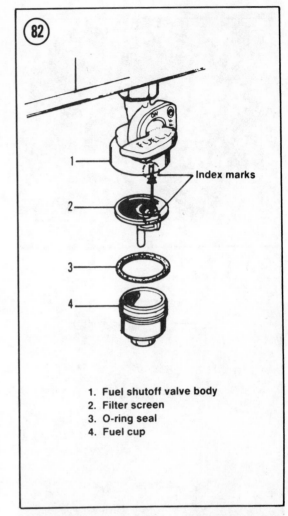

Index marks

1. Fuel shutoff valve body
2. Filter screen
3. O-ring seal
4. Fuel cup

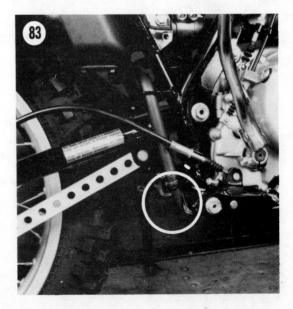

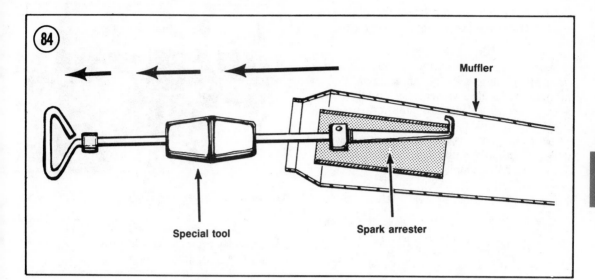

Muffler

Special tool

Spark arrester

3

Refer to Chapter Seven for more complete details on the breather system.

Evaporative Emission Control System (1983 Calif. XL250R Only)

Fuel vapor from the fuel tank is routed into a charcoal canister when the engine is stopped. When the engine is started these vapors are drawn into the air cleaner, through the carburetor and into the engine to be burned. Make sure that all vacuum hoses are correctly routed and attached. Inspect the hoses and replace if necessary. The charcoal canister must be replaced at the interval indicated in **Table 2**.

Spark Arrester Cleaning (U.S.A. Only)

The spark arrester should be cleaned at the interval listed in **Table 2**.

WARNING
To avoid burning your hands do not perform this cleaning operation with the exhaust system hot. Work in a well-ventilated area (outside your garage) that is free from fire hazards. Be sure to protect your eyes with safety goggles or glasses.

250 cc models

A special tool is required to remove the spark arrester from the muffler (**Figure 84**). Use an auto body slide hammer tool with a hook adapter. These are available from the following sources:
1. Flanders Co., P.O. Box 2297, Pasadena CA 91005:
   a. Slide hammer part No. 566-08980.
   b. Seal remover part No. 566-27840.
2. Precision Mfg. & Sales, P.O. Box 149, Clearwater FL 33517:
   a. Slide hammer part No. 202790.
   b. Seal and baffle remover part No. 202784.
Remove the arrester. Start the engine and rev it up about 20-25 times to blow out carbon deposits. Continue until carbon stops coming out.
Coat the spark arrester with a heat resistant sealant prior to installation. Tap the arrester into place with a hammer and piece of wood.

350-600 cc models

1A. On XL500S and XR500 models, remove the bolts securing the front and rear muffler port covers (**Figure 85**). Remove the covers and gaskets.
1B. On XR350R, XR500R and XL600R models, remove the bolts securing the rear muffler port cover (**Figure 86**). Remove the cover and gasket.

WARNING
Wear heavy gloves to protect your hands.

2. Start the engine and rev it up a couple of times. Momentarily place a wadded up shop cloth over the end of the muffler to create back pressure thus blowing the carbon deposits out the port(s). Repeat this step until carbon stops coming out.

Check the exhaust port gasket(s) and replace as necessary. Install the port cover(s) and gasket(s). Tighten the bolts securely.

Wheel Hubs, Rims and Spokes

Check wheel hubs and rims for bends and other signs of damage. Check both wheels for broken or bent spokes. Replace damaged or broken spokes as described under *Wheels* in Chapter Nine. Pluck each spoke with your finger like a guitar string or tap each one lightly with a small hammer. All spokes should emit the same sound. A spoke that is too tight will have a higher pitch than others; one that is too loose will have a lower pitch. If only one or two spokes are slightly out of adjustment, adjust with a spoke wrench made for this purpose. If more are affected, the wheel should be removed and trued. Refer to *Spoke Adjustment* in Chapter Nine.

On models so equipped, ensure that the rim locks are tight. If necessary, tighten to 7-11 ft.-lb. (9-15 N•m).

Front Suspension Check

1. Apply the front brake and pump the forks up and down as vigorously as possible. Check for smooth operation and check for any oil leaks.
2. Make sure the upper and lower fork bridge bolts are tight.
3. Check that the 4 bolts securing the handlebar are tight.
4. On XL250S models make sure the axle pinch bolt is tight; on all other models, check the 4 nuts securing the front axle holder for tightness. Also check the front axle nut on all models.

CAUTION
If any of the previously mentioned bolts and nuts are loose, refer to Chapter Nine for correct procedures and torque specifications.

Rear Suspension Check

1. Place a wooden block under the engine to raise the rear wheel of the ground.

2. Push hard on the rear wheel (sideways) to check for side play in the swing arm bushings. Remove the blocks from under the engine.
3. Check that the upper and lower shock absorber mounting bolts are tight.
4. Make sure the rear axle nut is tight and the cotter pin is still in place.
5. Check the tightness of the rear brake torque arm bolt.

CAUTION
If any of the previously mentioned nuts are loose, refer to Chapter Ten for correct procedures and torque specifications.

Nuts, Bolts and Other Fasteners

Constant vibration can loosen many fasteners on a motorcycle. Check the tightness of all fasteners, especially those on:
   a. Engine mounting hardware.
   b. Engine crankcase covers.
   c. Handlebars and front forks.
   d. Gearshift lever.
   e. Brake lever and pedal.
   f. Exhaust system.
   g. Lighting equipment (XL series only).

Wheel Bearings

The wheel bearings should be cleaned and repacked at the interval listed in **Table 2** or after crossing or riding small rivers or creeks. Refer to Chapter Nine and Chapter Ten for complete service procedures.

Side Stand Rubber (XL Series Only)

The rubber tip on the side stand kicks the stand up if you should forget. If it wears down to the molded line, replace the rubber as it will no longer be effective.

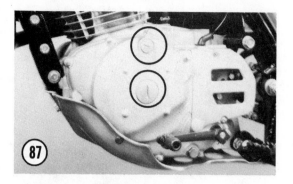

Steering Head Adjustment Check

The steering head is fitted with two ball bearings and should be checked for looseness at the interval listed in **Table 2**.

Jack up the bike so that the front wheel is off the ground.

Hold onto the front fork tubes and gently rock the fork assembly back and forth. If you can feel looseness refer to *Steering Head Adjustment* in Chapter Nine.

TUNE-UP

A complete tune-up should be performed on XL series models every 4,000 miles (6,400 km) and on XR series models every 1,000 miles (1,600 km). If you are using the XR series for racing, your bike should be tuned prior to each race. On XL series, more frequent tune-ups may be required if the bike is ridden primarily in stop-and-go traffic. The purpose of the tune-up is to restore the performance lost due to normal wear and deterioration of parts.

The spark plug should be routinely replaced at every other tune-up or if the electrodes show signs of erosion. In addition, this is a good time to clean the air cleaner element. Have the new parts on hand before you begin.

Because different systems in an engine interact, the procedures should be done in the following order:

  a. Tighten the cylinder head nuts.
  b. Adjust the valve clearances.
  c. Run a compression test.
  d. Check and adjust the ignition components and timing.
  e. Set carburetor idle speed and choke adjustment.

Cylinder Head Nuts

The cylinder head (not the cylinder head cover) is held in place with four acorn nuts. The two on the left-hand side are exposed but the two on the right-hand side are within the cylinder head cavity. On XL500S and XR500 models, it is necessary to remove the engine from the frame and remove the cylinder head cover to reach them.

The nuts should only be tightened on the first tune-up after purchase of a new bike or after the head has been removed for service. If you wish to tighten the four nuts, remove the cylinder head cover as described in Chapter Four.

Valve Clearance Adjustment

Valve clearance adjustment must be made with the engine cool, at room temperature (below 95° F/35° C). The correct valve clearance for all models is listed in **Table 12**. The exhaust valves are located at the front of the engine and the intake valves are at the rear of the engine.

> *NOTE*
> *Make sure there is free play in the starter decompressor lever. If not, it will hold down the exhaust valves and make the exhaust valve clearance incorrect. If necessary, adjust the decompressor as described in this chapter to allow sufficient slack. Readjust the decompressor after the valve clearance is correct.*

1. Place the bike on the side stand.
2. Remove the seat.
3. Remove the fuel tank as described in Chapter Seven.
4. Remove the 2 inspection covers (**Figure 87**) on the left-hand crankcase cover.

> *NOTE*
> *The following steps are shown with the engine removed from the frame for clarity. It is not necessary to remove the engine to perform this procedure.*

5A. On XR350R, XR500R and XL600R models, unscrew each valve adjustment cover.
5B. On all other models, remove the bolts (**Figure 88**) securing the front and rear valve adjustment covers and remove the covers.
6. Remove the spark plug (this will make it easier to rotate the engine).
7. Rotate the engine with the bolt or nut on the alternator rotor. Turn the engine *counterclockwise* until the piston is at top dead center (TDC) on the compression stroke.

> *NOTE*
> *A cylinder at TDC of its compression stroke will have free play in all of its*

rocker arms, indicating that all of the intake and exhaust valves are closed.

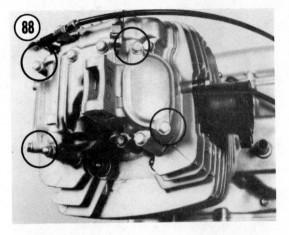

8. Make sure the "T" mark on the alternator rotor aligns with the index mark on the crankcase (**Figure 89**).

9. With the engine timing mark on the "T," if all rocker arms are not loose, rotate the engine an additional 180° until all valves have free play.

10. Check the clearance of both the intake and exhaust valves by inserting a flat feeler gauge between the adjusting screw and the valve stem (**Figure 90**). When the clearance is correct, there will be a slight resistance on the feeler gauge when it is inserted and withdrawn.

11. To correct the clearance perform the following:

   a. Back off the locknut.

   b. Screw the adjuster in or out so there is a slight resistance felt on the feeler gauge (**Figure 91**).

   c. Hold the adjuster to prevent it from turning further and tighten the locknut (**Figure 92**) to 11-13 ft.-lb. (15-18 N•m).

   d. Recheck the clearance to make sure the adjuster did not slip when the locknut was tightened. Readjust if necessary.

   e. Rotate the engine 360° and repeat Step 10 to make sure the adjustment is correct.

   f. Repeat for all 4 valves.

12. Inspect the rubber gaskets on all valve adjusting covers. Replace if they are starting to deteriorate or harden; replace as a set even if only one is bad. Install all covers.

13. Install the spark plug.

14. Adjust the decompressor free play as described in this chapter.

15. Install the inspection covers, fuel tank and seat.

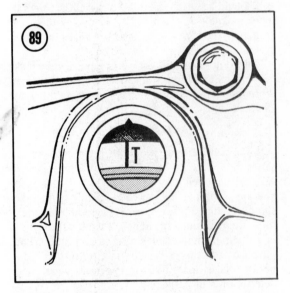

Compression Test

Every 6,000 miles, check cylinder compression. Record the results and compare them at the next 6,000 mile check. A running record will show trends in deterioration so that corrective action can be taken before complete failure.

The results, when properly interpreted, can indicate general cylinder, piston ring and valve condition.

1. Warm the engine to normal operating temperature, then shut it off. Ensure that the choke valve and throttle valve are completely open.

2. Turn off the engine and remove the seat, fuel tank and spark plug.

3. Connect the compression tester following the manufacturer's instructions.

4. Push the choke knob all the way in and open the throttle all the way.

5. Operate the kickstarter several times and check the gauge reading. The specifications are listed in **Table 12**.

If the compression reading is less than specified it indicates worn or broken rings, leaky or sticky valves, blown head gasket or a combination of all.

A reading of 10% or less indicates valve or ring trouble. To determine which, pour about a teaspoon of engine oil through the spark plug hole onto the top of the piston. Turn the engine over once to clear some of the excess oil, then take another compression test and record the reading. If the compression returns to normal, the valves are good but the rings are defective. If compression does not increase, the valves require servicing. A valve could be hanging open but not burned or a piece of carbon could be on a valve seat.

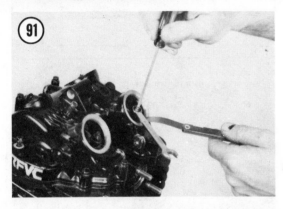

Spark Plug Heat Range

Spark plugs are available in various heat ranges, hotter or colder than plugs originally installed at the factory.

Select plugs of a heat range designed for the loads and temperature conditions under which the bike will run. Use of incorrect heat ranges can cause seized pistons, scored cylinder walls or damaged piston crowns.

In general, use a hot plug for low speeds, low loads and low temperatures. Use a cold plug for high speeds, high engine loads and high temperatures.

In areas where seasonal temperature variations are great, the factory recommends a "two-plug system"—a cold plug for hard summer riding and a hot plug for slower winter operation.

The reach (length) of a plug is also important. A longer than normal plug could interfere with the valves and pistons causing permanent and severe damage. Refer to **Figure 93**.

The recommended heat ranges are listed in **Table 12**.

Spark Plug Cleaning and Replacement

The spark plug should be inspected and cleaned at the interval listed in **Table 2**.

1. Grasp the spark plug lead as near the cap as possible and pull it off the plug.

2. Blow away any dirt and moisture that has accumulated in the spark plug well.

> *CAUTION*
> *Dirt could fall into the cylinder when the plug is removed, causing serious engine damage.*

3. Remove the spark plug with an 18 mm spark plug wrench.

3

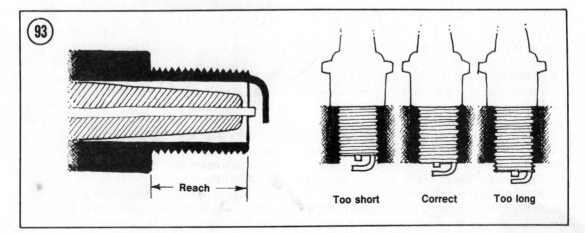

Reach

Too short   Correct   Too long

NOTE
If plug is difficult to remove, apply penetrating oil, such as WD-40 or Liquid Wrench, around base of the plug and let it soak in about 10-20 minutes.

4. Inspect the spark plug carefully. Look for a plug with broken center porcelain, excessively eroded electrodes and excessive carbon or oil fouling. Replace such a plug. If deposits are light, plug may be cleaned in solvent with a wire brush or cleaned in a special spark plug sandblast cleaner.

5. Gap the plug to the specification listed in **Table 12**. Use a wire feeler gauge (**Figure 94**).

6. Install plug with a *new* gasket. First, apply a *small* drop of oil to threads. Tighten the plug finger-tight, then tighten with a spark plug wrench an additional 1/2 turn. If you must reuse an old gasket, tighten only an additional 1/4 turn.

NOTE
Do not overtighten. This will only squash the gasket and destroy its sealing ability.

Reading Spark Plugs

Much information about engine and spark plug performance can be determined by careful examination of the spark plugs. This information is only valid after performing the following steps.

1. Ride the bike a short distance at full throttle in any gear.

2. Turn the kill switch to OFF before closing the throttle and simultaneously pull in the clutch; coast and brake to a stop.

3. Remove the spark plug and examine it. Compare it to those shown in **Figure 95**.

If insulator is white or burned, the plug is too hot and should be replaced with a colder one.

A too-cold plug will have sooty deposits ranging in color from dark brown to black. Replace with a hotter plug and check for too-rich carburetion or evidence of oil blow-by at the piston rings.

Ignition Timing

The Honda XL and XR series are equipped with a capacitor discharge ignition (CDI). This system, unlike a battery or magneto ignition system, uses no breaker points.

Since there are no components to wear, adjusting the ignition timing is not necessary even after engine disassembly. The timing should not change for the life of the bike.

Three items that could cause the timing to vary are the CDI unit, the advancer mechanism and/or the alternator. Check the timing with the following

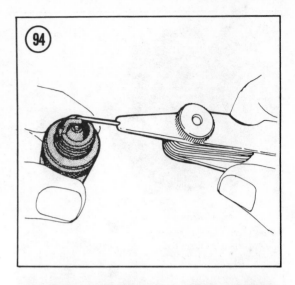

procedure; if it is incorrect, check out these units as described in Chapter Eight.

NOTE
Before starting on this procedure, check all electrical connections related to the ignition system. Make sure all connections are tight and free of corrosion and that all ground connections are tight.

1. Remove the timing inspection hole cover cap (**Figure 96**).

2. Connect a portable tachometer and timing light to the engine following the manufacturer's instructions.

(95)   **SPARK PLUG CONDITION**

NORMAL
• Identified by light tan or gray deposits on the firing tip.
• Can be cleaned.

GAP BRIDGED
• Identified by deposit buildup closing gap between electrodes.
• Caused by oil or carbon fouling. If deposits are not excessive, the plug can be cleaned.

OIL FOULED
• Identified by wet black deposits on the insulator shell bore electrodes.
• Caused by excessive oil entering combustion chamber through worn rings and pistons, excessive clearance between valve guides and stems, or worn or loose bearings. Can be cleaned. If engine is not repaired, use a hotter plug.

CARBON FOULED
• Identified by black, dry fluffy carbon deposits on insulator tips, exposed shell surfaces and electrodes.
• Caused by too cold a plug, weak ignition, dirty air cleaner, too rich a fuel mixture, or excessive idling. Can be cleaned.

LEAD FOULED
• Identified by dark gray, black, yellow, or tan deposits or a fused glazed coating on the insulator tip.
• Caused by highly leaded gasoline. Can be cleaned.

WORN
• Identified by severely eroded or worn electrodes.
• Caused by normal wear. Should be replaced.

FUSED SPOT DEPOSIT
• Identified by melted or spotty deposits resembling bubbles or blisters.
• Caused by sudden acceleration. Can be cleaned.

OVERHEATING
• Identified by a white or light gray insulator with small black or gray brown spots and with bluish-burnt appearance of electrodes.
• Caused by engine overheating, wrong type of fuel, loose spark plugs, too hot a plug, or incorrect ignition timing. Replace the plug.

PREIGNITION
• Identified by melted electrodes and possibly blistered insulator. Metallic deposits on insulator indicate engine damage.
• Caused by wrong type of fuel, incorrect ignition timing or advance, too hot a plug, burned valves, or engine overheating. Replace the plug.

3

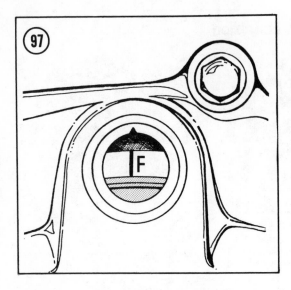

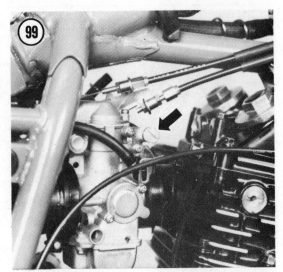

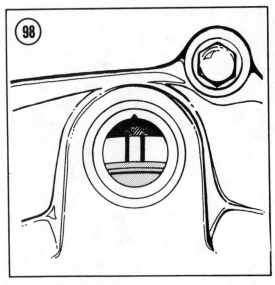

3. Place the bike on the side stand and start the engine. Let it warm up and idle at $1,200 \pm 100$ rpm; adjust if necessary as described under *Carburetor Idle Speed Adjustment* in this chapter.

4. Aim the timing light at the timing marks on the alternator flywheel. The timing is correct if the "F" on the alternator flywheel aligns with the index notch on the crankcase cover (**Figure 97**).

5. Increase engine speed and check that the advance timing marks (**Figure 98**) align with the index notch on the crankcase cover at 3,500 rpm.

Carburetor Idle Adjustment

Carburetor idle adjustment should be performed at the interval indicated in **Table 2**.

Before making this adjustment, the air filter element must be clean and the engine must have adequate compression. Otherwise, this procedure cannot be done properly.

1. Start the engine and let it reach normal operating temperature; 10-15 minutes of stop-and-go riding is usually sufficient.

2. Shut off the engine and connect a portable tachometer following the manufacturer's instructions.

3A. On XR350R, XR500R and XL600R models, turn the idle adjust screw (**Figure 99**) in to increase or out to decrease idle speed.

3B. On all other models, turn the black idle adjust knob (**Figure 100**) in to increase or out to decrease idle speed.

4. The correct idle speed is listed in **Table 12**.

5. Open and close the throttle a couple of times; check for variations in idle speed. Readjust if necessary.

> *WARNING*
> *With the engine at idle, move the handlebar from side to side. If idle speed increases during this movement, the throttle cables may need adjusting or they may be incorrectly routed through the frame. Correct this problem immediately. **Do not** ride the bike in this unsafe condition.*

Carburetor Idle Mixture

The idle mixture (pilot screw) is present at the factory and *is not to be reset*. Do not adjust the pilot screw unless the carburetor has been overhauled. If so, refer to Chapter Seven for service procedures.

Table 1 TIRE INFLATION PRESSURE*

Tire size	Air pressure	
	psi	kg/cm²
Front tire		
3.00-21 6PR	14	1.0
3.00-21 4PR	21	1.5
3.00-23 4 PR	21	1.5
90/80-21 6PR	15	1.03
Rear tire		
5.10-17 6PR	15	1.03
5.10-17 4PR	21	1.5
4.60-18 4PR	21	1.5
4.60-18 6PR	17	1.2
130/80-17 6PR	15	1.0

* Tire inflation pressure for factory equipped tires. Aftermarket tire inflation pressure may vary according to manufacturer's instructions.

Table 2 MAINTENANCE SCHEDULE*

XR SERIES MODELS

Every 300 miles (500 km) or when dry
    Lubricate and adjust the drive chain

Every 500 miles (800 km) or 6 months
    Clean air filter element
    Check engine oil level
    Lubricate all control cables
    Lubricate rear brake pedal and shift lever
    Lubricate side stand pivot point
    Inspect front steering for looseness
    Check wheel bearings for smooth operation
    Check ignition timing
    Check and adjust idle speed
    Check clutch lever free play
    Check fuel shutoff valve and filter
    Check wheel spoke condition
    Check wheel runout

(continued)

Table 2 MAINTENANCE SCHEDULE (continued)

XR SERIES MODELS

Every 1,000 miles (1,600 km)

Change engine oil
Lubricate swing arm bushings
Clean engine oil screen
Replace engine oil filter (XR350R, XR500R)
Inspect spark plug, regap if necessary
Check and adjust valve clearance
Adjust cam chain tension (models so equipped)
Adjust balancer chain tension (models so equipped)
Inspect decompressor free play, adjust if necessary
Inspect fuel lines
Inspect and repack wheel bearings
Inspect crankcase ventilation hoses, drain out all residue
Check engine mounting bolts for tightness
Check steering for free play
Check all suspension components
Adjust front and rear brake levers

Every 4,000 miles (6,400 km)

Check and adjust valve clearance
Adjust the cam chain tension (models so equipped)
Check and adjust ignition timing
Check and adjust the carburetor(s)
Replace spark plug
Dismantle and clean carburetor(s)
Change front fork oil
Inspect and repack swing arm bushings
Replace air filter element
Lubricate speedometer cable
Inspect brake shoes (or pads) for wear
Check engine mounting bolts for tightness
Check all suspension components
Inspect all drive chain roller tensioners and sliders
Lubricate control cables
Inspect and repack steering head bearings

XL SERIES MODELS

Every 300 miles (500 km) or when dry

Lubricate and adjust the drive chain

Every 500 miles (800 km) or 6 months

Clean air filter element
Check engine oil level
Lubricate all control cables
Lubricate rear brake pedal and shift lever
Lubricate side stand pivot point
Inspect front steering for looseness
Check wheel bearings for smooth operation
Check battery electrolyte level and condition
Check ignition timing
Check and adjust idle speed
Check clutch lever free play
Check fuel shutoff valve and filter
Check wheel spoke condition
Check wheel runout

(continued)

Table 2 MAINTENANCE SCHEDULE (continued)

XL SERIES MODELS

Every 1,000 miles (1,600 km)

Lubricate swing arm bushings

Every 1,800 miles (3,000 km)

Change engine oil

Every 4,000 miles (6,400 km)

Clean air filter element
Replace engine oil filter (XL600R)
Inspect spark plug, regap if necessary
Check and adjust valve clearance
Adjust cam chain tension (models so equipped)
Adjust balancer chain tension (models so equipped)
Inspect decompressor free play, adjust if necessary
Inspect fuel lines
Inspect and repack wheel bearings
Inspect crankcase ventillation hoses drain out all residue
Check engine mounting bolts for tightness
Check steering for free play
Check all suspension components
Adjust front and rear brake levers

Every 6,000 miles (10,000 km)

Check and adjust valve clearance
Adjust the cam chain tension (models so equipped)
Check and adjust ignition timing
Check and adjust the carburetor(s)
Replace spark plug
Dismantle and clean carburetor(s)
Change front fork oil
Inspect and repack swing arm bushings
Replace air filter element
Lubricate speedometer cable
Inspect brake shoes (or pads) for wear
Check engine mounting bolts for tightness
Check all suspension components
Inspect all drive chain roller tensioners and sliders
Lubricate control cables
Inspect and repack steering head bearings

Every 8,000 miles (12,800 km)

Remove and clean engine oil screen
Replace the spark plug

Every 12,000 miles (19,200 km)

Replace fuel evaporation canister (1983 XL250R only)

* This Honda Factory maintenance schedule should be considered as a guide to general maintenance and lubrication intervals. Harder than normal use and exposure to mud, water, sand, high humidity, etc. will naturally dictate more frequent attention to most maintenance items.

3

Table 3 COMPETITION PRE-RACE INSPECTION

Item	Inspection
Engine oil	Check for contamination, change if dirty
Fuel line	Check for leakage and deterioration, replace
Air cleaner	Check for tears and contamination, replace or clean
Valve clearance	Adjust if necessary to correct clearance
Cam chain tension	Check for abnormal noise, adjust if necessary
Carburetor idle speed	Check and adjust if necessary
Balancer chain tension	Adjust if necessary (check while inspecting the cluch disc)
Starter decompressor	Check for correct free play, adjust if necessary
Clutch disc wear	Check for abnormal wear and/or discoloration
Spark plug	Check for proper heat range, gap, tightness and plug cap tightness
Steering head	Check for free rotation of handlebar, check tightness of steering stem nut, adjust and/or tighten if necessary
Front suspension	Check for oil leaks, tight boot clamps and smooth action of forks
Rear suspension	Check for oil leaks and smooth operation
Swing arm bushings	Check for abnormal side play, replace if necessary
Brake shoes	Check wear indicators for wear beyond limits, replace brake shoes
Drive chain	Inspect for damage and chain stretch, replace if necessary
Sprockets (both)	Inspect for wear and tightness of installation
Seat	Check for tightness of mounting hardware
Control cables	Check for smooth operation and frayed outer sheath, lubricate or replace
Engine mounting bolts	Check for tightness and fractures on mounting hardware
Headlight	Proper headlight adjustment
Instrument lights	Check for proper operation
Tires	Check for proper inflation and inspect for cuts and deep abrasions, replace if necessary
Exterior of engine	Clean the entire engine and frame prior to a race

Table 4 STATE OF CHARGE

Specific Gravity	State of Charge
1.110-1.130	Discharged
1.140-1.160	Almost discharged
1.170-1.190	One-quarter charged
1.200-1.220	One-half charged
1.230-1.250	Three-quarters charged
1.260-1.280	Fully charged

Table 5 ENGINE OIL CAPACITY

Engine size	Oil Drain		Rebuild	
	U.S. qt.	Liter	U.S. qt.	Liter
250 cc	1.6	1.5	2.1	2.0
350 cc	1.9	1.8	2.1	2.0
500 cc (1979-1982)	1.6	1.5	2.1	2.0
500, 600 cc (1983)	2.1	2.0	2.6	2.5

Table 6 FRONT FORK OIL CAPACITY*

Model	Standard Capacity		Standard distance from top of fork	
	cc	fl. oz.	mm	in.
XL250S	190	6.4	–	–
XL250R	300	10.14	173	6.81
XR250R				
1981	368	12.4	152	6
1982	395	13.4	156	6.125
XR250	202	6.8	–	–
XR350R	553	18.7	132	5.2
XR500	202	6.8	–	–
XL500S	190	6.4	–	–
XL500R	379	12.75	163	6.42
XR500R				
1981-1982	345	11.7	181	7.1
1983	651	22	141	5.5
XL600R	455	15.4	150	5.9

* Capacity for each fork leg.

Table 7 SUSPENSION TORQUE SPECIFICATIONS

Item	ft.-lb.	N•m
Front fork cap bolt		
1978-1982 models	11-22	15-30
XR350R	11-14	15-20
XR500R, XL600R	11-18	15-25
Rear axle nut (Pro-Link models)		
1981	51-80	70-110
1982-1983	58-80	80-110

Table 8 FRONT FORK AIR PRESSURE

Model	psi	kg/cm²
1982 XL250R	0-2.8	0-0.2
1982 XL500R		
XL600R, XR350R	0	0
1983 XR500R	0-14	0.98

Table 9 DRIVE CHAIN SLACK

Model	in.	mm
Dual shock models		
XL series	0.6-0.8	15-20
XR series	0.8	20
Pro-Link models	1 3/8-1 3/4	35-45

Table 10 DRIVE CHAIN REPLACEMENT NUMBERS

Model	Standard
XL250S	102L
XL250R	520VC-102L
XR250	102L
XR250R	520DS-106RJ
XR350R	520MS-104FJ
XL500S	520KD-96
XL500R	520VS-100LE
XR500	DID520KD-100L or DID520KD-102L
XR500R	520KO-104FJ
XL600R	520VS-104CE or 520SO-104LE

Table 11 DRIVE CHAIN SERVICE LENGTH SPECIFICATIONS

Model	Number of pins	Dimension	
		in.	mm
XL250S	41	25.4	648
XL250R	NA		
XR250	102	64.4	1,635
XR250R	107	66.94	1,700
XR350R	105	66.94	1,700
XL500S	41	25.5	648
XL500R	NA		
XR500	100	76.5	1,944
XR500R			
1981-1982	105	64.75	1,645
1983	107	67.56	1,716
XL600R	NA		

* NA = Honda does not provide service information for all models.

Table 12 TUNE-UP SPECIFICATIONS

Valve clearance	
Intake	
XR250	0.003 in. (0.08 mm)
All other models	0.002 in. (0.05 mm)
Exhaust	
XR350R	0.003 in. (0.08 mm)
All other models	0.004 in. (0.10 mm)
Compression pressure	
XR250, XR250R	192 psi (13.5 kg/cm^2)
All other models	175 psi (12.5 kg/cm^2)
Spark plug type (standard)	
1978-1981	ND X24ES-U or NGK D8EA
1982	ND X24ESR-U or NGK DR8ES-L
1983	ND X24EPR-U9 or NGK DPR8EA-9
Spark plug gap	
1978-1982	0.6-0.7 mm (0.024-0.028 in.)
1983	0.8-0.9 mm (0.032-0.036 in.)
Ignition timing	"F" mark @ 1,200 ±100 rpm
Idle speed	1,200 ±100 rpm

3

CHAPTER FOUR

ALL 250 AND 1979-1982
500 CC ENGINES

This chapter covers the engine used in the following models:

a. XL250S.
b. XL250R.
c. XR250.
d. XR250R.
e. XL500S.
f. XL500R.
g. XR500.
h. 1981-1982 XR500R.

The 250 cc and 500 cc engines are basically the same. The exception is the larger piston, cylinder and cylinder head for the 500 cc version.

The engine is an air-cooled, four-stroke, single cylinder with a chain-driven overhead camshaft. The head incorporates a pair of dual valves, each set having its own rocker arm. Each valve has its own adjuster.

The crankshaft is supported by two large ball bearings and engine vibration is minimized by two counter-rotating balancers that are driven off the crankshaft by a chain or gears.

To ease starting the engine, it has a starter decompressor. As the kickstarter pedal is depressed, a cam on the pedal shaft operates a lever that transmits movement via a cable to the decompressor valve lifter on the cylinder head. This lifter opens the exhaust valves momentarily and then allows them to close as the pedal continues its downward travel.

The oil pump supplies oil under pressure throughout the engine and is driven by the kickstarter idle gear.

Table 1 at the end of this chapter provides complete specifications for the engine. Although the clutch and transmission are located within the engine, they are covered separately in Chapter Six to simplify the presentation of this material.

Service procedures for all models are virtually the same. The engine used in this chapter is from an XL500S; where differences occur they are identified.

Prior to removing the engine or any major assembly, clean the entire engine and frame with a good grade commercial degreaser, such as Gunk Cycle Degreaser or equivalent. It is easier to work on a clean engine and you will do a better job.

Make certain that you have all the necessary tools available, especially any special tools and purchase replacements for any know faulty parts prior to disassembly. Also make sure you have a clean place to work.

It is a good idea to identify and mark parts as they are removed so that errors will be avoided during assembly and installation. Clean all parts thoroughly upon removal, then place them in trays or boxes with their associated mounting hardware. Make certain all parts related to a particular cylinder, piston, connecting rod and/or valve assembly are identified for installation in the proper place. Do not rely on memory alone as it may be days or weeks before you complete the job.

Refer to **Table 2** at the end of the chapter for torque specifications on all engine components.

ENGINE PRINCIPLES

Figure 1 explains how the engine works. This will be helpful when troubleshooting or repairing your engine.

①

4-STROKE OPERATING PRINCIPLES

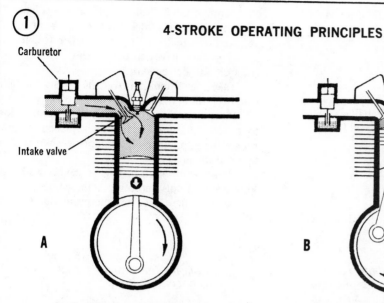

Carburetor

Intake valve

A

As the piston travels downward, the exhaust valve is closed and the intake valve opens, allowing the new fuel/air mixture from the **carburetor** to be drawn into the cylinder. When the piston reaches the bottom of its travel (BDC), the **intake valve** closes and remains closed for the next revolution-and-a-half of the crankshaft.

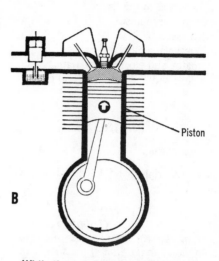

Piston

B

While the crankshaft continues to rotate, the **piston** moves upward, compressing the fuel/air mixture.

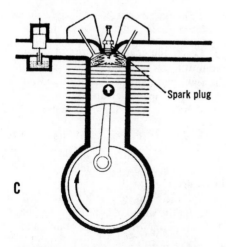

Spark plug

C

As the piston almost reaches the top of its travel, the **spark plug** fires, igniting the compressed fuel/air mixture. The piston continues to top dead center (TDC) and is pushed downward by the expanding gases.

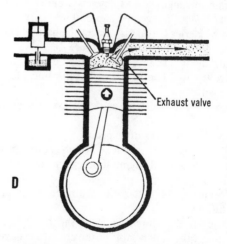

Exhaust valve

D

When the piston almost reaches BDC, the **exhaust valve** opens and remains open until the piston is near TDC. The upward travel of the piston causes the exhaust gases to be pushed out of the cylinder. After the piston has reached TDC, the exhaust valve closes and the cycle starts all over again.

4

SERVICING ENGINE IN FRAME

Many components can be serviced while the engine is mounted in the frame:

   a. Gearshift mechanism.
   b. Clutch assembly.
   c. Carburetor assembly.
   d. Alternator and electrical systems.
   e. Cylinder head and cylinder (250 cc only).

ENGINE

Removal/Installation

1. Remove the right- and left-hand side covers and seat.

CAUTION
On XL250S and XL500S models, reinstall the seat strap bolts as they also hold the upper portion of the shocks in place on the frame (Figure 2). Remove and reinstall one bolt at a time.

2. Remove the exhaust system as described in Chapter Seven.
3. Remove the carburetor assembly as described in Chapter Seven.
4. Remove the bolts (**Figure 3**) securing the skid plate and remove it.
5. Drain the engine oil as described under *Engine Oil and Filter Change* in Chapter Three.
6. On XL series bikes, disconnect the battery leads or disconnect the main fuse (**Figure 4**).
7. Turn the fuel shutoff valve to the OFF position; remove the fuel line to the carburetor and plug it with a golf tee.
8. Remove the fuel tank as described in Chapter Seven.
9. Remove the kickstarter pedal.
10. Disconnect the rear brake switch return spring and cable, front right-hand footpeg and rear brake pedal.
11. Remove the left-hand front footpeg and gearshift lever.
12. Slacken the clutch cable at the hand lever. Disconnect the clutch cable at the crankcase cover.
13. Disconnect the ignition pulser generator wires at the electrical connector. Refer to **Figure 5** or **Figure 6**.

NOTE
The electrical connector on all models contains 2 wires.

14. Disconnect the spark plug wire and tie it up out of the way.

15. Remove the 2 Phillips head screws (**Figure 7**) securing the drive sprocket cover and remove it.
16. Remove the 2 bolts and keeper (**Figure 8**) securing the drive sprocket and remove the sprocket and drive chain.
17. Take a final look all over the engine to make sure everything has been disconnected.
18. Place a suitable size jack, with a piece of wood to protect the crankcase, under the engine (A, **Figure 9**). Apply a small amount of jack pressure up on the engine.
19. Remove the 4 front engine hanger bolts (B, **Figure 9**) and nuts and remove the hanger.
20. Remove the upper rear mounting bolt (**Figure 10**).

NOTE
Don't lose the 2 spacers (Figure 10) between the frame and the engine. Be sure to reinstall them.

21. Remove the lower rear mounting bolt (C, **Figure 9**).
22. Remove the 3 upper bolts, nuts and plates (**Figure 11**).

CAUTION
Continually adjust the jack pressure during engine removal and installation to prevent damage to the mounting bolt threads and hardware.

CAUTION
The next step requires 2 people to safely remove the engine from the frame.

23. Lower the engine assembly to clear the frame mounting brackets and pull the engine out through the right-hand side of the frame. Take it to your workbench for further disassembly.
24. Install by reversing these removal steps. Note the following.
25. Tighten the engine hanger bolts to specifications. Refer to **Figure 12**. The letter designations on the figure relate to the letters listed in **Figure 12**.
26. Fill the crankcase with the recommended type and quantity of engine oil. Refer to Chapter Three.
27. Adjust the drive chain, clutch and rear brake pedal as described in Chapter Three.

CYLINDER HEAD COVER

Removal

The cylinder head cover can be removed with the engine in the frame on 250 cc models only.

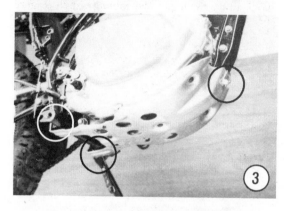

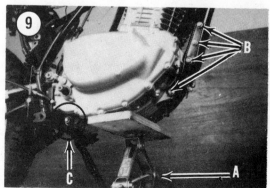

4

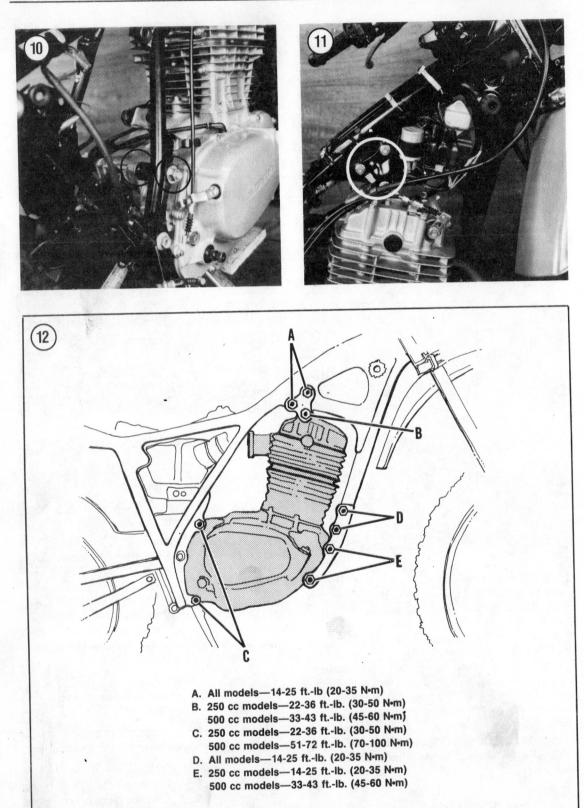

A. All models—14-25 ft.-lb (20-35 N•m)
B. 250 cc models—22-36 ft.-lb. (30-50 N•m)
   500 cc models—33-43 ft.-lb. (45-60 N•m)
C. 250 cc models—22-36 ft.-lb. (30-50 N•m)
   500 cc models—51-72 ft.-lb. (70-100 N•m)
D. All models—14-25 ft.-lb. (20-35 N•m)
E. 250 cc models—14-25 ft.-lb. (20-35 N•m)
   500 cc models—33-43 ft.-lb. (45-60 N•m)

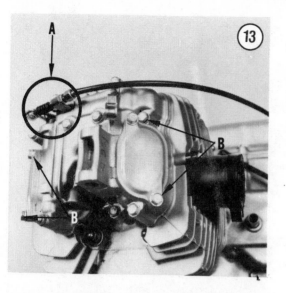

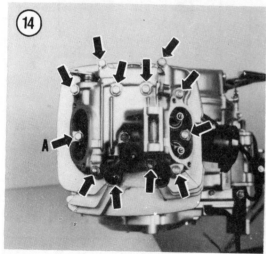

1. On 500 cc models, remove the engine from the frame as described in this chapter.

2. On 250 cc models, remove the seat, fuel tank, decompressor cable from the right-hand crankcase cover, upper engine mounting bolts and plates and the valve adjusting covers.

3. On 500 cc models, loosen the starter decompressor cable locknut and remove the cable from the lifter lever (A, **Figure 13**). Remove the bolts (B, **Figure 13**) securing each valve adjuster cover and remove them.

4. Remove the 11 bolts (**Figure 14**) and one acorn nut (A, **Figure 14**) securing the cylinder head cover and remove it.

NOTE
Don't lose the 2 locating dowels. •

CYLINDER HEAD COVER

Disassembly/Inspection/Assembly

Refer to **Figure 15** for this procedure.

1A. On XR250R, XR500R, XL500S and XL500R models, to remove the dowel pins securing the rocker arm shafts (**Figure 16**) perform the following:

   a. Cut a 2 mm notch (**Figure 17**) in each dowel pin with a small rotary grinder.

CAUTION
In the following step, do not overtighten the vise holding the cylinder head cover. Use the vise only as a holding fixture.

   b. Very carefully place the cylinder head cover in a vise with soft jaws.

   c. Insert a drift or chisel in through the valve adjustment cover opening in the cylinder head cover and tap out the dowel pins. Remove the dowel pins and discard them.

CAUTION
Be careful not to damage the cylinder head cover or rocker arms during the removal procedure.

NOTE
If these pins are difficult to remove, apply Liquid Wrench to the base of the pins and let sit for 10-15 minutes. This may help to loosen them.

1B. On all other models, remove the dowel pins securing the rocker arm shafts (A, **Figure 18**) and valve lifter lever (B, **Figure 18**).

2. Hold the cover upside down in your hand and tap on the engine mounting boss (C, **Figure 18**) with a plastic mallet several times. Tap on the side where the rocker shaft ends are exposed. This tapping will cause the rocker arm shafts to work their way out enough to get hold of with your fingers. Do not use pliers as there is an O-ring seal on each shaft at this end.

CAUTION
Do not use a metal hammer as the cover will be damaged.

3. Pull the rocker arm shaft out and remove the rocker arm and spring washer. Repeat for the other shaft.

NOTE
Mark the shafts with an "I" (intake) or "E" (exhaust) as they must be reinstalled into their original location.

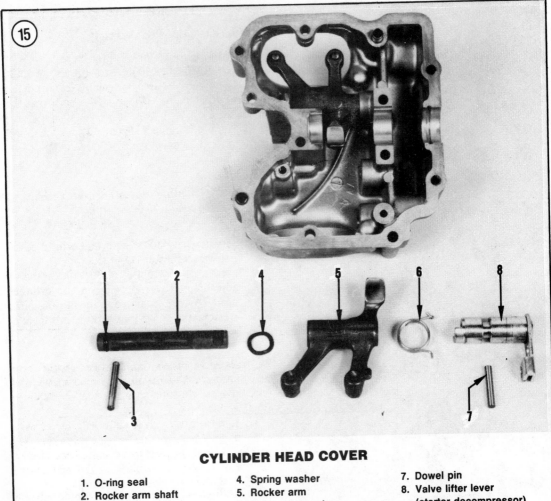

CYLINDER HEAD COVER

1. O-ring seal
2. Rocker arm shaft
3. Dowel pins
4. Spring washer
5. Rocker arm
6. Valve lifter spring
7. Dowel pin
8. Valve lifter lever
   (starter decompressor)

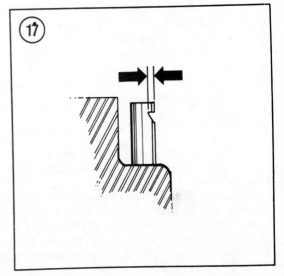

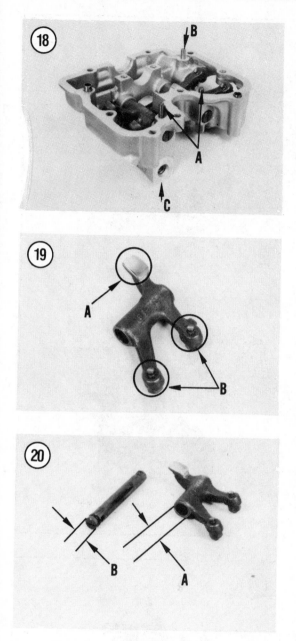

The rocker arms are not identical and need not be identified.

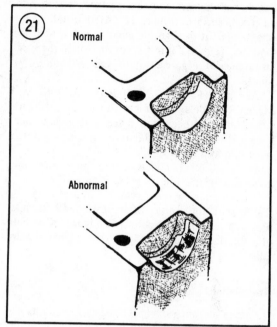

4. Pull the valve lifter lever out with the spring.

5. Wash all parts with solvent and thoroughly dry with compressed air.

6. Inspect the rocker arm pad where it rides on the cam lobe (A, **Figure 19**) and where the adjusters ride on the valve stem (B, **Figure 19**). If the pad is scratched or unevenly worn, inspect the cam lobe for scoring, chipping or flat spots. Replace the rocker arm if defective.

7. Measure the inside diameter of the rocker arm bore (A, **Figure 20**) with an inside micrometer and check against the dimensions given in **Table 1**. Replace if defective.

8. Inspect the rocker arm shafts for signs of wear or scoring. Measure the outside diameter (B, **Figure 20**) with a micrometer and check against dimensions given in **Table 1** at the end of the chapter. Replace if defective.

9. Inspect the camshaft bearing surfaces (**Figure 21**) for excessive wear.

10. Check the spring washers for breakage or distortion; replace if necessary.

11. Inspect the O-ring seals on the rocker arm shafts and valve lifter lever shaft. Replace if they have lost their resiliency.

12. Inspect the condition of the valve lifter lever shaft and the bearing surface in which it rides in the cover. Replace the valve lifter if damaged.

13. Coat the rocker arm shafts, rocker arm bores and shaft receptacles in the cover with assembly oil or clean engine oil.

14. Slide the rocker shaft into the cover while assembling the spring washer and rocker arm. Refer to marks made in Step 3, *Removal*, and be sure to reinstall the shafts into their original position.

NOTE
Make sure the O-ring seal is installed onto each rocker shaft.

15. Install the spring washer on the left-hand side of the rocker arm (**Figure 22**). After installing the shaft, rotate it to align the locating notch with the bolt hole (**Figure 23**) in the cover. Rotate the shaft using the slot (**Figure 24**) in the exposed end of the shaft.

16A. On XR250R, XR500R, XL500S and XL500R models, install new dowel pins (**Figure 16**). Hammer them into place with a hammer. Never reuse a dowel pin that has a removal notch ground into it.

16B. On all other models, install the locating pin to secure the shaft in place (A, **Figure 18**).

17. Repeat for the other rocker arm assembly.

18. Install the valve lifter lever and spring. Position the spring as shown in **Figure 25**. Install the locating dowel (B, **Figure 18**) securing it in place.

Installation

1. Make sure the slots in the rocker arm shafts are vertical (A, **Figure 26**) and that the locating notch aligns with the bolt hole in the cover (**Figure 23**). The dowel pins must be in place (B, **Figure 26**).

2. Clean the mating surface of the cylinder head and cover with contact cleaner.

3. Apply a light coat of non-hardening gasket sealer, such as Gasgacinch Gasket Sealer or equivalent, to the cover.

CAUTION
Do not apply gasket to the areas surrounding the camshaft bearing surfaces (Figure 27).

4. Install the camshaft plug (**Figure 28**).

5. Add fresh engine oil into the camshaft pocket in the cylinder head. The cam lobes must be submerged in oil or they will be damaged when the engine is first started up.

6. Make sure the 2 locating dowels (C, **Figure 26**) are in place.

7. Install the cylinder head cover bolts and acorn nut. Don't forget to install the cable clips on the right-hand side along with the 2 longest bolts (**Figure 29**).

8. Tighten the bolts in the sequence shown in **Figure 30**. Tighten to 7-10 ft.-lb. (10-14 N•m) on all models.

9. Inspect the O-ring seal on the valve adjuster covers. Replace if necessary. Tighten the bolts to 7-10 ft.-lb. (10-14 N•m) on all models.

10. On 500 cc models, install the engine as described in this chapter.

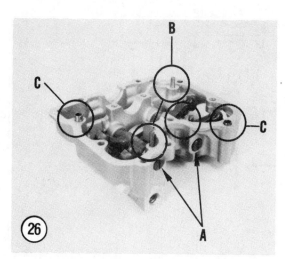

11. On 250 cc models, install the upper engine mounting plates, bolts and nuts. Tighten the bolts to 14-25 ft.-lb. (20-35 N•m). Attach the starter decompressor cable to the right-hand crankcase cover. Install the fuel tank and seat.

CYLINDER HEAD

NOTE
Cylinder head removal and inspection are the same for all engines. Installation differs because of a cam chain tensioner design change. Be sure to use the correct installation procedure for your particular bike.

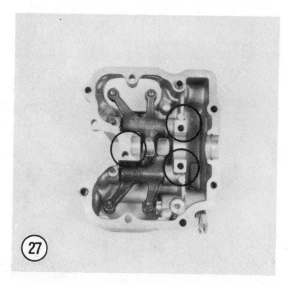

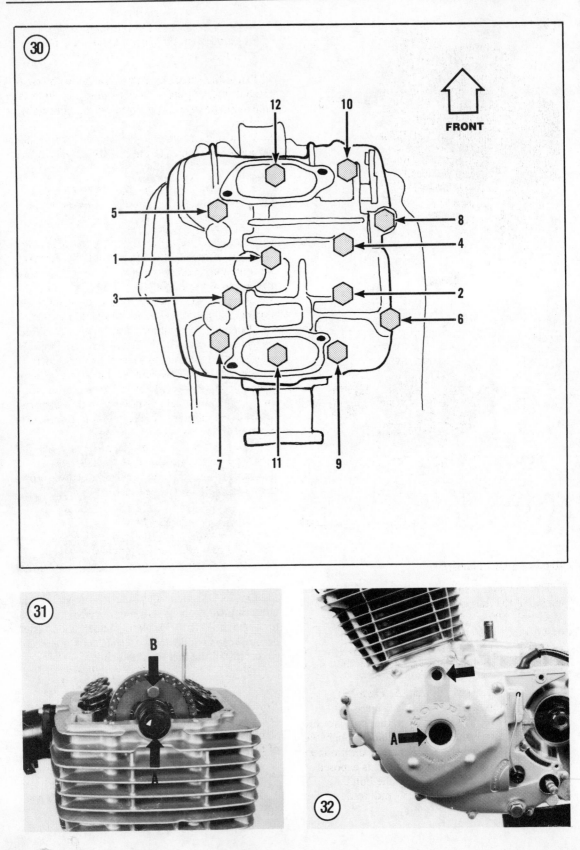

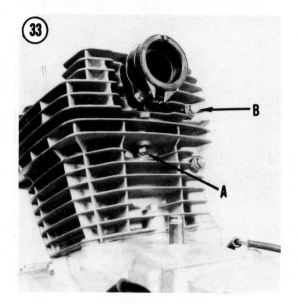

Removal (All Models)

The cylinder head can be removed with the engine in the frame on all 250 cc engines.

1. On all 500 cc engines, remove the engine as described in this chapter.

2. On all models, remove the cylinder head cover as described in this chapter. Remove the spark plug.

3. Remove the camshaft plug (A, **Figure 31**).

4. Remove the timing hole caps (**Figure 32**).

5. Rotate the crankshaft with the bolt on the alternator rotor, which is accessible through the bottom hole (A, **Figure 32**). Rotate it until one of the cam sprocket bolts (B, **Figure 31**) is exposed at the 12 o'clock position. Remove the bolt.

6. Rotate the crankshaft 180° and remove the other bolt.

NOTE
Don't drop these bolts in the camshaft chain cavity as they will fall into the crankcase.

7. Leave the sprocket in this position with one of the bolt holes at the 12 o'clock position. Slide the camshaft sprocket to the right, off the boss on the camshaft.

8. Tie a piece of wire to the camshaft chain and secure the other end to the exterior of the engine.

NOTE
This will prevent the chain from falling into the crankcase when the cam is removed.

9. Disengage the chain from the sprocket and place the chain to the left, behind the sprocket. Remove the sprocket.

10. Remove the camshaft.

11. Remove the 2 lower nuts and washers (A, **Figure 33**), one at the front and one at the rear.

12. Remove the upper cam chain tensioner lockbolt and washer (B, **Figure 33**). On XL250S and XR250 models, don't lose the O-ring seal.

13. On 250 cc models, remove the 4 cylinder head bolts in a crisscross pattern in 2 or 3 stages.

14. On 500 cc models, remove the 4 cylinder head acorn nuts and washers (**Figure 34**) in a crisscross pattern in 2 or 3 stages.

15. Loosen the head by tapping around the perimeter with a rubber or plastic mallet. If necessary, *gently* pry the head loose with a broad tipped screwdriver only in the ribbed areas of the fins.

CAUTION
Remember the cooling fins are fragile and may be damaged if tapped or pried on too hard. Never use a metal hammer.

NOTE
Sometimes it is possible to loosen the head with engine compression. Reinstall the spark plug. Rotate the engine with the kickstarter. As the piston reaches TDC on the compression stroke, it will pop the head loose.

16. Remove the head by pulling straight up and off the cylinder. Place a clean shop rag into the cam chain opening in the cylinder to prevent the entry of foreign matter.

Inspection (All Models)

1. Remove all traces of gasket material from head and cylinder mating surface.

2. Without removing the valves, remove all carbon deposits from the combustion chambers with a wire brush. A blunt screwdriver or chisel may be used if care is taken not to damage the head, valves and spark plug threads.

3. After all carbon is removed from combustion chambers and valve intake and exhaust ports, clean the entire head in solvent.

4. Clean away all carbon on the piston crowns.

5. Check for cracks in the combustion chamber and exhaust ports. A cracked head must be replaced.

6. After the head had been thoroughly cleaned, place a straightedge across the gasket surface at several points (**Figure 35**). Measure warp by inserting a feeler gauge between the straightedge and cylinder head at each location. There should be no warpage; if a small amount is present, it can be resurfaced by a Honda dealer or qualified machine shop.

7. Check the head cover mating surface using the procedure in Step 6. There should be no warpage.

8. Check the condition of the valves and valve guides as described under *Valve and Valve Components* in this chapter.

9. Check condition of the end seal plug (A, **Figure 31**). Make sure it fits tightly; if not, replace it.

10. Inspect the oil grooves (**Figure 36**) in the cam bearing surfaces. Make sure they are clean and that the surfaces are not scored or excessively worn.

Installation
(XR250R, XR500R, XL500S and XL500R)

1. Install the dowel pins (**Figure 37**). Install the O-ring seal on the dowel pin adjacent to the cam chain tensioner.

2. Install a new cylinder head gasket. Make sure the holes line up exactly.

3. Push the cam chain tensioner wedge "B" (**Figure 38**) down and pull up on wedge "A." Pull wedge "A" (A, **Figure 39**) up enough to expose the 2 mm hole in the wedge.

4. Insert a piece of wire (approximately 2 mm in diameter) into the hole to hold wedge "A" in the up position. Refer to B, **Figure 39**. A straightened No. 2 paper clip will work.

NOTE
Be careful that the piece of wire holding the cam tensioner wedge does not work loose while installing the cylinder head. If the wire jumps out of place it will fall down into the crankcase.

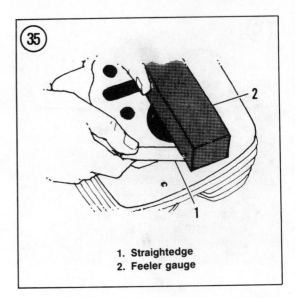

1. Straightedge
2. Feeler gauge

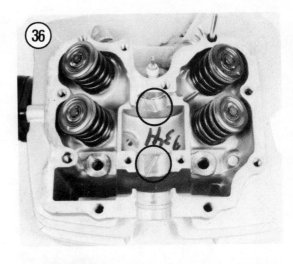

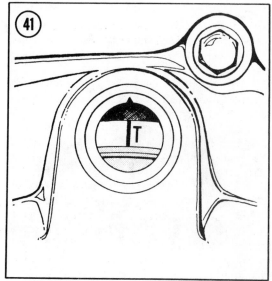

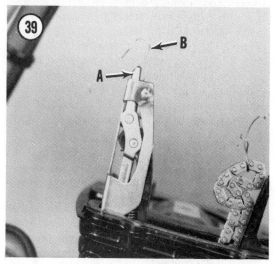

5. Carefully slide the cylinder head onto the cylinder. Feed the cam chain up through the chain cavity in the cylinder head and secure the other end of the wire again.

6. Apply oil to the threads of the cylinder studs or bolts.

7A. On 250 cc engines, install the cylinder bolts and washers and tighten in a crisscross pattern, in 2 or 3 stages, to the torque specification listed in **Table 2**.

7B. On 500 cc engines, install the washers and acorn nuts. Tighten them in a crisscross pattern, in 2 or 3 stages, to the torque specification listed in **Table 2**.

8. Install the 2 lower washers and nuts and tighten to the torque specification listed in **Table 2**.

9. Install the cam chain tensioner set bolt and sealing washer (**Figure 40**).

10. Pull up on the cam chain, making sure it is properly engaged on the crankshaft sprocket. Rotate the crankshaft until the "T" mark on the alternator rotor aligns with the fixed notch in the crankcase cover (**Figure 41**).

NOTE
Be sure to keep the cam chain taut while rotating the crankshaft.

11. Apply a light coat of molybdenum disulfide grease to the cam bearing journals.

12. Install the cam sprocket with the 2 timing marks facing toward the center of the engine and with the elongated notch up toward the top (**Figure 42**).

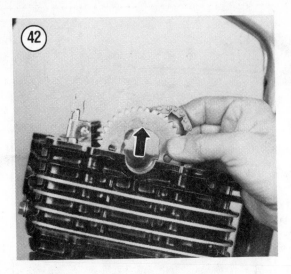

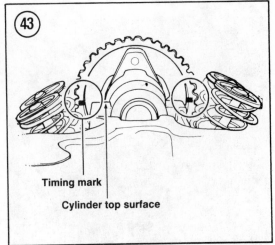

Timing mark

Cylinder top surface

13. Hold the cam sprocket and cam chain up in this position and feed the cam through the cam chain and sprocket. Rest the cam on the bearing surfaces in the cylinder head.

14. Rotate the cam sprocket until the 2 timing marks on the backside align with the top surface of the cylinder head (**Figure 43**).

15. Rotate the cam until the bolt mounting hole aligns with the cam sprocket—do not place the sprocket up on the cam boss at this time.

NOTE
The cam can be installed with the lobes up or down as long as the bolt holes align with the cam sprocket and the timing marks on the sprocket align with the cylinder head (Figure 43).

16. Install the cam chain onto the sprocket without rotating the sprocket. Slide the sprocket and cam chain up onto the cam boss. Recheck the alignment of the timing marks on the alternator rotor (**Figure 41**) and cam sprocket (**Figure 43**).

17. If alignment is incorrect, reposition the cam chain on the sprocket and recheck the alignment. Refer to **Figure 41** and **Figure 43**.

NOTE
If the engine is relatively new or a new cam chain or tensioner has been installed, Step 18 may be difficult. Carefully insert a long, broad tipped screwdriver down into the cam chain cavity and depress the tensioner from the inside. This will give you additional chain slack enabling the cam sprocket to slide up onto the cam boss. Be careful not to damage anything in the cam chain cavity with the screwdriver.

18. After alignment is correct, install one sprocket bolt only finger-tight, rotate the crankshaft and install the other bolt. Make sure the sprocket is correctly seated on the cam boss then tighten both bolts to the torque specification listed in **Table 2**.

19. After installation is complete, rotate the crankshaft several revolutions using the bolt on the alternator rotor. Make sure all timing marks align. If all marks align, the timing is correct.

CAUTION
*If there is any binding while rotating the crankshaft, **stop**. Determine the cause before proceeding.*

20. Remove the piece of 2 mm wire from the hole in wedge "A." Make sure that the cam chain tensioner wedge "A" is released (**Figure 44**).

21. Fill the oil pocket in the cylinder head with new engine oil so the cam lobes are submerged in oil.

22. Install the cylinder head cover as described in this chapter.

23. On 500 cc engines, install the engine as described in this chapter.

Installation (All Other Models)

1. Install the camshaft chain tensioner locknut (A, **Figure 45**); pull the tensioner assembly (B, **Figure 45**) all the way up and tighten the nut.

2. Install the 3 locating dowels (**Figure 46**). The rear right-hand side has an O-ring seal (A, **Figure 46**).

3. Install a new head gasket. Make sure all the holes line up exactly.

4. Carefully slide the cylinder head onto the cylinder. Feed the cam chain up through the chain

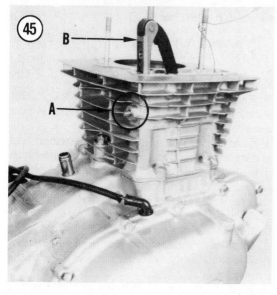

cavity in the head and secure the other end of the wire again.

5. Oil the threads of the cylinder studs or bolts.

6. On 250 cc models, install the 4 cylinder bolts and tighten them in a crisscross pattern, in 2 or 3 stages, to a final torque of 25-29 ft.-lb. (35-40 N•m).

7. On 500 cc models, install the 4 washers and acorn nuts. Tighten them in a crisscross pattern, in 2 or 3 stages, to a final torque of 16-20 ft.-lb. (22-28 N•m).

8. On all models, install the 2 lower washers and nuts (A, **Figure 33**) and tighten to 16-22 ft.-lb. (22-28 N•m).

9. Install the cam chain tensioner lockbolt and washer (B, **Figure 33**).

NOTE
On 250 cc models, make sure the O-ring seal is installed on the lockbolt.

10. Pull up on the cam chain making sure it is properly engaged on the sprocket on the crankshaft. Rotate the crankshaft until the "T" mark aligns with the fixed notch in the crankcase cover (**Figure 41**).

NOTE
Be sure to keep the cam chain taut while rotating the crankshaft.

11. Apply a light coat of molybdenum disulfide grease to the cam bearing journals.

12. Feed the cam through the chain. Let the chain rest on the cam behind the sprocket mounting flange.

13. Install the cam sprocket with the 2 timing marks facing toward the inside and in a horizontal position.

14. Rotate the cam until the bolt mounting hole aligns with the cam sprocket—do not place the sprocket up on the cam boss yet.

NOTE
*The cam can be installed with the lobes up or down as long as the bolt holes align and the timing marks on the sprocket align. Refer to **Figure 43**.*

15. Install the cam chain onto the sprocket without rotating the sprocket. Slide the sprocket and drive chain up onto the cam boss and recheck the alignment (**Figure 43**).

NOTE
If the engine is relatively new or a new cam chain or tensioner has been installed, Step 15 may be difficult. Carefully insert a long, broad tipped screwdriver down into the cam chain cavity and depress the tensioner from the inside. This will give you additional chain slack enabling the cam sprocket and chain to slide up onto the cam boss. Be carful not to damage anything in the chain cavity with the screwdriver.

16. If alignment is incorrect, reposition the cam chain on the sprocket and recheck the alignment Refer to **Figure 41** and **Figure 43**.

17. After alignment is correct, install one bolt only finger-tight, rotate the crankshaft and install the other bolt. Make sure the sprocket is correctly seated on the cam boss then tighten both bolts to 12-17 ft.-lb. (17-23 N•m) on all models.

18. After installation is complete, rotate the crankshaft several complete revolutions using the bolt on the alternator rotor (A, **Figure 32**). Make sure all timing marks align. If all marks align, the timing is correct.

CAUTION
*If there is any binding while rotating the crankshaft, **stop**. Determine the cause before proceeding.*

19. Install the cylinder head cover as described in this chapter.

20. On 500 cc models, install the engine as described in this chapter.

REED VALVE ASSEMBLY (XR500R)

The XR500R has a power reed valve assembly in the intake port of the cylinder head. The reed valve helps the engine achieve higher torque in the low to medium engine speed range. On a 4-stroke engine, part of the fuel-air mixture from the carburetor is forced back into the intake port and manifold during low to medium engine speed. This occurs because the fuel-air mixture enters the cylinder at a low velocity and the piston is trying to push it back out before the intake valve has completely closed.

The reed valve is a 1-way valve. It allows the fuel-air mixture to go past the reed valve assembly, the intake valves and into the combustion chamber. The reed valve prevents the fuel-air mixture from reversing its flow, thus keeping more of the fuel-air mixture in the combustion chamber to be burned.

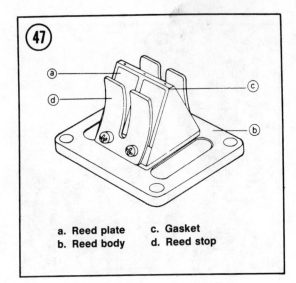

a. Reed plate   c. Gasket
b. Reed body   d. Reed stop

Removal/Installation

Particular care must be taken when handling the reed valve assembly.

1. Remove the carburetor as described in Chapter Seven.

2. Remove the bolts securing the rubber intake manifold and reed valve assembly to the cylinder head.

3. Carefully remove the reed valve assembly and gaskets from the cylinder head. If the assembly is difficult to remove, use a drift or broad tipped screwdriver and gently tap the side of the assembly to help break it loose from the gasket and cylinder head.

4. Inspect as described in this chapter.

5. Install a new gasket, the heat insulator, another new gasket and the reed valve assembly onto the cylinder head.

6. Inspect the O-ring seal on the rubber intake manifold. Replace if necessary.

7. Install the rubber intake manifold with the carburetor locating notch facing *up*. Insert the bolts and tighten securely.

8. Install the carburetor.

Inspection

Refer to **Figure 47** for basic reed valve construction.

Carefully examine the reed plate, reed stop and gasket. Check for signs of cracks, metal fatigue, distortion or damage from foreign matter. Pay particular attention to the rubber gasket seal. If any part of the original Honda reed valve assembly is damaged the assembly must be replaced as a unit; replacement parts are not available.

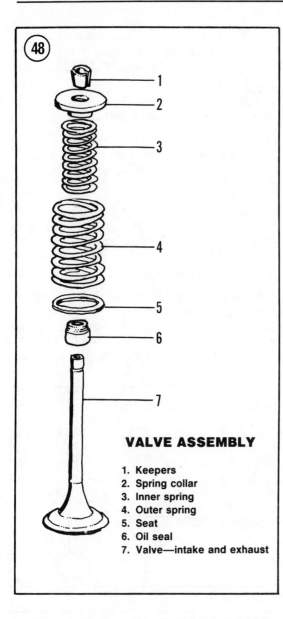

VALVE ASSEMBLY

1. Keepers
2. Spring collar
3. Inner spring
4. Outer spring
5. Seat
6. Oil seal
7. Valve—intake and exhaust

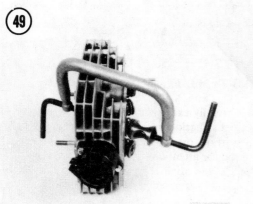

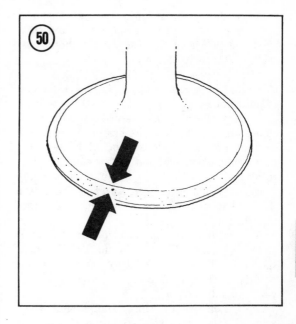

NOTE
Make sure that all parts are clean and free of any small dirt particles or lint from a shop cloth as they may cause distortion in the reed plate.

VALVE AND VALVE COMPONENTS

Removal

Refer to **Figure 48** for this procedure.
1. Remove the cylinder head as described in this chapter.
2. Compress springs with a valve spring compression tool (**Figure 49**). Remove the valve keepers and release compression.
3. Remove the valve spring caps, springs, and valves.

CAUTION
Remove any burrs from the valve stem grooves before removing the valve. Otherwise the valve guides will be damaged.

Inspection

1. Clean valves with a wire brush and solvent.
2. Inspect the contact surface of each valve for burning (**Figure 50**). Minor roughness and pitting can be removed by lapping the valve as described in this chapter. Excessive unevenness of the contact surface is an indication that the valve is not serviceable. The contact surface of the valve cannot be ground on a valve grinding machine because it is specially coated. You must replace a burned or damaged valve with a new one.

Inspect the valve stems for wear and roughness and measure the vertical runout of the valve stem as shown in **Figure 51**. The runout should not exceed 0.002 in. (0.05 mm).

3. Measure valve stems for wear (**Figure 52**). Compare with specifications in **Table 1** at the end of this chapter.

4. Remove all carbon and varnish from the valve guides with a stiff spiral wire brush.

5. Insert each valve in its guide. Hold the valve just slightly off its seat and rock it sideways. If it rocks more than slightly, the guide is probably worn and should be replaced. As a final check, take the head to a dealer and have the valve guides measured.

6. Measure the valve spring heights with a vernier caliper (**Figure 53**). All should be of length specified in **Table 1** (end of chapter) with no bends or other distortion. Replace defective springs in pairs (inner and outer).

7. Check the valve spring retainer and valve keepers. If they are in good condition, they may be reused.

8. Inspect the valve seats. If worn or burned, they must be reconditioned. This should be performed by your dealer or local machine shop, although the procedure is described in this section. Seats and valves in near-perfect condition can be reconditioned by lapping with fine carborundum paste. The valves are specially coated and cannot be ground.

Installation

1. Coat the valve stems with molybdenum disulfide grease and insert them into cylinder head.

2. Install bottom spring retainers and new seals.

3. Install the inner and outer valve springs and valve spring retainers.

NOTE
On 250 cc models, install the valve springs with the narrow pitch end (end with the coils closer together) facing the head.

4. Push down on the valve spring retainers with the valve compressor and install the keepers.

CAUTION
To avoid loss of spring tension, do not compress the springs any more than necessary to install the keepers.

5. After all springs have been installed, gently tap the valve stems with a plastic mallet to make sure the keepers are properly installed.

Valve Guide Replacement

When guides are worn so that there is excessive stem-to-guide clearance or valve tipping, they must be replaced. Replace all, even if only one is worn. This job should only be done by a Honda dealer as special tools are required.

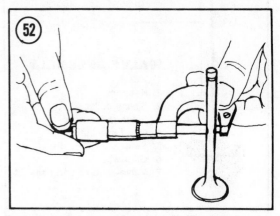

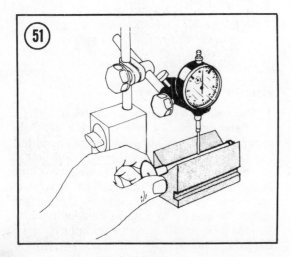

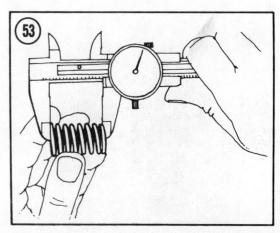

Valve Seat Reconditioning

This job is best left to your dealer or local machine shop. They have the special equipment and knowledge for this exacting job. You can still save considerable money by removing the cylinder head and taking just the head to the shop.

Valve Lapping

Valve lapping is a simple operation which can restore the valve seal without machining if the amount of wear or distortion is not too great.
1. Coat the valve seating area in the head with a lapping compound such as carborundum or Clover Brand.
2. Insert the valve into the head.
3. Wet the suction cup of the lapping stick (**Figure 54**) and stick it onto the head of the valve. Lap the valve to the seat by rotating the lapping stick in both directions. Every 5 to 10 seconds, rotate the valve 180° in the seat. Continue lapping until the contact surfaces of the valve and the valve seat are a uniform grey. Stop as soon as they are, to avoid removing too much material.
4. Thoroughly clean the valves and cylinder head in solvent to remove all grinding compound. Any compound left on the valves of the cylinder head will end up in the engine and will cause damage.

After the lapping has been completed and the valve assemblies have been reinstalled into the head, the valve seal should be tested. Check the seal of each valve by pouring solvent into each of the intake and exhaust ports. There should be no leakage past the seat. If fluid leaks past any of the seats, disassemble that valve assembly and repeat the lapping procedure until there is no leakage.

CAMSHAFT

Removal

The camshaft can be removed with the engine in the frame on all 250 cc engines.
1. On all 500 cc engines, remove the engine as described in this chapter.
2. On all models, remove the cylinder head cover as described in this chapter.
3. Remove the camshaft plug (A, **Figure 55**).
4. Remove the timing hole caps (**Figure 56**).
5. Rotate the crankshaft with the bolt on the alternator rotor, which is accessible through the bottom hole (A, **Figure 56**). Rotate it until one of the cam sprocket bolts (B, **Figure 55**) is exposed at the 12 o'clock position. Remove the bolt.
6. Rotate the crankshaft 180° and remove the other bolt.

54

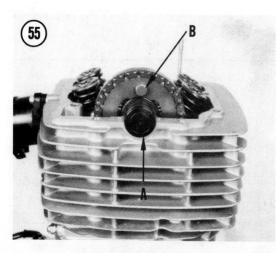

55

56

NOTE
Don't drop these bolts into the camshaft chain cavity as they will fall into the crankcase.

7. Leave the sprocket in this position with one of the bolt holes at the 12 o'clock position. Slide the camshaft sprocket to the right, off the boss on the camshaft.

8. Tie a piece of wire to the camshaft chain and secure the other end to the exterior of the engine.

NOTE
This will prevent the chain from falling into the crankcase when the cam is removed.

9. Disengage the chain from the sprocket and place the chain to the left, behind the sprocket. Remove the sprocket.

10. Remove the camshaft.

Inspection

1. Measure both bearing journals for wear. Measure both the right-hand and left-hand journals (**Figure 57**) with a micrometer. Replace the camshaft if either bearing journal is less than the wear limit given in **Table 1** (end of chapter).

NOTE
*Don't confuse the sprocket boss area (**Figure 58**) for the right-hand bearing journal.*

2. Check cam lobes for wear. The lobes should not be scored and the edges should be square. Slight. damage may be removed with a silicon carbide oilstone. Use No. 100-120 grit initially, then polish with a No. 280-320 grit.

NOTE
The cam is dark in color due to the manufacturing hardening process. It is not caused by lack of oil pressure or excessive engine heat.

3. Even though the cam lobe surfaces appear to ge satifactory, with no visible signs of wear, they must be measured with a micrometer as shown in **Figure 59**. Replace the shaft(s) if worn beyond the service limits given in **Table 1** at the end of this chapter.

4. Inspect the camshaft bearing bores in the cylinder head and cover. They should not be scored or excessively worn (**Figure 60**).

5. Remove the camshaft plug from the cylinder head. Install the cylinder head cover and tighten the bolts to 7-10 ft.-lb. (10-14 N•m) on all models. Use the sequence shown in **Figure 61**.

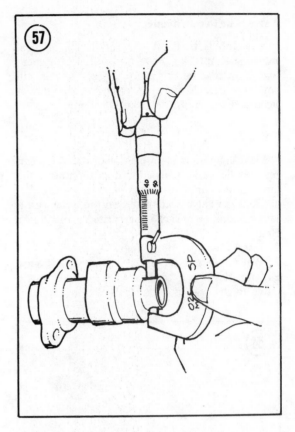

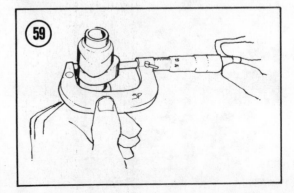

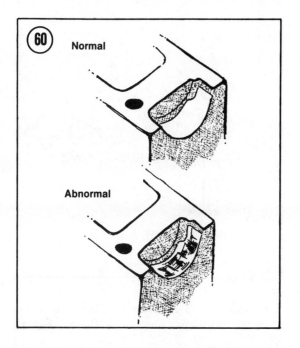

6. Measure the inside diameter of the bearing surfaces, both right and left side. Compare to dimensions given in **Table 1**. If either dimension exceeds wear limit in **Table 1**, the cylinder head and cylinder head cover must be replaced as a set. Remove the cylinder head cover.

NOTE
They must be replaced as a set as the
bearing surfaces are machined together
at time of manufacture.

7. Inspect the condition of the teeth on the sprocket. Replace if necessary.

Installation

1. Pull up on the cam chain making sure it is properly engaged on the crankshaft sprocket. Rotate the crankshaft until the "T" mark aligns with the fixed notch in the crankcase cover (**Figure 62**).

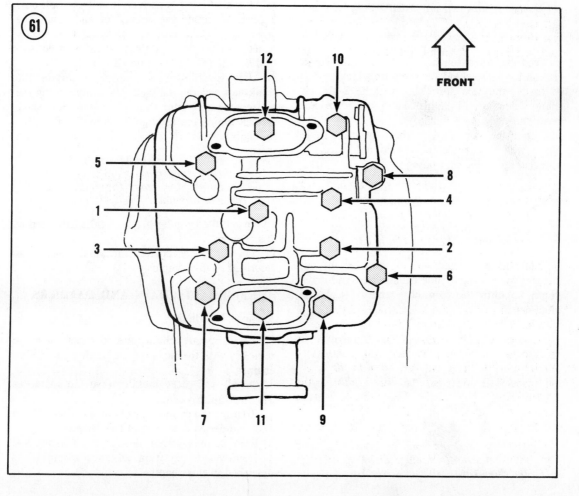

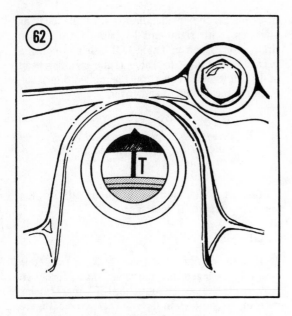

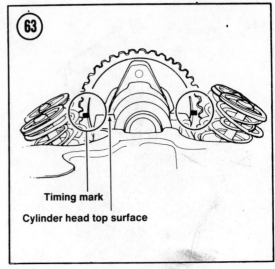

Timing mark

Cylinder head top surface

NOTE
Be sure to keep the cam chain taut while rotating the crankshaft.

2. Apply a light coat of molybdenum disulfide grease to the cam bearing journals.
3. Feed the cam through the chain. Let the chain rest on the cam behind the mounting flange.
4. Install the cam sprocket with the 2 timing marks facing toward the inside and in a horizontal position.
5. Rotate the cam until the bolt mounting hole aligns with the cam sprocket—do not place the sprocket up on the cam boss yet.

NOTE
*The cam can be installed with the lobes up or down as long as the bolt holes align and the timing marks on the sprocket align. Refer to **Figure 63**.*

6. Install the cam chain onto the sprocket without rotating the sprocket. Slide the sprocket and drive chain up onto the cam boss and recheck the alignment.

NOTE
If the engine is relatively new or a new cam chain or tensioner has been installed, Step 6 may be difficult. Carefully insert a long, broad tipped screwdriver down into the cam chain cavity and depress the tensioner from the inside. This will give you additional chain slack enabling the cam sprocket and chain to slide up onto the cam boss. Be careful not to damage anything in the chain cavity with the screwdriver.

7. If alignment is incorrect, reposition the cam chain on the sprocket and recheck. Refer to **Figure 62** and **Figure 63**.
8. After alignment is correct, install one bolt only finger-tight, rotate the crankshaft and install the other bolt. Make sure the sprocket is correctly seated on the cam boss, then tighten both bolts to 12-17 ft.-lb. (17-23 N•m) on all models.
9. After installation is complete, rotate the crankshaft several complete revolutions using the bolt on the alternator rotor (A, **Figure 56**). Make sure all timing marks align. If all marks align, the timing is correct.

CAUTION
*If there is any binding while rotating the crankshaft, **stop**. Determine the cause before proceeding.*

10. Install the cylinder head cover as described in this chapter.
11. On all 500 cc engines, install the engine as described in this chapter.

CAMSHAFT CHAIN AND DAMPERS

Removal/Installation

The camshaft chain and dampers can be removed with the engine in the frame on all 250 cc engines.
1. On all 500 cc engines, remove the engine as described in this chapter.
2. Remove the cylinder head cover, cylinder head and cylinder as described in this chapter.
3. Remove the clutch as described in Chapter Six.
4. Remove the ignition advance assembly as described in this chapter.

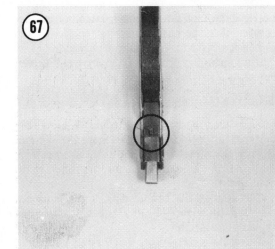

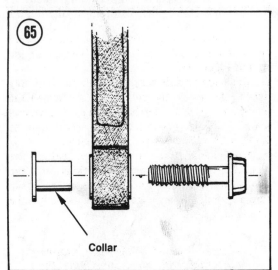

Collar

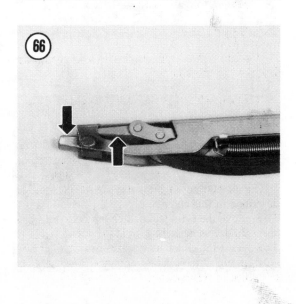

5. Remove the bolt (A, **Figure 64**) securing the cam chain tensioner and remove it.

NOTE
The cam chain guide was removed in
the cylinder removal sequence.

6. Disengage the cam chain from the crankshaft sprocket and remove it (B, **Figure 64**).
7. Install by reversing these removal steps. Tighten the cam chain tensioner bolt to 16-20 ft.-lb. (22-28 N•m).

CAUTION
Make sure the collar is in place in the
tensioner assembly prior to installation
*as shown in **Figure 65**.*

Inspection
(XR250R, XR500R,
XL500S and XL500R)

The upper end of the cam chain tensioner assembly is a set of sliding wedges that work together to maintain the correct tension on the cam chain, eliminating the need for periodic adjustment. Inspect the mating surfaces of both wedges (**Figure 66**) for uneven wear or damage. If either is damaged to the extent that they do not slide smoothly against each other, the tensioner assembly must be replaced.

Check the small spring (**Figure 67**) that holds the upper wedge up. If it is weak or broken, the tensioner assembly must be replaced.

The cam chain is a Hy-Vo type and rarely wears out, but will stretch with prolonged use. To check for chain wear remove the cylinder head cover as described in this chapter. Measure the distance that the upper wedge (wedge "B") protrudes above the upper surface of the tensioner assembly bracket (**Figure 68**). The chain must be replaced if the dimension is 0.35 in. (9.0 mm) or more.

If the chain is worn, check the drive and driven sprockets also; they may need to be replaced.

Inspection (All Other Models)

Check the top surface of the guide (A, **Figure 69**) and the tensioner assembly (B, **Figure 69**). If either is worn or disintegrating it must be replaced. This may indicate a worn chain or improper chain adjustment.

Check all of the components of the tensioner assembly (B, **Figure 69**); if any part is defective, replace the assembly.

The chain is a Hy-Vo type and rarely wears out. Check it thoroughly and if damaged, replace it. If it needs replacing, also check the drive sprocket on the crankshaft and the cam sprocket. They also may be defective.

CYLINDER

**Removal
(XR250R, XR500R,
XL500S and XL500R)**

1. Remove the cylinder head cover as described in this chapter.
2. Remove the cylinder head as described in this chapter.
3. Remove the cylinder head gasket, location dowels and the O-ring seal.
4. Remove the cam chain guide (**Figure 70**).
5. Remove the cam chain tensioner set bolt and copper washer (**Figure 71**) and push the tensioner assembly forward.
6A. On 250 cc engines, remove the cylinder bolts (**Figure 72**) on the right-hand side.
6B. On 500 cc engines, remove the cylinder bolts on the right-hand side. Also remove the nut and washer at the front and rear of the cylinder.

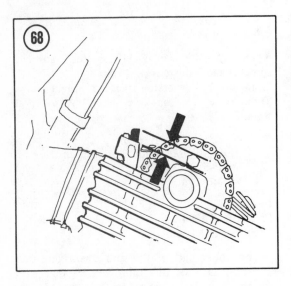

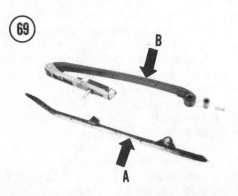

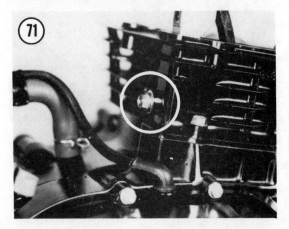

7. Loosen the cylinder by tapping around the perimeter with a rubber or plastic mallet. If necessary, *gently* pry the cylinder loose with a broad tipped screwdriver only in the ribbed areas of the fins.

CAUTION
Remember the cooling fins are fragile and may be damaged if tapped or pried too hard. Do not use a metal hammer.

8. Pull the cylinder straight up and off the piston (and cylinder studs on 500 cc engines).

NOTE
Be sure to keep the cam chain wired up to prevent it from falling into the crankcase.

9. Install a piston holding fixture under the piston.

NOTE
These fixtures may be purchased or may be homemade units of wood as shown in **Figure 73***.*

Removal
(All Other Models)

1. Remove the cylinder head cover as described in this chapter.
2. Remove the cylinder head as described in this chapter.
3. Remove the cylinder head gasket (A, **Figure 74**), location dowels and the O-ring (B, **Figure 74**) and the cam chain guide (C, **Figure 74**).
4. Remove the cam chain tensioner lock bolt and sealing washer (A, **Figure 75**). The 250 cc engines are equipped with an O-ring on the bolt; don't lose the O-ring.

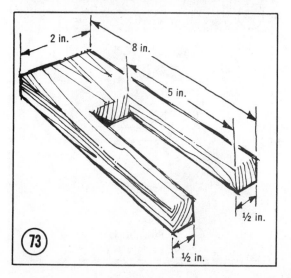

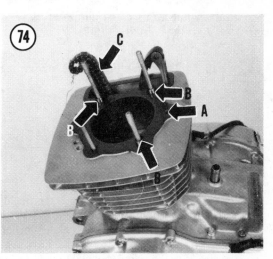

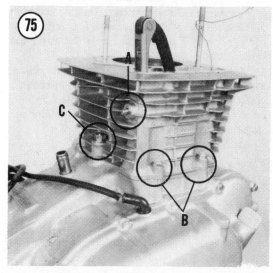

5. Push the tensioner assembly forward to move the stud out of the hole in the cylinder.

6. Remove the cylinder side bolts (B, **Figure 75**).

7. Remove the cylinder bolts or nuts and washers (C, **Figure 75**), one at the front and one at the rear.

8. Loosen the cylinder by tapping around the perimeter with a rubber or plastic mallet. If necessary, *gently* pry the cylinder loose with a broad tipped screwdriver only in the ribbed areas of the fins.

> **CAUTION**
> *Remember the cooling fins are fragile and may be damaged if tapped or pried too hard. Do not use a metal hammer.*

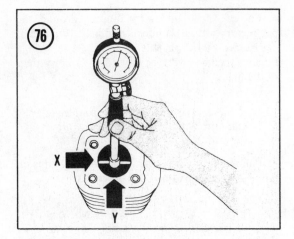

9. Pull the cylinder straight up and off the piston (and cylinder studs on 500 cc engines).

> **NOTE**
> *Be sure to keep the cam chain wired up to prevent it from falling into the crankcase.*

10. Install a piston holding fixture under the piston.

> **NOTE**
> *These fixtures may be purchased or may be homemade units of wood as shown in **Figure 73**.*

Inspection (All Models)

1. Wash the cylinder in solvent and thoroughly dry with compressed air.

2. Inspect the cylinder for signs of wear, distortion or damage. If the piston ever seizes, then it will be necessary to have the cylinder honed to remove the minute particles of aluminum from the wall and prevent further damage when the engine is rebuilt.

3. Measure the cylinder bore with a cylinder gauge in both X and Y directions (**Figure 76**) at the top, center, and bottom (**Figure 77**).

4. Measure in 2 axes—in line with piston pin and at 90° to the pin. If the taper or out-of-round is greater than 0.002 in. (0.05 mm), the cylinder must be rebored to the next oversize and new piston and rings installed.

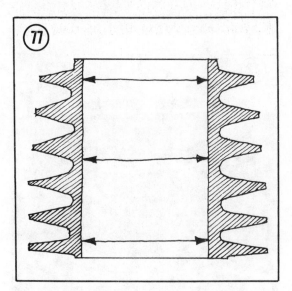

> **NOTE**
> *The new piston should be obtained first, before the cylinder is bored, so that the piston can be measured; slight manufacturing tolerances must be taken into account to determine the actual size and the working clearance. Piston-to-cylinder clearance should be 0.0004-0.0016 in. (0.010-0.040 mm).*

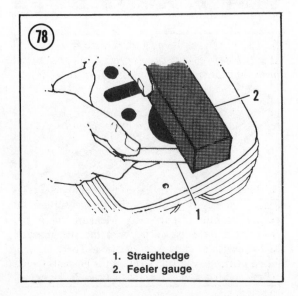

1. Straightedge
2. Feeler gauge

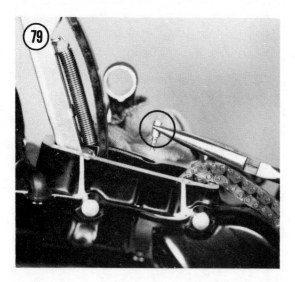

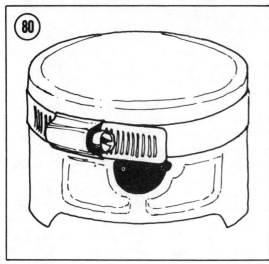

5. Check the cylinder wall for scratches; if evident, the cylinder should be rebored. The maximum wear limit on the cylinder is listed in **Table 1**.

NOTE
If the cylinder is worn to this limit, it must be replaced. Never rebore a cylinder if the finished rebore dimension will be this dimension or larger.

6. After the cylinder has been thoroughly cleaned, place a straightedge across the gasket surface at several points (**Figure 78**). Measure warp by inserting a feeler gauge between the straightedge and cylinder head at each location. There should be no warpage; if a small amount is present, it can be resurfaced by a Honda dealer or qualified machine shop.

Installation
(XR250R, XR500R, XL500S and XL500R)

1. Check that the top surface of the crankcase and the bottom surface of the cylinder are clean prior to installing a new gasket.
2. Make sure that the oil control orifice (**Figure 79**) is clean (not clogged) and is in place in the receptacle in the crankcase.
3. Install a piston holding fixture under the piston.
4. Install the locating dowels in the crankcase and install a new cylinder base gasket.
5. Make sure the O-ring seal is in place in the base of the cylinder.
6. Apply assembly oil or fresh engine oil to the piston, piston rings and to the cylinder wall.
7A. On 250 cc engines, slide the piston down over the piston until it bottoms out on the piston holding fixture.
7B. On 500 cc engines, slide the cylinder down over the piston and cylinder studs.
8. Compress each piston ring as it enters the cylinder either with your fingers, a piston ring compressor or by using aircraft type hose clamps (**Figure 80**) of the appropriate size.
9. Remove the piston holding fixture (and hose clamp if used) and push the cylinder down all the way.
10. Install the cylinder bolts or nuts and washers and tighten to the torque specification listed in **Table 2**.
11. Pull the cam chain tensioner to the rear and up and install the tensioner set bolt and copper washer (**Figure 71**).

NOTE
The tensioner has 2 set bolts that are of different lengths. Install the shorter one in the cylinder and the longer one in the cylinder head.

12. Install a new cylinder head gasket, locating dowels and O-ring seal. Install the cam chain guide.
13. Install the cylinder head and cylinder head cover as described in this chapter.

Installation
(All Other Models)

1. Check that the top surface of the crankcase and the bottom surface of the cylinder are clean prior to installing a new gasket.

NOTE
Make sure the oil control orifice is clean—not clogged.

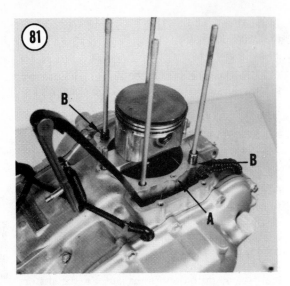

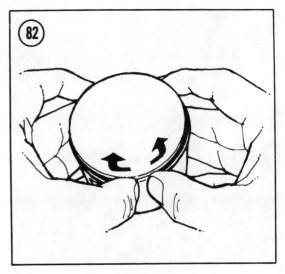

2. Install the oil control orifice (A, **Figure 81**) and locating dowels (B, **Figure 81**).

3. Install a new cylinder base gasket.

4. Make sure the O-ring is in place in the base of the cylinder.

5. Apply assembly oil or fresh engine oil to the piston, piston rings and to the cylinder wall.

6. Install a piston holding fixture under the piston.

7A. On 250 cc engines, slide the cylinder down over the piston.

7B. On 500 cc engines, slide the cylinder down over the piston and cylinder studs.

8. Compress each piston ring as it enters the cylinder either with your fingers, a piston ring compressor or by using aircraft type hose clamps (**Figure 80**) of the appropriate size.

9. Remove the piston holding fixture (and hose clamp if used) and push the cylinder down all the way.

10. Pull the cam chain tensioner to the rear until the stud comes through the hole in the cylinder.

11. Install the cylinder side bolts and the cylinder front and rear bolts or nuts and washers. Tighten to the torque specifications listed in **Table 2**.

12. Install a new cylinder head gasket, locating dowels and O-ring seal. Install the cam chain guide.

13. Install the cylinder head and cylinder head cover as described in this chapter.

PISTON, PISTON PIN AND PISTON RINGS

The piston can be removed with the engine in the frame on 250 cc engines only.

Piston Removal

WARNING
The rail portions of the oil scraper can be very sharp. Be careful when handling them to avoid cut fingers.

1. Remove the cylinder head and cylinder as described in this chapter.

2. Remove the top ring first by spreading the ends with your thumbs just enough to slide it up over the piston (**Figure 82**). Repeat for the remaining rings.

3. Before removing the piston, hold the rod tightly and rock piston as shown in **Figure 83**. Any rocking motion (do not confuse with the normal sliding motion) indicates wear on the piston pin, rod bushing, pin bore or, more likely, a combination of all three.

4. Remove the circlips from the piston pin bore (**Figure 84**). Wrap a clean shop cloth under the piston so that the clips will not fall into the crankcase.

5. Heat the piston and pin with a small butane torch. The pin will probably drop right out. If not, heat the piston to about 140°F (60°C), i.e., until it is too warm to touch, but not excessively hot. If the pin is still difficult to push out, use a homemade tool as shown in **Figure 85**.

Piston Inspection

1. Carefully clean the carbon from the piston crown with a chemical remover or with a soft scraper (**Figure 86**). Do not remove or damage the carbon ridge around the circumference of the piston above the top ring. If the piston rings and cylinder are found to be dimensionally correct and

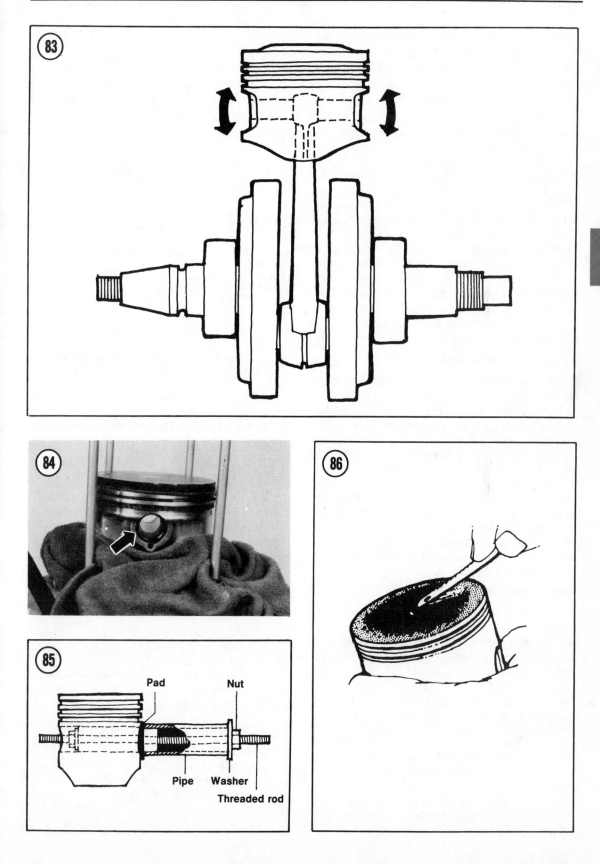

Pad   Nut

Pipe Washer

Threaded rod

can be reused, removal of the carbon ring from the top of piston or the carbon ridge from the top of cylinder will promote excessive oil consumption.

CAUTION
Do not wire brush piston skirts.

2. Examine each ring groove for burrs, dented edges and wide wear. Pay particular attention to the top compression ring groove, as it usually wears more than the others.

3. Measure piston-to-cylinder clearance as described in this chapter.

4. If damage or wear indicates piston replacement, select a new piston as described under *Piston-to-cylinder Clearance* in this chapter.

5. Measure the piston pin bore with a snap gauge (**Figure 87**) and measure the outside diameter of the piston pin with a micrometer (**Figure 88**). Compare against dimensions given in **Table 1** (end of chapter). Any machinist can do this for you if you do not have the measuring tools. Replace the piston and pin as a set if either or both are worn.

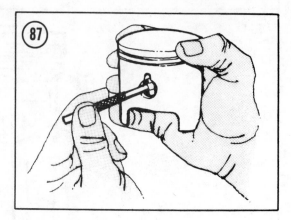

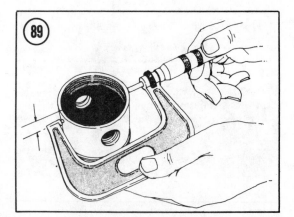

Piston-to-cylinder Clearance

1. Make sure the piston and cylinder wall are clean and dry.

2. Measure the inside diameter of the cylinder bore at a point 1/2 in. (13 mm) from the upper edge with a bore gauge.

3. Measure the outside diameter of the piston at a point 3/8 in. (10 mm) from the lower edge of the piston 90° to piston pin axis (**Figure 89**).

4. Subtract the piston diameter (Step 3) from the cylinder bore (Step 2). The difference is piston-to-cylinder clearance. Compare to specifications in **Table 1**; if clearance is too large, the piston should be replaced, the cylinder should be rebored or both.

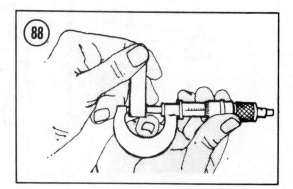

Piston Installation

1. Coat the connecting rod bushing, piston pin and piston bore with assembly oil or fresh engine oil.

2. Place the piston over the connecting rod with the "IN" mark (**Figure 90**) facing to the rear, toward the carburetor.

3. Insert the piston pin and tap it with a plastic mallet until it starts into the connecting rod bushing. If it does not slide in easily, heat the piston until it is too warm to touch but not excessively hot (140°F or 60°C). Continue to drive the pin while holding the piston so that the rod does not have to take any shock. Otherwise it may be bent. Drive the pin in until it is centered in the rod. If the pin is still difficult to install, use a homemade tool (**Figure 85**) but eliminate the piece of pipe.

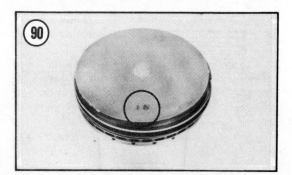

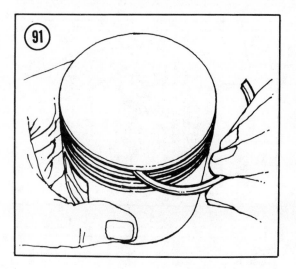

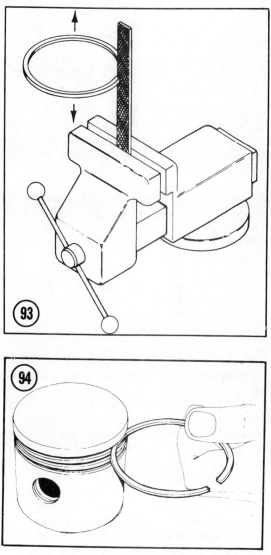

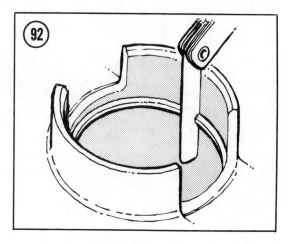

4. Install the rings as described in Steps 5-8 under *Piston Ring Replacement*.

5. Install the cylinder and cylinder head as described in this chapter.

Piston Ring Replacement

WARNING
The rail portions of the oil scraper can be very sharp. Be careful when handling them to avoid cut fingers.

1. Remove old rings with a ring expander tool or by spreading the ring ends with your thumbs and lifting the rings up evenly (**Figure 82**).

2. Carefully remove all carbon from the ring grooves with a broken piston ring (**Figure 91**). Inspect grooves carefully for burrs, nicks or broken and cracked lands. Recondition or replace piston if necessary.

3. Check end gap of each ring. To check ring, insert the ring into the bottom of the cylinder bore and square it with the wall by tapping with the piston. The ring should be in about 5/8 in. (15 mm). Insert a feeler gauge as shown in **Figure 92**. Compare gap with **Table 1** (end of chapter). If the gap is smaller than specified, hold a small file in a vise, grip the ends of the ring with your fingers and enlarge the gap. See **Figure 93**.

4. Roll each ring around its piston groove as shown in **Figure 94** to check for binding. Minor binding may be cleaned up with a fine-cut file.

NOTE
Install all rings with their markings facing up.

5. Install oil ring in oil ring groove with a ring expander tool or spread the ends with your thumbs.

6. Install 2 compression rings carefully with a ring expander tool or spread the ends with your thumbs.

7. Check side clearance of each ring as shown in **Figure 95**. Compare with specifications in **Table 1** (end of chapter).

8. Distribute the ring gaps around the piston as shown in **Figure 96**. The important thing is that the ring gaps do not align with each other when installed. Do not mix the top and second ring. Refer to **Figure 97**.

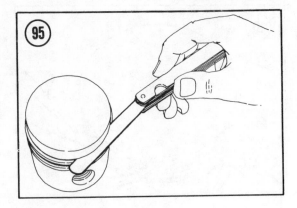

IGNITION ADVANCE MECHANISM

Removal

1. Remove both side covers and the seat.

> *CAUTION*
> *On XL250S and XL500S models, reinstall the seat strap bolts as they also hold the upper portion of the shocks to the frame (Figure 98). Remove and reinstall one bolt at a time.*

2. Remove the bolts securing the skid plate and remove the skid plate.

3. Drain the engine oil as described in Chapter Three.

4. Place wood block(s) under the frame to support the bike securely.

5. On XL models, disconnect the battery negative lead or disconnect the main fuse (**Figure 99**).

6. Remove the fuel tank as described in Chapter Seven.

7. Remove the kickstarter pedal (A, **Figure 100**).

8. Disconnect the rear brake switch return spring and cable (B, **Figure 100**), the front right-hand foot peg (C, **Figure 100**) and the rear brake pedal (D, **Figure 100**).

9. Slacken the clutch cable at the hand lever and disconnect the clutch cable at the crankcase cover (E, **Figure 100**).

10. Disconnect the decompressor cable at the crankcase cover (F, **Figure 100**).

11. Disconnect the electrical wires to the ignition pulse generator at the connector. Refer to **Figure 101** for XL series models or **Figure 102** for XR series models.

12. Remove the bolts securing the right-hand crankcase cover and remove the cover and gasket. Don't lose the locating dowels.

13. Place a copper washer (or penny) between the primary drive gear and the clutch outer housing gear. This will prevent the primary drive gear from turning while removing the locknut in Step 14.

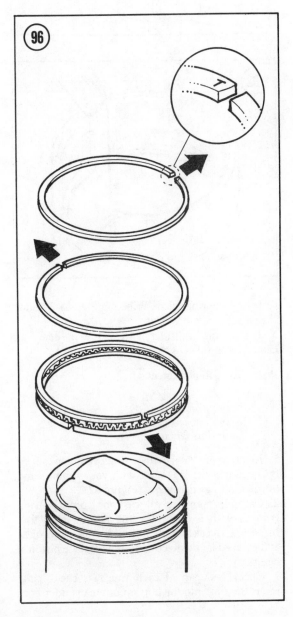

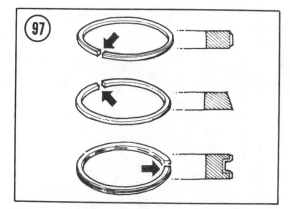

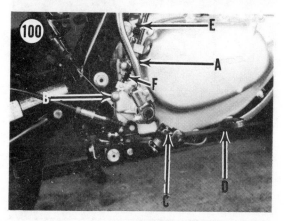

14A. On 1982-1983 XL250R and 1982 XL500R models (**Figure 103**), perform the following:
  a. Remove the 14 mm locknut and washer.
  b. Remove the stopper pin securing the oil pressure pad.
  c. Remove the oil pressure pad and spring.
  d. Slide off the pulse generator rotor from the crankshaft.

14B. On all other models, perform the following:
  a. Remove the 14 mm locknut (**Figure 104**).
  b. Remove the stopper pin securing the oil pressure pad (**Figure 105**).
  c. Remove the oil pressure pad and spring (A, **Figure 106**) and the washer (B, **Figure 106**).
  d. Slide off the pulse generator rotor from the crankshaft.

15. Inspect all components as described under *Ignition Advance Mechanism* in Chapter Eight.

Installation

1. Install by reversing the removal steps, noting the following.

2A. On 1982-1983 XL250R and 1982 XL500R models, align the cutout notch on the rotor with the dowel pin (**Figure 107**) on the crankshaft and slide on the rotor. Install the stopper pin (**Figure 108**).

(103) **PULSE GENERATOR ROTOR**

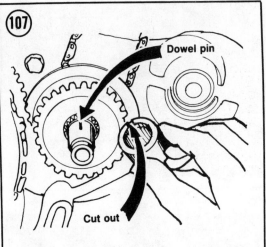

1. Oil pressure pad
2. Spring
3. Locknut
4. Lockwasher
5. Pulse generator rotor
6. Primary drive gear

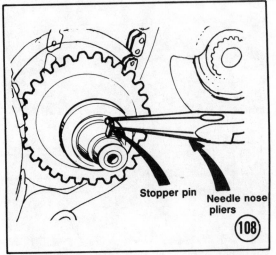

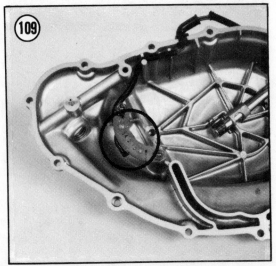

2B. On all other models, align the cutout notch on the rotor with the dowel pin on the crankshaft and slide on the rotor.

3. If either the advance rotor or pulse genertor have been replaced with new units, they must have the same identification marks (**Figure 109**). Failure to do so will result in poor engine performance.

4. Install the washer and the locknut. Tighten the locknut to the torque specification listed in **Table 2.**

5. Hold the compression release lever in the raised position and install the right-hand crankcase cover and gasket. Tighten all screws securely.

CAUTION
After the crankcase cover is installed, check the operation of the clutch and decompressor levers. They should operate without binding; if they do bind, remove the cover and correct the problem.

6. Connect the electrical wires to the pulse generator.

7. On XL models, connect either the battery lead or the main fuse.

8. Connect the clutch and decompressor cables.

9. Install the rear brake lever, front footpegs and kickstarter arm.

10. Install the skidplate, seat and side covers.

11. Install the fuel tank.

12. Fill the crankcase with the recommended type and quantity of engine oil; refer to Chapter Three.

13. Adjust the clutch cable, decompressor and rear brake as described in Chapter Three.

OIL PUMP

Removal/Installation

This procedure is shown with the engine removed for clarity. It is not necessary to remove it to remove the oil pump.

1. Remove the clutch as described in Chapter Six.

2. Remove the bolts (**Figure 110**) securing the set plate and remove it.

3. Remove the kickstarter idle gear (A, **Figure 111**) from the shift fork shaft (B, **Figure 111**).

4. Slide the oil pump assembly off of shaft and remove the two O-ring seals (A, **Figure 112**).

5. Slide out the oil filter screen (B, **Figure 112**) and clean it with solvent and medium soft toothbrush. Dry it carefully with compressed air. Inspect the screen; replace it if there are any breaks or holes in it.

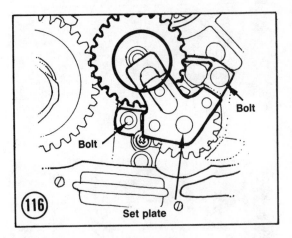

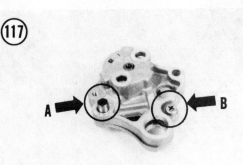

6. Thoroughly clean out the filter cavity (**Figure 113**) in the crankcase. Wipe it clean with a cloth saturated in solvent and dry it out with compressed air.

7. Install the oil filter screen with the thick side facing out (**Figure 114**).

8. Install the two O-ring seals (A, **Figure 112**) and make sure the locating dowel (**Figure 115**) is in place in the oil pump assembly.

9. Install the oil pump assembly and kickstarter idle gear.

10. Rotate the shift fork shaft (B, **Figure 111**) so that it aligns with the oil pump set plate. Install the set plate and bolts; refer to **Figure 116** for 250 cc engines or **Figure 110** for 500 cc engines.

CAUTION
The set plate must align with the shift fork shaft as shown in Figure 116 or Figure 110. On 250 cc engines, set it flush against the shaft so there is no clearance. If the shift fork shaft rotates (on all models), the lubrication passage within it will be blocked causing oil starvation to the transmission, resulting in transmission damage.

11. Retighten the exposed oil pump assembly screw.

12. Install the clutch assemby as described in Chapter Six.

Disassembly/Inspection/Assembly

1. Inspect the outer housing and cover for cracks.

2. Remove the locating dowel (A, **Figure 117**) and screws (B, **Figure 117**) securing the cover to the body and separate them.

3. Remove the inner and outer rotors and check for scratches or abrasion. Replace both parts if evidence is found of this.

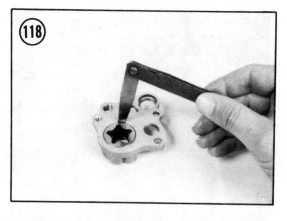

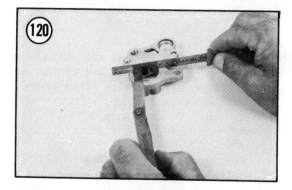

4. Install the outer rotor and measure the clearance between the body and outer rotor with a flat feeler gauge (**Figure 118**). The clearance should be 0.006-0.008 in. (0.15-0.21 mm). If the clearance is 0.01 in. (0.25 mm) or greater, replace the worn part.

5. Install the inner rotor and measure the clearance between the inner rotor and the outer rotor with a flat feeler gauge (**Figure 119**). The clearance should be 0.006 in. (0.15 mm). If the clearance is 0.008 in. (0.21 mm) or greater, replace the worn part.

6. Inspect the rotor side clearance with a straightedge and a flat feeler gauge (**Figure 120**). The clearance between the rotors and the top of the body should be 0.001-0.003 in. (0.02-0.08 mm). If the clearance is 0.005 in. (0.12 mm) or greater, replace either the rotors or the pump assembly.

7. Install the pump drive gear and shaft into the pump cover (**Figure 121**).

8. Install the inner and outer rotors onto it (**Figure 122**).

NOTE
Align the flat side on the pump shaft with the flat within the inner rotor.

9. Install the pump housing, locating dowel (A, **Figure 117**) and 2 screws (B, **Figure 117**). Tighten the 2 screws, one on each side.

10. Measure the inside diameter of the kickstarter idle gear. Compare with dimensions given in **Table 1** (end of chapter). Inspect the gear for excessive wear, burrs, pitting or chipped teeth. Replace if necessary.

11. Inspect the 2 small O-ring seals (A, **Figure 112**). Replace both if either has lost its resiliency or is deteriorated.

CRANKCASE
(1981-ON XL250R AND XR250R)

The only difference (relating to the crankcase) between the 1981-on XL250R and XR250R and the previous XR250 models is in the balancer system. The early balancer system consists of front and rear balancer weights that are chain-driven by the crankshaft. The later balancer system consists of 2 balancer weights on the front balancer shaft; it is gear-driven by the crankshaft. This later system makes crankcase separation much easier.

Disassembly

1. Remove the engine from the frame as described in this chapter.
2. Remove the cylinder head cover, cylinder head, cylinder, alternator, shift mechanism, clutch assembly and the ignition advance mechanism. Refer to the appropriate chapters in this book for details.
3. Remove the bolt securing the cam chain tensioner and remove the cam chain tensioner assembly.
4. Remove the cam drive chain and the balancer holder lockbolt.
5. Turn the engine upside down on the work bench.
6. Loosen the lower crankcase bolts in 2-3 stages in a crisscross pattern to avoid warpage. Remove all bolts.
7. Turn the engine right side up and set it on wood blocks.
8. Loosen the upper crankcase bolts in 2-3 stages in a crisscross pattern to avoid warpage. Remove all bolts.
9. Tap around the perimeter of the crankcase halves with a plastic mallet—do not use a metal hammer as it will cause damage.

> *CAUTION*
> *Honda's thin-walled crankcase castings are just that—thin. To avoid damage to the cases do not hammer on the projected walls that surround the clutch or alternator. These areas are easily damaged if stressed.*

> *CAUTION*
> *If it is necessary to pry the crankcase halves apart, do it very carefully so that you do not mar the gasket surfaces. If you do, they will leak and the crankcase halves must be replaced. They cannot be repaired.*

10. Lift up on the upper crankcase half and remove it from the lower one.

11. Remove the crankshaft assembly and both transmission shaft assemblies from the lower crankcase.
12. Remove the balancer assembly from the upper crankcase half as described in this chapter.
13. Remove the shift drum and shift fork shafts as described in Chapter Five.
14. Remove the kickstarter assembly as described in this chapter.
15. Remove the bolts securing the crankcase breather hose separator plate and remove the plate.

Assembly

Prior to installation of parts, coat all surfaces with assembly oil or engine oil. Do not get any oil on the sealing surfaces of the case halves.
1. Install the crankcase breather separator baffle plate and tighten the screws securely.
2. Install the kickstarter assembly and crankshaft assembly.
3. Install the transmission shaft assemblies as described in Chapter Six.
4. Install the balancer assembly into the upper crankcase half as described in this chapter.
5. If removed, install the 2 locating dowels in the lower crankcase half.
6. Apply a light coat of gasket sealer to the sealing surfaces of both halves. Coat only flat surfaces, not the curved bearing surfaces. Make the coating as thin as possible or the case can shift and hammer out the bearings.

> *NOTE*
> *Use Gasgacinch Gasket Sealer, 4-Three Bond or equivalent. When selecting an equivalent, avoid thick hard-setting materials.*

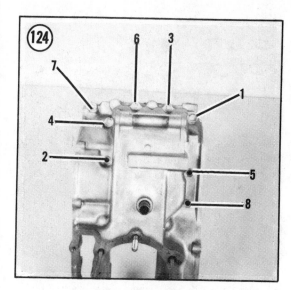

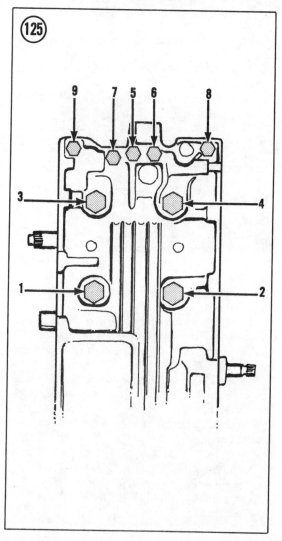

7. The counterbalance weights on the crankshaft assembly will locate the crankshaft at approximately bottom dead center (BDC). This will locate the punch mark on the balancer drive gear (attached to the crankshaft) at about the 10 o'clock position.

8. Position the upper crankcase half onto the lower half while aligning the punch mark (1981 models) or index line (1982-on models) on the balancer driven gear with the punch mark on the drive gear (**Figure 123**).

NOTE
Figure 123 shows a 1982 balancer driven gear. The 1981 gear is slightly different in construction but the alignment procedure is the same.

9. Lower the crankcase completely, making sure that the transmission bearing races are engaged into the dowel pins and 1/2 circlips. If not seated correctly this would keep the crankcase from completely seating.

CAUTION
Do not install any crankcase bolts until the sealing surface around the entire crankcase perimeter has seated completely.

10. Prior to installing the bolts, slowly spin the transmission main shaft and shift the transmission through all 6 gears. Also spin the crankshaft to make sure there is no binding.

11. Apply oil to the threads of all crankcase bolts. Install the bolts only finger-tight at this time.

12. Tighten the upper crankcase bolts in 2-3 stages in the sequence shown in **Figure 124**. Tighten the bolts to the torque specification listed in **Table 2**.

13. Turn the engine over and tighten the lower crankcase bolts in the sequence shown in **Figure 125**. Tighten the bolts to the torque specification listed in **Table 2**.

14. Make sure the collar is in place in the tensioner assembly prior to installation (**Figure 126**). Install the cam chain tensioner assembly and tighten the bolt to the torque specifications listed in **Table 2**.

15. Install the balancer holder lockbolt (**Figure 127**).

16. Adjust the balancer backlash as described in this chapter.

17. Install the cam drive chain and oil pipe.

18. Install all engine components that were removed.

19. Install the engine as described in this chapter.

20. Fill the crankcase with the recommended type and quantity of engine oil as described in Chapter Three.

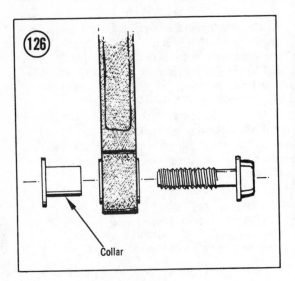

Collar

CRANKCASE
(ALL OTHER MODELS)

Service to the lower end requires that the crankcase be removed from the motorcycle frame.

Disassembly

1. Remove the engine as described in this chapter.
2. Remove the cylinder head, cylinder, piston, alternator and shift mechanism. Refer to the appropriate chapters in this book for details.
3. Remove the ignition advance mechanism (A, **Figure 128**), clutch assembly (B, **Figure 128**) and small oil pipe (C, **Figure 128**). Refer to Chapter Six for clutch removal.
4. Remove the bolt (**Figure 129**) securing the cam chain tensioner and remove it.
5. Remove the cam drive chain (A, **Figure 130**), the front balancer holder lockbolt (B, **Figure 130**) and spring (C, **Figure 130**).
6. Remove the 2 bolts (**Figure 131**) securing the balancer chain guide and remove it.
7. Turn the engine upside down on the workbench.

NOTE
On 500 cc engines, place the engine on wood blocks to protect the cylinder studs.

3. Remove the 8 (or 9) lower crankcase bolts (**Figure 132**). On 250 cc engines, there are only 4 bolts (not 5) across the front.

NOTE
Figure 132 shows bolt placement only—the bolts have been removed.

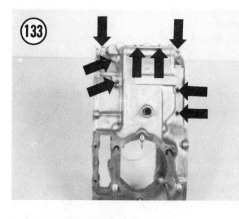

9. Turn the engine right side up and set it on wood blocks.

10. Remove the 8 upper crankcase bolts (**Figure 133**).

NOTE
Figure 133 shows bolt placement only—the bolts have been removed.

11. Carefully tap around the perimeter of the crankcase with a plastic mallet—do not use a metal hammer—to help separate the 2 case halves.

CAUTION
If it is necessary to pry the halves apart, do it very carefully so that you do not mar the gasket surfaces. If you do, the cases will leak and must be replaced.

12. Lift up on the upper crankcase and move it toward the rear (**Figure 134**).

13. Remove the balancer chain from the rear balancer on the transmission main shaft.

14. Remove the crankshaft assembly, transmission main shaft assembly and countershaft assembly from the lower crankcase.

15. Remove the front balancer assembly from the upper crankcase half.

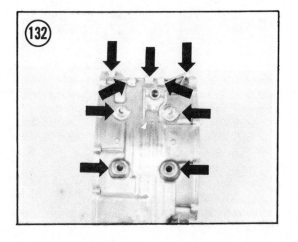

16. Remove the shift forks and shift drum assembly as described in Chapter Six.

17. Remove the kickstarter assembly as described in this chapter.

18. Remove the bolts (**Figure 135**) securing the crankcase breather oil separator plate and remove it and the hose.

Inspection

1. Thoroughly clean the inside and outside of both crankcase halves with cleaning solvent. Dry with compressed air. Make sure there is no solvent residue left in the cases as it will contaminate the engine oil.

2. Make sure all oil passages are clean; be sure to blow them out with compressed air.

3. Check the crankcases for possible damage such as cracks. Inspect the mating surfaces of both halves. They must be free of gouges, burrs or any damage that could cause an oil leak.

4. If any cracks are found, have them repaired immediately by a shop specializing in the repair of precision aluminum castings.

5. On 500 cc engines, make sure the cylinder studs are not bent and the threads are in good condition. Make sure they are screwed into the crankcase tightly.

6. Inspect all balancer components as described in this chapter.

Assembly

Prior to installation of parts, coat all surfaces with assembly oil or fresh engine oil. Do not get any oil on the sealing surfaces of the case halves.

1. Install the crankcase breather separator baffle plate (**Figure 135**).

> *NOTE*
> *Make sure the ears on the spring clip (A, Figure 135) securing the hose are facing toward the rear of the engine.*

2. Install the kickstarter assembly and crankshaft assembly.

3. Install the transmission assemblies, shift forks and shift drum as described in Chapter Six.

4. If the factory paint marks on the balancer chain have come off, they must be re-marked as follows. Refer to **Figure 136**. Lay the chain out flat in a loop. Make all the marks on the lower loop of the chain. Place a spot of quick drying paint on a link plate (start with any link—it makes no difference where you start); the pin on the left-hand side of this link plate will be pin No. 1. Count to the right until you reach pin No. 9 and mark that link plate with paint. The pin on the left-hand side of this

link plate will be pin No. 9. On 250 cc engines, continue counting to the right until you reach the 27th pin; mark that link plate with paint. The pin on the left-hand side of that link plate will be pin No. 27. On 500 cc engines, continue counting from pin No. 9 to the right to the 25th pin; mark that link plate with paint. The pin on the left-hand side of that link plate will be pin No. 25.

> *CAUTION*
> *This is very important for balancer timing; each mark must be accurate or extreme engine vibration will occur.*

> *CAUTION*
> ***Do not*** *disconnect or remove the balancer system from your motorcycle. The engine is designed to operate with it to reduce engine vibration. If the balancers are removed or disconnected an excessive amount of vibration could result in cracks or damage to the frame and/or engine. Also any applicable manufacturer's warranty will be voided.*

5. Install the 2 locating dowels (**Figure 137**) in the lower crankcase half.

6. Install the front balancer assembly into the upper crankcase half. Do not install the sprocket.

7. Install the balancer chain with the marks made in Step 4 on the lower half of the chain. Lift the transmission main shaft out and insert the chain over the rear balancer sprocket. Align the 27th link plate (250 cc engines) or 25th link plate (500 cc engines) with the punch mark on the sprocket (**Figure 138**). Reinstall the transmission main shaft.

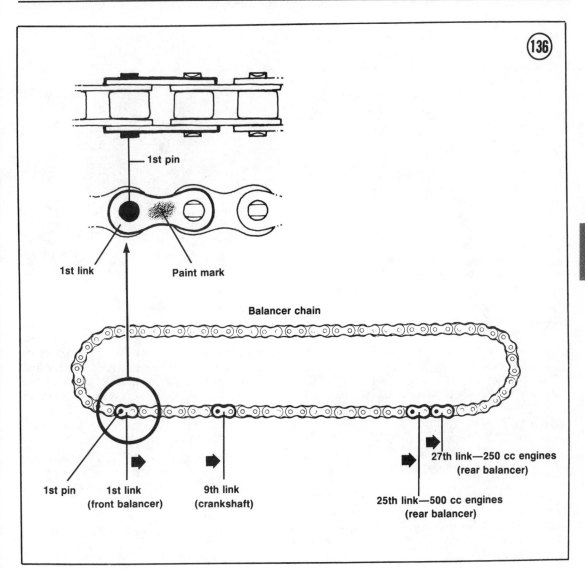

1st pin

1st link

Paint mark

Balancer chain

27th link—250 cc engines
(rear balancer)

1st pin

1st link
(front balancer)

9th link
(crankshaft)

25th link—500 cc engines
(rear balancer)

4

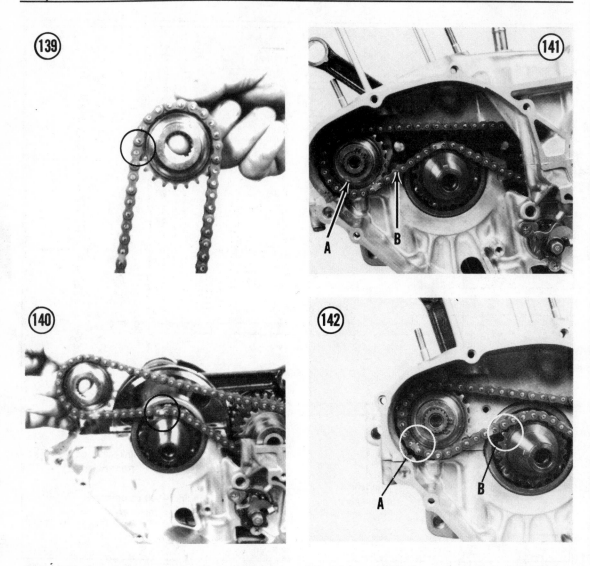

8. Install the chain onto the front balancer sprocket. Align the punch mark on the sprocket with the 1st link plate on the chain (**Figure 139**).

9. Pull the front balancer sprocket and chain forward and align the punch mark on the crankshaft sprocket with the 9th link plate on the chain (**Figure 140**). Let the front balancer sprocket and chain hang from the crankshaft sprocket.

10. Apply a light coat of gasket sealer to the sealing surfaces of both crankcase halves. Cover only flat surfaces, not curved bearing surfaces. Make the coating as thin as possible or the case can shift and hammer out the bearings.

> *NOTE*
> *Use Gasgacinch Gasket Sealer or equivalent. When selecting an equivalent, avoid thick or hard-setting materials.*

11. Make sure all alignments made in Steps 7-9 are still correct. If not, repeat Steps 7-9 until all are correct. Position the upper crankcase onto the rear of the lower crankcase and install the front balancer sprocket onto the balancer shaft.

> *CAUTION*
> *Make sure the punch marks on the front balancer shaft align with the punch mark on the balancer (A, **Figure 141**). Install the circlip.*

12. Completely join the 2 crankcase halves together. Again check the alignment of the punch marks and chain pins on the front balancer (A, **Figure 142**) and crankshaft (B, **Figure 142**). If alignment is incorrect, correct it before proceeding. Tap around the perimeter lightly with a plastic mallet—do not use a metal hammer as it will damage the cases.

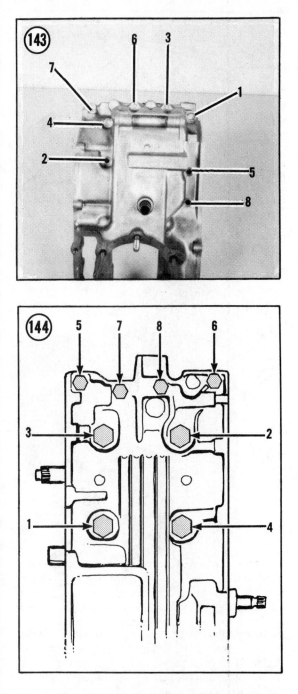

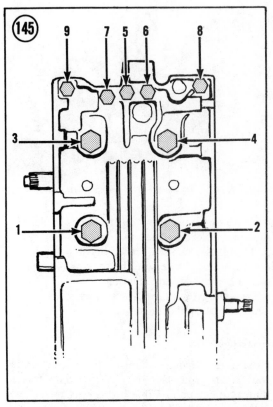

engines or **Figure 145** for 500 cc engines. Tighten the bolts to the torque specifications listed in **Table 2**.

15. Install the balancer chain guide (B, **Figure 141**).

16. Install the cam drive chain, front balancer holder lockbolt and spring (**Figure 130**).

17. Be sure to install the small oil pipe (C, **Figure 128**) prior to installing the right-hand crankcase cover.

18. Install all engine components that were removed.

19. Install the engine components that were removed.

20. Fill the crankcase with the recommended type and quantity of engine oil. Refer to Chapter Three.

CRANKSHAFT AND CONNECTING ROD

Removal/Installation

1. Split the crankcase as described under *Crankcase Disassembly* in this chapter.

2. Remove the crankshaft assembly from the lower crankcase half.

3. Prior to installing, lubricate the large ball bearings and connecting rod small end bearing with assembly oil or fresh engine oil.

13. Apply oil to the threads of all crankcase bolts; install them and tighten finger-tight only. Tighten the upper crankcase bolts in 2 or 3 stages in the sequence shown in **Figure 143**. Tighten the 6 mm bolts to 7-10 ft.-lb. (10-14 N•m) and the 8 mm bolts to 16-20 ft.-lb. (22-28 N•m) on all models.

14. Turn the engine over and install the lower crankcase bolts. Tighten the bolts in 2 or 3 stages in the sequence shown in **Figure 144** for 250 cc

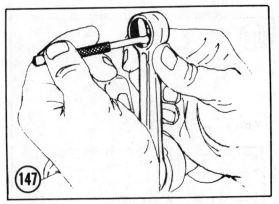

4. Make sure the set ring (**Figure 146**) is in place in the lower crankcase half.

5. Install the crankshaft assembly into the lower crankcase half. Make sure the set ring is properly seated into the bearing outer race.

6. Assembly the crankcase as described under *Crankcase Assembly* in this chapter.

Inspection

1. Measure the inside diameter of the connecting rod small end (**Figure 147**). Compare to dimensions given in **Table 1** (end of chapter).

2. Measure the side clearance of the connecting rod big end with a flat feeler gauge (**Figure 148**). Compare to dimensions given in **Table 1** (end of chapter).

3. Inspect the condition of both ball bearings (**Figure 149**). Make sure they rotate smoothly with no signs of wear or damage. These bearings are pressed into place; removal and installation should be entrusted to a Honda dealer or machine shop.

4. Mount the crankshaft assembly in a pair of V-blocks as shown in **Figure 150**. Rotate the crankshaft slowly several complete revolutions. Measure the runout, using a dial indicator, at each end. Replace the crankshaft assembly if the runout exceeds 0.004 in. (0.1 mm) at either end.

5. Mount the crankshaft assembly as in Step 4 and measure the clearance between the connecting rod and crankpin (**Figure 151**). Compare against dimensions given in **Table 1** (end of chapter).

> *NOTE*
> *Connecting rod replacement is a job for a Honda dealer. It requires a large press to separate and reassemble the crankshaft. In addition the runout (alignment) of the 2 crank halves must be within 0.0004 in. (0.01 mm) of each other. Play it safe and replace the entire assembly.*

6. Inspect the balancer drive gear (**Figure 152**) for excessive wear, burrs and pitted or missing teeth. If replacement is required, have it performed by a dealer. When installing the new gear make sure to align the punch mark on the gear with the Woodruff key (**Figure 153**).

7. Removal and replacement of the balancer and/or camshaft drive chain sprocket should be entrusted to a Honda dealer.

BALANCER SYSTEM

The balancer system eliminates the vibration normally associated with a large displacement

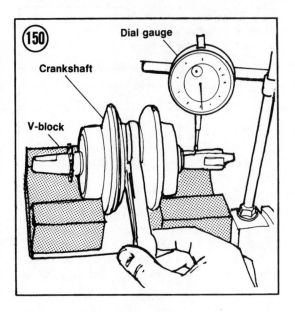

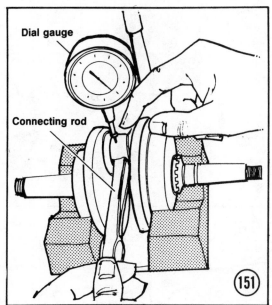

single cylinder engine. The engine and motorcycle frame are designed for use with this balancer system. If the balancers are disconnected or eliminated it will result in an excessive amount of engine vibration. This vibration will result in major fatigue to engine and frame components. *Do not eliminate* this feature.

CAUTION
Any applicable manufacturer's warranty will be voided if the balancer system is modified, disconnected or removed.

There are 2 types of balancer system used. The 1978-1980 250 cc and all 500 cc engines have front and rear balancer weights that are chain-driven by the crankshaft. The 1981-on 250 cc engines have a less complicated system that consists of 2 balancer weights on each end of the front balancer shaft. The balancer shaft is gear-driven by the crankshaft. There is no rear balancer on these late models 250 cc engines.

Front Balancer
Removal/Installation
(Chain-driven)

1. Remove the engine as described in this chapter.
2. Disassemble the crankcase as described in this chapter.

NOTE
The left-hand and right-hand side refers to the engine as it sits in the bike's frame—not as it sits on your workbench.

3. Remove the 20 mm circlip from the balancer shaft on the left-hand side of the engine. Remove the chain sprocket.

4. Slide the balancer and shaft (**Figure 154**) out the right-hand side.

5. Slide the balancer shaft holder (**Figure 155**) out the right-hand side.

6. Apply assembly oil to all rotating surfaces prior to installation.

7. Install by reversing these removal steps.

Front Balancer
Removal/Installation
(1981 Gear-driven)

1. Remove the engine as described in this chapter.

2. Disassemble the crankcase as described in this chapter.

> *NOTE*
> *The left-hand and right-hand side refers to the engine as it sits in the bike's frame—not as it sits on your workbench.*

3. On the left-hand side remove the circlip securing the balancer driven gear to the balancer shaft.

4. Remove the balancer gear. Remove the balancer shaft and holder from the right-hand side.

5. Apply assembly oil to the needle bearings and to all rotating surfaces prior to installation.

6. Install by reversing these removal steps, noting the following.

7. Align the punch marks on the balancer shaft and balancer driven gear and install the balancer driven gear onto the balancer shaft (**Figure 156**). Make sure these 2 marks align and install the circlip with the sharp edge facing toward the outside.

Front Balancer
Removal/Installation
(1982-on Gear-driven)

1. Remove the engine as described in this chapter.

2. Disassemble the crankcase as described in this chapter.

> *NOTE*
> *The left-hand and right-hand side refers to the engine as it sits in the bike's frame—not as it sits on your workbench.*

3. On the right-hand side remove the circlip (**Figure 157**) securing the right-hand balancer weight to the balancer shaft/gear unit. Slide off the balancer weight and thrust washer (**Figure 158**).

4. Remove the needle bearing and washer (**Figure 159**) located on the balancer shaft behind the thrust washer.

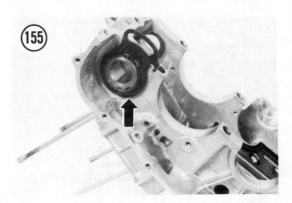
(155)

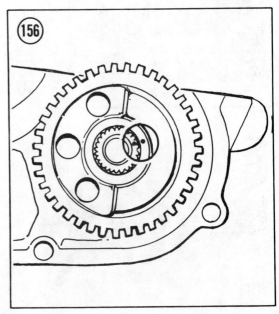
(156)

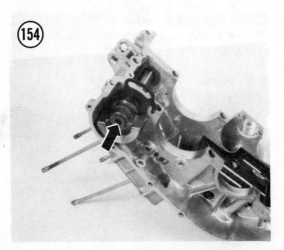
(154)

5. On the left-hand side, withdraw the balancer shaft/gear unit (**Figure 160**).

6. On the right-hand side remove the balancer shaft holder assembly (**Figure 161**).

7. Apply assembly oil to the needle bearings and to all rotating surfaces prior to installation.

8. Install by reversing these removal steps, noting the following.

9. Align the punch marks on the balancer shaft/gear unit with the right-hand balancer (**Figure 162**). Make sure these 2 marks align and install the circlip with the sharp edge facing toward the outside.

Front Balancer
Disassembly/Inspection/Assembly
(All Models)

Figure 163 shows the assembly used on 1981-on 250 cc engines.

1. If necessary, remove the circlip (**Figure 164**) securing the balancer holder flange to the shaft and remove the flange.

2A. On 1981 250 cc engines, remove the circlip (**Figure 165**) securing the balancer weight to the shaft and remove the balancer weight and the thrust washer. Slide off the needle bearing and special washer.

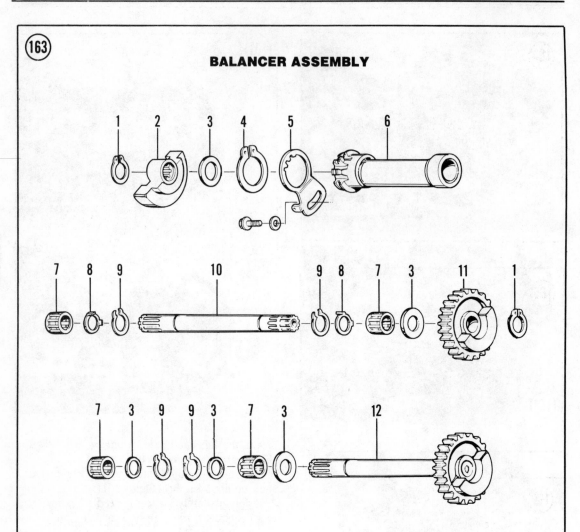

BALANCER ASSEMBLY

1. 20 mm circlip
2. Balancer weight
3. Thrust washer
4. Circlip
5. Balancer holder flange
6. Balancer shaft holder
7. Needle bearing
8. Special washer
9. Special circlip
10. Balancer shaft
11. Balancer driven weight
12. Balancer shaft/weight assembly

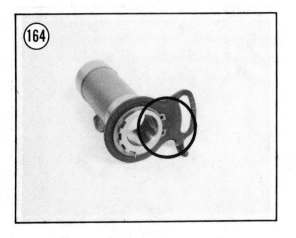

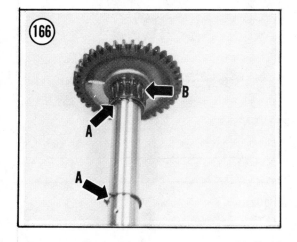

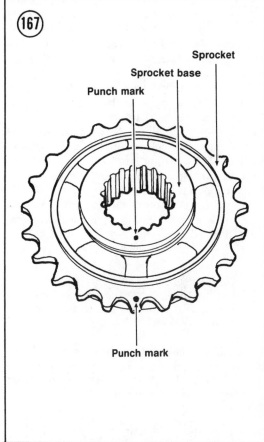

2B. On 1982-on 250 cc engines, remove both circlips (A, **Figure 166**) and remove the needle bearing next to the left-hand balancer weight/driven gear. Slide off the needle bearing (B, **Figure 166**).

NOTE
During the 1980 model year there was a running change to the XL250S. The rubber dampers used within both the front and rear sprocket/balancer assemblies have been eliminated. The new sprocket/balancer assemblies are a 1-piece unit and cannot be disassembled. Removal, inspection and installation are the same as on previous models.

3. On 1978-1981 250 cc engines, disassemble and assemble the sprocket/balancer assembly as follows:

a. Remove the circlip and side plate.

b. Note the location of the rubber dampers in relation to the sprocket and sprocket base. The rubber dampers must be reinstalled in the same locations. Remove the 6 rubber dampers from the sprocket base.

c. Remove the sprocket from the sprocket base.

d. Inspect the rubber dampers. If any are worn or disintegrating, replace all 6 as a set.

e. To reassemble, align the punch marks (**Figure 167**) of the sprocket and the sprocket base and install the sprocket onto the sprocket base.

f. Install the rubber dampers, the side plate and the circlip. Make sure the circlip is properly seated in the groove.

4. Inspect the needle bearings. Make sure they rotate smoothly with no signs of wear or damage. Replace as necessary.

5. Measure the inside diameter (A, **Figure 168**) of the balancer shaft holder. Replace if the diameter is 1.028 in. (26.10 mm) or greater. Measure the outside diameter (B, **Figure 168**) at each end of the bearing surfaces. Replace if either end is worn to 1.571 in. (39.91 mm) or less.

6. Inspect the sprocket teeth for wear or damage. Replace if necessary.

7. Inspect the teeth on the driven gear. Check for excessive wear, burrs, pitting or chipped or missing teeth. Replace if necessary.

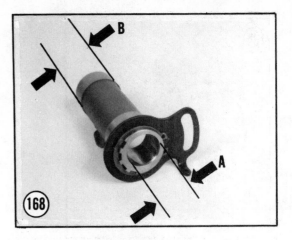

> *NOTE*
> *On 1982-on 250 cc engines, the gear is part of the shaft and cannot be removed. If damaged the entire unit must be replaced.*

8. Install the balancer holder flange with the bent-over ear (**Figure 169**) facing outward away from the shaft. Install the circlip with the sharp edge facing toward the outside.

> *NOTE*
> *In the following step there are 2 different width needle bearings. The narrow bearing (marked 20×26×17) is to be installed on the left-hand side (next to the gear-driven balancer). Refer to* **Figure 170**.

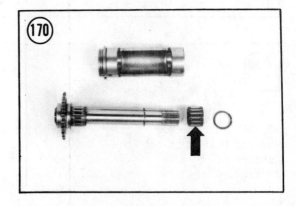

9A. On 1981 250 cc engines, install the circlips (A, **Figure 171**), special washers (B, **Figure 171**) and needle bearings (C, **Figure 171**) onto the shaft. Align the special washer tabs with the circlips so they are locked in place and will not spin. Apply a light coat of multipurpose grease to the inner side of the special washer to hold it in place during installation.

9B. On 1982-on 250 cc engines, slide on the narrow bearing (marked 20×26×17) next to the left-hand balancer weight/driven gear and install the circlip. Install the other circlip on the opposite end of the shaft.

> *NOTE*
> *If the wrong bearing is installed it will be impossible to install the circlip as the circlip groove in the shaft will not be exposed.*

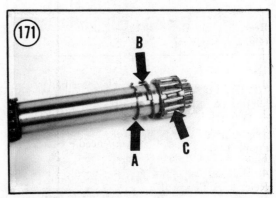

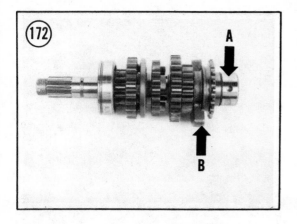

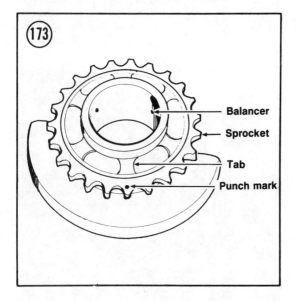

10. On 1981 250 cc engines, if the balancer weight was removed, align the punch marks on the balancer shaft with the balancer weight and install the balancer weight. Make sure these 2 marks align and install the circlip with the sharp edge facing toward the outside.

Rear Balancer Removal/Installation (Chain-driven Only)

1. Remove the engine from the frame and disassemble the crankcase as described in this chapter.
2. Remove the transmission main shaft from the lower crankcase.
3. Slide off the outer race and needle bearing (A, **Figure 172**) and thrust washer.
4. Slide off the outer race and needle bearing(s). Refer to B, **Figure 172**.

5. On 500 cc engines, remove the collar that is outside of the needle bearing. There are 2 needle bearings within the balancer on 250 cc engines.
6. Install by reversing these removal steps, noting the following.
7. On 500 cc engines, install in this order: thrust washer, needle bearing, collar, rear balancer, thrust washer, needle bearing and outer race.
8. On 250 cc engines, install in this order: thrust washer, needle bearing, needle bearing, rear balancer, thrust washer, needle bearing and outer race.

Rear Balancer Disassembly/ Inspection/Assembly (Chain-driven Only)

1. On 250 cc engines, disassemble the sprocket/balancer assembly. Remove the circlip, side plate, sprocket and 6 rubber dampers. If they are worn or disintegrating replace all 6 as a set. Reassemble by placing the sprocket onto the rear balancer while aligning the punch mark with the tab (**Figure 173**). Insert the 6 rubber dampers, the side plate and circlip.
2. On all models, measure the inside diameter of the rear balancer. Replace the balancer if the dimension is larger than the following:
   a. 250 cc engines—1.028 in. (26.10 mm).
   b. 500 cc engines—1.026 in. (25.05 mm).
3. Inspect the sprocket teeth for wear or damage and replace of necessary.

Balancer Backlash Adjustment (Gear-driven Only)

Whenever the balancer assembly has been removed (or if the balancer holder lockbolt is loosened or removed) the backlash must be adjusted. The most accurate way to measure is with a dial indicator; however, if you do not have an indicator, a modified feeler gauge can be used as described in the following steps.

NOTE
The engine must be at room temperature for this procedure to be accurate.

1. Measure backlash with a dial indicator as follows:
   a. Set the pointer of a dial indicator on a gear tooth of the balancer driven gear (A, **Figure 174**).
   b. Align the zero (B, **Figure 174**) on the dial gauge face exactly with the gauge needle. By hand, rotate the drive gear back and forth slightly to make sure gauge is centered on zero. Readjust the gauge face if necessary.

c. By hand, rotate the driven gear (C, **Figure 174**) back and forth slightly and check the amount of backlash between the driven gear and the drive gear. The specified backlash is 0.0002-0.005 in. (0.005-0.13 mm).

2. If you are unable to obtain a dial indicator, a modified flat feeler gauge may be used (the feeler gauge will have to be cut down narrow enough to fit into the meshed gear teeth). This method is not as accurate but it is better than guessing at the tolerance and being wrong. Insert a flat feeler gauge between the mating surfaces of the gear teeth (**Figure 175**). Nothing thicker than a 0.005 in. (0.13 mm) gauge should fit.

3. If the backlash is not within tolerance, loosen the balancer holder lockbolt (**Figure 176**) and rotate the balancer holder in either direction to achieve the correct amount of gear backlash. Tighten the lockbolt to the torque specification listed in **Table 2**.

> *CAUTION*
> *The most important thing is that there is some amount of backlash. If there is no backlash and the gears are tight against each other, wear will be rapid and excessive. If the backlash is greater than specified the gears will be noisy.*

KICKSTARTER

Removal

Refer to **Figure 177** for this procedure.
1. Remove the engine from the frame as described in this chapter.
2. Split the crankcase as described in this chapter.
3. Remove the thrust washer, kickstarter cam, spring and spring seat (**Figure 178**).
4. From within the crankcase, remove the kickstarter spring from the spring hook pin.
5. Remove the 16 mm circlip, thrust washer, collar and spring from the shaft.

Disassembly/Inspection/Assembly

1. Remove the thrust washer and ratchet spring (**Figure 179**) from the shaft.
2. Remove the 22 mm circlip, thrust washer and kickstarter gear, thrust washer and 24 mm circlip.
3. Measure the inside diameter of the kickstarter gear. If the dimension is 0.870 in. (22.10 mm) or greater, the gear must be replaced.
4. Measure the outside diameter of the kickstarter shaft where the gear rides. If this dimension is 0.863 in. (21.91 mm) or less, the shaft must be replaced.

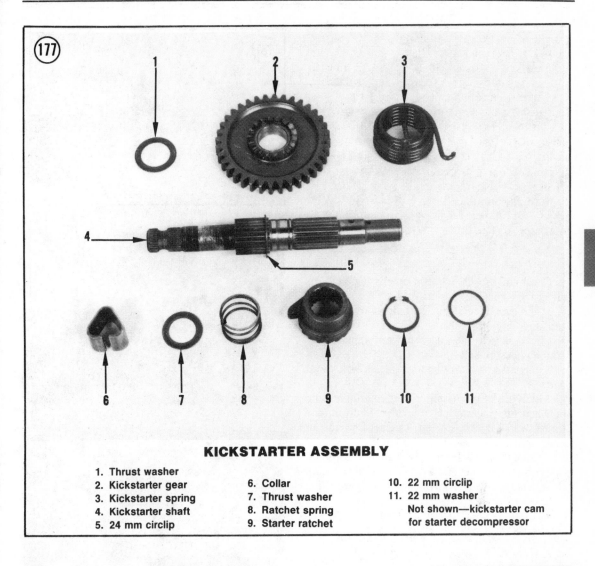

4

KICKSTARTER ASSEMBLY

1. Thrust washer
2. Kickstarter gear
3. Kickstarter spring
4. Kickstarter shaft
5. 24 mm circlip

6. Collar
7. Thrust washer
8. Ratchet spring
9. Starter ratchet

10. 22 mm circlip
11. 22 mm washer
Not shown—kickstarter cam
for starter decompressor

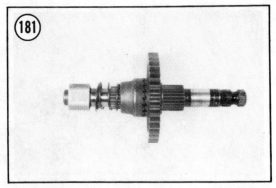

5. Check for broken, chipped or missing teeth on the gears. Replace any of necessary.

6. Make sure the ratchet gear operates properly and smoothly on its shaft.

7. Check all parts for uneven wear; replace any that are questionable.

8. Apply assembly oil to all sliding surfaces of all parts.

9. Install the 24 mm circlip on the right-hand side of where the kickstarter gear rides. Slide on the thrust washer, kickstarter gear (ratchet-free side on first), thrust washer and 22 mm circlip.

10. Install the starter ratchet; align the punch marks on the ratchet and shaft (**Figure 180**). Install the ratchet spring and thrust washer (**Figure 178**).

> *NOTE*
> *Prior to installing the shaft assembly into the crankcase half, check with **Figure 181** for correct placement of all components.*

Installation

1. Install the assembled shaft into the crankcase with the oil and spring holes facing up.

2. Pour a small amount of fresh engine oil into the oil hole (**Figure 182**).

3. Install the spring and collar (**Figure 183**).

4. Install the thrust washer and circlip.

> *NOTE*
> *Install the circlip with the chamfered edge toward the end of the shaft. Make sure the circlip is completely seated into the groove in the shaft.*

5. Pull the spring into position using a motorcycle muffler spring hook (**Figure 184**).

6. Install the spring seat, spring, kickstarter cam and thrust washer (**Figure 185**).

NOTE
*Align the punch mark on the shaft with the mark on the kickstarter cam (**Figure 186**), then slide the cam down onto the shaft splines.*

7. Reassembly the crankcase as described in this chapter.

BREAK-IN

Following cylinder servicing (boring, honing, new rings, etc.) and major lower end work, the engine should be broken in just as though it were new. The performance and service life of the engine depend greatly on a careful and sensible break-in.

The mono-grade oils recommended for break-in and normal use provide a better bedding pattern for rings and cylinders than do multi-grade oils. As a result, piston ring and cylinder bore life are

greatly increased. During this period, oil consumption will be higher than normal. It is therefore important to frequently check and correct the oil level. At no time, during break-in or later, should the oil level be allowed to drop below the bottom line on the dipstick; if the oil level is low, the oil will become overheated resulting in insufficient lubrication and increased wear.

500-mile Service

It is essential that oil and filter be changed after the first 500 miles. In addition, it is a good idea to change the oil and filter at the completion of break-in (about 1,500 miles) to ensure that all of the particles produced during break-in are removed from the lubrication system. The small added expense may be considered a smart investment that will pay off in increased engine life.

Tables are on the following pages.

Table 1 ENGINE SPECIFICATIONS*

Item	Specification	Wear limit
250 CC		
General		
Type	4-stroke, air-cooled, SOHC	
Number of cylinders	1	
Bore and stroke	74.0 x 57.8 mm (2.91 x 2.27 in.)	
Displacement	249 cc (15.1 cu. in.)	
Compression ratio		
XL series	9.1 to 1	
XR series	9.6 to 1	
Compression pressure		
XR250	192 ± 21 psi (13.5 ± 1.5 kg/cm^2)	
All other models	175 psi (12.5 kg/cm^2)	
Cylinder		
Bore	74.00-74.01 mm (2.913-2.914 in.)	74.11 mm (2.918 in.)
Out of round	–	0.05 mm (0.002 in.)
Piston/cylinder clearance	0.01-0.04 mm (0.0004-0.0016 in.)	0.1 mm (0.004 in.)
Warpage across top	–	0.1 mm (0.004 in.)
Piston		
Diameter	73.97-73.99 mm (2.912-2.913 in.)	73.89 mm (2.909 in.)
Clearance in bore	0.01-0.04 mm (0.0004-0.0016 in.)	0.10 mm (0.004 in.)
Piston pin bore	19.002-19.008 mm (0.7481-0.7483 in.)	19.08 mm (0.751 in.)
Piston pin outer diameter	18.994-19.000 mm (0.7478-0.7480 in.)	18.96 mm (0.747 in.)
Piston rings		
Number of rings		
Compression	2	
Oil control	1	
Ring end gap		
Top and second	0.15-0.35 mm (0.006-0.014 in.)	0.5 mm (0.02 in.)
Oil (side rail)	0.2-0.9 mm (0.007-0.035 in.)	NA
Ring side clearance		
Top and second ring	0.015-0.045 mm (0.006-0.0018 in.)	0.12 mm (0.006 in.)
Oil control	0.017 mm (0.0007 in.)	
Crankshaft/connecting rod		
Small end inner diameter	19.020-19.041 mm (0.7488-0.7496 in.)	19.07 mm (0.751 in).
Connecting rod big end side clearance	0.05-0.45 mm (0.002-0.017 in.)	0.60 mm (0.024 in.)
Connecting rod big end radial clearance	0.006-0.018 mm (0.0002-0.0007 in.)	0.05 mm (0.002 in.)
Camshaft		
Cam lobe height		
Intake	36.362 mm (1.4316 in.)	36.30 mm (1.429 in.)
Exhaust	36.256 mm (1.4274 in.)	36.20 mm (1.425 in.)

(continued)

Table 1 ENGINE SPECIFICATIONS* (continued)

Item	Specification	Wear limit
250 CC (cont.)		
Camshaft (cont.)		
Cam journal OD		
Left-hand end	19.954-19.975 mm (0.7856-0.7864 in.)	19.9 mm (0.78 in.)
Right-hand end	23.954-23.975 mm (0.9431-0.9439 in.)	23.9 mm (0.94 in.)
Cam bearing surface ID in cylinder head and cylinder head cover		
Left-hand side	20.000-20.021 mm (0.7874-0.7882 in.)	20.05 mm (0.789 in.)
Right-hand side	24.000-24.021 mm (0.9449-0.9457 in.)	24.05 mm (0.947 in.)
Valves		
Valve stem outer diameter		
Intake	5.475-5.490 mm (0.2037-0.2161 in.)	5.465 mm (0.2152 in.)
Exhaust	5.455-5.470 mm (0.2148-0.2154 in.)	5.445 mm (0.2144 in.)
Valve guide inner diameter	5.500-5.512 mm (0.2166-0.2170 in.)	5.53 mm (0.218 in.)
Stem to guide clearance	0.010-0.047 mm (0.0004-0.0019 in.)	0.06 mm (0.0024 in.)
Valve face width	1.2-1.4 mm (0.048-0.055 in.)	2.0 mm (0.08 in.)
Valve springs free length		
Inner	43.6 mm (1.72 in.)	42.5 mm (1.67 in.)
Outer	35.58 mm (1.40 in.)	34.5 mm (1.36 in.)
Rocker arm assembly		
Rocker arm bore ID	12.000-12.018 mm (0.4724-0.4731 in.)	12.05 mm (0.474 in.)
Rocker arm shaft OD	11.966-11.984 mm (0.4711-0.4718 in.)	11.91 mm (0.469 in.)
Oil pump		
Inner to outer rotor tip clearance	0.15 mm (0.006 in.)	0.20 mm (0.008 in.)
Outer rotor to body clearance	0.15-0.18 mm (0.006-0.007 in.)	0.25 mm (0.0010 in.)
Rotor to body clearance	0.01-0.07 mm (0.0004-0.0028 in.)	0.12 mm (0.0047 in.)
Counter balancer system		
Front		
Shaft holder ID	26.007-26.020 mm (1.0239-1.0244 in.)	26.05 mm (10.26 in.)
Shaft holder OD	39.964-39.980 mm (1.5734-1.5740 in.)	39.91 mm (1.571 in.)
Rear balancer ID	26.007-26.020 mm (1.0239-1.0244 in.)	26.05 mm (1.026 in.)
Kickstarter		
Gear ID	22.000-22.021 mm (0.8661-0.8670 in.)	22.10 mm (0.870 in.)
Shaft OD (where gear rides)	21.959-21.980 mm (0.8645-0.8654 in.)	21.91 mm (0.863 in.)

(continued)

4

Table 1 ENGINE SPECIFICATIONS* (continued)

Item	Specification	Wear limit
500 CC		
General		
Type	4-stroke, air-cooled, SOHC	
Number of cylinders	1	
Bore and stroke	89.0 x 80.0 mm (3.50 x 3.15 in.)	
Displacement	498 cc (30.37 cu. in.)	
Compression ratio	8.6 to 1	
Compression pressure	175 psi (12.5 kg/cm^2)	
Cylinder		
Bore	89.00-89.01 mm (3.5039-3.5041 in.)	89.11 mm (3.508 in.)
Out of round	–	0.05 mm (0.002 in.)
Piston/cylinder clearance	0.01-0.04 mm (0.0004-0.0016 in.)	0.1 mm (0.004 in.)
Warpage across top	–	0.1 mm (0.004 in.)
Piston		
Diameter	88.97-88.99 mm (3.503-3.504 in.)	88.88 mm (3.499 in.)
Clearance in bore	0.01-0.04 mm (0.0004-0.0016 in.)	0.10 mm (0.004 in.)
Piston pin bore	21.002-21.008 mm (0.8268-0.8271 in.)	21.08 mm (0.830 in.)
Piston pin outer diameter	20.994-21.000 mm (0.8265-0.8268 in.)	20.96 mm (0.825 in.)
Piston rings		
Number of rings		
Compression	2	
Oil control	1	
Ring end gap		
Top and second	0.30-0.50 mm (0.0118-0.0197 in.)	0.65 mm (0.026 in.)
Oil (side rail)	0.2-0.9 mm (0.007-0.035 in.)	NA
Ring side clearance		
Top ring	0.030-0.065 mm (0.0012-0.0026 in.)	0.12 mm (0.006 in.)
Second ring	0.015-0.045 mm (0.006-0.0018 in.)	0.12 mm (0.006 in.)
Oil control	NA	NA
Crankshaft/connecting rod		
Small end inner diameter	21.020-21.041 mm (0.8276-0.8284 in.)	21.07 mm (0.830 in.)
Connecting rod big end side clearance	0.05-0.65 mm (0.002-0.0256 in.)	0.80 mm (0.031 in.)
Connecting rod big end radial clearance	0.006-0.018 mm (0.0002-0.0007 in.)	0.05 mm (0.002 in.)
Camshaft		
Cam lobe height		
Intake	36.431 mm (1.4343 in.)	36.23 mm (1.426 in.)
Exhaust	36.466 mm (1.4357 in.)	36.27 mm (1.428 in.)

(continued)

Table 1 ENGINE SPECIFICATIONS* (continued)

Item	Specification	Wear limit
500 CC (cont.)		
Camshaft (cont.)		
Cam journal OD		
Left-hand end	19.954-19.975 mm (0.7856-0.7864 in.)	19.9 mm (0.78 in.)
Right-hand end	23.954-23.975 mm (0.9431-0.9439 in.)	23.9 mm (0.94 in.)
Cam bearing surface ID in cylinder head and cylinder head cover		
Left-hand side	20.000-20.021 mm (0.7874-0.7882 in.)	20.05 mm (0.789 in.)
Right-hand side	24.000-24.021 mm (0.9449-0.9457 in.)	24.05 mm (0.947 in.)
Valves		
Valve stem outer diameter		
Intake	6.575-6.590 mm (0.2589-0.2594 in.)	6.565 mm (0.258 in.)
Exhaust	6.560-6.570 mm (0.2583-0.2587 in.)	6.55 mm (0.2579 in.)
Valve guide inner diameter	6.600-6.615 mm (0.2598-0.2421 in.)	6.63 mm (0.261 in.)
Stem to guide clearance		
Intake	0.010-0.040 mm (0.0004-0.0016 in.)	0.065 mm (0.0026 in.)
Exhaust	0.030-0.055 mm (0.0012-0.0022 in.)	0.080 mm (0.0031 in.)
Valve face width		
Intake and exhaust	1.2-1.4 mm (0.048-0.055 in.)	2.0 mm (0.08 in.)
Valve springs		
Free length		
Inner	38.1 mm (1.50 in.)	37.0 mm (1.46 in.)
Outer	36.24 mm (1.43 in.)	35.3 mm (1.39 in.)
Rocker arm assembly		
Rocker arm bore ID	12.000-12.018 mm (0.4724-0.4731 in.)	12.05 mm (0.474 in.)
Rocker arm shaft OD	11.966-11.984 mm (0.4711-0.4718 in.)	11.91 mm (0.469 in.)
Oil pump		
Inner to outer rotor tip clearance	0.15 mm (0.006 in.)	0.20 mm (0.01 in.)
Outer rotor to body clearance	0.15-0.21 mm (0.006-0.008 in.)	0.25 mm (0.0010 in.)
Rotor to body clearance	0.02-0.08 mm (0.001-0.003 in.)	0.12 mm (0.005 in.)
Counter balancer system		
Front		
Shaft holder ID	26.007-26.020 mm (1.0239-1.0244 in.)	26.05 mm (10.26 in.)
Shaft holder OD	39.964-39.980 mm (1.5734-1.5740 in.)	39.91 mm (1.571 in.)

(continued)

Table 1 ENGINE SPECIFICATIONS* (continued)

Item	Specification	Wear limit
500 CC (cont.)		
Counter balancer system (cont.)		
Rear balancer ID	26.007-26.020 mm (1.0239-1.0244 in.)	26.05 mm (1.026 in.)
Kickstarter		
Gear ID	22.000-22.021 mm (0.8661-0.8670 in.)	22.10 mm (0.870 in.)
Shaft OD (where gear rides)	21.959-21.980 mm 0.8645-21.980 in.)	21.91 mm (0.863 in.)

* Honda does not provide service information for all items nor all models. All available information is included in this table. NA = Not available.

Table 2 ENGINE TORQUE SPECIFICATIONS

Item	ft.-lb.	N•m
Engine mounting bolts (upper 3)		
8 mm bolts	14-25	20-35
10 mm bolts		
XL series	22-36	30-50
XR series	33-43	45-60
Engine hanger bolts (front 4)		
Upper 8 mm bolts	22-36	30-50
Lower 10 mm bolts		
XL series	22-36	30-50
XR series	33-43	45-60
Engine mounting bolts		
10 mm (XL series)	22-36	30-50
12 mm (XR series)	51-72	70-100
Valve adjuster cover bolts	7-10	10-14
Cylinder head studs (XL250S, XR250)	25-29	35-40
Cylinder head nuts (XL500S, XR500, XR500R)	16-20	22-28
Cylinder head bolts and nuts (XL250S, 1981-on XR250)	25-29	35-40
Cylinder head cover bolts	7-10	10-14
Cylinder side bolts (XL250S, XR250)	7-10	10-14
Cylinder front, rear and side bolts	16-20	22-28
Cylinder nut (XR500R)	16-20	22-28
Cam sprocket bolts	12-17	17-23
Cam chain tensioner bolt	16-20	22-28
Ignition advance mechanism nut	33-43	45-60
Crankcase cover bolts	6-9	8-12
Alternator rotor bolt		
XL250S	61-69	85-105
XR250, XR250R	69-76	95-105
All 500 cc	72-87	100-120
Upper crankcase bolts		
6 mm bolts	7-10	10-14
8 mm bolts	16-20	22-28
Lower crankcase bolts		
6 mm bolts	7-10	10-14
8 mm bolts	16-20	22-28
9 mm bolts	20-23	27-32
10 mm bolts	24-27	33-37

CHAPTER FIVE

1983 350-600 CC ENGINES

The engine is an air-cooled, 4-stroke, single cylinder engine with a single overhead camshaft. The crankshaft is supported by 2 main ball bearings. The camshaft is chain-driven from the sprocket on the right-hand side of the crankshaft and operates sub-rocker arms and rocker arms that are individually adjustable.

Engine lubrication on the XR350R is by wet sump. On XR500R and XL600R models the engine is a dry-sump type with the oil reservoir stored in the front section of the frame tube. On all models the oil pump is located on the right-hand side of the engine next to the clutch. The oil pump delivers oil under pressure throughout the engine and is gear-driven by the crankshaft.

This chapter contains information for removal, inspection, service and reassembly of the engine. Although the clutch and transmission are located within the engine they are covered in Chapter Six to simplify this material. Ignition system and alternator components are covered in Chapter Eight.

Before beginning work, re-read Chapter One of this book. You will do a better job with this information fresh in your mind.

Throughout the text there is frequent mention of the right-hand and left-hand side of the engine. This refers to the engine as it sits in the bike's frame, not as it sits on your workbench. The right- and left-hand refers to a rider sitting on the seat facing forward.

Engine specifications and tightening torques are in **Table 1** and **Table 2** at the end of this chapter.

ENGINE PRINCIPLES

Figure 1 explains how the engine works. This will be helpful when troubleshooting or repairing the engine.

ENGINE COOLING

Cooling is provided by air passing over the cooling fins on the engine cylinder head and cylinder. It is very important to keep these fins free from buildup of dirt, oil, grease and other foreign matter. Brush out the fins with a whisk broom or small stiff paint brush.

> *CAUTION*
> *Remember, these fins are thin in order to dissipate heat and may be damaged if struck too hard.*

SERVICING ENGINE IN FRAME

The engine must be removed from the frame to remove the cylinder head, cylinder and piston.

The following components can be serviced while the engine is mounted in the frame (the bike's frame is a great holding fixture for breaking loose stubborn bolts and nuts):

a. Carburetor assembly.
b. Alternator.
c. Clutch.
d. Oil pump.
e. External shift mechanism.

① **4-STROKE OPERATING PRINCIPLES**

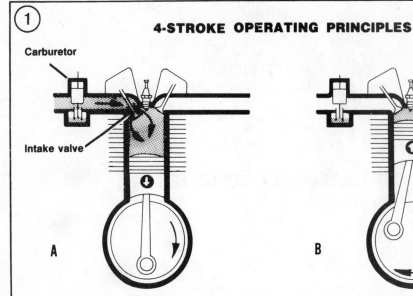

A

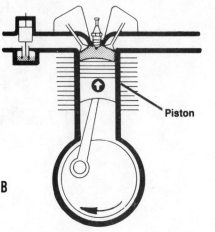

B

As the piston travels downward, the exhaust valve is closed and the intake valve opens, allowing the new air-fuel mixture from the carburetor to be drawn into the cylinder. When the piston reaches the bottom of its travel (BDC), the intake valve closes and remains closed for the next 1 1/2 revolutions of the crankshaft.

While the crankshaft continues to rotate, the piston moves upward, compressing the air-fuel mixture.

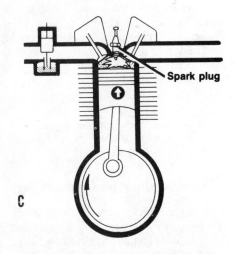

C

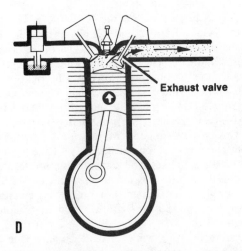

D

As the piston almost reaches the top of its travel, the spark plug fires, igniting the compressed air-fuel mixture. The piston continues to top dead center (TDC) and is pushed downward by the expanding gases.

When the piston almost reaches BDC, the exhaust valve opens and remains open until the piston is near TDC. The upward travel of the piston forces the exhaust gases out of the cylinder. After the piston has reached TDC, the exhaust valve closes and the cycle starts all over again.

ENGINE

Removal/Installation

1. Drain the engine oil as described in Chapter Three.

2. Remove the bolts securing the skid plate (**Figure 2**) and remove the skid plate.

3. Remove both side covers and the seat.

4. Remove the bolts securing the right-hand foot peg and remove the foot peg.

5. Remove the pivot bolt on the rear brake pedal. Move the brake pedal assembly to the rear. It is not necessary to completely remove the assembly.

6. Place wood block(s) under the frame to support the bike securely.

7. Remove the fuel tank as described in Chapter Seven.

8. Disconnect the spark plug lead and tie it up out of the way.

9. Remove the exhaust system as described in Chapter Seven.

10. Remove the carburetor assembly as described in Chapter Seven.

11. Remove the bolts (**Figure 3**) securing the external oil pipe and remove the oil pipe from the engine. Don't lose the sealing washers on each side of the fittings on the oil pipe.

12. Disconnect the manual and automatic decompressor cables (A, **Figure 4**) from the cylinder head cover.

13. On dry-sump models, disconnect the oil tank breather tube (B, **Figure 4**) from the cylinder head cover.

14. Remove the bolt securing the gearshift lever and remove the gear shift lever.

15. Remove the bolts securing the drive sprocket cover and remove the cover.

16. Remove the bolts (A, **Figure 5**) securing the drive sprocket. Remove the bolts.

17. Rotate the drive sprocket holder (B, **Figure 5**) in either direction and slide it off the shaft.

18. Loosen the rear axle nut and move the snail adjusters to loosen the drive chain.

19. Push the rear wheel forward and remove the drive sprocket and drive chain from the output shaft.

20. Remove the alternator as described in Chapter Eight.

21. Remove the clutch assembly as described in Chapter Six.

22. Disconnect the crankcase breather tube from the crankcase.

23. On dry-sump models, perform the following:

   a. Hold onto the fittings either on the metal oil line or the frame and unscrew the flexible oil lines from the frame (**Figure 6**).

b. Remove the bolts securing the oil line assemblies to the engine (**Figure 7**) and remove the oil lines. Don't lose the O-ring seals on the oil lines.

24. Remove the upper engine hanger bolts and nuts (**Figure 8**). Remove the upper hanger plates.

25. Place a suitable size hydraulic jack, with a piece of wood to protect the crankcase, under the engine. Apply a *small amount* of jack pressure up on the engine.

26. Remove the bolts (A, **Figure 9**) securing the front hanger plates to the frame on each side.

27. Remove the front through bolt (B, **Figure 9**) and nut. Remove the hanger plates.

28. Remove the bolts (**Figure 10**) securing the upper rear hanger plate on the right-hand side.

29. Remove the upper rear through bolt and nut (**Figure 11**) from the left-hand side. Remove the hanger plate on the right-hand side.

30. Remove the lower front through bolt (A, **Figure 12**) from the right-hand side. Don't lose the spacer (B, **Figure 12**) on the right-hand side.

CAUTION
The following steps require the aid of a helper to safely remove the engine assembly from the frame.

31. Pull the engine up and slightly forward. Remove the engine from the right-hand side. Take it to a workbench for further disassembly.

32. Install by reversing these removal steps, noting the following.

33. Be sure to install the spacer (B, **Figure 12**) on the right-hand side of the lower front through bolt.

34. Tighten the bolts and nuts to the torque specifications listed in **Table 2**.

35. Be sure to install a sealing washer on each side of the fittings on the oil pipe.

36. Fill the engine with the recommended type and quantity of engine oil; refer to Chapter Three.

37. Refer to Chapter Three and adjust the following:
   a. Clutch.
   b. Decompressor levers.
   c. Throttle grip free play.
   d. Drive chain slack.
   e. Rear brake pedal free play.

38. Start the engine and check for leaks.

CYLINDER HEAD COVER AND CAMSHAFT

The cylinder head cover carries the rocker arm assemblies and the decompressor lever.

The cam is held in place between the cylinder head cover and the cylinder head and is driven by a chain off of the sprocket on the crankshaft.

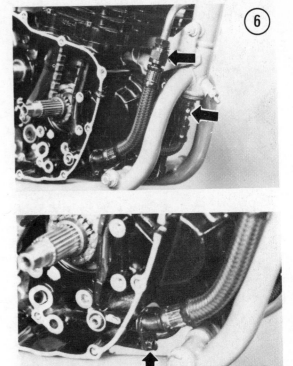

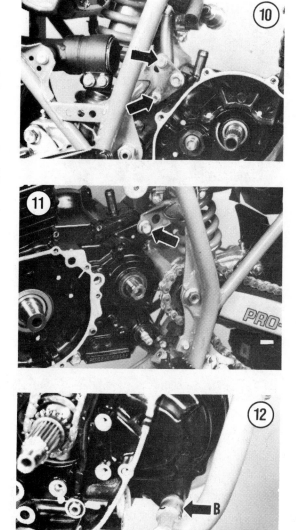

CAUTION
To prevent any warpage and damage, remove the cylinder head cover and cam only when the engine is at room temperature.

1. Remove the engine from the frame as described in this chapter.
2. Remove the spark plug. This will make it easier to rotate the engine by hand.
3. Temporarially install the alternator rotor.
4. Using the alternator rotor, rotate the crankshaft *counterclockwise* until the piston is at top dead center (TDC) on the compression stoke.

NOTE
A cylinder at TDC on its compression stroke will have free play in both of its rocker arms, indicating that both the intake and exhaust valves are closed.

5. Using a crisscross pattern, loosen the bolts (**Figure 13**) securing the cylinder head cover. Remove the bolts. Don't lose the dowel pin.
6. Remove the cylinder head cover and the gasket.
7. To remove the cam chain tensioner, perform the following:
   a. Remove the dowel pin (**Figure 14**) securing the cam chain tensioner.
   b. Screw a 6 mm bolt into the threaded hole (**Figure 15**) in the cam chain tensioner.
   c. Withdraw the cam chain tensioner shaft.

WARNING
In the next step, the cam chain tensioner is under spring tension. As the tensioner is removed from the cylinder head the spring will snap but will not fly out. It is captured on the tensioner. Do not put your fingers down into the cylinder cavity during this procedure as they may get cut by the spring.

   d. Carefully withdraw the cam chain tensioner from the cylinder head.

NOTE
Do not drop the cam sprocket bolts as they may become lodged in the cam chain tensioner slippers. If this happens further engine disassembly is necessary.

8. Using the alternator rotor, rotate the engine until one of the camshaft sprocket bolts is visible. Remove that bolt.

9. Again rotate the engine until the other camshaft sprocket bolt is visible. Remove that bolt.

10. Pull the cam sprocket and cam chain toward the center of the engine and off of the shoulder on the camshaft.

11. Tie a piece of wire to the cam chain and secure the loose end of the wire to the exterior of the engine. This will prevent the cam chain from falling into the crankcase.

12. Remove the cam and cam sprocket from the cylinder head.

CAUTION
If the crankshaft must be rotated when the camshaft is removed, pull up on the cam chain and keep it taut while rotating the crankshaft. Make certain that the chain is positioned onto the crankshaft sprocket. If this is not done, the chain may become kinked and may damage both the chain and the sprocket on the crankshaft.

Camshaft Inspection

1. Check the cam bearings (A, **Figure 16**) for roughness, pitting, galling and play by rotating them by hand. If any roughness or play can be felt in the bearing(s) it must be replaced.

2. Check the cam lobes for wear. The lobes should show no signs of scoring and the edges should be square. Slight damage may be removed with a silicone carbide oilstone. Use No. 100-120 grit stone initially, then polish with a No. 280-320 grit stone.

3. Even though the cam lobe surface appears to be satisfactory, with no visible signs of wear, the cam lobes must be measured with a micrometer or vernier caliper as shown in **Figure 17**.

4. Measure both the intake (B, **Figure 16**) and exhaust (C, **Figure 16**) lobes of the camshaft. Compare to dimensions given in **Table 1**. If any lobes are worn to the service limit the cam must be replaced.

NOTE
Position the cam with the cam sprocket boss on the right-hand side. The cam lobe locations from left to right are as follows; exhaust, intake, exhaust, intake.

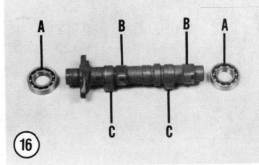

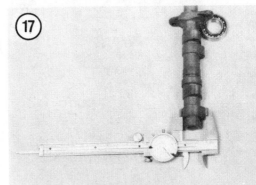

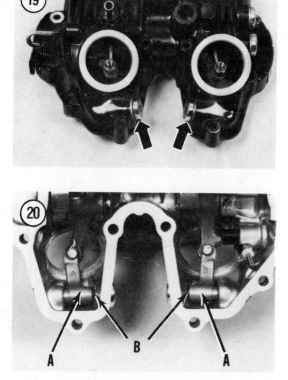

5. Inspect the cam sprocket for wear; replace if necessary.

Cylinder Head Cover
Disassembly/Inspection/Assembly

It is recommended that one rocker arm assembly be disassembled, inspected and then assembled to avoid the intermixing of parts. This is especially true on a well run-in engine as the different sets of parts have taken a set and wear pattern.

1. To remove the decompressor valve lifter lever, perform the following:

a. Remove the dowel pin (**Figure 18**) securing the lever.

b. Remove the lifter lever and return spring from the cylinder head cover.

2. Unscrew the valve adjuster covers.

3. To remove the sub-rocker arm assembly, perform the following:

a. Unscrew the exhaust valve sub-rocker arm shaft (**Figure 19**).

b. Remove the rocker arm shaft, copper sealing washer and wave washer.

c. Remove the sub-rocker arm (A, **Figure 20**).

d. Repeat Steps a-c for the intake valve sub-rocker arm shaft and sub-rocker arm.

4. To remove the main rocker arm assembly, perform the following:

a. Unscrew the main rocker arm shaft (**Figure 21**).

b. Remove the main rocker arm shaft, copper sealing washers and wave washers.

c. Remove the main rocker arms.

5. Wash all parts in cleaning solvent and thoroughly dry.

6. Inspect the sub-rocker arm components as follows:

a. Inspect the sub-rocker arm pad where it rides on the valve stem and main rocker arm adjuster. If the pad is scratched or unevenly worn, inspect the main rocker arm where the sub-rocker arm rides for scoring, chipping or flat spots. Replace the rocker arm if defective.

b. Measure the inside diameter of the rocker arm bore with an inside micrometer and check against dimensions in **Table 1**. Replace if worn to the service limit or greater.

c. Inspect the rocker arm shaft for signs of wear or scoring. Measure the outside diameter with a micrometer and check against dimensions in **Table 1**. Replace if worn to the service limit or less.

7. Inspect the main rocker arm components as follows:

a. Inspect the main rocker arm pad where it rides on the cam lobe and where the adjuster rides on the sub-rocker arm. If the pad is scratched or unevenly worn, inspect the cam lobe for scoring, chipping or flat spots. Replace the rocker arm if defective.

b. Measure the inside diameter of the main rocker arm bore with an inside micrometer and check against dimensions in **Table 1**. Replace if worn to the service limit or greater.

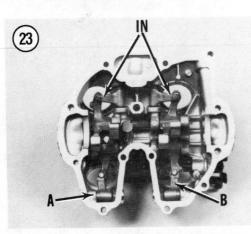

c. Inspect the rocker arm shaft for signs of wear or scoring. Measure the outside diameter with a micrometer and check against dimensions in **Table 1**. Replace if worn to the service limit or less.

8. Coat the rocker arm shaft and rocker arm bores with assembly oil.

9. To install the main rocker arm assemblies, perform the following:

    a. Position the rocker arms as shown in **Figure 22**. Each main rocker arm has its own identifying mark. The exhaust valves are marked "A" (A, **Figure 22**) and intake valves are marked "B" (B, **Figure 22**).

    b. Place a wave washer on the inboard side of each rocker arm (C, **Figure 22**).

    c. Place a copper sealing washer on each rocker arm shaft.

    d. Push the main rocker arm shaft through the cylinder head cover, rocker arm, wave washer, cover boss, wave washer and rocker arm.

    e. Screw in the main rocker arm shaft and tighten to the torque specification listed in **Table 2**.

10. To install the sub-rocker arm assemblies, perform the following:

    a. Position the sub-rocker arms as shown in **Figure 23**. Each sub-rocker arm has its own identifying mark. The exhaust valves are marked "A" (left-hand side) or "B" (right-hand side). The intake valves are marked "IN."

    b. Place a wave washer on the intake valve sub-rocker arm as shown in **Figure 24** and on the exhaust valve sub-rocker arm as shown in B, **Figure 20**.

    c. Place a copper sealing washer on each sub-rocker arm shaft.

    d. On the intake valve sub-rocker arm, push the sub-rocker arm shafts through the cylinder head cover, rocker arm, wave washer and cover boss.

    e. On the exhaust valve sub-rocker arm, push the sub-rocker arm shafts through the cylinder head cover, wave washer, rocker arm and cover boss.

    f. Screw in each sub-rocker arm shaft and tighten to the torque specification listed in **Table 2**.

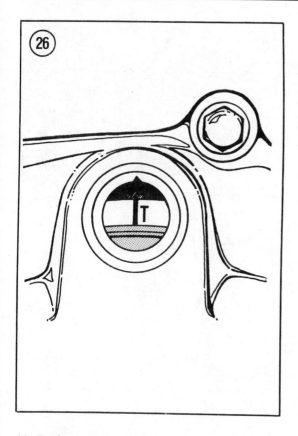

11. Perform Steps 3-10 for each rocker arm or sub-rocker arm assembly.

12. Inspect the cam chain tensioner lifter assembly (A, **Figure 25**) for wear or damage. Replace the O-ring seal (B, **Figure 25**) if it is starting to harden or deteriorate.

13. To install the decompressor lever, perform the following:

   a. Install the spring onto the lifter lever.

   b. Install the lifter lever into the cylinder head cover and position the spring onto the boss.

   c. Align the cutout notch in the lifter lever shaft with the dowel pin hole in the cylinder head cover.

   d. Apply a light coat of grease to the dowel pin. This will hold the dowel pin in place when the cylinder head cover is turned upside down during installation.

   e. Install the dowel pin (**Figure 18**) into the cylinder head cover and past the lifter lever shaft.

Installation

1. Lubricate all cam lobes with molybdenum disulfide grease. Apply clean engine oil to the bearings.

2. If removed, install the bearings onto the camshaft. The sealed bearing goes onto the sprocket boss end of the cam with the sealed side facing out.

> *CAUTION*
> *When rotating the crankshaft, keep the cam chain taut and engaged with the sprocket on the crankshaft.*

3. Temporarily install the alternator cover and remove the timing mark hole cap.

4. Using the alternator rotor, rotate the crankshaft *counterclockwise* until the "T" mark on the alternator rotor aligns with the stationary pointer (**Figure 26**).

5. Install the cam through the cam chain and into position in the cylinder head.

6. Position the cam sprocket with the flush side toward the left-hand side and install the cam sprocket onto the cam.

7. Position the cam sprocket so the alignment marks are aligned with the top surface of the cylinder head.

8. Make sure the cam chain is meshed properly with the drive sprocket on the crankshaft.

9. Pull the cam chain up and onto the cam sprocket.

10. Pull the cam chain and sprocket assembly up onto the shoulder on the cam. Check that the alignment marks are still aligned with the top surface of the cylinder head (**Figure 27**) and that the alternator rotor "T" mark is still aligned (**Figure 26**).

> *CAUTION*
> *Very expensive damage could result from improper cam and chain alignment. Recheck your work several times to be sure alignment is correct.*

11. Install one of the cam sprocket bolts only finger-tight at this time.

12. Rotate the crankshaft until the other bolt hole is visible. Install the other cam sprocket bolt and tighten to the torque specification listed in **Table 2**.

13. Again rotate the crankshaft until the other bolt is visible. Tighten the other cam sprocket bolt to the torque specification listed in **Table 2**.

14. After installation is complete, rotate the crankshaft several complete revolutions using the alternator rotor. Make sure all alignment marks align. If all marks align, the cam timing is correct.

CAUTION
*If there is any binding while rotating the crankshaft, **stop**. Determine the cause before proceeding.*

15. If removed, install the cam chain tensioner spring onto the tensioner as shown in **Figure 28**.

NOTE
A special tool may be used for the following step or you can improvise as described in Step 16B.

16A. If the special tool is used, proceed as follows:
 a. Partially install the tensioner lifter assembly into the cylinder head with the curved surface on the arm facing toward the cam chain.
 b. Insert special tool Honda tensioner setting holder (part No. 07973-MG30000) onto the tensioner as shown in **Figure 29**.
 c. Push the tensioner lifter assembly down until the hole aligns with the hole in the cylinder head.
 d. Apply clean engine oil to the O-ring seal on the tensioner shaft and install the tensioner shaft. Rotate the shaft until the shaft hole aligns with the hole in the cylinder head cover. Install the dowel pin (**Figure 30**) securing the tensioner shaft.
 e. Remove the special tool.

16B. If the special tool is not used, proceed as follows:
 a. Wrap a piece of wire around the tensioner lifter assembly and the spring and compress the spring (**Figure 31**).
 b. Partially install the tensioner lifter assembly into the cylinder head with the curved surface on the arm facing toward the cam chain.
 c. Push the tensioner lifter assembly down until the hole aligns with the hole in the cylinder head. You may have to use a long narrow-bladed screwdriver to help push the spring down into position onto the flat surface within the cylinder head.

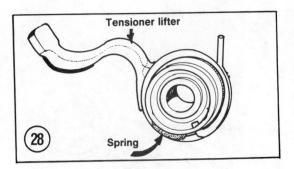

Tensioner lifter

Spring

(28)

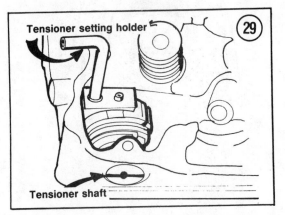

Tensioner setting holder

(29)

Tensioner shaft

(30)

(31)

d. Apply clean engine oil to the O-ring seal on the tensioner shaft and install the tensioner shaft. Use a wide-bladed screwdriver and rotate the shaft until the shaft hole aligns with the hole in the cylinder head cover. Install the dowel pin (**Figure 30**) and push it down all the way.

e. Cut the wire and pull it out. Make sure that all pieces of the wire are removed from the engine.

17. Fill the oil pocket with fresh engine oil so the cam lobes will be covered for the initial engine start up.

18. Make sure the locating dowel is in place in the cylinder head.

19. Loosen all valve adjusters fully. This is to relieve strain on the rocker arms and cylinder head cover during installation.

CAUTION
Do not destroy the silicone surface on the cylinder head cover gasket.

20. Wrap a small rubber band (**Figure 32**) around each sub-rocker arm and then attach it to the exterior of the engine. This will hold the main and sub-rocker arms up during cylinder head cover installation.

21. Install a new cylinder head cover gasket.

22. Clean the cylinder head cover mating surface.

23. Preload the decompressor lever and install the cylinder head cover.

24. Remove the small rubber bands.

25. Install the 6 mm and 8 mm bolts and tighten in a crisscross pattern in 2-3 steps to the torque specifications in **Table 2**.

26. Remove the alternator cover and rotor.

27. Adjust the valves as described in Chapter Three.

CYLINDER HEAD

Removal/Installation

CAUTION
To prevent any warpage and damage, remove the cylinder head only when the engine is at room temperature.

1. Remove the engine as described in this chapter.

2. Remove the cylinder head cover and camshaft as described in this chapter.

3. Remove the cylinder head bolt hole plug (**Figure 33**) and O-ring.

4. On 500 and 600 cc models, remove the nuts (**Figure 34**) on the right-hand side.

5. Loosen the cylinder head bolts (**Figure 35**) in a crisscross pattern in 2-3 steps.

6. Remove the cylinder head bolts and washers.

7. Loosen the head by tapping around the perimeter with a rubber or plastic mallet. If necessary, *gently* pry the head loose with a broad-tipped screwdriver.

CAUTION
Remember, the cooling fins are fragile and may be damaged if tapped or pried on too hard. Never use a metal hammer.

8. Untie the wire securing the cam chain and retie it to the cylinder head.

9. Remove the cylinder head by pulling it straight up and off the cylinder. Pull the cam chain and wire through the opening in the cylinder head and retie the cam chain to the engine.

10. Remove the cylinder head gasket and discard it.

NOTE
Don't lose the locating dowels.

11. Place a clean shop cloth into the cam chain opening in the cylinder block to prevent the entry of foreign matter.

NOTE
In the following step, removal of the sub-chamber cover is necessary so that any solvent and grinding residue can be removed from the chamber. Nothing mechanical is contained within the chamber.

12. On 500 and 600 cc models, if the valve seats are going to be ground perform the following:
   a. Remove the bolts securing the sub-chamber cover on the left-hand side.
   b. Remove the cover and gasket.

13. Install by reversing these removal steps; note the following.

14. Clean the mating surfaces of the head and cylinder of any gasket material.

15. Install locating dowels in the cylinder head.

16. Install a new head gasket.

17. Install the cylinder head and secure it with the bolts, washers and side nuts (on 500 and 600 cc models). Tighten the bolts to the torque specification listed in **Table 2**.

18. Make sure the O-ring seal is in good condition and is installed on the cylinder head bolt hole plug (**Figure 33**).

Inspection

1. Remove all traces of gasket material from the cylinder head mating surfaces.

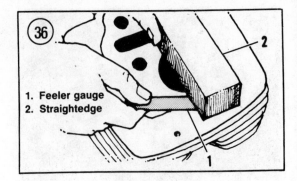

1. Feeler gauge
2. Straightedge

2. *Without removing the valves*, remove all carbon deposits from the combustion chambers and valve ports with a wire brush. A blunt screwdriver or chisel may be used if care is taken not to damage the head, valves and spark plug threads.

3. After the carbon is removed from the combustion chambers and the valve intake and exhaust ports, clean the entire head in cleaning solvent. Blow dry with compressed air.

4. Clean away all carbon from the the piston crown. Do not remove the carbon ridge at the top of the cylinder bore.

5. Check for cracks in the combustion chamber and exhaust ports. A cracked head must be replaced.

6. After the head has been thoroughly cleaned, place a straightedge across the cylinder head/cylinder gasket surface (**Figure 36**) at several points. Measure the warp by inserting a flat feeler gauge between the straightedge and the cylinder head at each location. There should be no warpage; if a small amount is present, it can be resurfaced by a dealer or qualified machine shop.

7. Check the cylinder head cover mating surface using the procedure in Step 6. There should be no warpage.

8. Check the valves and valve guides as described in this chapter.

9. On 500 and 600 cc models, inspect the reed valve as follows:
   a. Inspect the reed valve (A, **Figure 37**) for wear, burning or distortion.
   b. If necessary, remove the screw (B, **Figure 37**) securing the reed valve and reed stopper.
   c. Do not bend or distort the the reed stopper.
   d. Install a new reed valve and stopper. Tighten the screw securely.

VALVE AND VALVE COMPONENTS

Removal

Refer to **Figure 38** for this procedure.

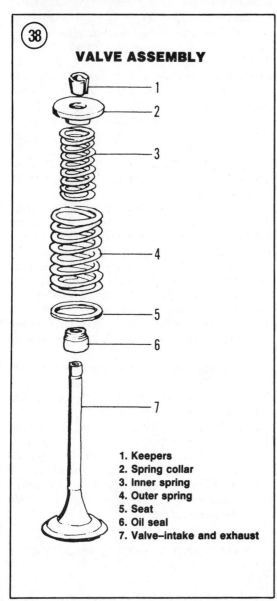

VALVE ASSEMBLY

1. Keepers
2. Spring collar
3. Inner spring
4. Outer spring
5. Seat
6. Oil seal
7. Valve–intake and exhaust

5

1. Remove the cylinder head as described in this chapter.

2. Compress the valve springs with a valve compressor tool (**Figure 39**). Remove the valve keepers and release the compression. Remove the valve compressor tool.

CAUTION
To avoid loss of spring tension, do not compress the springs any more than necessary to remove the keepers.

3. Remove the valve spring retainer and valve springs (**Figure 40**).

4. The spring seat (**Figure 41**) and the valve stem seal (**Figure 42**) may stay in the cylinder head.

5. Prior to removing the valve, remove any burrs from the valve stem (**Figure 43**). Otherwise the valve guide will be damaged.

6. On 600 cc models, perform the following to remove the decompression valve located at the rear of the cylinder head between the 2 intake valves:

    a. Hold onto the valve face with your hand and compress the valve spring with the fingers on your other hand.

    b. Slide the valve retainer from the groove in the valve.

    c. Remove the valve spring.

    d. Prior to removing the valve, remove any burrs from the valve stem (**Figure 43**). Otherwise the valve guide will be damaged.

7. Mark all parts as they are disassembled so that they will be installed in their same location.

Inspection

1. Clean valves with a wire brush and solvent.

2. Inspect the contact surface of each valve for burning (**Figure 44**). Excessive unevenness of the contact surface is an indication that the valve is not serviceable. The valve contact surface *cannot be ground* so replace a burned or damaged valve with a new valve.

3. Measure the valve stem for wear (**Figure 45**). Compare with specifications given in **Table 1**.

4. Remove all carbon and varnish from the valve guide with a stiff spiral wire brush.

5. Insert each valve in its guide. Hold the valve with the head just slightly off the valve seat and rock it sideways. If it rocks more than slightly, the guide is probably worn and should be replaced. As a final check, take the cylinder to a dealer and have the valve guides measured.

6. Measure the valve spring free length with a vernier caliper (**Figure 46**). All should be within the specifications in **Table 1** with no signs of bends or distortion. Replace defective springs in pairs (inner and outer).

7. Check the valve spring retainer and valve keepers. If they are in good condition they may be reused; replace as necessary.

8. Inspect the valve seats. If worn or burned, they must be reconditioned. This should be performed by a dealer or qualified machine shop.

Installation

1. Coat the valve stems with molybdenum disulfide grease. To avoid damage to the valve stem seal, turn the valve slowly while inserting the valve into the cylinder head.

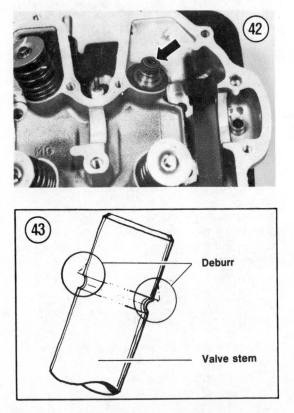

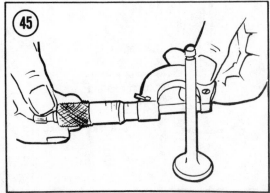

2. On all valves (except the 600 cc's decompression valve), install the valve springs with the narrow pitch end (coils closest together) facing the head.

3. Install the valve spring retainer.

4. Compress the valve springs with a compressor tool (**Figure 39**) and install the valve keepers.

CAUTION
To avoid loss of spring tension, do not compress the springs any more than necessary to install the keepers.

5. After all springs have been installed, gently tap the end of the valve stems with a soft aluminum or brass drift and hammer. This will ensure that the keepers are properly seated.

6. On 600 cc models, perform the following for the decompression valve:

  a. Install the valve into the cylinder head.

  b. Hold onto the valve face with one hand and compress the valve spring with the fingers on your other hand.

  c. Slide the valve retainer into the groove in the valve. Make sure the valve retainer is seated correctly in the groove.

Valve Guide Replacement

When valve guides are worn so that there is excessive stem-to-guide clearance or valve tipping, the guides must be replaced. Replace all, even if only one is worn. This job should ony be done by a dealer as special tools are required.

Valve Seat Reconditioning

This job is best left to a dealer or qualified machine shop. They have special equipment and knowledge for this exacting job. You can still save considerable money by removing the cylinder head and taking the head to the shop for repairs.

CYLINDER

Removal

1. Remove the cylinder head cover and cylinder head as described in this chapter.

2. Loosen the cylinder bolts (**Figure 47**) in a crisscross pattern in 2-3 stages.

3. Remove the cylinder bolts and washers.

4. Loosen the cylinder by tapping around the perimeter with a rubber or plastic mallet. If necessary, *gently* pry the cylinder block loose with a broad-tipped screwdriver.

5. Pull the cylinder straight up and off of the crankcase. Work the cam chain wire through the opening in the cylinder and retie the wire to the crankcase so the chain will not fall into the crankcase.

6. Remove the cylinder base gasket and discard it. Remove the dowel pins from the crankcase.

7. Install a piston holding fixture under the piston to protect the piston skirt from damage. This fixture may be purchased or may be a homemade unit of wood. See **Figure 48**.

5

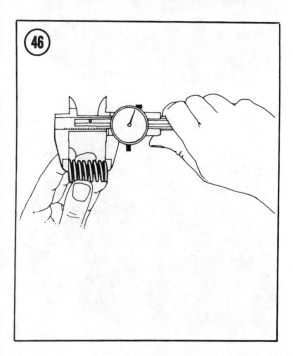

NOTE
If the following 2 items are to be removed, remove the clutch as described in Chapter Six and the oil pump as described in this chapter.

8. Remove the cam chain guide (**Figure 49**).
9. Remove the bolt (**Figure 50**) securing the cam chain tensioner slipper. Remove the slipper, bushing and washer.

Inspection

The following procedure requires the use of highly specialized and expensive measuring instruments. If such equipment is not readily available, have the measurements performed by a dealer or qualified machine shop.
1. Soak with solvent any old cylinder head gasket material on the cylinder. Use a broad-tipped *dull* chisel and gently scrape off all gasket residue. Do not gouge the sealing surface as oil and air leaks will result.
2. Measure the cylinder bore with a cylinder gauge or inside micrometer at the points shown in **Figure 51**. Measure in 2 axes—in line with the piston pin and at 90° to the pin. If the taper or out-of-round is 0.004 in. (0.10 mm) or greater, the cylinder must be rebored to the next oversize and a new piston installed.

NOTE
The new piston should be obtained before the cylinder is rebored so that the piston can be measured; slight manufacturing tolerances must be taken into account to determine the actual size and working clearance.

3. Check the cylinder wall for scratches; if evident, the cylinder should be rebored.

NOTE
The maximum wear limit on the cylinder is listed in Table 1. If the cylinder is worn to this limit, it must be replaced. Never rebore a cylinder if the finished rebore diameter will be this dimension or greater.

Installation

1. Check that the top surface of the crankcase and the bottom surface of the cylinder are clean prior to installing a new base gasket.
2. Install a new cylinder base gasket.

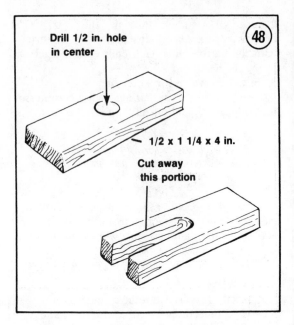

Drill 1/2 in. hole in center

1/2 x 1 1/4 x 4 in.

Cut away this portion

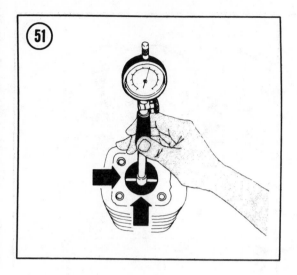

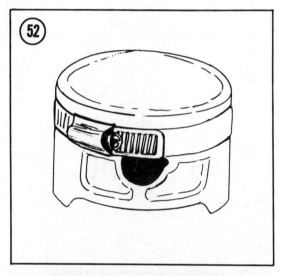

3. Install the dowel pins into the receptacles in the crankcase.

4. Install a piston holding fixture under the piston.

5. Make sure the end gaps of the piston rings are *not* lined up with each other—they must be staggered. Lightly oil the piston rings and the inside of the cylinder bore with assembly oil.

6. Untie the cam chain wire and tie it to the cylinder.

7. Carefully feed the cam chain and wire up through the opening in the cylinder and tie it to the engine.

8. Install the cylinder and start it down over the piston. Compress each piston ring as it enters the cylinder either with your fingers or by using aircraft type hose clamps (**Figure 52**) of the appropriate size.

9. Slide the cylinder down until it bottoms on the piston holding fixture.

10. Remove the piston holding fixture and slide the cylinder down into place on the crankcase.

11. Install the cylinder bolts and washers. Tighten in a crisscross pattern in 2-3 steps to the torque specification listed in **Table 2**.

12. If removed, install the cam chain guide (**Figure 49**). Make sure it seats correctly in the notch in the right-hand crankcase (**Figure 53**).

13. If removed, install the cam chain tensioner slipper, bushing and bolt. Tighten the bolt securely (**Figure 50**).

14. Install the cylinder head and cylinder head cover as described in this chapter.

15. Install the oil pump as described in this chapter and the clutch as described in Chapter Six if these items were removed.

16. Adjust the valves and ignition timing as described in Chapter Three.

PISTON, PISTON PIN AND PISTON RINGS

The piston is made of an aluminum alloy. The piston pin is made of steel and is a precision fit. It is held in place by a clip at each end.

Piston Removal

1. Remove the cylinder head cover, cylinder head and the cylinder as described in this chapter.

> *WARNING*
> *The edges of all piston rings are very sharp. Be careful when handling them to avoid cutting fingers.*

2. Remove the top ring with a ring expander tool or by spreading the ends with your thumbs just

5

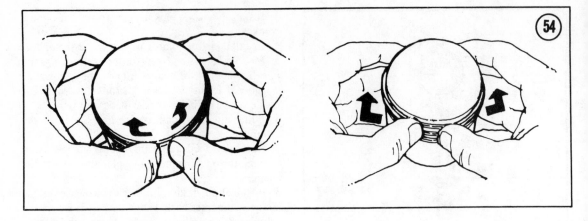

enough to slide the ring up over the piston (**Figure 54**). Repeat for the remaining rings.

3. Before removing the piston, hold the rod tightly and rock the piston as shown in **Figure 55**. Any rocking motion (do not confuse with the normal sliding motion) indicates wear on the piston pin, rod bearing or piston pin bore (more likely a combination of these).

> *NOTE*
> *Wrap a clean shop cloth under the piston so that the piston pin clip will not fall into the crankcase.*

4. Remove the clips from each side of the piston pin bore (**Figure 56**) with a small screwdriver or scribe. Hold your thumb over one edge of the clip when removing it to prevent it from springing out.

5. Use a proper size wooden dowel or socket extension and push out the piston pin.

> *CAUTION*
> *Be careful when removing the pin to avoid damaging the connecting rod. If it is necessary to gently tap the pin to remove it, be sure that the piston is properly supported so that lateral shock is not transmitted to the lower connecting rod bearing.*

6. If the piston pin is difficult to remove, heat the piston and pin with a butane torch. The pin will probably push right out. Heat the piston to only about 140° F (60° C), i.e., until it is too warm to touch, but not excessively hot. If the pin is still difficult to push out, use a homemade tool as shown in **Figure 57**.

> *NOTE*
> *A universal piston pin extractor is available from British Marketing, P.O. Box 219, San Juan Capistrano, CA 92693.*

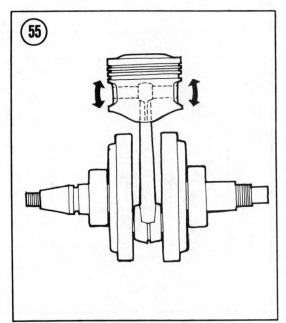

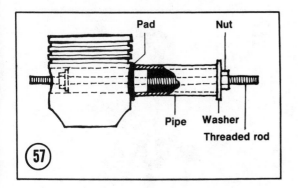

Pad   Nut
Pipe   Washer   Threaded rod

57

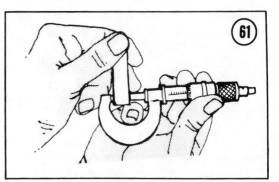

61

58

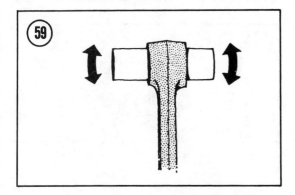

59

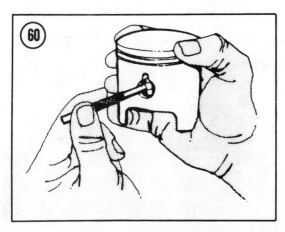

60

7. Lift the piston off the connecting rod.

8. If the piston is going to be left off for some time, place a piece of foam insulation tube over the end of the rod to protect it.

Inspection

1. Carefully clean the carbon from the piston crown with a chemical remover or with a soft scraper (**Figure 58**). Do not remove or damage the carbon ridge around the circumference of the piston above the top ring. If the piston, rings and cylinder are found to be dimensionally correct and can be reused, removal of the carbon ring from the top of the piston or the carbon ridge from the top of the cylinder will cause excessive oil consumption.

CAUTION
Do not wire brush the piston skirt.

2. Examine each ring groove for burrs, dented edges and wide wear. Pay particular attention to the top compression ring groove as it usually wears more than the others.

3. Measure piston-to-cylinder clearance as described under *Piston Clearance* in this chapter.

4. If damage or wear indicates piston replacement, select a new piston as described under *Piston Clearance* in this chapter.

5. Oil the piston pin and install it in the connecting rod. Slowly rotate the piston pin and check for radial and axial play (**Figure 59**). If any play exists, the piston pin should be replaced, providing the rod bore is in good condition. Measure the inside diameter of the piston pin bore with a snap gauge (**Figure 60**) and measure the outside diameter of the piston pin with a micrometer (**Figure 61**). Compare with dimensions, given in **Table 1**. Replace the piston and piston pin as a set if either or both are worn.

6. Check the piston skirt for galling and abrasion which may have been caused by piston seizure. If light galling is present, smooth the affected area

5

with No. 400 emery paper and oil or a fine oilstone. However, if galling is severe or if the piston is deeply scored, replace it.

Piston Clearance

1. Make sure the piston and cylinder walls are clean and dry.
2. Measure the inside diameter of the cylinder bore at a point 1/2 in. (13 mm) from the upper edge with a bore gauge (**Figure 62**).
3. Measure the outside diameter of the piston across the skirt at right angles to the piston pin. Measure at a distance 0.40 in. (10 mm) up from the bottom of the piston skirt (**Figure 63**).
4. Piston clearance is the difference between the maximum piston diameter and the minimum cylinder diameter. Subtract the dimension of the piston from the cylinder dimension. If the clearance exceeds 0.004 in. (0.10 mm) the cylinder should be rebored to the next oversize and a new piston installed.
5. To establish a final overbore dimension with a new piston, add the piston skirt measurement to the specified clearance. This will determine the dimension for the cylinder overbore size. Remember, do not exceed the cylinder maximum service limit listed in **Table 1**.

Piston Installation

1. Apply molybdenum disulfide grease to the inside surface of the connecting rod.
2. Oil the piston pin with assembly oil and install it in the piston until its end extends slightly beyond the inside of the boss (**Figure 64**).
3. Place the piston over the connecting rod with the "IN" on the piston crown directed rearward toward the intake port (**Figure 65**).
4. Line up the piston pin with the hole in the connecting rod. Push the piston pin through the connecting rod and into the other side of the piston until it is even with the piston pin clip grooves.

> *CAUTION*
> *If it is necessary to tap the piston pin into the connecting rod, do so gently with a block of wood or a soft-faced hammer. Make sure you support the piston to prevent the lateral shock from being transmitted to the lower connecting rod bearing.*

> *NOTE*
> *In the next step, install the clips with the gap away from the cutout in the piston (**Figure 66**).*

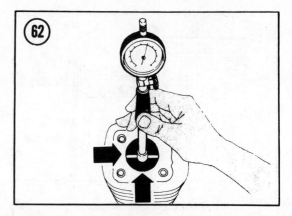

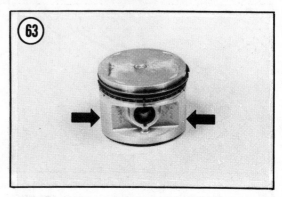

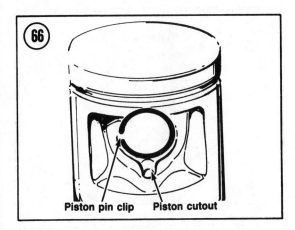

Piston pin clip   Piston cutout

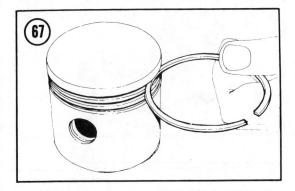

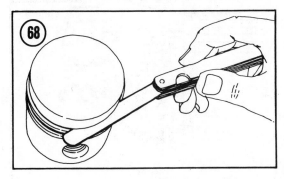

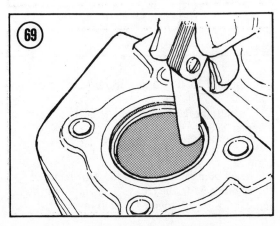

5. Install new piston pin clips in both ends of the pin boss. Make sure they are seated in the grooves.

6. Check the installation by rocking the piston back and forth around the pin axis and from side to side along the axis. It should rotate freely back and forth but not from side to side.

7. Install the piston rings as described in this chapter.

8. Install the cylinder, cylinder head and cylinder head cover as described in this chapter.

Piston Ring
Removal/Installation

> *WARNING*
> *The edges of all piston rings are very*
> *sharp. Be careful when handling them*
> *to avoid cut fingers.*

1. Remove the top ring by spreading the ends with your thumbs just enough to slide the ring up over the piston (**Figure 54**). Repeat for the remaining rings.

2. Carefully remove all carbon buildup from the ring grooves with a broken piston ring. Inspect the grooves carefully for burrs, nicks or broken and cracked lands. Recondition or replace the piston if necessary.

3. Roll each ring around its piston groove as shown in **Figure 67** to check for binding. Minor binding may be cleaned up with a fine-cut file.

4. Measure the side clearance of each ring in its groove with a flat feeler gauge (**Figure 68**) and compare to dimensions given in **Table 1**. If the clearance is greater than specified, the rings must be replaced. If the clearance is still excessive with the new rings, the piston must also be replaced.

5. Measure each ring for wear. Place each ring, one at a time, into the cylinder and push it in about 3/4 in. (20 mm) with the crown of the piston to ensure that the ring is square in the cylinder bore. Measure the gap with a flat feeler gauge (**Figure 69**) and compare to dimensions in **Table 1**. If the gap is greater than specified, the rings should be replaced. When installing new rings, measure their end gap in the same manner as for old ones. If the gap is less than specified, carefully file the ends with a fine-cut file (**Figure 70**) until the gap is correct.

6. Install the piston rings with their marks facing *up* in the order shown in **Figure 71**.

7. Install the piston rings—first the bottom one, then the middle one, then the top—by carefully spreading the ends of the ring with your thumbs and slipping the ring over the top of the piston. Remember that the marks on the piston rings are up toward the top of the piston.

5

8. Make sure the rings are seated completely in their grooves all the way around the piston and that the ends are distributed around the piston as shown in **Figure 72**. The important thing is that the ring gaps are not aligned with each other when installed.

9. If new rings were installed, measure the side clearance of each ring in its groove with a flat feeler gauge (**Figure 68**) and compare to dimensions given in **Table 1**.

PRIMARY DRIVE GEAR

Removal/Installation

> *NOTE*
> *Prior to removing the clutch assembly, place a copper washer between the clutch outer housing gear and the primary drive gear. Loosen the drive gear nut.*

1. Remove the clutch as described in Chapter Six.
2. Remove the oil pump drive gear (**Figure 73**).
3. Remove the primary drive gear locknut (**Figure 74**) and lockwasher.
4. Remove the oil pump drive gear and pulse generator rotor.
5. On 500 and 600 cc models, remove the bolts (**Figure 75**) securing the ignition pulse generator. Move the pulse generator assembly out of the way.
6. Remove the primary drive gear.

> *NOTE*
> *The primary drive gear, pulse generator rotor and oil pump drive gear can be installed onto the crankshaft in only one position. During installation match up the wide spline groove on the gears and rotor with the 2 matching splines on the crankshaft.*

7. Inspect the primary drive gear, oil pump drive gear and the pulse generator rotor for wear or damage. Replace any worn or damaged part.
8. Align the splines of the primary drive gear and slide it onto the crankshaft (**Figure 76**).
9. On 500R and 600 cc models, install the pulse generator assembly and tighten the bolts securely.
10. Align the splines of the pulse generator rotor and slide it onto the crankshaft (**Figure 77**).
11. Install the oil pump drive gear (**Figure 73**).
12. Install the lockwasher with the "OUTSIDE" mark (**Figure 78**) facing out toward the outside.
13. Install the locknut (**Figure 74**) and tighten only finger tight at this time.
14. Prior to installing the clutch cover, place a copper washer between the clutch outer housing gear and the drive gear. Tighten the primary drive

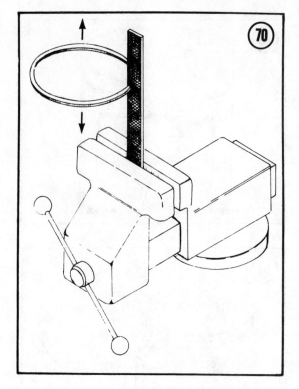

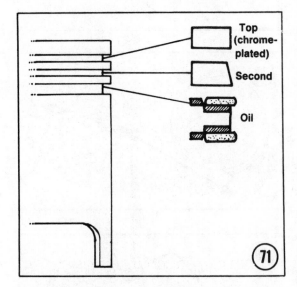

gear locknut to the torque specification listed in **Table 2**.
15. Install the clutch assembly as described in Chapter Six.

OIL PUMP

The oil pump is located on the right-hand side of the engine next to the clutch. The oil pump can be removed with the engine in the frame.

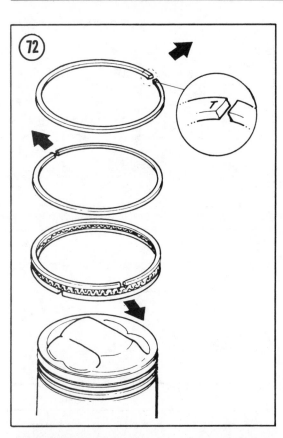

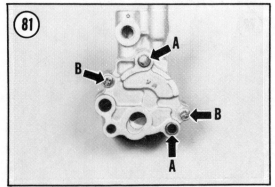

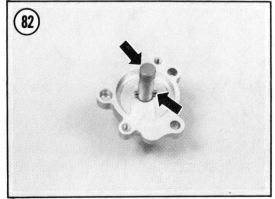

A 2-stage pump is used on dry-sump models to pull the oil from the reservoir in the frame tubes, through the oil pump and into the engine. This procedure is shown with a 2-stage oil pump.

Removal/Installation

1. Remove the clutch as described in Chapter Six.
2. Remove the oil pump drive gear (**Figure 73**).
3. Remove the bolts (A, **Figure 79**) securing the oil pipe and remove the oil pipe.
4. Remove the bolts (B, **Figure 79**) securing the oil pump to the crankcase and remove the oil pump assembly.
5A. On 350 cc models, make sure the large O-ring seal is installed in the inlet on the crankcase.
5B. On 500 and 600 cc models, make sure the oil control orifice and O-ring (**Figure 80**) are installed in the inlet on the crankcase.
6. Install the locating dowels either in the oil pump (A, **Figure 81**) or in the crankcase.
7. Install the oil pump assembly and tighten the screws securely.
8. Make sure the O-ring seals are in place on each end of the oil pipe.
9. Install the oil pipe and bolts. Tighten the bolts securely.

Disassembly/Inspection/Assembly (2-stage Pump)

1. Remove the Phillips head screws (B, **Figure 81**) securing the pump cover to the body and remove the cover.
2. Remove the outer rotor "A" and inner rotor "A."
3. Turn the assembly over and remove the base, outer rotor "B," inner rotor "B" and the pump shaft from the body.
4. Inspect the inner and outer rotors for scratches and abrasions. Replace both parts if evidence of this is found.
5. Clean all parts in solvent and thoroughly dry. Coat all parts with fresh engine oil prior to assembly.
6. Inspect the teeth on the driven gear. Replace the driven gear if the teeth are damaged or any are missing.
7. Into the pump base, install the pump shaft and dowel pin (**Figure 82**).
8. Install the inner rotor "B" (**Figure 83**) and the outer rotor "B" (**Figure 84**).
9. Measure the clearance between the inner rotor tip and the outer rotor with a flat feeler gauge. If

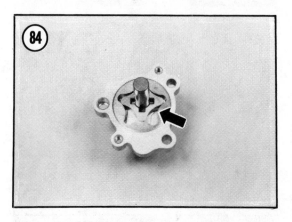

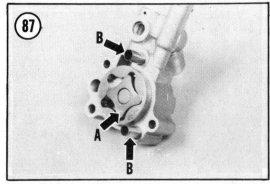

5

the clearance is 0.008 in. (0.20 mm) or greater, replace the worn part.

14. Measure the clearance between the outer rotor and the oil pump body with a flat feeler gauge. If the clearance is 0.010 in. (0.25 mm) or greater, replace the worn part.

15. Measure the clearance between both rotors and the oil pump base with a flat feeler gauge. If the clearance is 0.005 in. (0.12 mm) or greater, replace the worn part.

16. Remove both rotors from the cover.

17. Install the body onto the base assembly (**Figure 85**).

18. Install the washer onto the pump shaft.

19. Install the dowel pin into the pump shaft (**Figure 86**).

20. Install the inner and outer rotors (A, **Figure 87**) and the locating dowels (B, **Figure 87**).

21. Install the cover and turn the assembly over.

22. Install the screws (B, **Figure 81**) and tighten securely.

Disassembly/Inspection/Assembly (Single-stage Pump)

1. Remove the Phillips head screws securing the pump cover to the body and remove the cover.

the clearance is 0.008 in. (0.20 mm) or greater, replace the worn part.

10. Measure the clearance between the outer rotor and the oil pump body with a flat feeler gauge. If the clearance is 0.010 in. (0.25 mm) or greater, replace the worn part.

11. Measure the clearance between both rotors and the oil pump base with a flat feeler gauge. If the clearance is 0.005 in. (0.12 mm) or greater, replace the worn part.

12. Into the oil pump cover, install the inner rotor "A" and the outer rotor "A."

13. Measure the clearance between the inner rotor tip and the outer rotor with a flat feeler gauge. If

2. Remove the outer and inner rotors.

3. Inspect the inner and outer rotors for scratches and abrasions. Replace both parts if evidence of this is found.

4. Clean all parts in solvent and thoroughly dry. Coat all parts with fresh engine oil prior to assembly.

5. Inspect the teeth on the driven gear. Replace the driven gear if the teeth are damaged or any are missing.

6. Into the pump body, install the inner rotor and the outer rotor.

7. Measure the clearance between the inner rotor tip and the outer rotor with a flat feeler gauge. If the clearance is 0.010 in. (0.25 mm) or greater, replace the worn part.

8. Measure the clearance between the outer rotor and the oil pump body with a flat feeler gauge. If the clearance is 0.008 in. (0.20 mm) or greater, replace the worn part.

9. Measure the end clearance between both rotors and the oil pump body with a flat feeler gauge. If the clearance is 0.005 in. (0.12 mm) or greater, replace the worn part.

10. Install the driven gear shaft assembly into the oil pump cover.

11. Make sure the small locating dowel is in place.

12. Align the flat on the driven gear shaft with the flat in the inner rotor and install the oil pump cover assembly onto the body assembly.

13. Push the 2 assemblies together and install the Phillips screws. Tighten the screws securely.

13. Remove the driven gear shaft from the assembled oil pump.

OIL LINES
(DRY-SUMP MODELS)

With a dry sump engine, the engine oil is stored in the bike's frame. Engine oil is transferred from the the bike's frame to the engine via flexible and metal oil lines.

Removal/Inspection/Installation

1. Drain the engine oil as described in Chapter Three.

2. Hold onto the fitting, either on the frame or the metal oil line, with a wrench and unscrew the flexible oil lines from these fittings (**Figure 88**).

3. Remove the bolts (**Figure 89**) securing the plate that secures the oil lines to the crankcase.

4. Remove the plate and the oil lines.

5. Inspect the oil lines for damage or leakage. If damaged, replace both lines.

6. Inspect the O-ring seals on the engine end of the lines. If damaged or starting to deteriorate, replace the O-ring on each oil line.

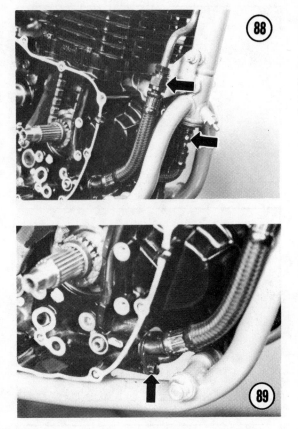

7. To remove the metal oil line, perform the following:

    a. Remove the clamping band on the frame.

    b. Disconnect the fitting on the metal oil line from the bike's frame tube.

8. Install by reversing these removal steps, noting the following.

9. Make sure the O-ring seals (**Figure 90**) are installed on the flexible oil lines where they enter the engine.

10. When installing the flexible oil lines, hold onto the fitting (either on the frame or the metal oil line) with a wrench and screw the flexible oil lines to these fittings. Let the flexible oil lines flow in a natural curve; make sure they are not kinked. Tighten the fittings securely.

CAMSHAFT CHAIN

Removal/Installation

1. Remove the cylinder head cover and camshaft as described in this chapter.

2. Remove the clutch assembly as described in Chapter Six.

3. Remove the primary drive gear and oil pump as described in this chapter.

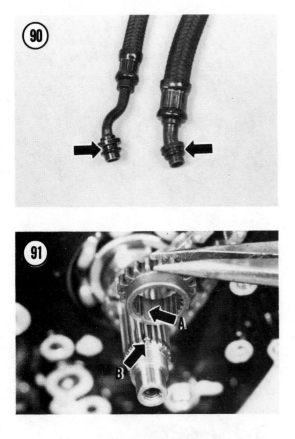

NOTE
In the following steps the cylinder head and cylinder have been removed for clarity. It is not necessary to remove them for this procedure.

4. Let the cam chain drop down through the passageway in the cylinder head and cylinder and into the right-hand crankcase.

5. Remove the cam chain from the cam chain drive sprocket on the crankshaft.

6. Remove the cam chain drive sprocket from the crankshaft.

7. Inspect the cam drive chain for wear and damage. If the chain needs replacing, also check the drive sprocket and cam sprocket. They may require replacement also.

8. Install by reversing these removal steps, noting the following.

9. The cam chain drive gear can be installed onto the crankshaft in only one position. Align the wide spline groove on the cam drive gear (A, **Figure 91**) with the 2 matching splines on the crankshaft (B, **Figure 91**) and slide it onto the crankshaft.

10. Attach a piece of wire to the cam chain and pull the cam chain up through the passageway in the cylinder head and cylinder.

CRANKCASE AND CRANKSHAFT

Disassembly of the crankcase (splitting the cases) and removal of the crankshaft assembly require that the engine be removed from the frame.

The crankcase is made in 2 halves of precision diecast aluminum alloy and is of the "thin-walled" type. To avoid damage do not hammer or pry on any of the interior or exterior projected walls. These areas are easily damaged. They are assembled with a gasket between the 2 halves and dowel pins align the crankcase halves when they are bolted together.

The crankshaft assembly is made up of 2 full-circle flywheels pressed together on a hollow crankpin. The connecting rod big end bearing on the crankpin is a needle bearing assembly. The crankshaft assembly is supported in 2 ball bearing in the crankcase. Service to the crankshaft is limited to removal and replacement.

The procedure which follows is presented as a complete, step-by-step, major lower end rebuild that should be followed if an engine is to be completely reconditioned. However, if you're replacing a part that you know is defective, the disassembly should be carried out only until the failed part is accessible; there is no need to disassemble the engine beyond that point so long as you know the remaining components are in good condition and that they were not affected by the failed part.

5

Disassembly

This procedure is shown on a XR500R. Crankcase bolt locations are different among the various models. Make sure that you have removed all bolts prior to trying to separate the crankcase halves.

1. Remove all exterior engine assemblies as described in this chapter and other related chapters:
   a. Cylinder head cover and camshaft.
   b. Cylinder head.
   c. Cylinder and piston.
   d. Cam chain and cam chain tensioner.
   e. Clutch assembly.
   f. Alternator assembly.
   g. External shift mechanism.
   h. Primary drive gear.
   i. Drive sprocket.
   j. Oil lines (dry-sump models).

2. On the left-hand crankcase side, remove the bolts securing the crankcase halves together (**Figure 92**). To prevent warpage, loosen them in a crisscross pattern.

NOTE
*Set the engine on wood blocks or fabricate a holding fixture of 2 X 4 inch wood as shown in **Figure 93**.*

3. On the right-hand crankcase side, remove the bolts securing the crankcase halves together (**Figure 94**).

CAUTION
*Perform the next step directly over and close to the workbench as the crankcase halves may easily separate. **Do not** hammer on the crankcase halves or they will be damaged.*

4. Set the crankcase down on the left-hand side. Hold onto the right-hand crankcase and tap on the right-hand end of the crankshaft and transmission shafts with a plastic or rubber mallet until the crankshaft and crankcase separate.

5. If the crankcase and crankshaft will not separate using this method, check to make sure that all screws are removed. If you still have a problem, take the crankcase assembly to a dealer and have it separated.

NOTE
Never pry between case halves. Doing so may result in oil leaks, requiring replacement of the case halves.

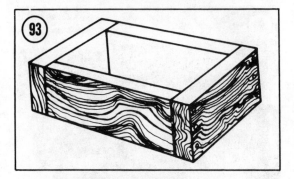

6. Remove the gasket and locating dowels. The locating dowels do not have to be removed from the case if they are secure.

7A. On 350 cc models, rotate the crankshaft until the balancer does not interfere with the counterbalance weights on the crankshaft. Remove the balancer weight assembly.

7B. On 500 and 600 cc models, remove the balancer weight assembly.

8. Lift up and carefully remove the transmission, shift drum and shift fork shaft assemblies.

CAUTION
The crankshaft assembly is pressed into the left-hand crankcase half. Do not try to remove it or the crankcase will be damaged. If removal is necessary, take the crankcase and crankshaft to a dealer or competent machine shop and have it pressed out.

9. Inspect the crankcase halves and crankshaft as described in this chapter.

Assembly

1. Apply assembly oil to the inner race of all bearings in both crankcase halves.

NOTE
Set the crankcase half assembly on wood blocks or the wood holding fixture shown in the disassembly procedure.

2A. On 350 cc models, perform the following:
   a. Rotate the crankshaft until the connecting rod is at top dead center.
   b. Install the balancer weight assembly with the gear end in first.
   c. Align the index marks on the balancer weight gear and crankshaft driven gear.

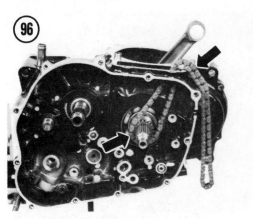

d. Install the balancer weight assembly completely into position in the left-hand crankcase half.

e. Rotate the crankshaft and balancer several times. Make sure there is no interference between the balancer weight and the crankshaft.

2B. On 500 and 600 cc models, perform the following:

a. Align the index marks on the balancer weight assembly and the crankshaft (**Figure 95**).

b. Install the balancer weight assembly completely into position in the left-hand crankcase half.

c. Rotate the crankshaft and balancer several times. Make sure there is no interference between the balancer weight and the crankshaft.

3. Install the transmission assemblies, shift forks and shafts and shift drum in the right-hand crankcase half and lightly oil all shaft ends. Refer to Chapter Six for the correct procedures.

NOTE
Make sure the mating surfaces are clean and free of all old gasket

material. Make sure you get a leak-free seal.

4. Install the 2 locating dowels if they were removed.

5. Install a new crankcase gasket.

6. Set the right-hand crankcase half over the left-hand crankcase half. Push it down squarely into place until it reaches the crankshaft bearing. There is usually about 1/2 inch left to go.

7. Lightly tap the case halves together with a plastic or rubber mallet until they seat.

CAUTION
Crankcase halves should fit together without force. If the crankcase halves do not fit together completely, do not attempt to pull them together with the crankcase screws. Separate the crankcase halves and investigate the cause of the interference. If the transmission shafts were disassembled, recheck to make sure that a gear is not installed backwards. Do not risk damage by trying to force the cases together.

8. Into the left-hand crankcase, install all of the crankcase screws (**Figure 92**) and tighten only finger-tight.

9. Securely tighten the screws in 2 stages in a crisscross pattern to the torque specification listed in **Table 2**.

10. Turn the crankcase over and install the crankcase screws on the right-hand side (**Figure 94**). Tighten the screws to the torque specification listed in **Table 2**.

11. After the crankcase halves are completely assembled, rotate the crankshaft and transmission shafts to make sure there is no binding. If any is present, disassemble the crankcase and correct the problem.

NOTE
After a new crankcase gasket is installed, it must be trimmed. Carefully trim off all excess crankcase gasket material where the cylinder base gasket comes in contact with the crankcase. If it is not trimmed the cylinder base gasket will not seal properly.

12. Feed the cam chain down through the top of the chain opening in the crankcase and install the cam chain onto the crankshaft sprocket (**Figure 96**). Make sure it is correctly engaged with the sprocket.

13. Install all exterior engine assemblies as described in this chapter and other related chapters:
   a. Cylinder head cover and camshaft.
   b. Cylinder head.
   c. Cylinder and piston.
   d. Cam chain and cam chain tensioner.
   e. Clutch assembly.
   f. Alternator assembly.
   g. External shift mechanism.
   h. Primary drive gear.
   i. Drive sprocket.
   j. Oil lines (dry-sump models).

Inspection

1. Clean both crankcase halves inside and out with cleaning solvent. Thoroughly dry with compressed air and wipe off with a clean shop cloth. Be sure to remove all traces of old gasket material from all mating surfaces.

2. Check the transmission and shift drum bearings (A, **Figure 97**) for roughness, pitting, galling and play by rotating them slowly by hand. If any roughness or play can be felt in the bearings they must be replaced.

3. Carefully inspect the cases for cracks and fractures, especially in the lower areas; they are vulnerable to rock damage. Also check the areas around the stiffening ribs, bearing bosses and threaded holes. If any damage is found, have them repaired by a shop specializing in the repair of precision aluminum castings or replace them.

4. Check the right-hand crankshaft main bearing (B, **Figure 97**) for roughness, pitting, galling and play by rotating it slowly by hand. If any roughness or play can be felt in the bearing it must be replaced.

5. On the left-hand crankcase half, check the crankshaft bearing by rotating the crankshaft by hand. If the bearing requires replacement take the crankcase to a dealer. The crankshaft assembly must be removed and installed with a hydraulic press.

6. Check the balancer shaft bearings (C, **Figure 97**) for roughness, pitting, galling and play by rotating them slowly by hand. If any roughness or play can be felt in the bearings they must be replaced.

7. Inspect the balancer gear (A, **Figure 98**) for wear or missing teeth. If either are damaged, replacement must be performed by a dealer.

8. Measure the inside diameter of the connecting rod small end (**Figure 99**) with an inside micrometer. Compare to dimensions given in **Table 1**. If worn to the service limit the crankshaft assembly must be replaced.

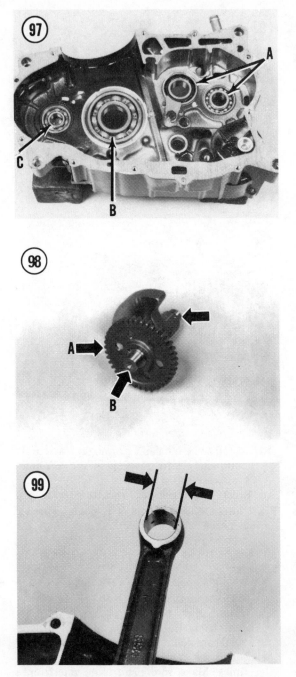

9. Check the condition of the connecting rod big end bearing by grasping the rod in one hand and lifting up on it. With the heel of your other hand, rap sharply on the top of the rod. A sharp metallic sound, such as a click, is an indication that the bearing or crankpin or both are worn and the crankshaft assembly should be replaced.

10. Check the connecting rod to crankshaft side clearance with a flat feeler gauge (**Figure 100**).

Compare to dimensions given in **Table 1**. If the clearance is greater than specified the crankshaft assembly must be replaced.

NOTE
Other inspections of the crankshaft assembly involve accurate measuring equipment and should be entrusted to a dealer or competent machine shop. The crankshaft assembly operates under severe stress and dimensional tolerances are critical. These dimensions are given in Table 1. If any are off by the slightest amount it may cause a considerable amount of damage or destruction of the engine. The crankshaft assembly must be replaced as a unit as it cannot be serviced without the aid of a 10-12 ton (9,000-11,000 kilogram) capacity press, holding fixtures and crankshaft jig.

11. Inspect the oil seals. They should be replaced every other time the crankcase is disassembled.

Refer to *Bearing and Oil Seal Replacement* in this chapter.

Bearing and Oil Seal Replacement

NOTE
This procedure relates only to the left-hand crankcase half. If bearings and oil seals need replacing in the right-hand crankcase half it must be performed by a dealer since the crankshaft must be removed with a hydraulic press.

1. Pry out the oil seals with a small screwdriver, taking care not to damage the crankcase bore. If the seals are old and difficult to remove, heat the cases as described in Step 3 and use an awl to punch a small hole in the steel backing of the seal. Install a small sheet metal screw part way into the seal and pull the seal out with a pair of pliers.

CAUTION
Do not install the screw too deep or it may contact and damage the bearing behind it.

2. Remove the bolt and retainer (**Figure 101**) securing the bearing into the crankcase.
3. The bearings are installed with a slight interference fit. The crankcase must be heated in an oven to a temperature of about 212° F (100° C). An easy way to check the proper temperature is to drop tiny drops of water on the case; if they sizzle and evaporate immediately, the temperature is correct. Heat only one case at a time.

CAUTION
Do not heat the cases with a torch (propane or acetylene); never bring a flame into contact with the bearing or case. The direct heat will destroy the case hardening of the bearing and will likely cause warpage of the case.

4. Remove the case from the oven and hold onto the crankcase with kitchen pot holders, heavy gloves or heavy shop cloths—*it is hot.*
5. Remove the oil seals if not already removed (see Step 1).
6. Hold the crankcase with the bearing side down and tap it squarely on a piece of soft wood. Continue to tap until the bearing(s) fall out. Repeat for the other half.

CAUTION
Be sure to tap the crankcase squarely on the piece of wood. Avoid damaging the sealing surface of the crankcase.

5

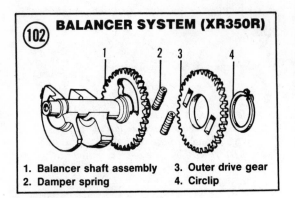

BALANCER SYSTEM (XR350R)

1. Balancer shaft assembly
2. Damper spring
3. Outer drive gear
4. Circlip

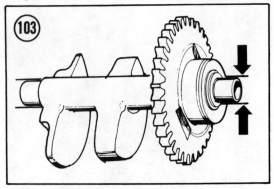

7. If the bearings are difficult to remove, they can be gently tapped out with a socket or piece of pipe the same size as the bearing outer race.

> *CAUTION*
> *If the bearings or seals are difficult to remove or install, don't take a chance on expensive damage. Have the work performed by a dealer or competent machine shop.*

8. While heating up the crankcase halves, place the new bearings in a freezer. Chilling them will slightly reduce their overall diameter while the hot crankcase is slightly larger due to heat expansion. This will make installation much easier.

9. While the crankcase is still hot, press each new bearing into place in the crankcase by hand until it seats completely. Do not hammer it in. If the bearing will not seat, remove it and cool it again. Reheat the crankcase and install the bearing again.

10. Oil seals are best installed with a special tool available at a dealer or motorcycle supply store. However, a proper size socket or piece of pipe can be substituted. Make sure that the bearings and seals are not cocked in the crankcase hole and that they are seated properly.

BALANCER SYSTEM

The balancer system eliminates the vibration normally associated with a large displacement single cylinder engine. The engine and the frame are designed to be compatible with this balancer system. If the balancer is eliminated it will result in an excessive amount of engine vibration. This vibration will result in major fatigue to engine and frame components. *Do not eliminate* this feature.

> *CAUTION*
> *Any applicable manufacturer's warranty will be voided if the balancer system is modified, disconnected or removed.*

The balancer system consists of a balancer weight that is gear-driven by the crankshaft assembly. The balancer construction varies slightly among the different models.

Removal/Installation

Remove and install the balancer assembly as described under *Crankcase and Crankshaft* in this chapter.

> *NOTE*
> *Honda does not provide service specifications for all models. All available factory inspection information is included in this manual.*

Disassembly/Inspection/Assembly (350 cc Models)

1. Remove the circlip and remove the outer driven gear and damper springs from the balancer shaft assembly (**Figure 102**).

2. Check for broken, chipped or missing teeth on the outer driven gear and the gear on the balancer shaft assembly.

3. Check the damper springs. Make sure they are not broken or have sagged. Replace as a set even if only one requires replacement.

4. Measure the outside diameter of the balancer shaft at each end (**Figure 103**) with a micrometer. Compare to the dimensions listed in **Table 1**. Replace if worn to the service limit or less.

5. Install the damper springs into the balancer shaft assembly.

6. Align the index marks on both gears and install the outer driven gear.

7. Install the circlip with the sharp side facing out. Make sure it is completely seated in the groove in the shaft assembly.

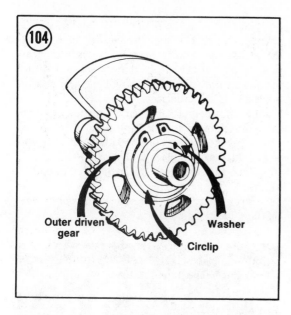

Outer driven gear   Washer   Circlip

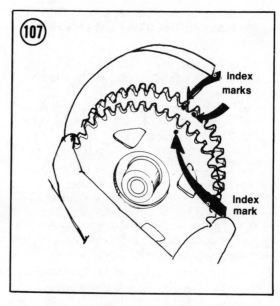

Index marks

Index mark

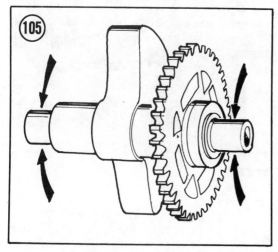

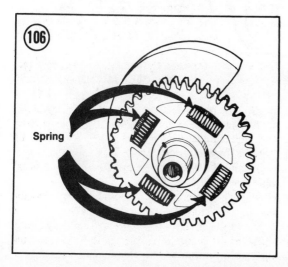

Spring

Disassembly/Inspection/Assembly (500 cc Models)

1. Check for broken, chipped or missing teeth on the balancer shaft assembly (A, **Figure 98**). Replace the balancer shaft assembly if the teeth are damaged.

2. Inspect the balancer shaft at each end (B, **Figure 98**) for wear or damage. Replace the balancer shaft assembly if wear is evident.

Disassembly/Inspection/Assembly (600 cc Models)

1. Remove the circlip and washer (**Figure 104**).

2. Remove the outer driven gear and damper springs from the balancer shaft assembly.

3. Check for broken, chipped or missing teeth on the outer driven gear and the gear on the balancer shaft assembly.

4. Check the damper springs. Make sure they are not broken or have sagged. Replace as a set even if only one requires replacement.

5. Measure the outside diameter of the balancer shaft at each end (**Figure 105**) with a micrometer. Compare to the dimensions listed in **Table 1**. Replace if worn to the service limit or less.

6. Install the damper springs into the balancer shaft assembly (**Figure 106**).

7. Align the index marks on both gears and install the outer driven gear (**Figure 107**).

8. Install the washer.

9. Install the circlip with the sharp side facing out. Make sure it is completely seated in the groove in the shaft assembly.

5

KICKSTARTER

Removal

1. Remove the clutch as described in Chapter Six.
2. Remove the kickstarter idle gear and bushing (**Figure 108**).
3. Unhook the return spring from the boss on the crankcase and withdraw the kickstarter shaft assembly from the crankcase.

Disassembly/Inspection

Refer to **Figure 109** for this procedure.
1. Clean the assembled shaft in solvent and dry with compressed air.
2. Slide off the thrust washer, kickstarter cam, spring and spring seat.
3. Remove the circlip.
4. From the other end of the shaft, remove the spring collar, return spring and spring seat.
5. Remove the kickstarter ratchet.
6. Remove the circlip and slide off the thrust washer, the kickstarter gear and the other thrust washer.
7. Measure the inside diameter of the kickstarter idle gear (A, **Figure 110**) and the inside (B, **Figure 110**) and outside (C, **Figure 110**) diameter of the kickstarter idle gear bushing. If the dimensions differ from the service limits in **Table 1** the gear and/or bushing must be replaced.

8. Measure the inside diameter of the kickstarter gear (A, **Figure 111**) and the outside diameter of the kickstarter shaft where the kickstarter gear rides (B, **Figure 111**). If the dimensions differ from the service limits listed in **Table 1** the gear and/or the shaft must be replaced.
9. Check for chipped, broken or missing teeth on the gears. Replace as necessary.
10. Inspect the splines on the kickstarter shaft for wear or damage. Replace if necessary.
11. Make sure the ratchet gear operates smoothly on the shaft.
12. Check all parts for uneven wear; replace any that are questionable.

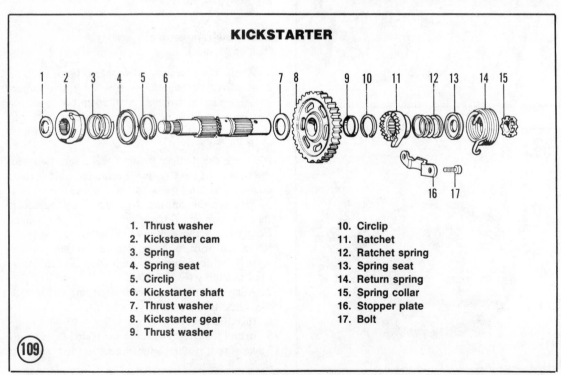

KICKSTARTER

1. Thrust washer
2. Kickstarter cam
3. Spring
4. Spring seat
5. Circlip
6. Kickstarter shaft
7. Thrust washer
8. Kickstarter gear
9. Thrust washer
10. Circlip
11. Ratchet
12. Ratchet spring
13. Spring seat
14. Return spring
15. Spring collar
16. Stopper plate
17. Bolt

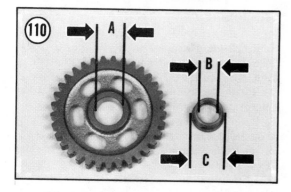

Figure 110

Assembly

1. Apply assembly oil to all sliding surfaces of all parts prior to assembly.

2. Install the thrust washer and kickstarter gear onto the shaft (**Figure 112**).

3. Install the thrust washer and the circlip (**Figure 113**). Make sure the circlip is correctly seated in the groove in the kickstarter shaft.

4. Align the punch marks on kickstarter ratchet and the punch mark on the shaft (**Figure 114**). Slide on the ratchet.

5. Install the ratchet spring and spring seat (**Figure 115**).

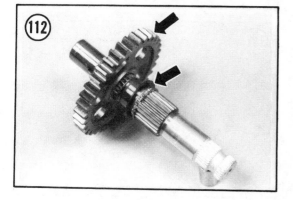

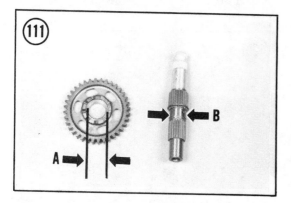

6. Install the return spring. Place the hook into the hole in the shaft (**Figure 116**).

7. Slide on the collar and push the collar into place within the return spring (**Figure 117**).

8. Onto the other end of the shaft, install the spring seat and spring (**Figure 118**).

9. Align the punch marks on kickstarter cam and the punch mark on the shaft (**Figure 119**) and slide on the cam.

10. Install the thrust washer (**Figure 120**).

11. Prior to installing the assembled shaft into the crankcase half, check **Figure 121** for correct placement of all components.

Installation

1. Install the assembled shaft into the crankcase. Insert the drive ratchet pawl against the ratchet guide plate on the crankcase.

2. Rotate the assembly clockwise and hook the return spring into the rib on the crankcase.

3. Install the kickstarter idle gear bushing with the shoulder side on first (**Figure 122**).

4. Install the kickstarter idle gear onto the bushing (**Figure 108**).

5. Install the clutch assembly as described in Chapter Six.

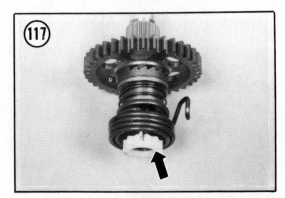

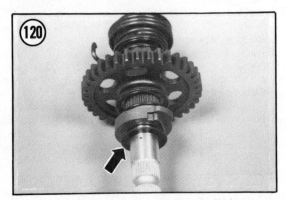

Table 1 ENGINE SPECIFICATIONS*

Item	Specifications	Wear limit
350 CC		
General		
Type	4-stroke, air-cooled, SOHC	
Number of cylinders	1	
Bore and stroke	84.0 x 61.3 mm (3.31 x 2.41 in.)	
Displacement	339 cc (20.7 cu. in.)	
Compression ratio	9.5 to 1	
Compression pressure	175 psi (12.5 kg/cm²)	
Cylinder		
Bore	84.00-84.01 mm (3.3071-3.3074 in.)	84.11 mm (3.311 in.)
Out of round	–	0.05 mm (0.002 in.)
Piston/cylinder clearance	0.01-0.04 mm (0.0004-0.0016 in.)	0.1 mm (0.004 in.)
Warpage across top	–	0.1 mm (0.004 in.)
Piston		
Diameter	83.96-83.98 mm (3.3057-3.3065 in.)	83.87 mm (3.302 in.)
Clearance in bore	0.01-0.04 mm (0.0004-0.0016 in.)	0.10 mm (0.004 in.)
Piston pin bore	21.002-21.008 mm (0.8268-0.8271 in.)	21.08 mm (0.830 in.)
Piston pin outer diameter	20.994-21.000 mm (0.8265-0.8268 in.)	20.96 mm (0.825 in.)
Piston rings		
Number of rings		
Compression	2	
Oil control	1	
Ring end gap		
Top and second	0.20-0.40 mm (0.0079-0.0157 in.)	0.55 mm (0.0216 in.)
Oil (side rail)	0.2-0.9 mm (0.007-0.035 in.)	NA
Ring side clearance		
Top ring	0.030-0.065 mm (0.0012-0.0026 in.)	0.12 mm (0.006 in.)
Second ring	0.015-0.045 mm (0.0006-0.0018 in.)	0.12 mm (0.006 in.)
Oil control	NA	NA
Crankshaft/connecting rod		
Small end inner diameter	19.020-19.041 mm (0.7488-0.7496 in.)	19.07 mm (0.751 in).
Connecting rod big end side clearance	0.05-0.65 mm (0.002-0.0256 in.)	0.80 mm (0.031 in.)
Connecting rod big end radial clearance	0.006-0.018 mm (0.0002-0.0007 in.)	0.05 mm (0.002 in.)
Camshaft		
Cam lobe height		
Intake	30.569 mm (1.2035 in.)	30.37 mm (1.195 in.)
Exhaust	30.575 mm (1.2037 in.)	30.38 mm (1.196 in.)
Cam journals OD	19.972-19.993 mm (0.7863-0.7871 in.)	19.92 mm (0.784 in.)

(continued)

5

Table 1 ENGINE SPECIFICATIONS* (continued)

Item	Specifications	Wear limit
350 CC (cont.)		
Camshaft bearing ID	19.99-20.00 mm (0.7870-0.7874 in.)	20.049 mm (.0789 in.)
Valves		
Valve stem outer diameter		
Intake	5.475-5.490 mm (0.2155-0.2161 in.)	5.46 mm (0.215 in.)
Exhaust	5.467-5.477 mm (0.2152-0.2156 in.)	5.45 mm (0.214 in.)
Valve guide inner diameter	5.500-5.512 mm (0.2166-0.2170 in.)	5.53 mm (0.218 in.)
Stem to guide clearance	0.010-0.047 mm (0.0004-0.0019 in.)	0.06 mm (0.0024 in.)
Valve face width	1.2-1.4 mm (0.048-0.055 in.)	2.0 mm (0.08 in.)
Valve springs		
free length		
Inner	35.7 mm (1.4055 in.)	34.6 mm (1.362 in.)
Outer	41.1 mm (1.6181 in.)	40.16 mm (1.575 in.)
Main rocker arm assembly		
Rocker arm bore ID	11.482-11.500 mm (0.4520-0.4527 in.)	10.53 mm (0.454 in.)
Rocker arm shaft OD	11.466-11.484 mm (0.4514-0.4521 in.)	11.41 mm (0.449 in.)
Sub-rocker arm assembly		
Rocker arm bore ID		
Intake	8.00-8.015 mm (0.3150-0.3155 in.)	8.05 mm (0.317 in.)
Exhaust	7.00-7.015 mm (0.2756-0.2761 in.)	7.05 mm (0.277 in.)
Rocker arm shaft OD		
Intake	7.969-7.972 mm (0.3137-0.3139 in.)	7.916 mm (0.312 in.)
Exhaust	6.969-6.972 mm (0.2744-0.2745 in.)	6.916 mm (0.272 in.)
Rocker arm to shaft clearance (all)	0.016-0.052 mm (0.0006-0.0020 in.)	0.14 mm (0.006 in.)
Oil pump		
Inner to outer rotor tip clearance	0.15 mm (0.006 in.)	0.20 mm (0.008 in.)
Outer rotor to body clearance	0.15-0.21 mm (0.006-0.008 in.)	0.25 mm (0.0010 in.)
Rotor to body clearance	0.02-0.08 mm (0.001-0.003 in.)	0.12 mm (0.005 in.)
Counter balancer system		
Shaft OD (each end)	11.972-11.99 mm (0.4713-0.4720 in.)	11.95 mm (0.471 in.)
Kickstarter		
Gear ID	22.020-22.041 mm (0.8669-0.8679 in.)	22.12 mm (0.871 in.)
Shaft OD (where gear rides)	21.959-21.980 mm (0.8645-0.8645 in.)	21.91 mm (0.863 in.)

(continued)

Table 1 ENGINE SPECIFICATIONS* (continued)

Item	Specifications	Wear limit
500 AND 600 CC		
General		
Type	4-stroke, air-cooled, SOHC	
Number of cylinders	1	
Bore and stroke		
500 cc	92.0 x 75.0 mm (3.62 x 2.95 in.)	
600 cc	100.0 x 75.0 mm (3.93 x 2.95 in.)	
Displacement		
500 cc	498 cc (30.37 cu. in.)	
600 cc	589 cc (35.91 cu. in.)	
Compression ratio		
500 cc	9.2 to 1	
600 cc	8.6 to 1	
Compression pressure	175 psi (12.5 kg/cm²)	
Cylinder		
Bore		
500 cc	91.00-91.01 mm (3.5827-3.5831 in.)	91.12 mm (3.587 in.)
600 cc	101.00-101.01 mm (3.9337-3.9375 in.)	100.12 mm (3.942 in.)
Out of round	–	0.05 mm (0.002 in.)
Piston/cylinder clearance	0.01-0.04 mm (0.0004-0.0016 in.)	0.1 mm (0.004 in.)
Warpage across top	–	0.1 mm (0.004 in.)
Piston		
500 cc		
Diameter	90.95-90.98 mm (3.5807-3.5819 in.)	90.85 mm (3.577 in.)
Clearance in bore	0.01-0.04 mm (0.0004-0.0016 in.)	0.10 mm (0.004 in.)
Piston pin bore	22.002-22.008 mm (0.8662-0.8665 in.)	22.08 mm (0.869 in.)
Piston pin outer diameter	21.995-21.989 mm (0.8659-0.8657 in.)	21.95 mm (0.864 in.)
600 cc		
Diameter	99.95-99.98 mm (3.9535-3.936 in.)	99.85 mm (3.93 in.)
Clearance in bore	0.01-0.04 mm (0.0004-0.0016 in.)	0.10 mm (0.004 in.)
Piston pin bore	24.002-24.008 mm (0.9450-0.9452 in.)	24.03 mm (0.946 in.)
Piston pin outer diameter	NA	23.96 mm (0.943 in.)
Piston rings		
Number of rings		
Compression	2	
Oil control	1	
Ring end gap		
Top and second	0.20-0.40 mm (0.0097-0.0157 in.)	0.50 mm (0.020 in.)
Oil (side rail)	0.2-0.9 mm (0.007-0.035 in.)	NA
Ring side clearance		
Top ring	0.030-0.065 mm (0.0012-0.0026 in.)	0.12 mm (0.006 in.)

(continued)

5

Table 1 ENGINE SPECIFICATIONS* (continued)

Item	Specifications	Wear limit
500 AND 600 CC (cont.)		
Piston rings		
Ring side clearance (cont.)		
Second ring	0.015-0.045 mm (0.006-0.0018 in.)	0.12 mm (0.006 in.)
Oil control	NA	NA
Crankshaft/connecting rod		
Small end inner diameter		
500 cc	22.020-22.041 mm (0.8669-0.8678 in.)	22.07 mm (0.869 in.)
600 cc	24.020-24.041 mm (0.9457-0.9465 in.)	24.07 mm (0.948 in.)
Connecting rod big end side clearance	0.05-0.65 mm (0.002-0.0256 in.)	0.80 mm (0.031 in.)
Connecting rod big end radial clearance	0.006-0.018 mm (0.0002-0.0007 in.)	0.05 mm (0.002 in.)
Camshaft lobe height		
500 cc		
Intake	34.023 mm (1.3394 in.)	33.85 mm (1.334 in.)
Exhaust	33.976 mm (1.3376 in.)	33.81 mm (1.331 in.)
Camshaft lobe height		
600 cc		
Intake	31.023 mm (1.2214 in.)	31.85 mm (1.215 in.)
Exhaust	30.976 mm (1.2195 in.)	30.81 mm (1.213 in.)
Valves		
Valve stem outer diameter		
Intake	6.575-6.590 mm (0.2589-0.2594 in.)	6.565 mm (0.258 in.)
Exhaust	6.565-6.575 mm (0.2585-0.2589 in.)	6.55 mm (0.2579 in.)
Sub-chamber (600 cc)	4.97-4.985 mm (0.1957-0.1963 in.)	4.96 mm (0.195 in.)
Valve guide inner diameter		
Intake and exhaust	6.600-6.615 mm (0.2598-0.2421 in.)	6.63 mm (0.261 in.)
Sub-chamber (600 cc)	5.010-5.028 mm (0.1972-0.1980 in.)	5.02 mm (0.199 in.)
Stem to guide clearance		
Intake	0.010-0.040 mm (0.0004-0.0016 in.)	0.065 mm (0.0026 in.)
Exhaust	0.025-0.050 mm (0.0010-0.0020 in.)	0.080 mm (0.0031 in.)
Sub-chamber (600 cc)	NA	NA
Valve face width		
Intake	1.20-1.85 mm (0.047-0.071 in.)	2.6 mm (0.10 in.)
Exhaust	0.90-1.70 mm (0.040-0.067 in.)	2.4 mm (0.09 in.)
Sub-chamber (600 cc)	1.00-1.40 mm (0.039-0.551 in.)	2.0 mm (0.08 in.)

(continued)

Table 1 ENGINE SPECIFICATIONS* (continued)

Item	Specifications	Wear limit
500 AND 600 CC (cont.)		
Valve springs free length intake and exhaust		
Inner	35.1 mm (1.240 in.)	34.1 mm (1.34 in.)
Outer	36.0 mm (1.417 in.)	35.0 mm (1.38 in.)
Sub-chamber (600 cc)	40.5 mm (1.5494 in.)	39.3 mm (1.55 in.)
Main rocker arm assemby		
Rocker arm bore ID	11.50-11.518 mm (0.4528-0.4535 in.)	11.55 mm (0.455 in.)
Rocker arm shaft OD	11.466-11.484 mm (0.4514-0.4521 in.)	11.41 mm (0.449 in.)
Sub-rocker arm assemby		
Rocker arm bore ID		
Intake	8.00-8.015 mm (0.3150-0.3155 in.)	8.05 mm (0.317 in.)
Exhaust	7.00-7.015 mm (0.2756-0.2761 in.)	7.05 mm (0.277 in.)
Rocker arm shaft OD		
Intake	7.972-7.967 mm (0.3137-0.3139 in.)	7.92 mm (0.312 in.)
Exhaust	6.972-6.969 mm (0.2744-0.2745 in.)	6.92 mm (0.272 in.)
Main rocker arm to shaft clearance	0.016-0.052 mm (0.0006-0.0020 in.)	0.14 mm (0.006 in.)
Sub-rocker arm to shaft clearance	0.033-0.043 mm (0.0013-0.0017 in.)	0.08 mm (0.003 in.)
Oil pump (A and B rotors)		
Inner to outer rotor tip clearance	0.15 mm (0.006 in.)	0.20 mm (0.01 in.)
Outer rotor to body clearance	0.15-0.21 mm (0.006-0.008 in.)	0.25 mm (0.0010 in.)
Rotor to body clearance	0.02-0.08 mm (0.001-0.003 in.)	0.12 mm (0.005 in.)
Counter balancer system		
Shaft OD each end		
600 cc	16.977-16.995 mm (0.6684-0.6691 in.)	16.95 mm (0.667 in.)
500 cc	NA	NA
Kickstarter		
Idle gear ID	20.00-20.021 mm (0.7874-0.7882 in.)	20.11 mm (0.792 in.)
Idle gear bushing		
ID	16.00-16.018 mm (0.6299-0.6366 in.)	16.03 mm (0.631 in.)
OD	19.959-19.98 mm (0.7858-0.7866 in.)	19.90 mm (0.793 in.)
Gear ID	22.000-22.033 mm (0.8661-0.8674 in.)	22.12 mm (0.871 in.)
Shaft OD (where gear rides)	21.959-21.980 mm (0.8645-21.980 in.)	21.91 mm (0.863 in.)

5

* NA Honda does not provide service information for all items nor all models. All available information is included in this table. NA = Not available.

Table 2 ENGINE TORQUE SPECIFICATIONS

Item	ft.-lb.	N•m
Engine mounting bolts and nuts (8 mm)	22-27	30-37
Engine mounting bolts (10 mm)	40-48	55-65
Valve adjuster locknuts	13-16	18-22
Cylinder head cover bolts		
6 mm	7-10	10-14
8 mm	15-19	20-26
Cylinder head bolts	19-22	26-30
Cylinder bolts	34-38	47-53
Cam sprocket bolts	13-16	18-22
Main rocker arm shafts	18-22	25-30
Sub-rocker arm shafts		
Intake	18-22	25-30
Exhaust	15-18	20-25
Drive gear locknut	36-43	50-60
Crankcase bolts	6-9	8-12
Crankcase cover bolts	6-9	8-12
Alternator cover bolts	6-9	8-12
Alternator rotor bolt	72-87	100-120

CHAPTER SIX

CLUTCH AND TRANSMISSION

Clutch and transmission specifications are in **Tables 1-3** at the end of the chapter.

CLUTCH OPERATION

The clutch is a wet multi-plate type which operates immersed in an oil supply shared with the transmission. It is mounted on the end of the transmission main shaft. The inner clutch hub is splined to the main shaft and the outer clutch housing can rotate freely on the main shaft. The outer clutch housing is geared to the crankshaft.

The clutch release mechanism is mounted within the crankcase and is operated by the clutch cable and hand lever mounted on the handlebar.

> *NOTE*
> *Honda has indicated that some 1983 models may have an oil leak problem on the lower rear portion of the right-hand crankcase cover. Return the bike to your dealer for inspection and correction if you have not already done so.*

CLUTCH REMOVAL/INSTALLATION (1983 350-600 CC MODELS)

Removal/Disassembly

Refer to **Figure 1** for XR350R models or **Figure 2** for XR500R and XL600R models for this procedure.

The clutch assembly can be removed with the engine in the frame.

1. Remove the seat and side covers.
2. Drain the engine oil as described in Chapter Three.
3. Remove the bolts securing the skid plate and remove the skid plate.
4. Place wood block(s) under the engine to support the bike securely.
5. Remove the bolts securing the right-hand front footpeg and remove the footpeg.
6. Loosen the brake adjust nut (**Figure 3**) on the end of the rear brake rod.
7. Remove the rear brake pedal pivot bolt (**Figure 4**). Move the brake pedal assembly back and out of the way. It is not necessary to remove the assembly from the frame.
8. Remove the bolt securing the kickstarter lever and remove the lever.
9. Disconnect the decompression cable (A, **Figure 5**) from the lever on the crankcase cover.
10. Remove the bolts securing the clutch cover (B, **Figure 5**) and remove the cover and gasket. Don't lose the locating dowels.

> *NOTE*
> *Note the location of the conical washers on the lower rear 3 bolts. To help prevent an oil leak, these conical washers must be reinstalled on these 3 bolts.*

11A. On XR350R models, perform the following:
   a. Remove the lifter rod, stopper ring, washer and bearing from the lifter plate.
   b. Using a crisscross pattern, remove the clutch bolts securing the lifter plate and remove the springs and the lifter plate.
   c. Place a copper washer (or copper penny) between the gears on the clutch outer housing and the primary drive gear.
   d. Remove the clutch locknut and washer.
   e. Remove the clutch center, friction discs, clutch plates and the clutch pressure plate.
   f. Slide off the clutch outer housing and guide.

11B. On XR500R and XL600R models, perform the following:
   a. Using a crisscross pattern, remove the clutch bolts securing the clutch pressure plate and remove the springs and the pressure plate.
   b. Remove the friction discs and clutch plates.

6

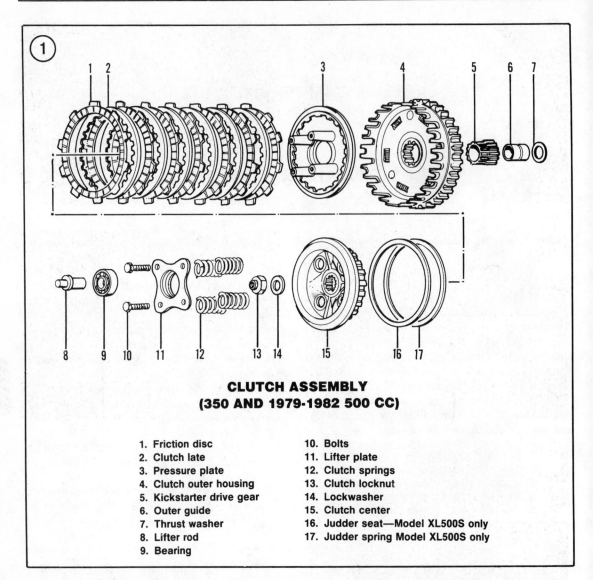

CLUTCH ASSEMBLY
(350 AND 1979-1982 500 CC)

1. Friction disc
2. Clutch late
3. Pressure plate
4. Clutch outer housing
5. Kickstarter drive gear
6. Outer guide
7. Thrust washer
8. Lifter rod
9. Bearing
10. Bolts
11. Lifter plate
12. Clutch springs
13. Clutch locknut
14. Lockwasher
15. Clutch center
16. Judder seat—Model XL500S only
17. Judder spring Model XL500S only

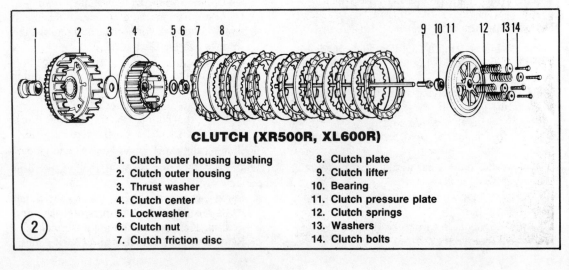

CLUTCH (XR500R, XL600R)

1. Clutch outer housing bushing
2. Clutch outer housing
3. Thrust washer
4. Clutch center
5. Lockwasher
6. Clutch nut
7. Clutch friction disc
8. Clutch plate
9. Clutch lifter
10. Bearing
11. Clutch pressure plate
12. Clutch springs
13. Washers
14. Clutch bolts

c. Remove the clutch lifter (**Figure 6**) and the clutch pushrod (**Figure 7**) from the transmission shaft.

d. To keep the clutch center from turning in the next step, attach a special tool such as the "Grabbit" (**Figure 8**) to it.

NOTE
The "Grabbit" (part No. 969103) is available from Precision Mfg. and Sales Co. Inc., P.O. Box 149, Clearwater, FL 33517.

e. Remove the clutch nut and lockwasher.

f. Remove the clutch center, thrust washer and clutch outer housing.

g. Slide off the clutch outer housing guide.

12. Inspect the clutch parts as described in this chapter.

**Assembly/Installation
(XR350R)**

CAUTION
If new friction discs or clutch plates are being installed, apply new engine oil to all surfaces to avoid having the clutch lock up when used for the first time.

1. Position the clutch outer housing guide with the flange side on first and slide it onto the transmission shaft (**Figure 9**).

2. Onto the clutch center install first a friction disc and then a clutch plate. Continue to install the friction discs and clutch plates, alternating them until all are installed. The last item installed is a friction disc.

3. Align the friction disc tabs (this will make installation easier).

4. Install the pressure plate.

5. Install all items assembled in Steps 2-4 into the clutch outer housing.

6. Install the clutch outer housing assembly onto the transmission main shaft.

7. Install the lockwasher with the "OUTSIDE" mark facing toward the outside.

8. To prevent the clutch center from turning in the next step, use the same tool set-up used in *Removal/Disassembly.*

9. Install the clutch nut and tighten to 36-43 ft.-lb. (50-60 N•m).

10. Install the clutch springs and lifter plate.

11. Install the clutch bolts and tighten in a crisscross pattern in 2-3 steps. Tighten the bolts securely.

12. Install the bearing, washer and stopper ring.

13. Install the lifter rod.

14. Make sure the locating dowels are installed on the crankcase. Install a new crankcase gasket.

15. Hold the decompressor cam follower lever in the raised position and install the crankcase cover.

16. Install the crankcase screws and tighten the screws securely.

NOTE
After the crankcase cover is installed, check the operation of the decompressor lever. It should operate without binding. If there is any binding, remove the crankcase cover and correct the problem.

17. Install the decompressor cable to the lever on the crankcase cover.

18. Install the gearshift lever and tighten the bolt securely.

19. Install the rear brake pedal and the pivot bolt. Tighten the bolt securely.

20. Install the right-hand front footpeg and tighten the bolts securely.

21. Install the skid plate and tighten the screws securely.

22. Refill the engine with the recommended type and quantity of oil as described in Chapter Three.

23. Adjust the clutch and rear brake as described in Chapter Three.

1. Position the clutch outer housing guide with the flange side on first and slide it onto the transmission shaft (**Figure 9**).

2. Install the clutch outer housing (A, **Figure 10**) and the thrust washer (B, **Figure 10**).

3. Install the clutch center (**Figure 11**).

4. Install the lockwasher (**Figure 12**) with the "OUTSIDE" mark facing toward the outside.

5. To prevent the clutch center from turning in the next step, use the same tool set-up used in *Removal/Disassembly.*

6. Install the clutch nut (**Figure 13**) and tighten to 36-43 ft.-lb. (50-60 N•m).

7. Install the clutch pushrod (**Figure 7**).

8. Install the clutch lifter (**Figure 6**).

9. Onto the clutch center install first a friction disc and then a clutch plate. Continue to install the friction discs and clutch plates, alternating them until all are installed. The last item installed is a friction disc.

10. Install the pressure plate (A, **Figure 14**) and the clutch springs (B, **Figure 14**).

11. Install the clutch bolts (**Figure 15**). Tighten the bolts securely in a crisscross pattern in 2 or 3 stages.

12. Make sure the locating dowels are installed on the crankcase. Install a new crankcase gasket.

13. Hold the decompressor cam follower in the down position and install the crankcase cover.

14. Clean the threads of the 3 lower rear crankcase screws that are used with the conical washers. Apply Loctite Lock N' Seal to the threads of these 3 screws only. Place the conical washers on these 3 screws with the cupped side of the washer facing toward the cover. Install these screws and washers on the 3 lower rear holes in the cover, and then install the remainder of the crankcase screws. Tighten the screws securely.

> *NOTE*
> *After the crankcase cover is installed, check the operation of the decompressor lever. It should operate without binding. If there is any binding, remove the crankcase cover and correct the problem.*

15. Install the decompressor cable to the lever (**Figure 16**) on the crankcase cover.

16. Install the gearshift lever and tighten the bolt securely.

17. Install the rear brake pedal and the pivot bolt. Tighten the bolt securely.

18. Install the right-hand front footpeg and tighten the bolts securely.

Assembly/Installation (XR500R and XL600R)

> *CAUTION*
> *If new friction discs or clutch plates are being installed, apply new engine oil to all surfaces to avoid having the clutch lock up when used for the first time.*

6

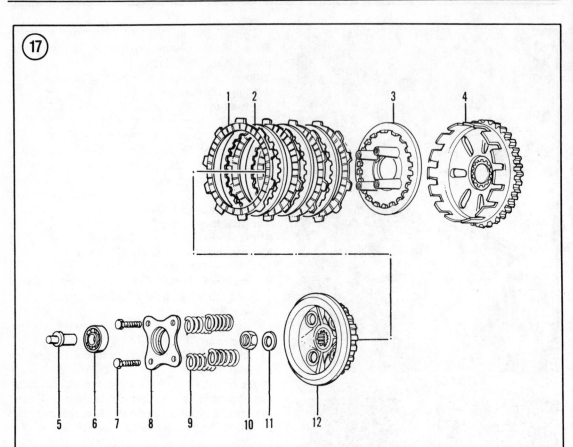

CLUTCH ASSEMBLY
(1979-1980 XL250S, 1977-1981 XR250)

1. Friction disc (4)
2. Clutch plate (3)
3. Pressure plate
4. Clutch outer housing
5. Lifter rod
6. Bearing
7. Bolts
8. Lifter plate
9. Clutch springs
10. Clutch nut
11. Lockwasher
12. Clutch center

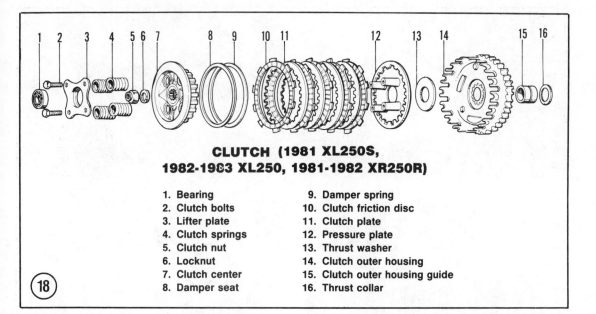

CLUTCH (1981 XL250S, 1982-1983 XL250, 1981-1982 XR250R)

1. Bearing
2. Clutch bolts
3. Lifter plate
4. Clutch springs
5. Clutch nut
6. Locknut
7. Clutch center
8. Damper seat
9. Damper spring
10. Clutch friction disc
11. Clutch plate
12. Pressure plate
13. Thrust washer
14. Clutch outer housing
15. Clutch outer housing guide
16. Thrust collar

19. Install the skid plate and tighten the screws securely.

20. Refill the engine with the recommended type and quantity of oil as described in Chapter Three.

21. Adjust the clutch and rear brake as described in Chapter Three.

CLUTCH REMOVAL/INSTALLATION (ALL OTHER MODELS)

The clutch mechanism used on these models is basically the same but minor variations exist among the different models. Where differences occur they are identified.

The following models are covered in this procedure:

a. **Figure 17**—1979-1980 XL250S, 1977-1981 XR250.

b. **Figure 18**—1981 XL250S, 1982-1983 XL250, 1981-1982 XR250R.

c. **Figure 1**—1979-1982 500 cc models.

Removal/Disassembly

The clutch assembly can be removed with the engine in the frame.

1. Remove the right- and left-hand side covers and seat.

CAUTION
On XL250S and XL500S models, reinstall the seat strap bolts as they also hold the upper portion of the shocks to the frame (Figure 19). Remove and reinstall one bolt at a time.

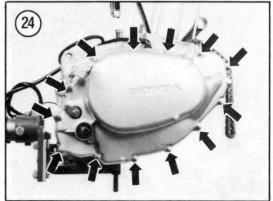

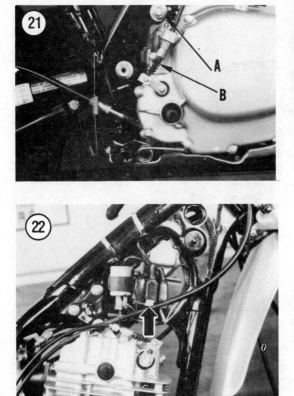

2. Remove the bolts securing the skid plate and remove it.

3. Drain the engine oil as described in Chapter Three.

4. Place block(s) of wood under the engine to properly secure it.

5. On XL series models, disconnect the battery leads or disconnect the main fuse.

6. Remove the fuel tank as described in Chapter Seven.

7. Remove the kickstarter pedal.

8. Disconnect the rear brake switch return spring and cable, front right-hand footpeg and rear brake pedal.

9. Slacken the clutch cable at the hand lever (**Figure 20**).

10. Disconnect the clutch cable at the crankcase cover (A, **Figure 21**).

11. Disconnect the decompressor cable at the crankcase cover (B, **Figure 21**).

12. Disconnect the ignition pulser generator wires at the electrical connector. Refer to **Figure 22** or **Figure 23**.

NOTE
The electrical connector on all models
contains 2 wires.

13. Remove the bolts (**Figure 24**) securing the crankcase cover and remove it and the gasket.

NOTE
Don't lose the 2 locating dowels and
small oil control pipe.

14. Remove the lifter rod and bearing (**Figure 25**). Remove the 4 bolts (**Figure 26**) securing the lifter plate in a crisscross pattern and remove the plate. Loosen the bolts evenly in 2-3 steps.

15. Remove the 4 clutch springs (**Figure 27**).

16. On 500 cc models, straighten the locking tab on the clutch nut (**Figure 28**).

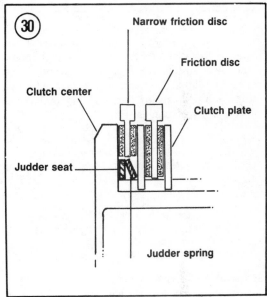

Narrow friction disc

Friction disc

Clutch center

Clutch plate

Judder seat

Judder spring

6

NOTE
250 cc models are not equipped with this type of locking clutch nut.

17. Remove the clutch nut and lockwasher.

NOTE
To prevent the clutch assembly from rotating, wedge a soft aluminum or brass bar between the clutch outer housing gear and the drive gear or kickstarter gear.

18. Pull the entire clutch assembly (clutch center, friction plates, clutch plates, pressure plate and

clutch outer housing) off of the transmission main shaft.

19. Remove the clutch outer housing guide and thrust washer.

20. Separate the clutch components removed in Step 18.

21. Inspect the clutch parts as described in this chapter.

Assembly/Installation

1. On all models except the 1978-1980 XL250S and 1979-1980 XR250, perform the following:
   a. Install the flat judder seat (**Figure 29**).
   b. Install the judder spring onto the clutch center with the dished side facing up as shown in **Figure 30**.
   c. Install the only *narrow* friction disc (**Figure 31**) onto the clutch center with the judder seat and spring seat inboard of it. Refer to **Figure 30**.

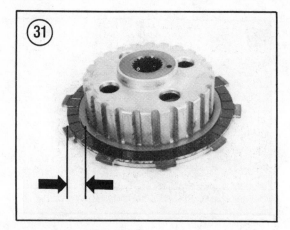

2. On all other models, onto the clutch center first install a friction disc and then a clutch plate. Continue to install the friction discs and clutch plates, alternating them until all are installed. Align the friction disc tabs as shown in **Figure 32**. This will make installation easier.

NOTE
The number of friction discs and clutch plates varies among the different models.

CAUTION
If new friction discs or clutch plates are being installed, apply new engine oil to all surfaces to avoid having the clutch lock up when used for the first time.

3. Install the pressure plate.
4. Install the thrust washer and clutch outer housing guide (**Figure 33**) on the transmission main shaft.
5. Install the kickstarter drive gear into the back of the clutch outer housing and install the assembly (**Figure 34**). Make sure the gears mesh properly with the drive gear on the crankshaft.
6. Install a couple of clutch springs, washers and clutch bolts (A, **Figure 35**) to hold the assembly, made up in Steps 2 and 3, together. This will aid in installation. Slide the assembly into the clutch outer housing (**Figure 35**).

NOTE
Do not tighten the bolts as some play is needed for final alignment of friction plate tabs into the clutch outer housing.

7. Remove the bolts, washers and springs.
8. Install the lockwasher with the marking "OUTSIDE" facing toward the outside (**Figure 36**).
9. Install the clutch nut and tighten to 33-43 ft.-lb. (45-60 N•m) on all models.

6

NOTE
To prevent the clutch outer housing from turning, wedge a soft aluminum or brass bar between the housing gear and the drive gear as shown in **Figure 37**.

10. On 500 cc engines, lock the nut in place by staking the rim of the locknut into the groove in the main shaft (**Figure 38**). Use a punch and hammer.

NOTE
250 cc engines are not equipped with this type of locknut.

11. Install the clutch springs, lifter plate and clutch bolts. Tighten the bolts in a crisscross pattern, in 2-3 stages, until tight.
12. Install the ball bearing and lifter rod (A, **Figure 39**).

NOTE
Make sure the oil screen (B, **Figure 39***) is still in place. This is a good time to remove and clean the screen. Refer to Chapter Three.*

13. Install the small oil control pipe (**Figure 40**); install a new gasket and make sure the 2 locating dowels are in place.
14. Install the crankcase cover while holding the decompressor cam follower lever in position. Install the bolts and tighten to 6-9 ft.-lb. (8-12 N•m).

CAUTION
After the cover is completely installed, check the operation of the clutch and decompressor levers. They should operate without binding; if they bind, remove cover and correct the problem.

15. Connect the clutch and decompressor cables (**Figure 21**).

16. Install the rear brake lever, front footpegs and kickstarter arm.

17. Install the skid plate. On XR250 and XR500 models, make sure all rubber spacers (**Figure 41**) are installed onto the skid plate prior to installation.

18. Install the seat and side covers.

19. Fill the crankcase with the recommended type and quantity of engine oil. Refer to Chapter Three.

20. Adjust the clutch, decompressor and rear brake as described in Chapter Three.

CLUTCH INSPECTION
(ALL MODELS)

1. Clean all parts in a petroleum based solvent such as kerosene and thoroughly dry with compressed air.

2. Measure the free length of each clutch spring as shown in **Figure 42**. If any of the springs are worn to the service limit shown in **Table 1**, they should be replaced. Replace all springs as a set.

3. Measure the thickness of each friction disc at several places around the disc as shown in **Figure 43**. Replace any disc that is worn to the service limit shown in **Table 1**. For optimum performance, replace all discs as a set even if only a few need replacement.

4. Check the clutch plates for warpage on a surface plate such as a piece of plate glass (**Figure 44**). Replace any that are warped to the service limit listed in **Table 1**. For optimum performance, replace all plates as a set even if only a few need replacement.

5. Inspect the grooves in the clutch outer housing (**Figure 45**) for cracks, nicks or galling where they come in contact with the friction disc tabs. If any severe damage is evident, the clutch housing must be replaced.

6. Inspect the teeth on the clutch outer housing and clutch outer housing inner gear (**Figure 46**). Remove any small nicks on the gear teeth with an oilstone. If damage is severe the clutch outer

43

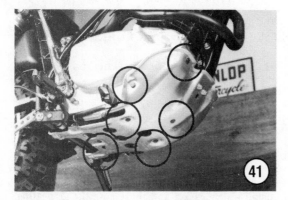

41

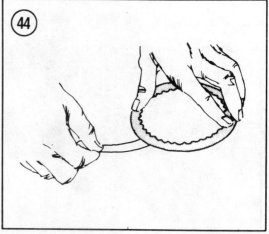

44

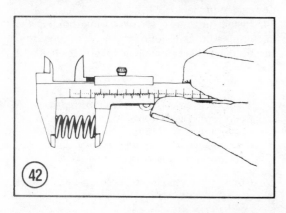

42

housing and inner gear should be replaced. Also check the teeth on the primary drive gear on the crankshaft.

7. On 350 and 500 cc engines, inspect the damper springs (**Figure 47**). If they have sagged or broken the housing must be replaced.

8. On 350 and 500 cc engines, inspect the inner spline (A, **Figure 48**) of the clutch outer housing and the outer splines of the kickstarter driven gear (B, **Figure 48**). Replace damaged parts.

9. Measure the inside diameter of the kickstarter driven gear (A, **Figure 49**). Measure the inside diameter (B, **Figure 49**) and the outside diameter

(C, **Figure 49**) of the outer guide. Compare to the service limit dimensions listed in **Table 1**. Replace any worn part.

10. Inspect the grooves and studs in the pressure plate (A, **Figure 50**). If either show signs of wear or galling the pressure plate should be replaced.

11. Inspect the inner splines and outer grooves in the clutch center (B, **Figure 50**), if damaged the clutch center should be replaced.

12. Inspect the clutch lifter rod for bending. Roll it on a surface plate such as a piece of plate glass. Honda does not provide service specifications for this component, but if the rod is bent or deformed

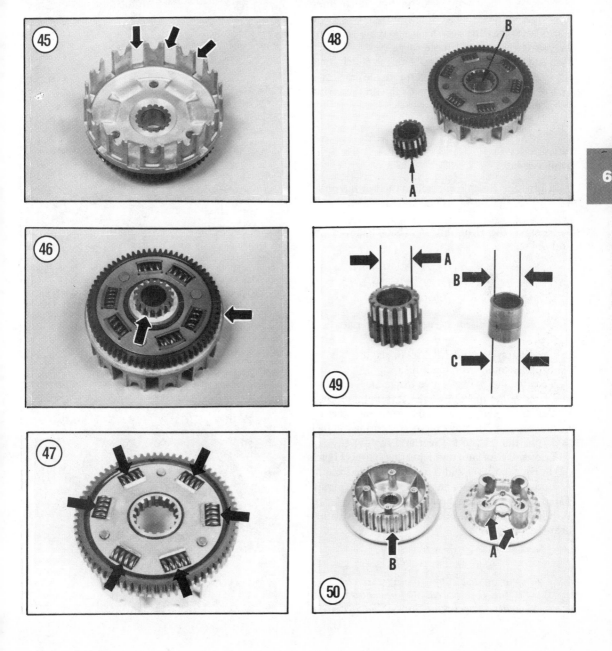

6

in any way it must be replaced. Otherwise it may hang up in the channel within the transmission shaft, causing erratic clutch operation.

13. Check the movement of the clutch lifter mechanism in the crankcase cover. If the arm binds or the return spring is weak or broken, it must be replaced. To remove the mechanism perform the following:

    a. Remove the clutch lifter from the lifter arm.

    b. Remove the spring pin (A, **Figure 51**) and withdraw the lifter arm (B, **Figure 51**) from the cover.

    c. Remove the spring.

    d. Inspect the O-ring seal on the clutch lifter mechanism; replace if necessary.

    e. Check that the return spring is not bent or broken, replace if necessary.

    f. Apply multipurpose grease to the clutch lifter mechanism and reinstall it into the crankcase cover. Secure the mechanism with the spring pin.

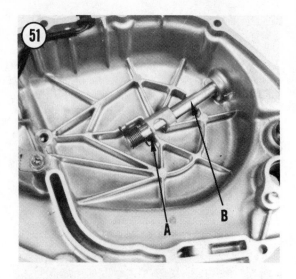

CLUTCH CABLE

Replacement

In time the clutch cable will stretch to the point where it is no longer useful and will have to be replaced.

1. Remove the right- and left-hand side covers and the seat.

> *CAUTION*
> *On XL250 and XL500S models, reinstall the seat strap bolts as they also hold the upper portion of the shock to the frame. Remove and reinstall one bolt at a time.*

2. On XL series models, disconnect the battery leads or disconnect the main fuse.

3. Turn the fuel shutoff valve to the OFF position and remove the fuel line to the carburetor.

4. Pull the fuel cap vent tube from the steering head receptacle. Remove the bolt securing the fuel tank, pull the tank to the rear and remove it.

5. Loosen the locknut and adjusting barrel (**Figure 52**) at the hand lever and remove the cable from it.

6. Loosen the locknut and adjusting nut (A, **Figure 53**) at the frame lower bracket.

7. Slip the cable end out of the clutch activating arm (B, **Figure 53**).

> *NOTE*
> *Prior to removing the cable, make a drawing of the cable routing through the frame. It is very easy to forget how it was, once it has been removed. Replace*

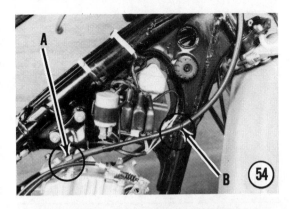

Figure 54

Figure 55

Figure 56

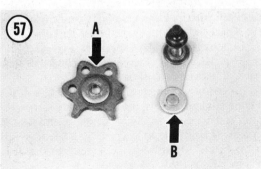

Figure 57

it exactly as it was, avoiding any sharp turns.

8. Pull the cable out of the retaining clip (A, **Figure 54**) on the cylinder head cover.

9. Pull the hand lever end of the cable from the handlebar/steering head area and out of the retaining loop on the frame (B, **Figure 54**).

10. Remove the cable and replace it with a new one.

11. Install by reversing these removal steps.

12. Adjust the clutch cable as described in Chapter Three.

EXTERNAL SHIFT MECHANISM (1983 XR350R, XR500R, XL600R)

The external shift mechanism is located on the same side of the crankcase as the clutch assembly. To remove the internal shift mechanism (shift lever, shift drum and shift forks), it is necessary to remove the engine and split the crankcase. This procedure is covered *Transmission and Internal Shift Mechanism* in this chapter.

Removal

1. Remove the clutch assembly described in this chapter.

2. Remove the kickstarter as described in Chapter Five.

NOTE
In the following steps the oil pump assembly is shown removed for clarity. It is not necessary to remove it but additional room is gained if the pump is removed.

3. Remove the bolts securing the oil line from the oil pump to the crankcase.

4. Remove the bolt (**Figure 55**) securing the shift drum stopper plate and remove the stopper plate.

5. Remove the bolt (**Figure 56**) securing the neutral stopper arm. Remove the neutral stopper arm and its return spring.

Inspection

1. Inspect the ramps of the shift drum stopper plate (A, **Figure 57**). They must be smooth and free from burrs or wear. Replace if necessary.

2. Inspect the roller on the neutral stopper arm (B, **Figure 57**). It must rotate freely with no signs of binding. Replace if necessary.

Installation

1. Install the neutral stopper arm and spring (**Figure 56**) onto the crankcase. Tighten the bolt securely.

6

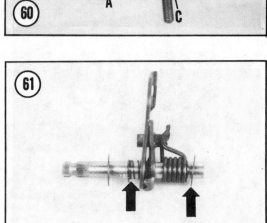

2. Hold the neutral stopper arm back out of the way with a screwdriver (A, **Figure 58**).

3. Align the hole in the backside of the shift drum stopper plate with the dowel pin on the shift drum. Install the shift drum stopper plate and bolt (B, **Figure 58**). Tighten the bolt securely.

4. Remove the screwdriver and index the stopper arm onto the shift drum stopper plate.

5. Install the oil line from the oil pump to the crankcase. Install and tighten the bolts securely.

6. Install the kickstarter as described in Chapter Five.

7. Install the clutch assembly as described in this chapter.

8. Refill the engine with the correct type and quantity of oil. Refer to Chapter Three.

9. Adjust the clutch as described in Chapter Three.

EXTERNAL SHIFT MECHANISM (ALL OTHER MODELS)

The external shift mechanism is located under the left-hand crankcase cover. Removal and installation can be accomplished with the engine in the frame. This procedure is shown with the engine removed for clarity. To remove the internal shift mechanism (shift lever, shift drum and shift forks), it is necessary to remove the engine and split the

crankcase. That procedure is covered under *Transmission and Internal Shift Mechanism* in this chapter.

Removal/Installation

1. Remove the alternator as described in Chapter Four.

CAUTION
On XL models shift the transmission into 1st gear. This will align the neutral indicator rotor with the open area of the shift plate. Do not damage this rotor during removal and installation.

2. Remove the thrust washer (A, **Figure 59**) and carefully withdraw the gearshift spindle assembly (B, **Figure 59**) and the inner thrust washer.

3. Unhook the shift pawl spring (A, **Figure 60**) and remove the bolt (B, **Figure 60**) securing the shift pawl. Remove the shift pawl.

4. If necessary, remove the stopper plate bolt (C, **Figure 60**) and remove the neutral indicator rotor.

5. If spindle disassembly is necessary, remove the circlips (**Figure 61**) at each end and remove all components. Assemble in the same order shown in **Figure 61**.

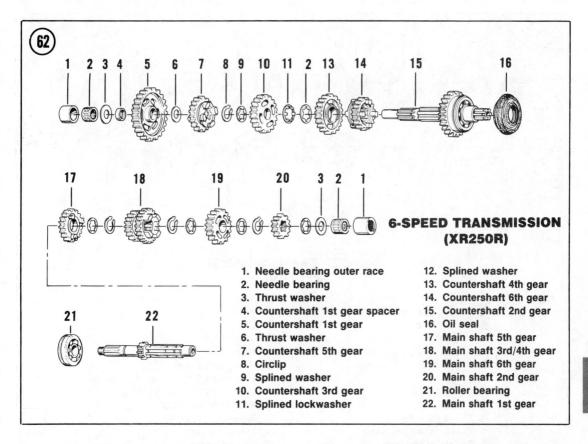

(62)

6-SPEED TRANSMISSION (XR250R)

1. Needle bearing outer race
2. Needle bearing
3. Thrust washer
4. Countershaft 1st gear spacer
5. Countershaft 1st gear
6. Thrust washer
7. Countershaft 5th gear
8. Circlip
9. Splined washer
10. Countershaft 3rd gear
11. Splined lockwasher
12. Splined washer
13. Countershaft 4th gear
14. Countershaft 6th gear
15. Countershaft 2nd gear
16. Oil seal
17. Main shaft 5th gear
18. Main shaft 3rd/4th gear
19. Main shaft 6th gear
20. Main shaft 2nd gear
21. Roller bearing
22. Main shaft 1st gear

6. Install by reversing these removal steps. Make sure the transmission is in 1st gear when installing the gearshift spindle. Slide the inner thrust washer onto the spindle assembly prior to installation.

TRANSMISSION

To gain access to the transmission and internal shift mechanism it is necessary to remove the engine and split the crankcase. Once the crankcase is split, removal of the transmission assemblies is a simple task of pulling the assemblies up and out of the crankcase. Installation is more complicated and is covered in more detail than the removal sequence.

Pay particular attention to the location of spacers, washers and bearings during disassembly. If disassembling a used, well run-in engine for the first time by yourself, pay particular attention to any additional shims that may have been added by a previous owner. These may have been added to take up the tolerance of worn components and must be reinstalled in the same position since the shims have developed a wear pattern. If new parts are going to be installed these shims may be eliminated. This is something you will have to determine upon reassembly.

There are 4 different transmissions used among the various models. Be sure to use the correct procedure for your specific bike.

Specifications for the transmission components are in **Table 2** at the end of the chapter.

6-SPEED TRANSMISSION (250 CC MODELS)

The transmission shown in **Figure 62** is used on the 1981-1982 XR250R. The transmission shown in **Figure 63** is used on the 1982-1983 XL250R.

These 2 transmission assemblies are basically identical except that bushings are used on the XL250R main shaft 5th and 6th gears.

Removal/Installation

1. Remove the engine and split the crankcase as described in Chapter Four.
2. Remove the countershaft assembly (A, **Figure 64**).
3. Remove the main shaft assembly (B, **Figure 64**).

NOTE
Prior to installation, coat all bearing surfaces with assembly oil.

6

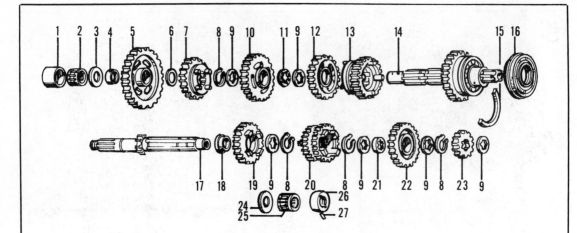

6-SPEED TRANSMISSION
(XL250R)

1. Needle bearing outer race
2. Needle bearing
3. Washer
4. Countershaft 1st gear bushing
5. Countershaft 1st gear
6. Washer
7. Countershaft 5th gear
8. Circlip
9. Splined washer
10. Countershaft 3rd gear
11. Splined lockwasher
12. Countershaft 4th gear
13. Countershaft 6th gear
14. Countershaft/2nd gear

15. 1/2 clip
16. Oil seal
17. Main shaft
18. Main shaft 5th gear bushing
19. Main shaft 5th gear
20. Main shaft 3rd/4th combination gear
21. Main shaft 6th gear bushing
22. Main shaft 6th gear
23. Main shaft 2nd gear
24. Thrust washer
25. Needle bearing
26. Needle bearing outer race
27. Pin

(63)

(64)

(65)

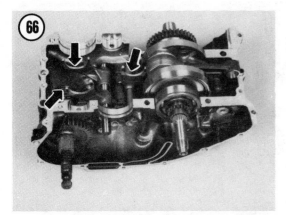

6

4. Turn the shift drum to the neutral position (**Figure 65**). This will correctly position the shift forks (**Figure 66**) to allow easy installation of the transmission shaft assemblies.

5. Install the 2 bearing set rings (A, **Figure 67**) and roller bearing outer race locating dowels (B, **Figure 67**) in the lower crankcase half.

NOTE
The locating dowel on the left-hand side is also an oil control orifice (Figure 68).

6. Install the main shaft assembly (**Figure 69**). Make sure that the shift fork properly engages with the groove in the gear and that the bearings are properly indexed into the set ring and oil control orifice.

7. Install the countershaft assembly (**Figure 70**). Make sure that the shift forks properly engage with the groove in the gears and that the bearings are properly indexed into the set ring and locating dowel.

CAUTION
The sealing ridge on the oil seal must be correctly seated into the groove (Figure 71) in the crankcase or the crankcase halves will not join and seat properly.

8. After both transmission assemblies have been installed, spin the transmission shafts and shift through the gears using the shift drum. Make sure you can shift into all gears. This is the time to find that something may be installed incorrectly—not after the crankcase is completely assembled.

9. Assemble the crankcase as described in Chapter Four.

Main Shaft Disassembly/ Inspection/Assembly

Refer to **Figure 62** or **Figure 63** during this procedure.

> *NOTE*
> *A helpful "tool" that should be used for transmission disassembly is a large egg flat (the type that restaurants get their eggs in). As you remove a part from the shaft set it in one of the depressions in the same position from which it was removed (**Figure 72**). This is an easy way to remember the correct relationship of all parts.*

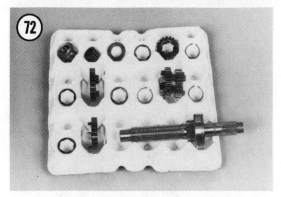

1. Place the assembled shaft into a large can or plastic bucket and thoroughly clean with solvent and a stiff brush. Dry with compressed air or let it sit on rags to drip dry.
2. Slide off the needle bearing outer race and the needle bearing.
3. Slide off the thrust washer, the splined washer and the 2nd gear.
4. Remove the circlip.
5A. On XR250R models, slide off the splined washer and the 6th gear.
5B. On XL250R models, slide off the splined washer, the 6th gear and the 6th gear bushing.
6. Slide off the splined washer and remove the circlip.
7. Slide off the 3rd/4th combination gear.
8. Remove the circlip and splined washer.
9A. On XR250R models, slide off the 5th gear.
9B. On XL250R models, slide off the 5th gear and 5th gear bushing.
10. If necessary remove the ball bearing (A, **Figure 73**) from the shaft.
11. Check each gear for excessive wear, burrs, pitting or chipped or missing teeth. Make sure the lugs on the gears are in good condition.

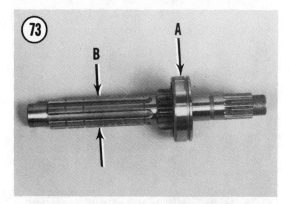

> *NOTE*
> *Defective gears should be replaced. It is a good idea to replace the mating gear on the countershaft even though it may not show as much wear or damage.*

> *NOTE*
> *The 1st gear is part of the shaft. If the gear is defective the shaft must be replaced.*

12. Make sure that all gears slide smoothly on the main shaft splines.
13. Measure the outside diameter of the main shaft (B, **Figure 73**). The shaft must be replaced if worn to less than the service limit listed in **Table 2**.

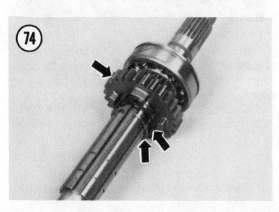

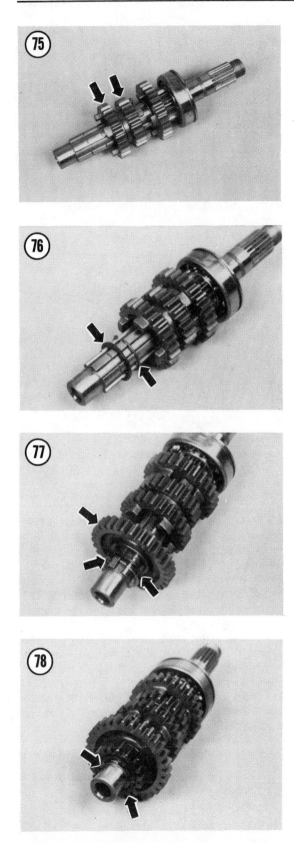

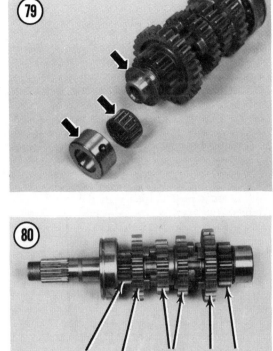

1st   5th   3rd/4th   6th   2nd

14. Check the condition of the ball bearing (A, **Figure 73**). Make sure it rotates smoothly with no signs of wear or damage. Replace if necessary.

NOTE
It is a good idea to replace all circlips every other time the transmission is disassembled to ensure proper gear alignment.

15A. On XR250R models, slide on the 5th gear and install the splined washer and circlip (**Figure 74**).
15B. On XL250R models, slide on the 5th gear bushing and the 5th gear. Install the splined washer and circlip.
16. Position the 3rd/4th combination gear with the smaller 3rd gear going on first. Slide on the 3rd/4th combination gear (**Figure 75**).
17. Install the circlip and the splined washer (**Figure 76**).
18. Install the 6th gear and the splined washer and circlip (**Figure 77**).
19. Slide on the 2nd gear and splined washer (**Figure 78**).
20. Slide on the thrust washer, needle bearing and needle bearing outer race (**Figure 79**).
21. After assembly is complete refer to **Figure 80** for the correct placement of all gears. Make sure all

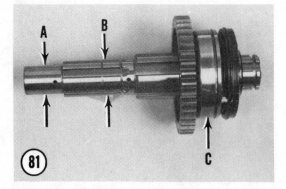

circlips are seated correctly in the main shaft grooves.

**Countershaft Disassembly/
Inspection/Assembly**

Refer to **Figure 62** or **Figure 63** during this procedure.

> *NOTE*
> *Use the same large egg flat (used on the main shaft disassembly) during the countershaft disassembly. This is an easy way to remember the correct relationship of all parts.*

1. Place the assembled shaft into a large can or plastic bucket and thoroughly clean with solvent and a stiff brush. Dry with compressed air or let it sit on rags to drip dry.
2. Slide off the needle bearing outer race and the needle bearing.
3. Slide off the thrust washer, 1st gear, the 1st gear bushing and the thrust washer.
4. Slide off the 5th gear.
5. Remove the circlip and splined washer and slide off the 3rd gear.
6. Slide off the splined lockwasher. Rotate the splined washer in either direction to disengage the tangs from the raised splines on the transmission shaft. Slide off the splined washer.
7. Slide off the 4th gear.
8. Slide off the 6th gear.
9. Check each gear for excessive wear, burrs, pitting or chipped or missing teeth. Make sure the lugs on the gears are in good condition.

> *NOTE*
> *Defective gears should be replaced. It is a good idea to replace the mating gear on the main shaft even though it may not show as much wear or damage.*

> *NOTE*
> *The 2nd gear is part of the shaft. If the gear is defective the shaft must be replaced.*

10. Make sure that all gears slide smoothly on the countershaft splines.
11. Measure the outside diameter of the countershaft at points "A" and "B" shown in **Figure 81**. The shaft must be replaced if worn to less than the service limit listed in **Table 2**. The clearance limit between any gear and the shaft is 0.006 in. (0.15 mm).
12. Measure the inside diameter (ID) and the outside diameter (OD) of the 1st gear spacer. If worn to the service listed in **Table 2** the spacer must be replaced.
13. Check the ball bearing (C, **Figure 81**). Make sure it rotates smoothly with no signs of wear or damage. Replace if necessary.

> *NOTE*
> *It is a good idea to replace the circlip every other time the transmission is disassembled to ensure proper gear alignment.*

14. Slide on the 6th gear (**Figure 82**).

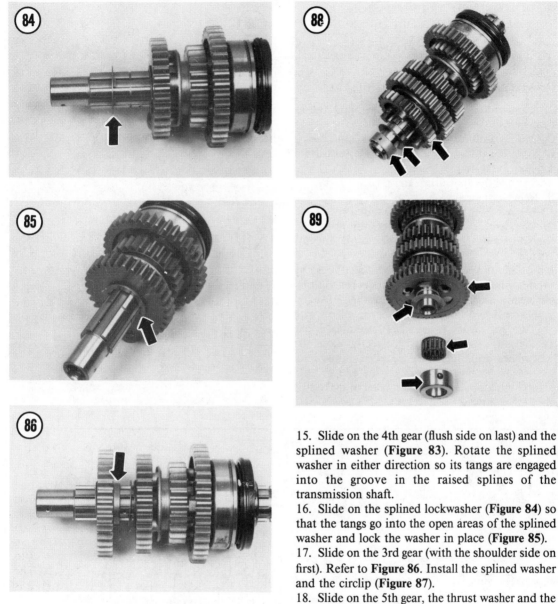

15. Slide on the 4th gear (flush side on last) and the splined washer (**Figure 83**). Rotate the splined washer in either direction so its tangs are engaged into the groove in the raised splines of the transmission shaft.

16. Slide on the splined lockwasher (**Figure 84**) so that the tangs go into the open areas of the splined washer and lock the washer in place (**Figure 85**).

17. Slide on the 3rd gear (with the shoulder side on first). Refer to **Figure 86**. Install the splined washer and the circlip (**Figure 87**).

18. Slide on the 5th gear, the thrust washer and the 1st gear spacer (**Figure 88**).

19. Slide on the 1st gear (flush side on last), thrust washer, needle bearing and needle bearing outer race (**Figure 89**).

20. After assembly is complete refer to **Figure 90** for the correct placement of all gears. Make sure the circlip is seated correctly in the countershaft groove.

21. After both transmission shafts have been assembled, mesh the 2 assemblies together in the correct position (**Figure 91**). Check that all gears meet correctly. This is your last check prior to installing the assemblies into the crankcase; make sure they are correctly assembled.

6-SPEED TRANSMISSION
(350 CC MODELS)

The transmission shown in **Figure 92** is used on the 1983 XR350R.

Removal/Installation

1. Remove the engine and split the crankcase as described in Chapter Five.
2. Pull the shift fork shaft out of the crankcase.
3. Pivot the shift forks away from the shift drum to allow for shift drum removal.
4. Remove the shift drum and the shift forks.
5. Remove the gearshift assembly.
6. Remove both transmission assemblies.
7. Disassemble and inspect the shift forks and transmission assemblies as described in this chapter.
8. Install the 2 transmission assemblies by meshing them together in their proper relationship to each other. Install them in the left-hand crankcase. Hold the thrust washer in place, with your fingers, on the countershaft assembly. Make sure it is still positioned correctly after the assemblies are completely installed. After both assemblies are installed, tap on the end of both shafts with a plastic or rubber mallet to make sure they are completely seated.

1st   5th   3rd   4th   6th   2nd

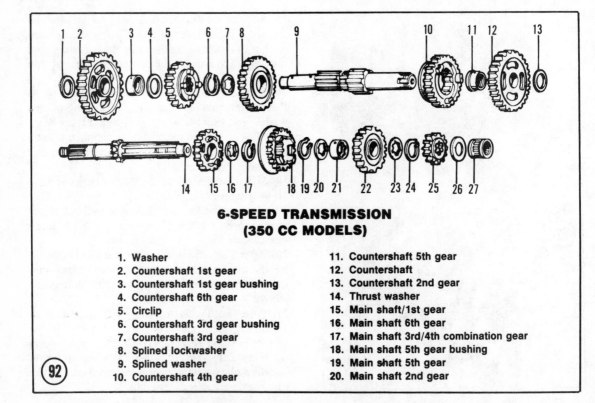

6-SPEED TRANSMISSION
(350 CC MODELS)

1. Washer
2. Countershaft 1st gear
3. Countershaft 1st gear bushing
4. Countershaft 6th gear
5. Circlip
6. Countershaft 3rd gear bushing
7. Countershaft 3rd gear
8. Splined lockwasher
9. Splined washer
10. Countershaft 4th gear
11. Countershaft 5th gear
12. Countershaft
13. Countershaft 2nd gear
14. Thrust washer
15. Main shaft/1st gear
16. Main shaft 6th gear
17. Main shaft 3rd/4th combination gear
18. Main shaft 5th gear bushing
19. Main shaft 5th gear
20. Main shaft 2nd gear

NOTE
If the thrust washer on the end of the transmission shaft is not seated correctly it will hold the transmission shaft up a little and prevent the crankcase halves from seating completely.

9. Install the gearshift assembly with the splined end (for the gearshift pedal) into the left-hand crankcase half.
10. Each shift fork is marked with either an "R" (right-hand side), "C" (center) or "L" (left-hand side). Install the shift forks with these marks facing *down* toward the left-hand crankcase half.
11. Install the shift forks in this sequence—"L," "C" and then "R." Engage the shift forks into the grooves in the gears but do not insert the shift fork shaft(s).
12. Coat all bearing and sliding surfaces of the shift drum with assembly oil and install the shift drum. Make sure it engages properly with the gearshift assembly.
13. Pivot each shift fork into mesh with the shift drum.
14. Install the shift fork shaft.
15. Make sure all 3 cam pin followers are in mesh with the shift drum grooves.
16. Spin the transmission shafts and shift through the gears using the shift drum. Make sure you can shift into all gears. This is the time to find that something may be installed incorrectly—not after the crankcase is completely assembled.

NOTE
This procedure is best done with the aid of a helper as the assemblies are loose and won't spin very easily. Have the helper spin the transmission shaft while you turn the shift drum through all the gears.

17. Make sure that the thrust washer is installed on the countershaft.

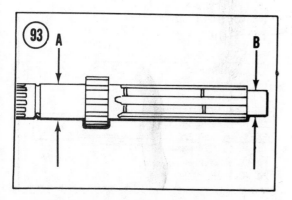

Main Shaft Disassembly/ Inspection/Assembly

Refer to **Figure 92** for this procedure.

NOTE
A helpful "tool" that should be used for transmission disassembly is a large egg flat (the type that restaurants get their eggs in). As you remove a part from the shaft set it in one of the depressions in the same position from which it was removed. This is an easy way to remember the correct relationship of all parts.

1. Place the assembled shaft into a large can or plastic bucket and thoroughly clean with solvent and a stiff brush. Dry with compressed air or let it sit on rags to drip dry.
2. Slide off the 2nd gear, the 5th gear and the 5th gear bushing.
3. Slide off the splined washer and remove the circlip.
4. Slide off the 3rd/4th combination gear.
5. Remove the circlip and splined washer.
6. Slide off the 6th gear.
7. Check each gear for excessive wear, burrs, pitting or chipped or missing teeth. Make sure the lugs on the gears are in good condition.

CAUTION
Defective gears should be replaced. It is a good idea to replace the mating gear on the countershaft even though it may not show as much wear or damage.

NOTE
The 1st gear is part of the shaft. If the gear is defective the shaft must be replaced.

8. Make sure that all gears slide smoothly on the main shaft splines.
9. Measure the outside diameter of the main shaft at locations "A" and "B" as shown in **Figure 93**. Refer to dimensions listed in **Table 2** for this specific model. If the shaft is worn to less than the service limit, the shaft must be replaced.
10. Measure the inside diameter of the main shaft 5th gear. Refer to dimensions listed in **Table 2** for this specific model. If the gear is worn to the service limit, the gear must be replaced.

NOTE
It is a good idea to replace all circlips every other time the transmission is disassembled to ensure proper gear alignment.

11. Slide on the 6th gear and install the splined washer and circlip.

12. Position the 3rd/4th combination gear with the smaller diameter gear side on first. Slide on the 3rd/4th combination gear and install the circlip and splined washer.

13. Slide on the 5th gear and 5th gear bushing.

14. Slide on the 2nd gear.

15. Make sure all circlips are seated correctly in the main shaft grooves.

Countershaft Disassembly/ Inspection/Assembly

Refer to **Figure 92** for this procedure.

NOTE
Use the same large egg flat (used on the main shaft disassembly) during the countershaft disassembly. This is an easy way to remember the correct relationship of all parts.

1. Place the assembled shaft into a large can or plastic bucket and thoroughly clean with solvent and a stiff brush. Dry with compressed air or let it sit on rags to drip dry.

2. Slide off the thrust washer and the 2nd gear.

3. From the other end of the shaft, slide off the thrust washer, the 1st gear and 1st gear bushing.

4. Slide off the 6th gear.

5. Remove the circlip and slide off the 3rd gear and 3rd gear bushing.

6. Remove the splined lockwasher. Rotate the splined washer in either direction to disengage the tangs from the raised splines on the transmission shaft. Slide off the splined washer.

7. Slide off the 4th gear.

8. Slide off the 5th gear.

9. Check each gear for excessive wear, burrs, pitting or chipped or missing teeth. Make sure the lugs on the gears are in good condition.

CAUTION
Defective gears should be replaced. It is a good idea to replace the mating gear on the main shaft even though it may not show as much wear or damage.

10. Make sure that all gears slide smoothly on the countershaft splines.

11. Measure the outside diameter of the countershaft at locations "C" and "D" as shown in **Figure 94**. Refer to dimensions listed in **Table 2** for this specific model. If the shaft is worn to less than the service limit, the shaft must be replaced.

12. Measure the inside diameter of the countershaft 1st, 2nd, 3rd and 4th gears. Refer to

dimensions listed in **Table 2** for your specific model. If the gear is worn to the service limit, the gear must be replaced.

NOTE
It is a good idea to replace the circlip every other time the transmission is disassembled to ensure proper gear alignment.

13. Slide on the 5th gear.

14. Slide on the 4th gear and install the splined washer. Rotate the splined washer in either direction so its tangs are engaged into the groove in the raised splines of the transmission shaft.

15. Slide on the splined lockwasher so that the tangs go into the open areas of the splined washer and lock the washer in place.

15. Slide on the 3rd gear (flush side on first) and the 3rd gear bushing.

16. Install the circlip.

17. Slide on the 6th gear.

18. Slide on the 1st gear bushing.

19. Slide on the 1st gear (flush side on last) and thrust washer.

20. Onto the other side of the shaft, slide on the 2nd gear (flush side on last) and the thrust washer.

21. Make sure the circlip is seated correctly in the countershaft groove.

NOTE
After both transmission shafts have been assembled, mesh the 2 assemblies together in the correct position. Check that all gears meet correctly. This is your last check prior to installing the assemblies into the crankcase; make sure they are correctly assembled.

5-SPEED TRANSMISSION (1978-1982)

The 5-speed transmission shown in **Figure 95** is used on the following models:
a. 1978-1981 XL250S.
b. 1979-1980 XR250.
c. 1979-1981 XL500S.
d. 1981-1982 XL500R.
e. 1979-1980 XR500.
f. 1981-1982 XR500R.

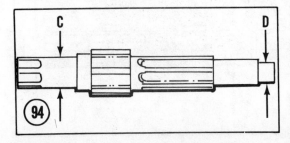

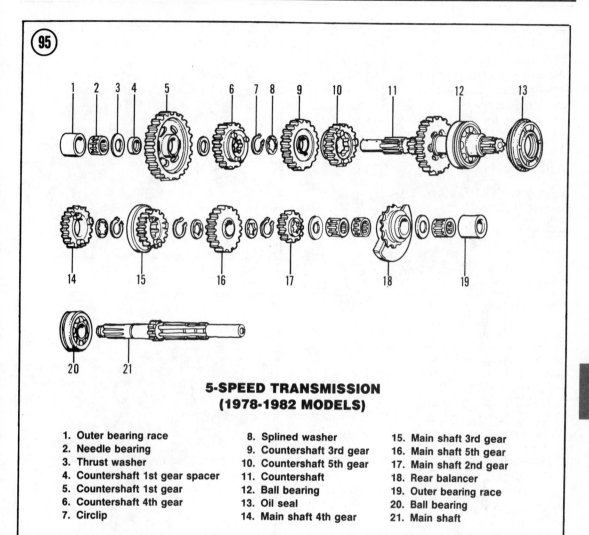

**5-SPEED TRANSMISSION
(1978-1982 MODELS)**

1. Outer bearing race
2. Needle bearing
3. Thrust washer
4. Countershaft 1st gear spacer
5. Countershaft 1st gear
6. Countershaft 4th gear
7. Circlip
8. Splined washer
9. Countershaft 3rd gear
10. Countershaft 5th gear
11. Countershaft
12. Ball bearing
13. Oil seal
14. Main shaft 4th gear
15. Main shaft 3rd gear
16. Main shaft 5th gear
17. Main shaft 2nd gear
18. Rear balancer
19. Outer bearing race
20. Ball bearing
21. Main shaft

6

Removal/Installation

1. Remove the engine and disassemble the crankcase as described in Chapter Four.
2. Remove the main shaft assembly (A, **Figure 96**) and countershaft assembly (B, **Figure 96**).
3. Install by reversing these steps, noting the following.

> *NOTE*
> *Prior to installation, coat all bearing surfaces with assembly oil.*

4. Position the shift forks as shown in A, **Figure 97**.
5. Install the 2 bearing set rings (B, **Figure 97**) and bearing locating dowel (C, **Figure 97**) in the lower crankcase half.

6. Engage the balancer chain onto the sprocket on the left-hand end of the main shaft assembly and install it (**Figure 98**).

NOTE
Make sure the shift fork engages properly and that the bearings are properly indexed into the set ring and oil control orifice on the left-hand side.

7. Install the countershaft assembly (**Figure 99**).

NOTE
*Make sure the shift forks engage properly and that the bearings are properly indexed into the set ring and locating dowel. The sealing ridge on the oil seal must be correctly seated into the groove (A, **Figure 99**) or the crankcase halves will not join properly.*

NOTE
When a new oil seal is installed, apply a light coat of grease to the lips prior to installation.

8. After both transmission assemblies are installed, rotate both by hand. Make sure there is no binding. Also shift through all 5 gears to make sure the shift forks are operating properly and that the transmission gears are properly installed on their respective shafts.
9. Reassembly the crankcase as described in Chapter Four.

**Main Shaft Disassembly/
Inspection/Assembly**

Refer to **Figure 95** for this procedure.

1. Remove the outer bearing race, needle bearing and thrust washer (1, **Figure 100**).
2. Remove the rear balancer weight (2).
3. On XL250S and XR250 models, remove the 2 roller bearings.
4. On XL500S, XL500R and XR500 models, remove the spacer, needle bearing and washer (3).
5. Slide off 2nd gear (4).
6. Remove the circlip and splined washer and slide off 5th gear (5).
7. Remove the splined washer and circlip and slide off 3rd gear (6).
8. Remove the circlip and splined washer and slide off 4th gear (7).
9. If necessary, remove the ball bearing from the shaft (**Figure 101**).
10. Clean all parts in cleaning solvent and thoroughly dry.

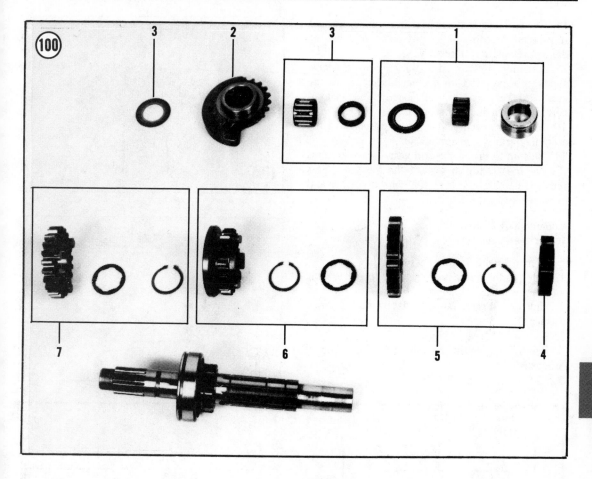

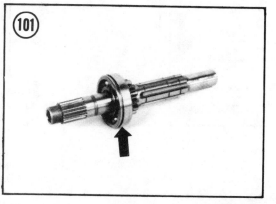

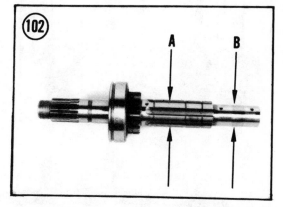

11. Check each gear for excessive wear, burrs, pitting or chipped or missing teeth. Make sure the lugs on ends of gears are in good condition.

NOTE
Defective gears should be replaced. It is a good idea to replace the mating gear on the countershaft even though it may not show as much wear or damage.

12. Make sure all gears slide smoothly on the main shaft splines.

13. Measure the outside diameter of the main shaft at points "A" and "B." Refer to **Figure 102**. The service limit for all models is listed in **Table 2**.

If the dimension anywhere within both areas is this dimension or less, the shaft must be replaced. The clearance limit between any gear and shaft is 0.006 in. (0.15 mm).

14. Check the condition of the bearing. Make sure it rotates smoothly with not signs of wear or damage. Replace if necessary.

15. Assemble by reversing these removal steps. Refer to **Figure 103** for correct placement of the gears. Make sure that all circlips are seated correctly in the main shaft grooves.

16. Make sure each gear engages properly to the adjoining gear where applicable.

17. Be sure to install the 2nd gear with the recess (**Figure 104**) facing in toward the 5th gear. This recess is necessary to clear the splined washer and circlip securing the 5th gear.

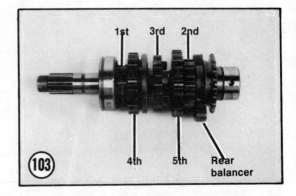

Countershaft Disassembly/ Inspection/Assembly

Refer to **Figure 95** for this procedure.

1. Remove the outer bearing race, needle bearing and thrust washer (1, **Figure 105**).

2. Slide off 1st gear, 1st gear spacer and the thrust washer (2).

3. Slide off 4th gear (3).

4. Remove the circlip and splined washer; slide off 3rd gear (4).

5. Slide off 5th gear (5).

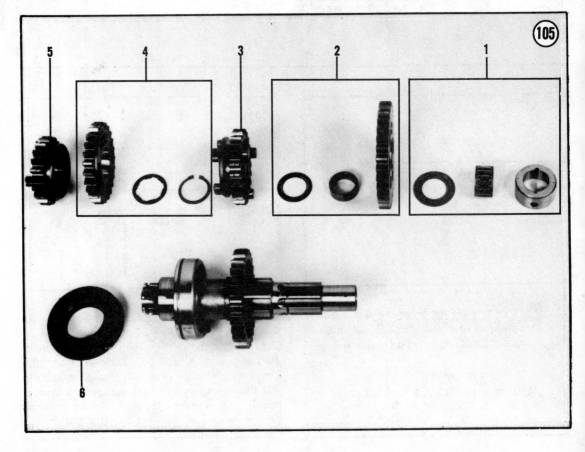

6. Remove 2nd gear and/or the ball bearing if necessary (**Figure 106**).

> *NOTE*
> *These 2 components are pressed into place on the countershaft and removal should be entrusted to a Honda dealer or machine shop.*

7. Carefully slide off the oil seal (6).
8. Clean all parts in solvent and thoroughly dry.
9. Check each gear for excessive wear, burrs, pitting or chipped or missing teeth. Make sure the lugs on ends of gear are in good condition.

> *NOTE*
> *Defective gear should be replaced. It is a good idea to replace the mating gear on the main shaft even though it may not show signs of wear or damage.*

10. Make sure all gears slide smoothly on the countershaft splines.
11. Measure the outside diameter of the countershaft at points "A," "B" and "C." Refer to **Figure 107**. The service limit is listed in **Table 2**.

If the dimension anywhere within any of these areas is this dimension or less, the shaft must be replaced. The clearance limit between any gear and shaft is 0.006 in. (0.15 mm).

12. Measure the inside diameter (ID) and outside diameter (OD) of the 1st gear spacer. The service limits are listed in **Table 2**.

If either dimension is to this service limit the spacer must be replaced.

13. Check the condition of the bearing. Make sure it rotates smoothly with no signs of wear or damage. Replace it if necessary.

14. Assemble by reversing these removal steps. Refer to **Figure 108** for correct placement of the gears. Make sure all circlips are seated correctly in the countershaft grooves.

15. Make sure each gear engages properly to the adjoining gear where applicable.

5-SPEED TRANSMISSION (1983)

The transmission shown in (**Figure 109**) is used on the following models:

   a. 1983 XR500R.
   b. 1983 XL600R.

Removal/Installation

1. Remove the engine and split the crankcase as described in Chapter Five.
2. Pull back on the gear shift plate of the gearshift mechanism to disengage it from the shift drum. Remove the gearshift assembly.
3. Bend down the locking tab on the lockwasher and remove the bolt and lockwasher securing the center shift fork to the shift fork shaft. Discard the lockwasher (never reuse an old lockwasher).

6

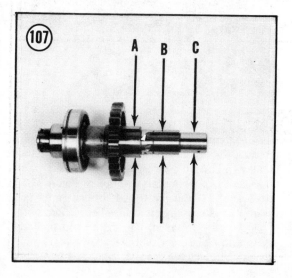

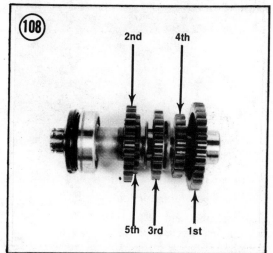

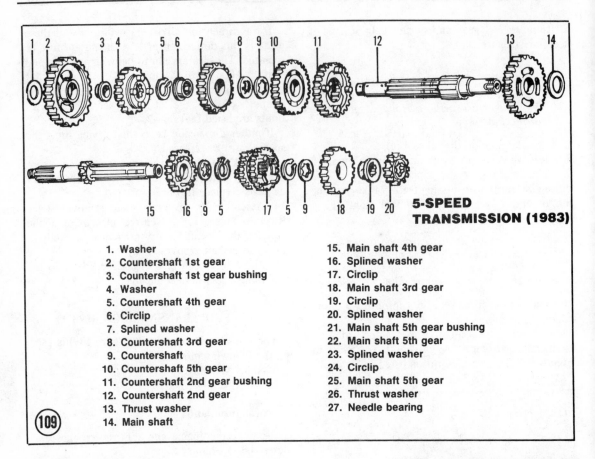

5-SPEED TRANSMISSION (1983)

1. Washer
2. Countershaft 1st gear
3. Countershaft 1st gear bushing
4. Washer
5. Countershaft 4th gear
6. Circlip
7. Splined washer
8. Countershaft 3rd gear
9. Countershaft
10. Countershaft 5th gear
11. Countershaft 2nd gear bushing
12. Countershaft 2nd gear
13. Thrust washer
14. Main shaft
15. Main shaft 4th gear
16. Splined washer
17. Circlip
18. Main shaft 3rd gear
19. Circlip
20. Splined washer
21. Main shaft 5th gear bushing
22. Main shaft 5th gear
23. Splined washer
24. Circlip
25. Main shaft 5th gear
26. Thrust washer
27. Needle bearing

4. Pull the shift fork shaft out of the crankcase.

5. Pivot the shift forks away from the shift drum to allow room for shift drum removal.

6. Remove the shift drum and the shift forks.

7. Remove both transmission assemblies.

8. Disassemble and inspect the shift forks and transmission assemblies as described in this chapter.

9. Install the 2 transmission assemblies by meshing them together in their proper relationship to each other. Install them in the left-hand crankcase. Hold the thrust washers in place, with your fingers, on both shaft assemblies (**Figure 110**). Make sure it is still positioned correctly after the assemblies are completely installed. After both assemblies are installed, tap on the end of both shafts with a plastic or rubber mallet to make sure they are completely seated.

NOTE
If the thrust washer on the end of the transmission shaft is not seated correctly it will hold the transmission shaft up a little and prevent the crankcase halves from seating completely.

10. Coat all bearing and sliding surfaces of the shift drum with assembly oil and install the shift drum (**Figure 111**).

11. Install the left-hand shift fork (**Figure 112**), center shift fork (**Figure 113**) and the right-hand shift fork (**Figure 114**). Make sure each shift fork is engaged in its respective gear and that all 3 cam pin followers are in mesh with the shift drum grooves.

12. Align the bolt hole in the shift fork shaft and the hole in the center shift fork and install the shift fork (A, **Figure 115**).

13. Install the shift fork shaft bolt and lockwasher (B, **Figure 115**) and tighten to 9-12 ft.-lb. (13-17 N•m).

14. Bend up one of the tabs on the new lockwasher onto the bolt.

15. Partially install the gearshift assembly with the splined end (for the gearshift pedal) into the left-hand crankcase half. Pull back on the shift plate and push the shift mechanism all the way down into position. Release the shift plate and engage it correctly into the shift drum (**Figure 116**).

16. Spin the transmission shafts and shift through the gears using the shift drum. Make sure you can shift into all gears. This is the time to find that something may be installed incorrectly—not after the crankcase is completely assembled.

NOTE
This procedure is best done with the aid of a helper as the assemblies are loose and won't spin very easily. Have the helper spin the transmission shaft while you turn the shift drum through all the gears.

6

17. Make sure that the thrust washer is installed on the countershaft.

Main Shaft Disassembly/ Inspection/Assembly

Refer to **Figure 109** for this procedure.

> *NOTE*
> *A helpful "tool" that should be used for transmission disassembly is a large egg flat (the type that restaurants get their eggs in). As you remove a part from the shaft set it in one of the depressions in the same position from which it was removed (Figure 117). This is an easy way to remember the correct relationship of all parts.*

1. Place the assembled shaft into a large can or plastic bucket and thoroughly clean with solvent and a stiff brush. Dry with compressed air or let it sit on rags to drip dry.
2. Slide off the needle bearing and thrust washer.
3. Slide off the 2nd gear.
4. Remove the circlip and slide off the splined washer.
5. Slide off the 5th gear and the 5th gear bushing.
6. Slide off the splined washer and remove the circlip.
7. Slide off the 3rd gear.
8. Remove the circlip and splined washer.
9. Slide off the 4th gear.
10. Check each gear for excessive wear, burrs, pitting or chipped or missing teeth. Make sure the lugs on the gears are in good condition.

> *CAUTION*
> *Defective gears should be replaced. It is a good idea to replace the mating gear on the countershaft even though it may not show as much wear or damage.*

> *NOTE*
> *The 1st gear is part of the shaft. If the gear is defective the shaft must be replaced.*

11. Make sure that all gears slide smoothly on the main shaft splines.
12. Measure the outside diameter of the main shaft at location "A" as shown in **Figure 118**. Refer to dimensions listed in **Table 2** for your specific model. If the shaft is worn to the service limit, the shaft must be replaced.
13. Measure the inside diameter of the main shaft 4th and 5th gear. Refer to dimensions listed in **Table 2** for your specific model. If the gear is worn to the service limit, the gear must be replaced.

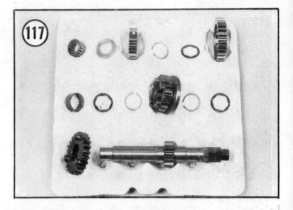

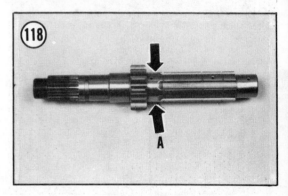

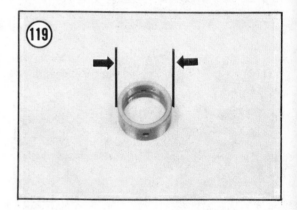

14. Measure the outside diameter of the main shaft 5th gear bushing (**Figure 119**). Refer to dimensions listed in **Table 2** for your specific model. If the gear is worn to the service limit, the gear must be replaced.

> *NOTE*
> *It is a good idea to replace all circlips every other time the transmission is disassembled to ensure proper gear alignment.*

15. Slide on the 4th gear and install the splined washer and circlip (**Figure 120**).

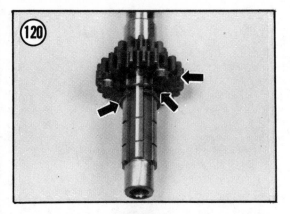

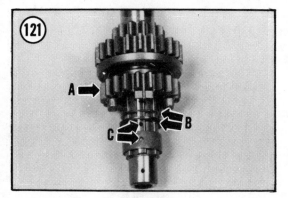

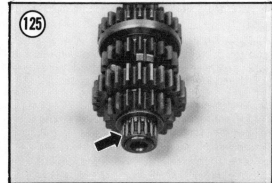

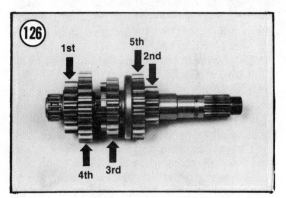

6

16. Slide on the 3rd gear (A, **Figure 121**) and install the circlip and splined washer (B, **Figure 121**).

17. Align the oil hole in the 5th gear bushing (C, **Figure 121**) with the oil hole in the main shaft and slide on the bushing.

18. Install the 5th gear and the splined washer (**Figure 122**).

19. Install the circlip (**Figure 123**).

20. Slide on the thrust washer (**Figure 124**) and needle bearing (**Figure 125**).

21. After assembly is complete, refer to **Figure 126** for the correct placement of all gears. Make sure all

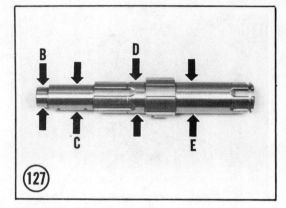

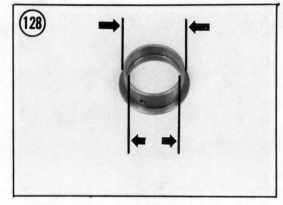

circlips are seated correctly in the main shaft grooves.

Countershaft Disassembly/Inspection/Assembly

Refer to **Figure 109** for this procedure.

> *NOTE*
> *Use the same large egg flat (used on the main shaft disassembly) during the countershaft disassembly. This is an easy way to remember the correct relationship of all parts.*

1. Place the assembled shaft into a large can or plastic bucket and thoroughly clean with solvent and a stiff brush. Dry with compressed air or let it sit on rags to drip dry.
2. Slide off the thrust washer, the 2nd gear and the 2nd gear bushing.
3. Slide off the 5th gear.
4. From the other end of the shaft, slide off the thrust washer, the 1st gear and 1st gear bushing.
5. Slide off the thrust washer and the 4th gear.
6. Remove the circlip and slide off splined washer and the 3rd gear.
7. Check each gear for excessive wear, burrs, pitting or chipped or missing teeth. Make sure the lugs on the gears are in good condition.

> *CAUTION*
> *Defective gears should be replaced. It is a good idea to replace the mating gear on the main shaft even though it may not show as much wear or damage.*

8. Make sure that all gears slide smoothly on the countershaft splines.
9. Measure the outside diameter of the countershaft at locations "B," "C," "D" and "E" as shown in **Figure 127**. Refer to dimensions listed in **Table 2** for your specific model. If the shaft is worn to the service limit, the shaft must be replaced.

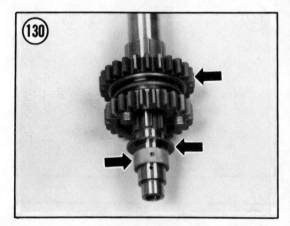

10. Measure the inside diameter of the countershaft 1st, 2nd and 3rd gears. Refer to dimensions listed in **Table 2** for your specific model. If the gear is worn to the service limit, the gear must be replaced.
11. Measure the inside and outside diameter of the countershaft 1st and 2nd gear bushings (**Figure 128**). Refer to dimensions listed in **Table 2** for your specific model. If the bushing is worn to the service limit, the bushing must be replaced.

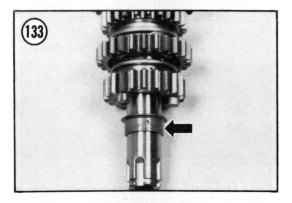

NOTE
It is a good idea to replace the circlip every other time the transmission is disassembled to ensure proper gear alignment.

12. Slide on the 3rd gear (flush side on first), splined washer and circlip (**Figure 129**).
13. Slide on the 4th gear, thrust washer and the 1st gear bushing (**Figure 130**).
14. Install the 1st gear (with the higher boss side on first) and the thrust washer (**Figure 131**).
15. Onto the other end of the shaft, install the 5th gear (**Figure 132**).
16. Slide on the 2nd gear bushing (**Figure 133**).
17. Install the 2nd gear (with the higher boss side on first) and thrust washer (**Figure 134**).
18. After assembly is complete, refer to **Figure 135** for the correct placement of all gears. Make sure all circlips are seated correctly in the shaft grooves.
19. After both transmission shafts have been assembled, mesh the 2 assemblies together in the correct position (**Figure 136**). Check that all gears meet correctly. This is your last check prior to installing the assemblies into the crankcase; make sure they are correctly assembled.

INTERNAL SHIFT MECHANISM
(1983 350-600 CC MODELS)

Removal and installation is described under transmission removal/installation in this chapter.

Inspection

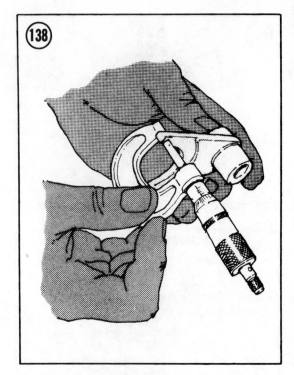

NOTE
Prior to removal or disassembly of any of the components, lay the assembly down on a piece of paper or cardboard and carefully trace around it. Write down the identifying numbers and letters next to the item. This will take a little extra time now but it may save some time and frustration later.

1. Inspect each shift fork for signs of wear or cracking. Check for bending and make sure the end shift forks slide smoothly on the shaft. Replace any worn or damaged forks.
2. Check for any arc-shaped wear or burned marks on the shift forks. This indicates that the shift fork has come in contact with the gear. The fork fingers have become excessively worn and the fork must be replaced.
3. Measure the inside diameter of each shift fork with an inside micrometer or snap gauge (**Figure 137**). Replace any that are worn to the service limit listed in **Table 3**.
4. Measure the width of the gearshift fork fingers with a micrometer (**Figure 138**). Replace any that are worn to the service limit listed in **Table 3**.
5. Check the shift drum dowel pin (**Figure 139**) on each shift fork for wear or damage; replace the shift fork as necessary.

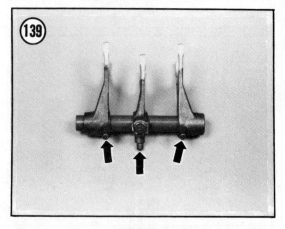

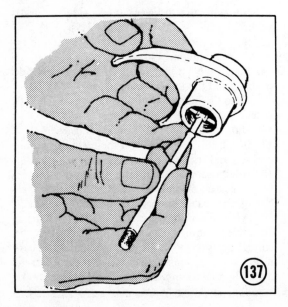

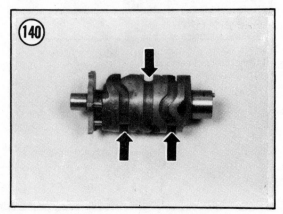

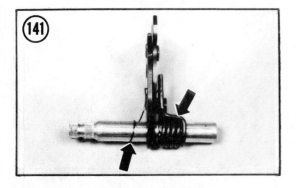

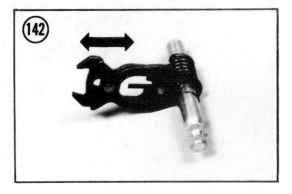

6. Roll the shift fork shaft on a flat surface such as a piece of plate glass and check for any bends. If the shaft is bent, it must be replaced.

7. Measure the outside diameter of the shift fork shaft with a micrometer. Replace if worn to the service limit listed in **Table 3**.

8. Check the grooves in the shift drum (**Figure 140**) for wear or roughness. If any of the groove profiles have excessive wear or damage, replace the shift drum.

9. Apply a light coat of oil to the shift fork shafts and the inside bores of the shift forks prior to installation.

10. Inspect the shift mechanism for wear or damage. Make sure the return springs (**Figure 141**) have not sagged or broken. Replace if necessary.

11. Move the shift plate back and forth (**Figure 142**). It must move freely with no binding. Replace the shift mechanism if necessary.

INTERNAL SHIFT MECHANISM (ALL OTHER MODELS)

Refer to **Figure 143** and **Figure 144** for this procedure. Refer to **Table 3** for shift drum, forks and shaft specifications.

6

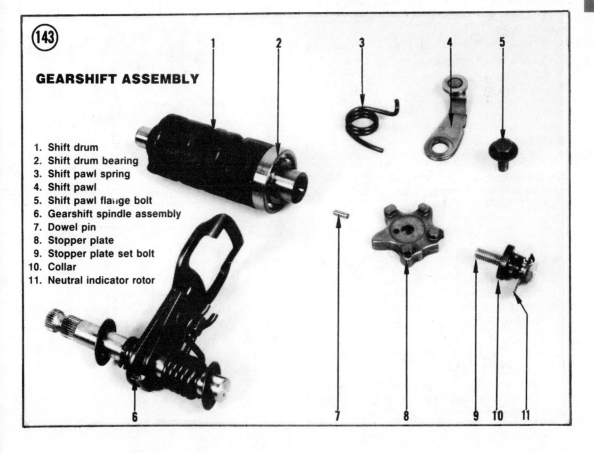

GEARSHIFT ASSEMBLY

1. Shift drum
2. Shift drum bearing
3. Shift pawl spring
4. Shift pawl
5. Shift pawl flange bolt
6. Gearshift spindle assembly
7. Dowel pin
8. Stopper plate
9. Stopper plate set bolt
10. Collar
11. Neutral indicator rotor

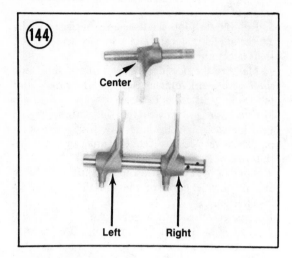

Center

Left   Right

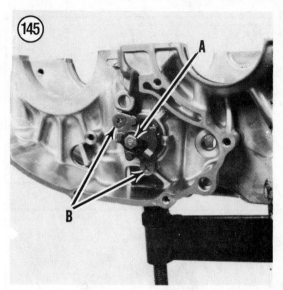

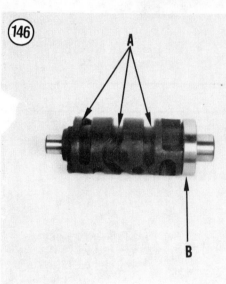

Removal/Disassembly

1. Remove the external shifting mechanism as described in this chapter.
2. Perform Steps 1 and 2 of *Transmission Removal/Installation* for your specific model in this chapter.
3. Withdraw the shift fork shafts, one at a time, from the right-hand side. Remove the shift forks.
4. Remove the bolt (A, **Figure 145**) securing the neutral indicator rotor, collar and stopper plate and remove them.
5. Remove the 2 screws (B, **Figure 145**) securing the bearing set plate and remove the plate.
6. Carefully withdraw the shift drum from the left-hand side.
7. Wash all parts in solvent and thoroughly dry.

Inspection

1. Inspect each shift fork for signs of wear of cracking. Make sure the forks slide smoothly on their respective shafts. Make sure the shafts are not bent.

> *NOTE*
> *Check for any arc-shaped wear or burned marks on the shift forks. If this is apparent, the shift fork has come in contact with the gear, indicating that the fingers are worn beyond use and fork must be replaced.*

2. Check grooves in the shift drum (A, **Figure 146**) for wear or roughness.
3. Check the shift drum bearing (B, **Figure 146**). Make sure it operates smoothly with no signs of wear or damage.

4. Check the cam pin follower in each shift fork. It should fit snugly but not be too tight. Check the end that rides in the shift drum for wear or burrs. Replace as necessary.
5. Check the stopper plate for wear; replace as necessary.
6. Measure the inside diameter of the shift forks with an inside micrometer (**Figure 137**). Replace the ones worn beyond the wear limits given in **Table 3**.
7. Measure the width of the gearshift fork fingers with a micrometer (**Figure 138**). Replace the ones that are worn beyond the wear limit given in **Table 3**.

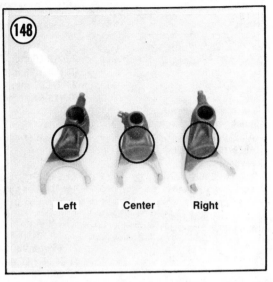

8. Measure the outside diameter of the shift fork shafts with a micrometer. Replace the ones worn beyond the wear limits given in **Table 3**.

Assembly/Installation

1. Coat all bearing surfaces with assembly oil.
2. Install the shift drum from the left-hand side and install the bearing set plate as shown in **Figure 145**. Tighten the screws to 7-9 ft.-lb. (9-13 N•m).

NOTE
After installing the shift drum, make sure it rotates smoothly with no binding.

3. Align the dowel pin in the stopper plate with the notch on the end of the shift drum and install it. Install the collar, neutral indicator rotor and stopper plate set bolt. Tighten the bolt securely.

4. Install the right- and left-hand shift forks and rear shaft (A, **Figure 147**).
5. Install the center shift fork and front shaft (B, **Figure 147**).

NOTE
The shift forks have an identification mark cast into them: "L"—left-hand; "C"—center; and "R"—right-hand (Figure 148).

NOTE
Make sure the shift fork guide pins are properly meshed with the grooves in the shift drum and correctly positioned on their respective shafts (Figure 144).

6. Complete the assembly as described during transmission installation in this chapter.

6

Table 1 CLUTCH SPECIFICATIONS

Item	Standard	Wear limit
Friction disc thickness		
250 and 500 cc	2.62-2.78 mm (0.102-1.09 in.)	2.3 mm (0.091 in.)
350 and 600	2.92-3.08 mm (0.115-0.121 in.)	2.6 mm (0.10 in.)
Clutch plate warpage	–	0.30 mm (0.01 in.)
Clutch springs free length		
All 250-500 cc; 1979-1982 500 cc (except XL500R)	37.3 mm (1.46 in.)	35.8 mm (1.41 in.)
1982 XL500R	44.1 mm (1.74 in.)	42.5 mm (1.67 in.)
1978-1982 XR350	33.7 mm (1.32 in.)	32.2 mm (1.27 in.)
1983 XR350	35.9 mm (1.41 in.)	34.4 mm (1.35 in.)
1983 500 and 600 cc	44.3 mm (1.744 in.)	42.7 mm (1.68 in.)
Clutch outer guide		
OD	26.959-26.980 mm (1.0614-1.0622 in.)	26.91 mm (10.59 in.)
ID	26.000-22.035 mm (0.8661-0.8675 in.)	22.05 mm (0.968 in.)
Length		
All 250 cc; 1979-1982 500 cc	33.20-33.30 mm (1.307-1.311 in.)	33.10 mm (1.303 in.)
350 cc	29.20-29.30 mm (1.150-1.154 in.)	29.1 mm (1.15 in.)
1983 500 and 600 cc	31.30-31.40 mm (1.2322-1.2362 in.)	31.2 mm (1.229 in.)

Table 2 TRANSMISSION SPECIFICATIONS

Item	Standard	Service limit
6-SPEED (XL250R)		
Transmission gears ID		
Main shaft		
5th gear	28.020-28.041 mm (1.1032-1.1040 in.)	28.10 mm (1.106 in.)
6th gear	28.020-28.053 mm (1.1032-1.1045 in.)	28.12 mm (1.107 in.)
Countershaft		
1st, 4th gear	25.020-25.041 mm (0.9850-0.9859 in.)	25.10 mm (0.988 in.)
2nd gear	27.020-27.053 mm (1.0638-1.0651 in.)	27.12 mm (1.068 in.)
3rd gear	28.020-28.053 mm (1.1032-1.1045 in.)	28.12 mm (1.107 in.)
Gear bushing OD		
Main shaft 6th, Countershaft 3rd	27.969-27.980 mm (1.1011-1.1016 in.)	27.90 mm (1.098 in.)

(continued)

Table 2 TRANSMISSION SPECIFICATIONS (continued)

6-SPEED (XR250R)		
Transmission gears ID		
Main shaft 5th, 6th gear	25.020-25.041 mm (0.9850-0.9859 in.)	25.10 mm (0.988 in.)
Countershaft 1st, 2nd, 3rd gear	25.020-25.041 mm (0.9850-0.9859 in.)	21.10 mm (0.988 in.)
Countershaft 1st gear bushing		
ID	20.020-20.041 mm (0.7866-0.7890 in.)	20.10 mm (0.791 in.)
OD	25.005-25.016 mm (0.9846-0.9849 in.)	24.96 mm (0.982 in.)
Gear to bushing clearance	0.004-0.036 mm (0.0002-0.0014 in.)	0.15 mm (0.006 in.)
Main shaft OD	24.959-24.980 mm (0.9826-0.9835 in.)	24.91 mm (0.981 in.)
Countershaft OD @ locations:		
A	24.959-24.980 mm (0.9826-0.9835 in.)	24.91 mm (0.981 in.)
B	19.987-20.000 mm (0.7869-0.7874 in.)	19.95 mm (0.785 in.)

5-SPEED (1981-1982)		
Transmission gears ID		
Main shaft 4th, 5th gear	25.020-25.041 mm (0.9850-0.9859 in.)	25.10 mm (0.988 in.)
Countershaft 1st, 3rd gear	25.020-25.041 mm (0.9850-0.9859 in.)	21.10 mm (0.988 in.)
Countershaft 1st gear bushing		
ID	20.020-20.041 mm (0.7866-0.7890 in.)	20.10 mm (0.791 in.)
OD	25.005-25.016 mm (0.9846-0.9849 in.)	24.96 mm (0.982 in.)
Shaft to bushing clearance	0.020-0.054 mm (0.0008-0.0021 in.)	0.15 mm (0.006 in.)
Main shaft OD @ locations:		
A	24.959-24.980 mm (0.9826-0.9835 in.)	24.91 mm (0.981 in.)
B	19.987-20.000 mm (0.7869-0.7874 in.)	19.95 mm (0.785 in.)
Countershaft OD @ locations:		
A	26.959-26.980 mm (1.0614-1.0622 in.)	26.91 mm (1.059 in.)
B	24.959-24.980 mm (0.9826-0.9835 in.)	24.91 mm (0.981 in.)
C	19.987-20.000 mm (0.7869-0.7874 in.)	19.95 mm (0.785 in.)

(continued)

6

Table 2 TRANSMISSION SPECIFICATIONS (continued)

Item	Standard	Service limit
6-SPEED (XR350R)		
Transmission gears ID		
Main shaft 5th gear	24.020-24.041 mm (0.9457-0.9465 in.)	24.10 mm (0.949 in.)
Countershaft 1st, 4th gear	22.020-22.041 mm (0.8669-0.8678 in.)	22.10 mm (0.870 in.)
2nd, 3rd gear	24.020-24.041 mm (0.9457-0.9465 in.)	24.10 mm (0.949 in.)
Countershaft 1st gear bushing		
ID	17.014-17.020 mm (0.6698-0.670 in.)	17.08 mm (0.672 in.)
OD	21.984-22.000 mm (0.8655-0.8663 in.)	21.93 mm (0.863 in.)
Shaft to countershaft 1st gear bushing clearance	0.020-0.054 mm (0.0008-0.0021 in.)	0.10 mm (0.004 in.)
Main shaft OD @ locations:		
A	21.959-21.980 mm (0.8645-0.8653 in.)	21.91 mm (0.862 in.)
B	16.966-16.984 mm (0.6691-0.6687 in.)	16.93 mm (0.667 in.)
Countershaft OD @ locations:		
C	19.959-19.980 mm (0.7858-0.7866 in.)	19.92 mm (0.784 in.)
D	16.966-16.984 mm (0.6680-0.6687 in.)	16.93 mm (0.667 in.)
5-SPEED (XR500R, XL600R)		
Transmission gears ID		
Main shaft		
4th gear	25.020-25.041 mm (0.9850-0.9859 in.)	25.10 mm (0.988 in.)
5th gear	28.000-28.021 mm (1.1024-1.1032 in.)	28.08 mm (1.106 in.)
Countershaft		
1st, 3rd gear	25.021-25.041 mm (0.9850-0.9859 in.)	25.10 mm (0.988 in.)
2nd gear	28.020-28.041 mm (1.1031-1.1040 in.)	28.10 mm (1.106 in.)
Gear bushing		
Main shaft 5th gear OD	27.949-27.980 mm (1.1004-1.1016 in.)	27.90 mm (1.1098 in.)
Countershaft		
1st gear ID	20.024-20.041 mm (0.7880-0.7890 in.)	20.01 mm (0.791 in.)
1st gear OD	24.984-25.005 mm (0.9836-0.9844 in.)	24.93 mm (0.981 in.)
2nd gear ID	25.020-25.041 mm (0.9850-0.9859 in.)	25.10 mm (0.988 in.)
2nd gear OD	27.979-28.000 mm (1.1015-1.1024 in.)	27.93 mm (1.100 in.)
Gear to bushing clearance		
Mainshaft 5th gear	0.020-0.072 mm (0.0008-0.0028 in.)	0.10 mm (0.004 in.)

(continued)

Table 2 TRANSMISSION SPECIFICATIONS (continued)

5-SPEED (XR500R, XR600R) (continued)		
Countershaft		
1st gear	0.015-0.057 mm (0.0006-0.0022 in.)	0.10 mm (0.004 in.)
2nd gear	0.020-0.062 mm (0.0008-0.0024 in.)	0.10 mm (0.004 in.)
Main shaft OD @ location: A	24.972-24.993 mm (0.9831-0.9840 in.)	24.92 mm (0.981 in.)
Countershaft OD @ locations:		
B	15.966-15.984 mm (0.6286-0.6293 in.)	15.93 mm (0.627 in.)
C	19.980-19.993 mm (0.7866-0.7871 in.)	19.94 mm (0.785 in.)
D	24.972-24.993 mm (0.9831-0.9840 in.)	24.92 mm (0.981 in.)
E	24.959-24.980 mm (0.9826-0.9835 in.)	24.92 mm (0.981 in.)

Table 3 SHIFT FORK AND SHAFT SPECIFICATIONS

Item	Specification	Wear limit
ALL 250, 1979-1982 500 CC		
Shift fork ID		
Center fork	12.000-12.021 mm (0.4724-0.4733 in.)	12.05 mm (0.474 in.)
Right-hand, left-hand	15.000-15.021 mm (0.5906-0.5914 in.)	15.05 mm (0.592 in.)
Shift fork finger thickness	4.93-5.00 mm (4.93-5.00 in.)	4.50 mm (0.18 in.)
Shift fork shaft OD		
At center fork	11.966-11.984 mm (0.4711-0.4718 in.)	11.91 mm (0.469 in.)
At right-hand, left-hand	14.966-14.984 mm (0.5892-0.5899 in.)	14.91 mm (0.587 in.)
Gear shift drum OD	11.966-11.984 mm (0.4711-0.4718 in.)	11.91 mm (0.469 in.)
350 CC		
Shift fork ID	13.000-13.021 mm (0.5118-0.5126 in.)	13.05 mm (0.514 in.)
Shift fork finger thickness	4.93-5.00 mm (4.93-5.00 in.)	4.50 mm (0.18 in.)
Shift fork shaft OD	12.966-12.984 mm (0.5105-0.5111 in.)	12.90 mm (0.508 in.)
Shift drum OD	11.966-11.984 mm (0.4711-0.4718 in.)	11.91 mm (0.469 in.)
1983 500 AND 600 CC		
Shift fork ID		
All	14.000-14.018 mm (0.5512-0.5519 in.)	14.05 mm (0.553 in.)
Shift fork finger thickness	4.93-5.00 mm (4.93-5.00 in.)	4.50 mm (0.18 in.)
Shift fork shaft OD	13.966-13.984 mm (0.5498-0.5506 in.)	13.90 mm (0.547 in.)

6

CHAPTER SEVEN

FUEL AND EXHAUST SYSTEMS

The fuel system consists of a fuel tank, shutoff valve, fuel filter and a single or dual carburetor depending on model. There are slight differences among the various models. Where differences occur they are identified.

The exhaust system consists of a dual exhaust pipe and a muffler. The muffler can be partially disassembled for carbon removal.

This chapter includes service procedures for all parts of the fuel and exhaust systems.

CARBURETOR OPERATION

For proper operation a gasoline engine must be supplied with fuel and air mixed in proper proportions by weight. A mixture in which there is an excess of fuel is said to be rich. A lean mixture is one which contains insufficient fuel. A properly adjusted carburetor supplies the proper mixture to the engine under all operating conditions.

The carburetor consists of several major systems. A float and float valve mechanism maintain a constant fuel level in the float bowl(s). The pilot system supplies fuel at low speeds. The main fuel system supplies fuel at medium and high speeds. A starter (choke) system supplies the very rich mixture needed to start a cold engine.

The 1983 XR350R, XR500R and XL600R models have 2 carburetors. The primary carburetor operates by itself at low- to mid-range for smooth, precise throttle control. The secondary carburetor opens (along with the primary carburetor) at high-range to provide a large volume of fuel-air mixture for maximum power.

During the low- to mid-range the fuel-air mixture enters the engine through both intake valves. The secondary carburetor is closed at this time. There is a small reed valve within the cylinder head that allows some of the fuel mixture from the primary carburetor to flow from the primary intake port to the secondary intake port. However, the majority of the mixture flows through the primary intake port.

As the throttle is opened from mid-range to high-range the secondary carburetor starts to open. The reed valve closes at this time and each carburetor feeds directly into its own intake port and intake valve.

The progressive linkage connecting the 2 carburetors is mechanical; linkage adjustment is covered in this chapter.

CARBURETOR SERVICE

Major carburetor service (removal and cleaning) should be performed at the intervals indicated in Table 2 in Chapter Three or when poor engine performance, hesitation and little or no response to mixture adjustment is observed. Alterations in jet size and throttle slide cutaway and changes in jet needle position, etc., should be attempted only if you're experienced in this type of "tuning" work; a bad guess could result in costly engine damage or, at least, poor performance. If, after servicing the carburetor and making the adjustments described in this chapter, the bike does not perform correctly (and assuming that other factors affecting performance are correct, such as ignition timing

and condition, etc.), the bike should be checked by a dealer or a qualified performance tuning specialist.

Carburetor specifications are covered in **Table 1** at the end of this chapter.

Removal/Installation (Dual Carburetors)

1. Remove both side covers and the seat.
2. Remove the fuel tank as described in this chapter.
3. Loosen the screws on the clamping bands (A, **Figure 1**) on each end of both carburetors. Slide the clamping bands away from the carburetors.
4. Remove the bolts (B, **Figure 1**) securing the intake tube and insulator to the cylinder head. Remove the intake tube and insulator from the engine and carburetor assembly.

NOTE
There is 1 bolt on the bottom in the center of the intake tubes. It's very difficult to remove.

5. Pull the carburetor assembly forward and out of the air cleaner intake tubes (**Figure 2**).
6. Loosen the throttle cable locknuts (**Figure 3**) at the carburetor assembly.
7. Partially pull the carburetor assembly out through the left-hand side.
8. Disconnect the "pull" cable (A, **Figure 4**) and the "push" cable (B, **Figure 4**) from the throttle wheel.
9. Remove the carburetor assembly.
10. Install by reversing these removal steps, noting the following.
11. Inspect the O-ring seals in the intake tube (A, **Figure 5**) and the insulator (B, **Figure 5**). Replace if necessary.

12. When installing the throttle cables be sure to install the "pull" cable (A, **Figure 4**) to the bottom receptacle on the throttle wheel and the "push" cable (B, **Figure 4**) to the upper receptacle on the throttle wheel.

13. Adjust the throttle cable as described in Chapter Three.

Removal/Installation
(Single Carburetor)

1. Remove both side covers and the seat.

> *NOTE*
> *On some early XL250S and XL500R models, reinstall the seat strap bolts as they also hold the upper portion of the shocks to the frame (**Figure 6**). Remove and install one bolt at a time.*

2. On XL series models, disconnect the battery negative lead and remove the battery.

3. Remove the fuel tank as described in this chapter.

4. It is recommended that the air cleaner box be removed as it makes carburetor removal and installation much simplier.

5. Disconnect the breather hose (A, **Figure 7**) from the air box.

6. Loosen the screws on the clamping bands on the rear rubber boot (**Figure 8**) and slide the clamping band away from the carburetor.

7. Remove the bolts securing the air box to the frame (B, **Figure 7** and **Figure 9**) and remove the air box.

8. Disconnect the "pull" cable and the "push" cable from the throttle wheel (**Figure 10**).

9. Loosen the clamping screw (**Figure 11**) on the choke cable and remove the choke cable end from the link plate on the carburetor (A, **Figure 12**).

10. Loosen the screws on the clamping bands on the rubber intake tube (B, **Figure 12**) and slide the clamping band away from the carburetor.

11. Withdraw the carburetor drain tube from the frame.

12. Pull the carburetor assembly to the rear and remove it.

13. Install by reversing these removal steps, noting the following.

14. Install the carburetor so that the boss on the carburetor aligns with the notch in the rubber intake tube.

15. When installing the throttle cables be sure to install the "pull" cable to the bottom receptacle on the throttle wheel and the "push" cable to the upper receptacle on the throttle wheel.

16. Adjust the throttle cable as described in Chapter Three.

Disassembly/Assembly

The carburetor on all models is basically the same unit. Slight variations exist on dual-

carburetor designs. Refer to **Table 1** for all carburetor specifications. All XL series models are equipped with an accelerator pump system.

Dual carburetors (**Figure 13**) are used on 1983 XR350R, XR500R and XL600R models. The single carburetor (**Figure 14**) is used on all other models.

On models with dual carburetors it is recommended that only one carburetor be disassembled at a time. This will prevent a mixup of parts. The primary carburetor is located on the left-hand side and the secondary carburetor is on the right-hand side.

1. On dual-carburetor models, separate the carburetors as described in this chapter.

NOTE
Carburetor separation is necessary to gain access to the air cutoff valve on the left-hand carburetor.

2. Remove the vent and overflow tubes (**Figure 15**).

3. Remove the screws (**Figure 16**) securing the top cover and remove the cover and the gasket.

4. Remove the screws (**Figure 17**) securing the link arm assembly to the throttle valve and pivot the link arm assembly back out of the way.

5. Remove the throttle valve and needle jet.

6. On models equipped with an air cutoff valve, perform the following:
   a. Remove the screws (**Figure 18**) securing the air cutoff valve cover and remove the cover.
   b. Remove the spring and diaphragm (**Figure 19**).
   c. Remove the small O-ring seal (**Figure 20**).

7. On models equipped with an accelerator pump, perform the following:
   a. Remove the screws (**Figure 21**) securing the accelerator pump cover and remove the cover.
   b. Remove the spring (**Figure 22**).
   c. Carefully withdraw the accelerator pump rod assembly (A, **Figure 23**) and remove the rubber boot (B, **Figure 23**).

8. Remove the screws securing the float bowl and remove the float bowl. Refer to **Figure 24** for models with an accelerator pump or A, **Figure 25** for all other models.

9. On models so equipped, unscrew the main jet cover (B, **Figure 25**) from the float bowl.

10. Remove the plastic ferrule (**Figure 26**) from the main jet stanchion.

7

DUAL CARBURETORS

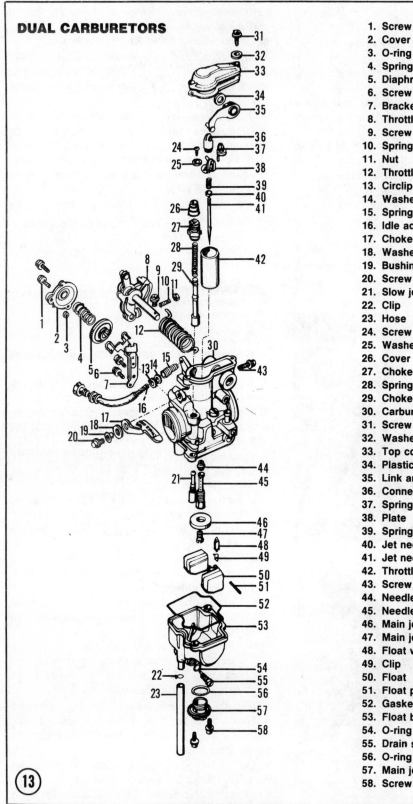

1. Screw
2. Cover
3. O-ring
4. Spring
5. Diaphragm
6. Screw
7. Bracket
8. Throttle wheel
9. Screw
10. Spring
11. Nut
12. Throttle return spring
13. Circlip
14. Washer
15. Spring
16. Idle adjust cable
17. Choke lever
18. Washer
19. Bushing
20. Screw
21. Slow jet
22. Clip
23. Hose
24. Screw
25. Washer
26. Cover
27. Choke valve nut
28. Spring
29. Choke valve
30. Carburetor body
31. Screw
32. Washer
33. Top cover
34. Plastic washer
35. Link arm
36. Connector
37. Spring
38. Plate
39. Spring
40. Jet needle clip
41. Jet needle
42. Throttle valve
43. Screw
44. Needle jet
45. Needle jet holder
46. Main jet holder
47. Main jet
48. Float valve
49. Clip
50. Float
51. Float pivot pin
52. Gasket
53. Float bowl
54. O-ring
55. Drain screw
56. O-ring
57. Main jet cover
58. Screw

(13)

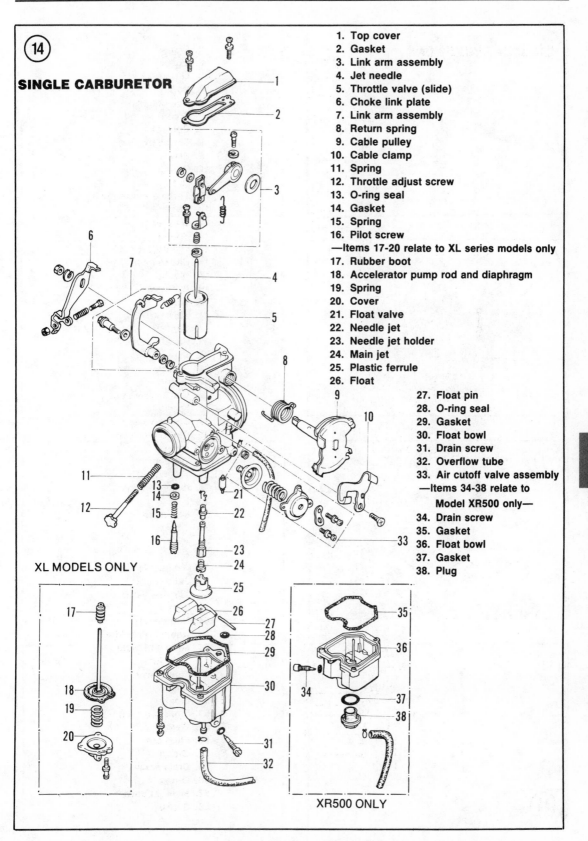

SINGLE CARBURETOR

1. Top cover
2. Gasket
3. Link arm assembly
4. Jet needle
5. Throttle valve (slide)
6. Choke link plate
7. Link arm assembly
8. Return spring
9. Cable pulley
10. Cable clamp
11. Spring
12. Throttle adjust screw
13. O-ring seal
14. Gasket
15. Spring
16. Pilot screw
—Items 17-20 relate to XL series models only
17. Rubber boot
18. Accelerator pump rod and diaphragm
19. Spring
20. Cover
21. Float valve
22. Needle jet
23. Needle jet holder
24. Main jet
25. Plastic ferrule
26. Float

27. Float pin
28. O-ring seal
29. Gasket
30. Float bowl
31. Drain screw
32. Overflow tube
33. Air cutoff valve assembly
—Items 34-38 relate to
   Model XR500 only—
34. Drain screw
35. Gasket
36. Float bowl
37. Gasket
38. Plug

XL MODELS ONLY

XR500 ONLY

7

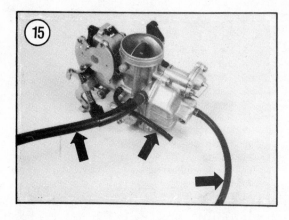

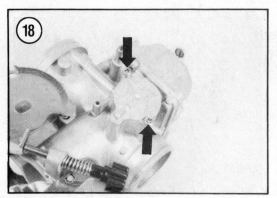

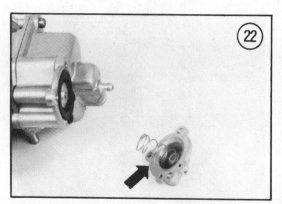

NOTE
*Prior to removing the pilot screw,
carefully screw it in until it **lightly** seats.
Count and record the number of turns
so it can be installed in the same
position.*

11. Unscrew the pilot screw and spring (**Figure 27**).

12. Remove the small O-ring seal (**Figure 28**) located within the pilot screw receptacle.

13. Remove the float pivot pin (**Figure 29**).

14. Remove the float and float valve needle (**Figure 30**).

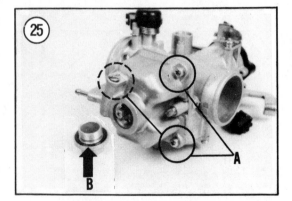

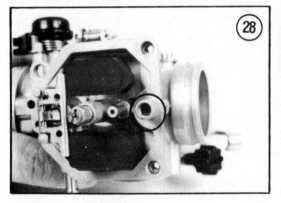

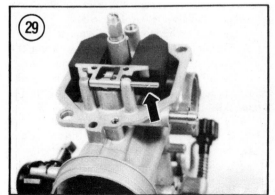

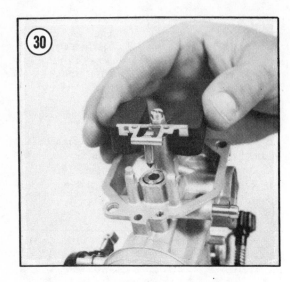

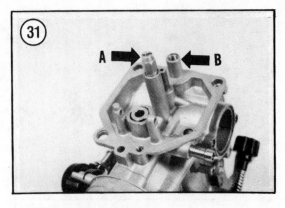

NOTE
*Prior to removing the air screw, carefully screw it in until it **lightly** seats. Count and record the number of turns so it can be installed in the same position.*

15. Remove the air screw on dual-carburetor models; the secondary carburetor is not equipped with an air screw.

NOTE
On XL600R models, if the air screw is to be removed, use a pair of pliers and break off the limiter cap. If removed, a new air screw and limiter cap must be installed.

16. Remove the main jet (A, **Figure 31**), needle jet holder (**Figure 32**) and needle jet.

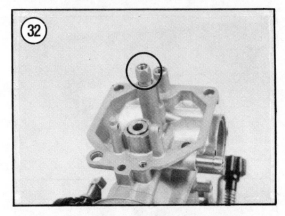

NOTE
Turn the carburetor over and catch the needle jet as it falls out into your hand.

17. On models equipped with a removable slow jet, remove the slow jet (B, **Figure 31**).
18A. On dual-carburetor models, on the primary carburetor only, remove the screw securing the starter choke and remove the choke assembly.
18B. On all other models, unhook the choke return spring and remove the plastic link arm (A, **Figure 33**).
19. Unscrew the throttle adjust screw (B, **Figure 33**) and remove the spring and the throttle adjust screw.
20. Remove the float bowl seal from the float bowl.
21. Unscrew the main jet cover and O-ring seal.

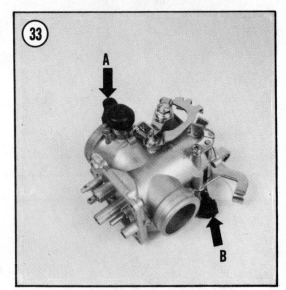

NOTE
Further disassembly is neither necessary nor recommended. If throttle shaft or butterfly is damaged, take the carburetor body to a dealer for replacement.

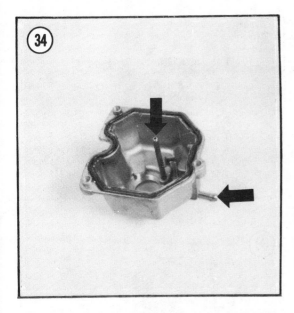

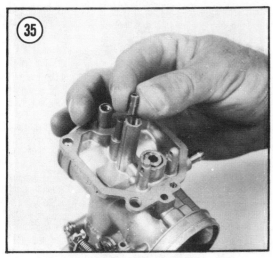

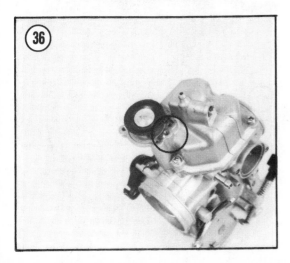

22. Clean all parts, except rubber or plastic parts, in a good grade of carburetor cleaner. This solution is available at most automotive or motorcycle supply stores in a small, resealable tank with a dip basket for just a few dollars. If it is tightly sealed when not in use, the solution will last for several cleanings. Follow the manufacturer's instructions for correct soak time (usually about 1/2 hour).

23. Remove all parts from the cleaner and blow dry with compressed air. Blow out the jets with compressed air. *Do not* use a piece of wire to clean them as minor gouges in the jet can alter flow rate and upset the fuel-air mixture. Blow out all passages in the carburetor body with compressed air.

24. Be sure to clean out the overflow tube (**Figure 34**) from both ends.

25. Inspect the end of the float valve needle and seat for wear or damage; replace either or both parts if necessary.

26. Inspect all O-ring seals. O-ring seals tend to become hardened after prolonged use and heat and therefore lose their ability to seal properly.

27. Assembly is the reverse of these disassembly steps, noting the following.

28. Install the needle jet (**Figure 35**) with the chamfered end facing *up* toward the needle jet holder.

29. If removed, install the jet needle clip in the correct groove. Refer to **Table 1** for correct stock position.

30. Install the plastic ferrule (**Figure 26**) with the cutout notch facing toward the float pin. This notch is for the overflow tube in the float bowl.

31. Check the float height and adjust if necessary as described in this chapter.

32. On models equipped with an accelerator pump, perform the following:
   a. Make sure the tabs on the accelerator pump diaphragm are positioned correctly in the float bowl (**Figure 36**).
   b. Make sure that the rubber boot is completely seated in the carburetor body flange (**Figure 37**).

CAUTION
The boot must be correctly seated as it seals off the pump shaft to keep dirt out of the diaphragm area.

33. Ensure that any small O-ring seals removed are correctly installed and not forgotten.

34. On dual-carburetor models, repeat for the other carburetor.

35. After the carburetor has been disassembled the pilot screw, the air screw and the idle speed should be adjusted.

DUAL-CARBURETOR SEPARATION

1. Remove the carburetor assembly as described in this chapter.

2. Remove the screws (**Figure 38**) securing the throttle adjust screw bracket and remove the bracket assembly.

3. Remove the screws (A, **Figure 39**) securing the 2 carburetor bodies together.

4. Carefully separate the ball stud from the ball joint (**Figure 40**) on the throttle drum of the secondary carburetor.

5. Carefully pull the 2 carburetor bodies apart. Do not damage the air joint (**Figure 41**) nor the fuel joint (B, **Figure 39**) joining the 2 carburetors.

6. Install new O-ring seals on both the air and fuel joints.

7. Apply a light coat of grease to the O-ring seals on the air and fuel joints.

8. Insert the air and fuel joints into their receptacles on the primary carburetor.

9. Place the secondary carburetor onto the primary carburetor, carefully aligning the air joint (**Figure 41**) and fuel joint (B, **Figure 39**). Make sure that the O-ring seals are in place on both joints.

10. Push the 2 carburetor bodies together until they are completely seated.

11. Push the ball stud onto the ball joint (**Figure 40**).

12. Install the screws (A, **Figure 39**) securing the 2 carburetor bodies together.

13. Align the groove in the throttle adjust screw bracket with the tab on the air vent tube. Install the screws and tighten securely.

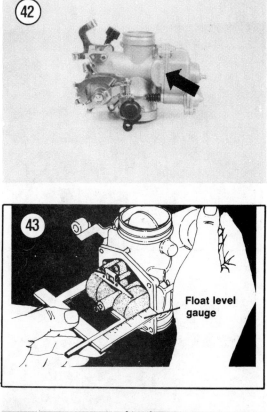

Float level gauge

14. Check the operation of the throttle as follows:
  a. Move the throttle plate and open and close the throttle a couple of times. It should move freely from open to closed with no binding.
  b. If movement is not free, make sure the ball stud is correctly seated on the throttle drum. Apply a few drops of oil.
  c. Loosen the carburetor attachment screws a little and slightly move each carburetor body.
  d. Retighten the screws and recheck the movement.

CARBURETOR ADJUSTMENTS

Float Adjustment

The carburetor assembly has to be removed and partially disassembled for this adjustment.
1. Remove the carburetor as described in this chapter.
2A. On dual-carburetor models, remove the screws securing both float bowls. Remove both float bowls.
2B. On all other models, remove the screws securing the float bowl. Remove the float bowl (**Figure 42**).
3. Hold the carburetor so the float arm is just touching the float needle—not pushing it down. Use a float level gauge (**Figure 43**), vernier caliper or small ruler and measure the distance from the carburetor body to the float. The correct height (**Figure 44**) is listed in **Table 1**.
4. Adjust by carefully bending the tang on the float arm. If the float level is set too high, the result will be a rich fuel-air mixture. If it is set too low the mixture will be too lean.

NOTE
Both float chambers must be at the same height.

5. Reassemble and install the carburetor.

Needle Jet Adjustment (XR Series Models)

NOTE
The needle on XL series models has only one groove for the clip and so is non-adjustable.

Needle position can be adjusted to affect the fuel-air mixture for medium throttle openings.
The carburetor will have to be removed and partially disassembled for this adjustment.
1. Remove the carburetor as described in this chapter.

7

2. Remove the 2 screws (**Figure 45**) securing the top cover and remove it and the gasket.

3. Remove the 2 screws (**Figure 46**) securing the link arm assembly to the throttle valve and pivot the link assembly back out of the way.

4. Remove the throttle valve and needle jet.

5. Remove the needle valve and note the original position of the needle clip. The standard setting is listed in **Table 1**. Raising the needle (lowering the clip) will enrich the mixture during mid-throttle opening, while lowering it (raising the clip) will lean the mixture.

6. Reassemble and install the carburetor by reversing these steps.

Pilot Screw Adjustment (1978-1979)

NOTE
The pilot jet is pre-set at the factory and adjustment is not necessary unless the carburetor has been overhauled or someone has misadjusted it.

1. For the preliminary adjustment, carefully turn the pilot screw (**Figure 47**) in until it seats lightly and then back it out the number of turns listed in **Table 2**.

CAUTION
The pilot jet screw seat will be damaged if the pilot screw is tightened too hard against the seat.

2. Start the engine and let it reach normal operating temperature. Stop-and-go driving for approximately 10 minutes is sufficient.

3. Turn the engine off and connect a portable tachometer following the manufacturer's instructions.

4. Start the engine and adjust the idle speed as listed in **Table 1**. Use the throttle adjust screw (**Figure 48**).

NOTE
Figure 48 is shown with some components removed for clarity only; it is not necessary to remove them for this adjustment.

5A. On XL models, turn the pilot screw clockwise slowly until the engine stops running. On XL250S models back it out 2 full turns and on XL500S models back it out one full turn. Restart the engine and proceed to Step 6.

5B. On XR models, turn the pilot screw either way until the highest idle speed is obtained.

6. On all models reset the idle speed; refer to Step 4. Open and close the throttle a couple of times; check for variations in idle speed. Readjust if necessary.

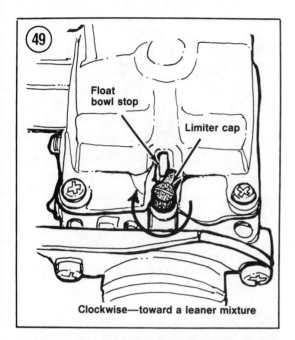

Clockwise—toward a leaner mixture

readjusting the factory setting. The limiter cap will allow a maximum of 7/8 of a turn of the pilot screw *to a leaner mixture only*. The pilot screw is preset at the factory and should not be reset unless the carburetor has been overhauled.

CAUTION
Do not try to remove the limiter cap from the pilot screw as it is bonded in place and will break off and damage the pilot screw if removal is attempted.

The air cleaner must be cleaned before starting this procedure or the results will be inaccurate.
1. For the preliminary adjustment, carefully turn the pilot screw in until it *lightly seats* and then back it out the number of turns listed in **Table 2**.
2. Start the engine and let it reach normal operating temperature. Stop-and-go riding for approximately 10 minutes is sufficient.
3. Turn the engine off and connect a portable tachometer following the manufacturer's instructions.
4. Start the engine and turn the idle adjust screw (**Figure 48**) in or out to achieve the idle speed listed in **Table 1**.
5. Turn the pilot screw *in* slowly until the engine stops.
6. Turn the pilot screw *out* the number of turns listed in **Table 2**.
7. Start the engine and turn the idle adjust screw in or out again to achieve the idle speed listed in **Table 1**.
8. Perform this step only if a new limiter cap is to be installed. Apply Loctite No. 601 or equivalent to the limiter cap and install it on the pilot screw. Make sure the pilot screw does not move while installing the limiter cap. Position the limiter cap against the stop on the float bowl (**Figure 49**) so that the pilot screw can only turn *clockwise*, not counterclockwise.

WARNING
With the engine idling, move the handlebar from side to side. If idle speed increases during this movement, the throttle cable needs adjustment or it may be incorrectly routed through the frame. Correct this problem immediately. Do not ride the bike in this unsafe condition.

9. Turn the engine off and disconnect the portable tachometer.
10. After this adjustment is completed, test ride the bike. Throttle response from idle should be rapid and without any hesitation.

WARNING
With the engine idling, move the handlebar from side to side. If idle speed increases during this movement, the throttle cables may need adjusting or they may be incorrectly routed through the frame. Correct this problem immediately. Do not ride the bike in this unsafe condition.

7. If necessary, repeat Step 5 and Step 6 until the engine runs smoothly at the correct idle speed.
8. Disconnect the portable tachometer.

Pilot Screw Adjustment
(1980-1981 XL250S and XL500S)

To comply with U.S. and Canadian emission control standards, a limiter cap is attached to the pilot screw. This is to prevent the owner from

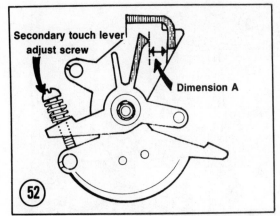

Air Screw Adjustment
(XR350R, XR500R)

The air cleaner must be cleaned before starting this procedure or the results will be inaccurate.

1. For the preliminary adjustment, carefully turn the air screw (**Figure 50**) in until it *lightly seats* and then back it out the number of turns listed in **Table 2**.

2. Start the engine and let it reach normal operating temperature. Stop-and-go riding for approximately 10 minutes is sufficient.

3. Turn the engine off and connect a portable tachometer following the manufacturer's instructions.

4. Start the engine and turn the idle adjust screw (**Figure 51**) in or out to achieve the idle speed listed in **Table 1**.

5. Open and close the throttle a couple of times. Engine speed should increase smoothly with no hesitation.

6. Turn the air screw in or out to obtain the highest idle speed.

7. Turn the idle adjust screw to achieve the idle speed listed in **Table 1**.

> *WARNING*
> *With the engine idling, move the handlebar from side to side. If idle speed increases during this movement, the throttle cable needs adjustment or it may be incorrectly routed through the frame. Correct this problem immediately. Do not ride the bike in this unsafe condition.*

8. Turn the engine off and disconnect the portable tachometer.

9. After this adjustment is completed, test ride the bike. Throttle response from idle should be rapid and without any hesitation.

Air Screw Adjustment
and New Limiter Cap Installation
(XL600R)

The air cleaner must be cleaned before starting this procedure or the results will be inaccurate.

1. For the preliminary adjustment, carefully turn the air screw (**Figure 50**) in until it *lightly seats* then back it out the number of turns listed in **Table 2**.

2. Start the engine and let it reach normal operating temperature. Stop-and-go riding for approximately 10 minutes is sufficient.

3. Turn the engine off and connect a portable tachometer following the manufacturer's instructions.

4. Start the engine and turn the idle adjust screw (**Figure 51**) in or out to achieve the idle speed listed in **Table 1**.

5. Turn the air screw in or out to obtain the highest idle speed.

6. Turn the idle adjust screw to achieve the idle speed listed in **Table 1**.

7. Turn the air screw in until the idle speed drops by 100 rpm.

8. Turn the air screw out 1 full turn from the position obtained in Step 7.

9. Turn the idle adjust screw in or out again to achieve the idle speed listed in **Table 1**.

> *WARNING*
> *With the engine idling, move the handlebar from side to side. If idle speed increases during this movement, the throttle cable needs adjustment or it may be incorrectly routed through the frame. Correct this problem immediately. Do not ride the bike in this unsafe condition.*

10. Perform this step only if a new limiter cap is to be installed. Apply Loctite No. 601 or equivalent

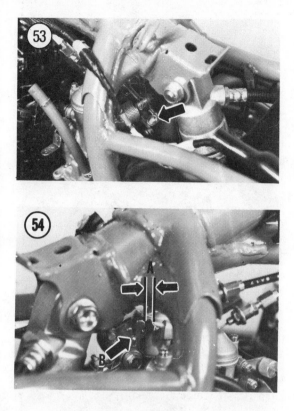

to the limiter cap and install it on the air screw. Make sure the air screw does not move while installing the limiter cap. Position the limiter cap against the stop on the carburetor body so that the air screw can only turn *counterclockwise*, not clockwise.

11. Turn the engine off and disconnect the portable tachometer.

12. After this adjustment is completed, test ride the bike. Throttle response from idle should be rapid and without any hesitation.

Secondary Carburetor Touch Lever Adjustment (XR350R, XL600R)

Refer to **Figure 52** for this procedure.

1. Turn the throttle adjust screw (**Figure 51**) *counterclockwise* until it stops. Record the number of turns.

2. Turn the secondary touch lever adjust screw *out* until the stopper on the secondary touch lever lightly bottoms out on the lug on the throttle lever.

3. Turn the secondary touch lever adjust screw *in* until the clearance (dimension A) between the stopper and the lug is as follows:

   a. XR350R: 0.177-0.207 in. (4.5-5.0 mm).
   b. XL600R: 0.323-0.343 in. (8.2-8.7 mm).

4. Turn the throttle adjust screw (**Figure 51**) *clockwise* to the position recorded in Step 1.

5. Adjust the idle speed as described in this chapter.

Carburetor Synchronization (XR500R)

The 1983 XR500R is the only model with dual carburetors that can be synchronized.

1. Remove both side covers and the seat.

2. Loosen the adjusting screw (**Figure 53**) on the secondary throttle drum.

3. Make sure both throttle valves are in the closed position.

4. Measure the distance between the primary and secondary throttle drums (A, **Figure 54**). The correct clearance is 0.30-0.32 in. (7.8-8.0 mm).

5. If adjustment is necessary, carefully bend (open or close) the fork end (B, **Figure 54**) of the secondary throttle drum.

6. Screw in the adjusting screw until it just comes in contact with the primary throttle drum.

Fast Idle Adjustment (XL250S and XL500S Only)

1. Start the engine and let it reach normal operating temperature. Stop-and-go riding for approximately 10 minutes is sufficient.

2. Turn the engine off and connect a portable tachometer following the manufacturer's instructions.

3. Start the engine and pull the choke knob out (**Figure 55**) to its detent position. The correct high speed idle is 2,000-2,500 rpm for both models.

4. Adjust by loosening the locknut and turning the adjustment screw (**Figure 56**) until the fast idle speed is correct. Open and close the throttle a couple of times; check for variations. Readjust if necessary.

7

NOTE
Figure 56 is shown with the fuel tank and side cover removed for clarity only; do not remove them for this adjustment.

NOTE
The locknut and adjustment screw are covered with locking paint at the factory so they will be difficult to adjust the first time.

5. Turn the engine off and disconnect the portable tachometer.

High Altitude Adjustment (1978-1980 XR250 and XR500)

If the bike is going to be ridden for any sustained period of time at elevations above 5,000 ft. (1,500 m), the main jet must be changed to a smaller jet. The engine will run too rich and carbon up if run with the standard jet.

The standard jet is sufficient for riding up to a maximum of 6,500 ft. (2,000 m) and the high altitude jet is okay for operation down to a minimum of 5,000 ft. (1,500 m).

CAUTION
If the bike has been rejetted for high altitude operation (smaller jet), it must be changed back to the standard main jet if riding at altitudes lower than 5,000 ft. (1,500 m). Engine overheating and piston seizure will occur if the engine runs too lean with the smaller jet.

1. Remove the carburetor as described in this chapter.
2. Remove the screws securing the float bowl and remove it.
3. Remove the standard main jet (**Figure 57**) and install the new, smaller one. The sizes are listed in **Table 1**.
4. Reassemble and install the carburetor.
5. Adjust the idle speed as described in Chapter Three. Idle speed is the same as with the standard main jet.
6. If the engine idle is rough or the engine misses or stalls, adjust the pilot screw as described in this chapter. On XR250 models, the pilot screw mut be backed out 1 3/4 turns instead of 2 1/2 turns with the standard main jet. Refer to Step 1 of *Pilot Screw Adjustment*. On XR500 models, the adjustment is the same as with the standard main jet.

High-altitude and Temperature Adjustment (1981-on XR250R and XR500R)

High-altitude and temperature adjustment consists of 3 different changes to the carburetor: main jet size change, a different location of the clip on the jet needle and a different pilot screw setting. Refer to **Figure 58**.

If the bike is going to be ridden for any sustained period at high elevations (above 5,000 ft.—1,500 m), the main jet should be changed to a 1-step smaller jet. Never change the jet by more than one size at a time without test riding the bike and running a spark plug test. Refer to *Reading Spark Plugs* in Chapter Three.

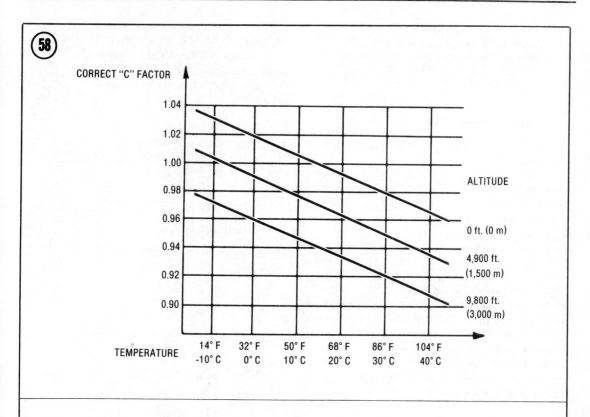

Use the information in this table to determine what carburetor adjustments are necessary for proper engine operation in various areas.

The chart in the table is divided in 2 directions:

    Horizontal—for various ambient temperatures

    Vertical (right-hand side)—various altitudes

    Vertical (left-hand side)—for the "C" factor

Determine the approximate altitude and surrounding air temperature of the area where you are going to ride. Locate these 2 factors on the chart. Where these 2 factors intersect (vertical and horizontal), closest to one of the angled lines, will establish the "C" factor. Use this established "C" factor for the following steps:

To Determine Main Jet Size

Multiply the standard main jet number (No. 138) by the "C" factor. Use the main jet number closest to the number in the answer.

EXAMPLE

Main jet number times the "C" factor—i.e.

(138 X 0.96 = 132.48)—use main jet number 132.

To Determine the Pilot Screw Setting and Jet Needle Clip Position

If the determined "C" factor is above 0.95 (left-hand side of the chart) no adjustment is necessary to the pilot screw or clip position change on the jet needle for proper engine operation.

If the determined "C" factor is 0.95 (left-hand side of the chart) or anywhere below, turn the pilot screw *out* by 1/2 turn and raise the clip on the jet needle by one groove.

EXAMPLE

Pilot screw opening (+) plus 1/2 turn—i.e.

(2 1/2 + 1/2 turn = 3). Turn the pilot screw out 3 turns from the *lightly seated position*.

EXAMPLE

Jet needle clip standard position minus 1 position—i.e.

(4 - 1 = 3). Move the jet needle clip to the No. 3 position on the jet needle.

7

CAUTION
If the carburetor has been adjusted for high-altitude operation, it must be changed back to standard settings when ridden at altitudes below 5,000 ft. (1,500 m). Engine overheating and piston seizure will occur if the engine runs too lean.

1. Remove the carburetor as described in this chapter.
2. Remove the float bowl or main jet cover from the float bowl.
3. Remove the main jet (**Figure 59**) and replace it with the factory recommended size as indicated in **Table 1**.
4. Make sure the main jet cover gasket is in place and in good condition. Install the main jet cover.
5. Remove the screws securing the carburetor top cover and remove the top cover and the gasket.
6. Remove the screws (**Figure 60**) securing the link arm assembly to the throttle valve and pivot the link assembly back out of the way.
7. Remove the throttle valve and the needle jet.
8. Remove the jet needle and note the original position of the needle clip. The standard position for all models is listed in **Table 1**.

9. Reposition the clip according to the factory information listed in **Figure 58**.
10. Reassemble the throttle valve assembly and install it into the carburetor.
11. The pilot screw opening should be increased according to the factory information listed in **Figure 58**.
12. Start the engine and adjust the idle speed as described in Chapter Three.
13. Test ride the bike and perform a spark plug test; refer to *Reading Spark Plugs* in Chapter Three.

FUEL TANK (METAL)

Removal/Installation

1. Remove the right- and left-hand side covers and seat.

CAUTION
*On XL250S and XL500S models, reinstall the seat strap bolts as they also hold the upper portion of the shocks to the frame (A, **Figure 61**). Remove and reinstall one bolt at a time.*

2. On XL models, disconnect the battery electrical lead or main fuse (**Figure 62**).

3. Turn the fuel shutoff valve to the OFF position (**Figure 63**); remove the fuel line to the carburetor.
4. Pull the fuel fill cap vent tube from the steering head receptacle (**Figure 64**).
5. Remove the bolt (B, **Figure 61**) securing the fuel tank; pull the tank to the rear and remove it.
6. Install by reversing these removal steps.

FUEL TANK (PLASTIC)

Removal/Installation

1. Place wood block(s) under the engine to support the bike securely.

2. Turn the fuel shutoff valve to the OFF position and remove the fuel line to the carburetor.
3. Remove both side covers and the seat.
4. Unhook the rubber strap (A, **Figure 65**) securing the rear of the fuel tank. Remove the bolt and spacer on each side of the front of the fuel tank (B, **Figure 65**). Pull the fuel fill cap vent tube (C, **Figure 65**) free from the steering head area. Pull the tank up and toward the rear and remove the tank.
5A. On 1983 350-600 cc models, inspect the protective bands (**Figure 66**) on the frame. Replace if damaged or starting to deteriorate.
5B. On all other models, inspect the rubber covers (**Figure 67**) over the bolts and nuts on the upper engine hanger plate. Replace as a set if any are damaged or starting to deteriorate.

> *WARNING*
> *If the protective bands or rubber covers are worn through or not installed, the bolt heads and nuts may wear a hole through the fuel tank. This presents a real fire danger.*

6. Install by reversing these removal steps.

7

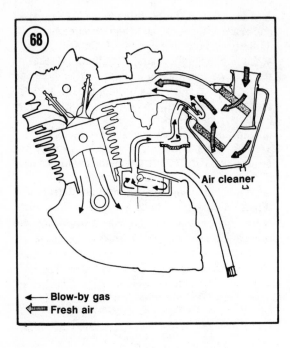

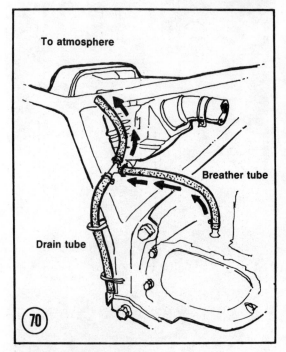

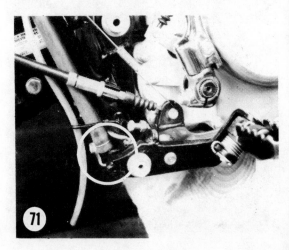

FUEL FILTER

The bike is fitted with a small fuel filter screen in the shutoff valve. Considering the dirt and residue that is often found in today's gasoline, it is a good idea to install an inline fuel filter to help keep the carburetor clean.

A good quality inline fuel filter (A.C. part No. GF453 or equivalent) is available at most auto and/or motorcycle supply stores. Just cut the flexible fuel line from the fuel tank to the carburetor and install the filter. Cut out a section of the fuel line the length of the filter so the fuel line does not kink and restrict fuel flow.

CRANKCASE BREATHER SYSTEM

In order to comply with air pollution standards, the XL series models are equipped with a closed crankcase breather system. The system shown in **Figure 68** has a breather separator unit (A, **Figure 69**) and the gases are burned. The system used on the XR series differs in that the gases are not routed into the air cleaner air box nor are they burned in the engine. They are routed as shown in **Figure 70** and are vented into the atmosphere.

Inspection

Make sure all hose clamps (B, **Figure 69**) are tight and check all hoses for deterioration. Replace as necessary. Check that hoses are not clogged or crimped.

Figure 69 *shows the system used on the*
XL series as it is the most complex.

Remove the plug on the XL series (**Figure 71**) or
XR series (**Figure 72**) from the drain hose and
clean out all residue. This cleaning procedure is
needed more frequently if a considerable amount
of riding is done at full throttle or in the rain.

NOTE
Be sure to install the plugs and clamps.

EXHAUST SYSTEM

The exhaust system is a vital performance
component and frequently, because of its design, it
is a vulnerable piece of equipment. Check the
exhaust system for deep dents and fractures and
repair or replace them immediately. Check the
muffler frame mounting flanges for fractures and
loose bolts. Check the cylinder head mounting
flanges for tightness. A loose exhaust pipe
connection will not only rob the engine of power, it
could also damage the piston and cylinder.

The exhaust system consists of a dual exhaust
pipe, a single muffler and spark arrrestor.

Removal/Installation

1. Place wood block(s) under the engine to support
the bike securely.
2. Remove the side covers and the seat.
3. Remove the fuel tank as described in this
chapter.
4. Remove the nuts (**Figure 73**) securing the dual
exhaust pipe to the cylinder head.
5. Loosen the clamping bolts (**Figure 74**) securing
the exhaust pipe to the muffler. Withdraw the
exhaust pipe from the muffler and the cylinder
head and remove it.

NOTE
Don't lose the 2 collars at each exhaust
port when the exhaust pipe is removed
from the cylinder head.

7. Remove the bolts and washers securing the
front of the muffler to the frame.
8. Remove the bolt and washer securing the rear
of the muffler to the frame. Withdraw the muffler
out through the rear and remove it.
9. Inspect the gaskets at all joints; replace as
necessary.
10. Make sure the cylinder head exhaust port
gasket is in place.
11. Install the muffler into the frame.

7

12. Install the exhaust pipe assembly into position and install one cylinder head nut (at each exhaust port) only finger tight until the muffler bolts and washers are installed.

13. Install the muffler attachment bolts and washers; do not tighten at this time. Make sure the head pipe inlet is correctly seated in the exhaust port.

14. Remove both cylinder head nuts. Install the 4 collars into place (2 collars per exhaust port) and slide the exhaust pipe flange into position. Install the 4 nuts and tighten securely. Make sure the collars are correctly seated into the cylinder head exhaust port.

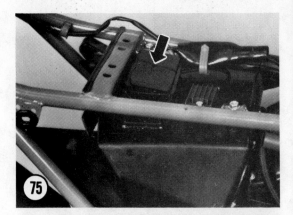

NOTE
Tightening the cylinder head nuts first will minimize exhaust leaks at the cylinder head.

15. Tighten the muffler bolts securely.

16. Install the fuel tank, the seat and side covers.

17. After installation is complete, start the engine and make sure there are no exhaust leaks.

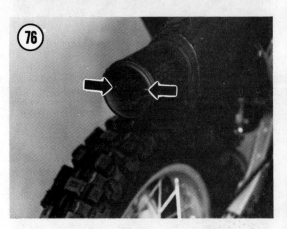

INLET DUCT CAP AND MUFFLER DIFFUSER PIPE

State noise regulations may require that motorcycle models be equipped with the inlet duct cap and muffler diffuser. When these 2 items are installed the noise level is reduced to 86 dB(A).

These 2 items are furnished with U.S. XR500R models by the factory and are stored in the tool bag on the rear fender.

1. Remove both side covers and the seat.

2. Install the air inlet duct into the opening of the air box (**Figure 75**). Push it down until it seats correctly.

3. Remove the screws (**Figure 76**) in the end of the muffler.

4. Insert the diffuser pipe (**Figure 77**) into the end of the muffler.

5. Secure the diffuser pipe with the screws removed in Step 3.

6. Install the seat and both side covers.

Table 1 CARBURETOR SPECIFICATIONS*

Item	1978-1979 XL250S	1980-1981 XL250S
Model No.	PD 03A	PD 10A
Main jet No.	120	115
Slow jet No.	40	38
Initial pilot screw opening	1 3/8 turns	1 3/4 turns
Needle jet clip position from top	Fixed	Fixed
Float level	14.5 mm (0.57 in.)	14.5 mm (0.57 in.)
Idle speed	1,200 ±100 rpm	1,200 ±100 rpm

Item	1982 XL250R	1979 XR250
Model No.	PD 74A	PD 02A
Main jet No.	110	122
High altitude jet	NA	118
Slow jet No.	38	40
Initial pilot screw opening	1 3/4 turns	2 1/8 turns
Needle jet clip position from top	Fixed	4th groove
Float level	14.0 mm (0.55 in.)	14.5 mm (0.57 in.)
Idle speed	1,200 ±100 rpm	1,200 ±100 rpm

Item	1980 XR250	1981-1982 XR250R
Model No.	PD 12A	PD 71A
Main jet No.	120	130
High altitude jet	115	115, 118, 120, 122, 125, 128, 132, 135
Slow jet No.	40	40
Initial pilot screw opening	1 1/4 turns	2 1/2 turns
Needle jet clip position from top	4th groove	3rd groove
Float level	14.5 mm (0.57 in.)	12.5 mm (0.49 in.)
Idle speed	1,300 ±100 rpm	1,300 ±100 rpm

Item	XR350R
Model No.	PD 01A
Main jet No.	
Primary	112
Secondary	105
High altitude jet	90, 98, 100, 102, 108, 110 115, 118, 120
Slow jet No.	45
Initial pilot screw opening	1 1/4 turns
Needle jet clip position from top	
Primary	2nd groove
Secondary	3rd groove
Float level	18.0 mm (0.71 in.)
Idle speed	1,300 ±100 rpm

7

(continued)

Table 1 CARBURETOR SPECIFICATIONS* (continued)

Item	1979 XL500S	1980 XL500S
Model No.	PD 07A	PD 07B
Main jet No.	155	155
Slow jet No.	55	55
Initial pilot screw opening	2 1/4 turns	2 3/8 turns
Needle jet clip position from top	Fixed	Fixed
Float level	14.5 mm (0.57 in.)	14.5 mm (0.57 in.)
Idle speed	1,200 ± 100 rpm	1,200 ± 100 rpm

Item	1979 XR500	1980 XR500
Model No.	PD 06A	PD 11B
Main jet No.	158	155
High altitude jet	152	150, 152, 158, 160
Slow jet No.	55	55
Initial pilot screw opening	2 turns	2 1/4 turns
Needle jet clip position from top	3rd groove	3rd groove
Float level	14.5 mm (0.57 in.)	14.5 mm (0.57 in.)
Idle speed	1,200 ± 100 rpm	1,200 ± 100 rpm

Item	1981-1982 XR500R	1982 XL500R
Model No.	PD 11B	PD 77A
Main jet No.	152	135
High altitude jet	138, 140, 142, 145, 148, 150, 155, 158	130
Slow jet No.	55	52
Initial pilot screw opening	2 1/4 turns	1 3/4 turns
Needle jet clip position from top	3rd groove	Fixed
Float level	14.5 mm (0.57 in.)	18.0 mm (0.70) in.)
Idle speed	1,200 ± 100 rpm	1,200 ± 100 rpm

Item	1983 XR500R	XL600R
Model No.	PD 50A	PH 60A
Main jet No.		
Primary	135	125
Secondary	108	112
Slow jet No.	55	55
Initial pilot screw opening	1 1/8 turns	1 1/8 turns
Needle jet clip position from top		
Primary	4th groove	NA
Secondary	2nd groove	NA
Float level	20.0 mm (0.79 in.)	18.0 mm (0.71 in.)
Idle speed	1,300 ± 100 rpm	1,200 ± 100 rpm

* Honda does not provide service information for all items nor all models. NA = Not available.

Table 2 CARBURETOR PILOT SCREW INITIAL OPENING

Model	Turns out
XL250S	
1978-1979	1 3/8
1980-1981	1 3/4
XL250R	
1982-1983	1 3/4
XR250	
1979	2 1/8
1980	1 1/4
XR250R	2 1/2
XL500S	
1979 and 1981	2 1/4
1980	2 3/8
XR500	
1979	2
1980	2 1/4
XL500R	2 1/4
XR500R	
1981-1982	2 1/4
1983	1 1/8
XR350R	1 1/4
XL600R	1 1/8

7

CHAPTER EIGHT

ELECTRICAL SYSTEMS

This chapter contains operating principles and service and test procedures for all electrical and ignition components. The electrical systems vary between the XL and XR series as the XL is equipped with components approved for street-legal operation. These consist of a battery, voltage regulator/rectifier, approved headlight, taillight/brakelight, directional signals and a horn.

The XR series is equipped only with a headlight and taillight (no battery) and is for off-road use only.

Where differences occur between the XL and XR series they are identified.

The electrical system includes the following systems (each is described in detail in this chapter):

a. Charging system (XL series models).
b. Ignition system.
c. Lighting system.

d. Directional signals (XL series models).
e. Horn (XL series models).

Full color wiring diagrams are located at the end of this book.

CHARGING SYSTEM (XL SERIES MODELS)

The charging system consists of the battery, alternator and solid state, non-adjustable voltage regulator/rectifier. See **Figures 1-3**.

The alternator generates an alternating current (AC) which the rectifier converts to direct current (DC). The voltage regulator maintains the voltage to the battery and load (lights, ignition, etc.) at a constant voltage, regardless of variations in engine speed and load.

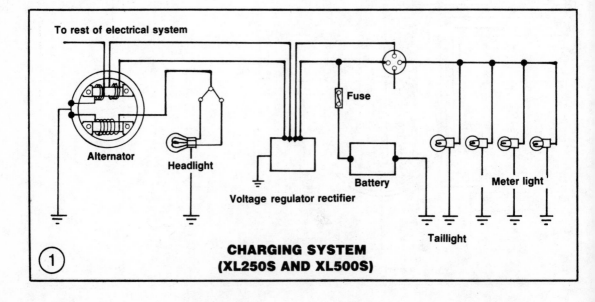

To rest of electrical system

Fuse

Alternator   Headlight

Voltage regulator rectifier   Battery   Meter light

Taillight

**CHARGING SYSTEM
(XL250S AND XL500S)**

①

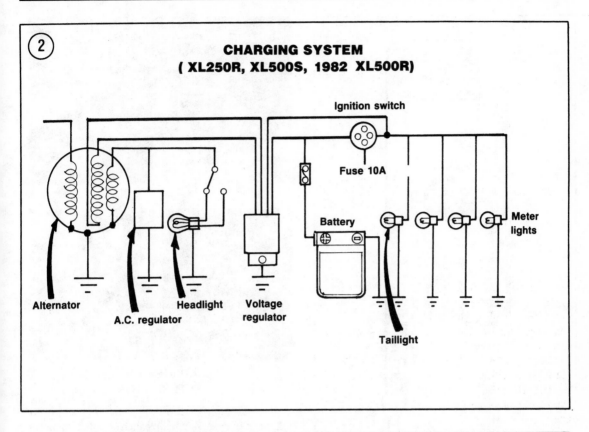

CHARGING SYSTEM
(XL250R, XL500S, 1982 XL500R)

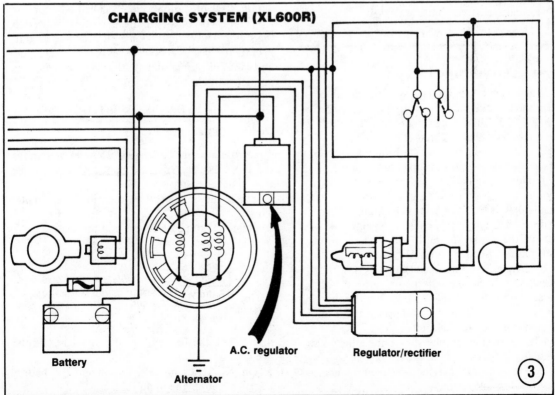

CHARGING SYSTEM (XL600R)

8

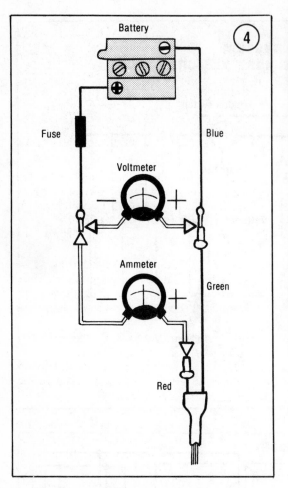

Battery

4

Fuse

Blue

Voltmeter

Ammeter

Green

Red

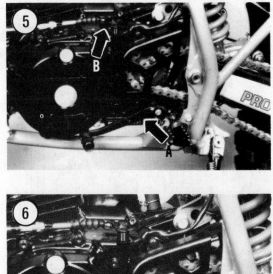

5

B

A

6

Testing Charging System

Whenever a charging system trouble is suspected, make sure the battery is good before going any further. Clean and test the battery as described in Chapter Three.

Prior to starting the test, start the bike and let it reach normal operating temperature; shut it off.

To test the chargine system, disconnect the battery wires leading to the voltage regulator/rectifier. Connect a 0-15 DC voltmeter and 0-10 DC ammeter as shown in **Figure 4**.

Start the engine and let it idle. Check output at the rpm described in **Table 1**.

If charging current is considerably lower than specified, check the alternator and/or voltage regulator/rectifier. It is less likely that the charging current is too high; in that case, the voltage regulator is probably at fault.

After the test is completed, reconnect the voltage regulator/rectifier leads to the battery.

Test the separate charging system components as described in this chapter.

ALTERNATOR

An alternator is a form of electrical generator in which a magnetized field called a rotor revolves within a set of stationary coils called a stator. As the rotor revolves, alternating current is induced in the stator. The current is then rectified and used to operate the electrical accessories on the motorcycle and for charging the battery. The rotor is permanently magnetized.

ALTERNATOR ROTOR

Removal/Installation

1. On models other than 1983 350-600 cc, remove the bolts securing the skid plate and remove the skid plate.
2. Drain the engine oil as described in Chapter Three.
3. Remove both side covers and the seat.

> *NOTE*
> *On early XL250S and XL500S models, reinstall the seat strap bolts as they also hold the upper portion of the shocks to the frame. Remove and reinstall one bolt at a time.*

4. Remove the fuel tank as described in Chapter Six.
5. On XL series models, disconnect the battery negative lead or the main fuse.

6. Disconnect the alternator's stator assembly electrical connector containing 2 wires.

7. Remove the bolt securing the gearshift lever (A, **Figure 5**) and remove the gearshift lever.

8. On 1983 350-600 cc models, perform the following:

   a. Loosen the locknut on the clutch cable at the hand lever to allow slack in the clutch cable.

   b. Disconnect the clutch cable from the actuating arm (B, **Figure 5**) on the alternator cover.

9. Remove the bolts securing the drive sprocket cover (**Figure 6**) and remove the cover.

10. Remove the screws securing the alternator cover (**Figure 7**). Remove the cover and gasket. Don't lose the locating dowels.

11. Shift the transmission into any gear and have an assistant apply the rear brake. Remove the shoulder bolt (**Figure 8**) securing the rotor in place.

12. Screw a flywheel puller (**Figure 9**) into the rotor until it stops. Use the Honda flywheel puller (part No. 07733-0020001), K & N (part No. 81-0170) or equivalent. Refer to **Figure 10** for 1983 350-600 cc models or **Figure 11** for all other models.

> *CAUTION*
> *Do not try to remove the rotor without a puller; any attempt to do so will lead to some form of damage to the engine and/or rotor. Many aftermarket types of pullers are available from most motorcycle dealers or mail order houses. The cost of a puller is about $10 and it makes an excellent addition to any mechanic's tool box. If you can't borrow one, have a dealer remove the rotor for you.*

13. Turn the puller until the rotor disengages from the crankshaft.

14. Remove the rotor and puller. Don't lose the Woodruff key on the crankshaft.

> *CAUTION*
> *Carefully inspect the inside of the rotor (Figure 12) for small bolts, washers, or other metal "trash" that may have been*

picked up by the magnets. These small metal bits can cause severe damage to the stator assembly components.

15. Make sure the Woodruff key is in place in the slot in the crankshaft. Refer to **Figure 13** for 1983 350-600 cc models or **Figure 14** for all other models.

16. Align the keyway in the rotor with the key when installing the rotor.

17. Install the rotor shoulder bolt.

18. To keep the rotor from turning hold the rotor with a flywheel holder (Honda part No. 07725-004000), strap wrench (**Figure 15**) or equivalent.

19. Tighten the rotor bolt to the torque specification listed in **Table 2**.

20. Make sure the locating dowels are in place. Install the alternator rotor cover and gasket. Tighten the screws securely.

21. Install the drive sprocket cover and tighten the screws securely.

22. On 1983 350-600 cc models, connect the clutch cable to the actuating arm (B, **Figure 5**) on the alternator cover.

23. Install the gearshift lever and tighten the bolt securely.

24. Connect the alternator's stator assembly electrical connector.

25. On XL series models, connect the battery negative lead.

26. Install the fuel tank as described in Chapter Six.

27. Install both side covers and the seat.

28. Fill the engine with the recommended type and quantity of engine oil as described in Chapter Three.

29. On 1983 350R-600 cc models, adjust the clutch as described in Chapter Three.

Testing

The rotor is permanently magnetized and cannot be tested except by replacement with a rotor known to be good. A rotor can lose magnetism from old age or a sharp blow. If defective, the rotor must be replaced; it cannot be remagnetized.

ALTERNATOR STATOR

Removal/Installation

1. Perform Steps 1-10 of *Alternator Rotor Removal/Installation* in this chapter.

2A. On 1983 350-600 cc models, perform the following:

    a. Remove the bolts (A, **Figure 16**) securing the stator assembly to the alternator cover.

    b. Remove the rubber grommet (B, **Figure 16**) and electrical wire harness from the notch in the cover.

    c. Remove the stator assembly.

Figure 16

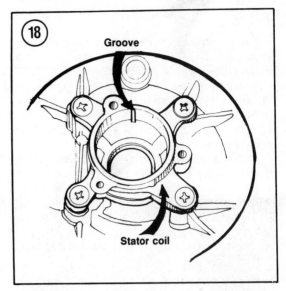

Figure 18 — Groove, Stator coil

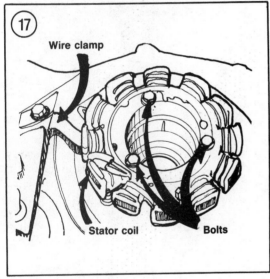

Figure 17 — Wire clamp, Stator coil, Bolts

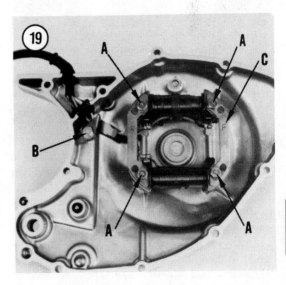

Figure 19

8

2B. On 1982 XL500S and XL500R models, perform the following:

a. Remove the bolts (**Figure 17**) securing the stator assembly to the stator coil base in the alternator cover.

b. Remove the bolt securing the wire clamp (**Figure 17**) and remove the stator assembly.

c. Remove both rubber grommets and electrical wire harness from the 2 notches in the alternator cover.

d. To remove the stator coil base, remove the screws securing the base to the alternator cover. To install the base, position the groove on the base facing upward (**Figure 18**). Tighten the screws securely.

2C. On all other models, perform the following:

a. Remove the bolts (A, **Figure 19**) securing the stator assembly and set plates to the alternator cover.

b. Remove the bolt (B, **Figure 19**) securing the wire clamp and remove the wire clamp.

c. Remove both rubber grommets and electrical wire harness from the 2 notches in the alternator cover.

d. Remove the stator assembly.

e. Be sure to install the assembly with the "F" mark (C, **Figure 19**) facing toward the front of the alternator cover.

3. Install by reversing these removal steps, noting the following.

4. Make sure all electrical connections are tight.

Testing

It is not necessary to remove the stator assembly to perform the following tests. It is shown removed in the following procedure for clarity.

In order to get accurate resistance measurements, the stator assembly must be warm (minimum temperature is 68° F/20° C). If necessary, start the engine and let it reach normal operating temperature.

1. Remove the side covers, seat and fuel tank.
2. On XL series models, disconnect the battery negative lead or disconnect the main fuse (**Figure 20**).
3. Disconnect the electrical wires coming from the alternator stator assembly.

Lighting coil

Use an ohmmeter set at R×1 and check for continuity between the following wires (A, **Figure 21**):

    a. XR series: Blue wire and ground.
    b. XL series: White/yellow wire and ground.

If there is continuity (low resistance) the coil is good. If there is no continuity (infinite resistance) the coil is bad and the stator assembly must be replaced (the individual coil cannot be replaced).

Exciter coil

On XL series models, use an ohmmeter set at R×1 and check for continuity between the pink/yellow wire and ground (B, **Figure 21**).

On XR series models, use an ohmmeter set at R×10 and check for continuity between the black/red wire and ground.

If there is continuity (low resistance) the coil is good. If there is no continuity (infinite resistance) the coil is bad and the stator assembly must be replaced (the individual coil cannot be replaced).

VOLTAGE REGULATOR/RECTIFIER (XL SERIES)

Removal/Installation

1. Remove the seat and fuel tank.
2. Disconnect the battery leads or disconnect the main fuse (**Figure 20**).
3. Remove the bolts and disconnect the wires from the voltage regulator/rectifier and remove it.
4. Install by reversing these steps.

Voltage Regulator Performance Test

Connect a voltmeter to the battery negative and positive terminals. Leave the battery cables

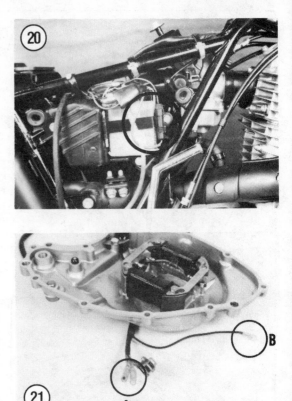

attached. Start the engine and let it idle; increase engine speed until the voltage going to the battery reaches 8.0-8.9 volts. At this point, the voltage regulator should prevent any further increase in voltage. If this does not happen and voltage increases above specifications, the voltage regulator/rectifier is faulty and must be replaced.

IGNITION SYSTEM

The ignition systems used among the various models are shown in the following illustrations:

    a. **Figure 22**—XL250S and XL500S.
    b. **Figure 23**—XR250 and XR500.
    c. **Figure 24**—1981-1982 XR250R, 1981-1982 XR500R and XR350R.
    d. **Figure 25**—1982-1983 XL250R, XL500R.
    e. **Figure 26**—1983 XR500R.
    f. **Figure 27**—1983 XL600R.

Ignition Coil
Removal/Installation

1. Remove the side covers and the seat.
2. Remove the fuel tank as described in Chapter Seven.

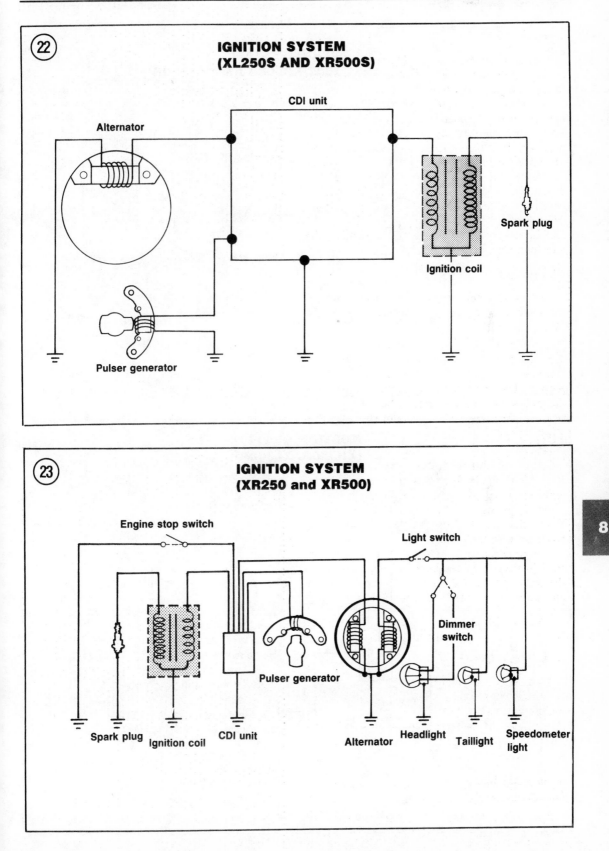

**IGNITION SYSTEM
(XL250S AND XR500S)**

22

CDI unit

Alternator

Spark plug

Ignition coil

Pulser generator

**IGNITION SYSTEM
(XR250 and XR500)**

23

Engine stop switch

Light switch

Dimmer switch

Pulser generator

Spark plug

Ignition coil

CDI unit

Alternator

Headlight

Taillight

Speedometer light

8

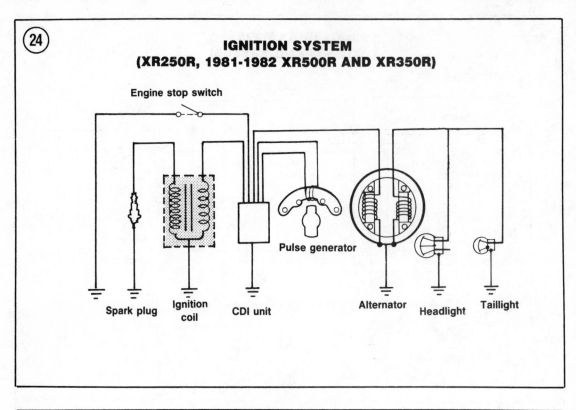

(24)

IGNITION SYSTEM
(XR250R, 1981-1982 XR500R AND XR350R)

Engine stop switch

Pulse generator

Spark plug   Ignition   CDI unit   Alternator   Headlight   Taillight
              coil

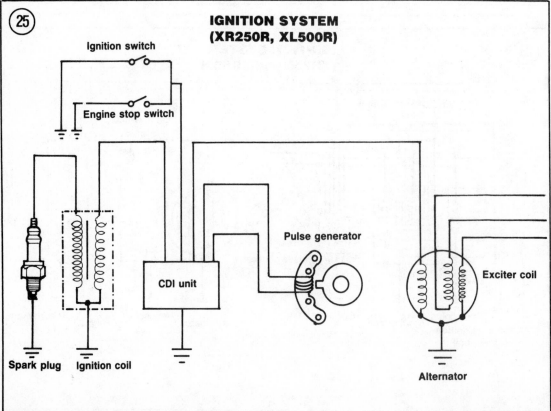

(25)

IGNITION SYSTEM
(XR250R, XL500R)

Ignition switch

Engine stop switch

Pulse generator

CDI unit

Exciter coil

Spark plug   Ignition coil

Alternator

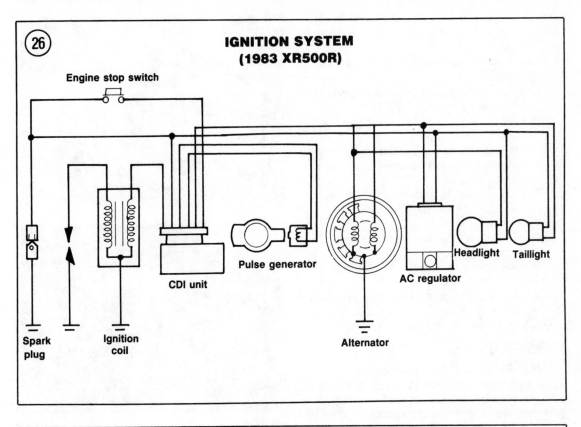

(26)

IGNITION SYSTEM
(1983 XR500R)

Engine stop switch

Spark plug

Ignition coil

CDI unit

Pulse generator

Alternator

AC regulator

Headlight   Taillight

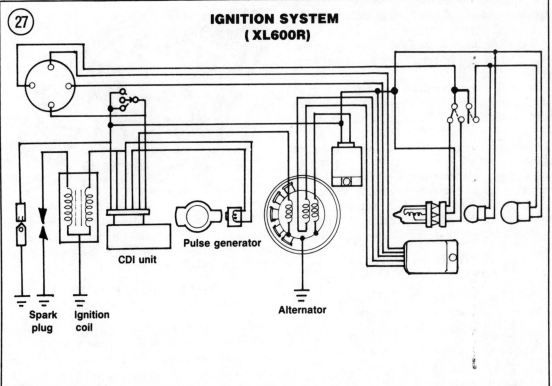

(27)

IGNITION SYSTEM
(XL600R)

Spark plug

Ignition coil

CDI unit

Pulse generator

Alternator

8

3. On XL series models, disconnect the battery negative lead or disconnect the main fuse (**Figure 28**).

4A. On XR500R and XL600R models, perform the following:

    a. Disconnect the primary wires (**Figure 29**) from the ignition coil.

    b. Disconnect the secondary (spark plug) wire from the spark plug.

    c. Pull the ignition coil and secondary from the frame (the coil is not mounted to the frame as on other models).

4B. On all other models, perform the following:

    a. Disconnect the primary wires from the ignition coil.

    b. Disconnect the secondary (spark plug) wire from the spark plug.

    c. Remove the bolts (**Figure 30**) securing the ignition coil to the frame.

    d. Remove the coil and the secondary wire from the frame.

5. Install by reversing these removal steps.

Ignition Coil Testing

Refer to **Figure 31** for this procedure.

The ignition coil is a form of transformer which develops the high voltage required to jump the spark plug gap. The only maintenance required is that of keeping the electrical connections clean and tight and occassionally checking to see that the coil is mounted securely.

If coil condition is doubtful, there are several checks which may be made. Disconnect coil wires before testing.

1. Measure the coil primary resistance using an ohmmeter set at R X1. Measure the resistance between the primary terminal and the mounting flange. The value is listed in **Table 3**.

2. Measure the secondary resistance, using an ohmmeter set at R X1. Measure the resistance between the secondary (spark plug lead) and the mounting flange. The value is listed in **Table 3**.

3. If the coil resistance does not meet these specifications, the coil must be replaced. If the coil exhibits visible damage, it should be replaced.

SOLID-STATE IGNITION ADVANCE MECHANISM

Ignition timing advance on the following models is electronically controlled and maintenance free:

    a. XL250R.

    b. XR350R.

    c. XL500R.

    d. XR500R.

    e. XL600R.

An ignition timing advance circuit has been added to the CDI unit. This circuit senses speed of the pulse generator rotor as it passes the pulse generator and changes ignition timing accordingly.

MECHANICAL IGNITION ADVANCE MECHANISM

The mechanical ignition advance mechanism advances the ignition (fires the spark plug sooner) as engine speed increases. If if does not advance properly and smoothly, the ignition will be incorrect at high engine rpm. It must be inspected

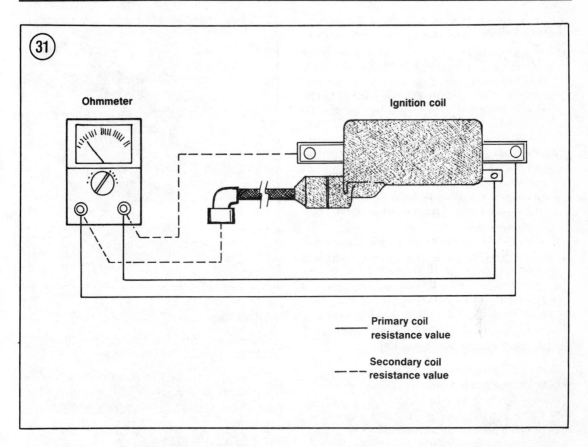

Ohmmeter

Ignition coil

_____ Primary coil
resistance value

_ _ _ _ Secondary coil
resistance value

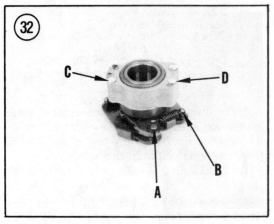

periodically to make certain it operates smoothly.

1. Remove the ignition advance mechanism as described in Chapter Four.

2. Inspect the rotor pivot points (A, **Figure 32**) of each weight. The rotor must pivot freely to maintain proper ignition advance. Apply lightweight grease to the pivot pins.

3. Inspect the rotor return springs (B, **Figure 32**). Make sure they are taut and return the rotor to its fully retarded position completely.

4. If the rotor is removed from the base, install it, aligning the punch mark (C, **Figure 32**) with the hole in the base.

NOTE
*If the ignition advancer rotor is replaced, the new one must have the same letter designation stamped on it. Refer to D, **Figure 32**. Failure to do so will result in poor engine performance.*

5. Install by reversing these removal steps.

CAPACITOR DISCHARGE IGNITION

All models are equipped with a capacitor discharge ignition (CDI) system. This solid state system uses no breaker points.

Alternating current from the alternator is rectified and used to charge the capacitor. As the piston approaches the firing position, pulse from the signal coil is rectified, shaped and then used to trigger the silicon controlled rectifier (SCR). This in turn allows the capacitor to discharge quickly into the primary circuit of the ignition coil, where the voltage is stepped up in the secondary circuit to a value sufficient to fire the spark plug.

8

CDI Precautions

Certain measures must be taken to protect the capacitor discharge system. Instantaneous damage to the semiconductors in the system will occur if the following precautions are not observed. The majority of these precautions relate to the XL series.

1. Never connect the battery backward. If battery polarity is wrong, damage will occur to the voltage regulator/recifier, alternator and CDI system.
2. Do not disconnect the battery when the engine is running. A voltage surge will occur which will damage the voltage regulator/rectifier and possibly burn out the lights.
3. Keep all connections between the various units clean and tight. Be sure that the wiring connectors are pushed together firmly.
4. Do not substitute another type of ignition coil or battery.
5. The CDI unit is mounted with a rubber vibration isolator. Always be sure that the isolators are in place when replacing the unit.

CDI Troubleshooting

Problems with the capacitor discharge system usually fall into one of the following categories. See **Table 4**.

a. Weak spark.
b. No spark.

Pulse Generator Testing/Replacement

Inspect the pulse generator in the right-hand crankcase cover. Use an ohmmeter, set at R X 10, and check the resistance between the green and blue/yellow wire in the electrical terminal. The value should be between 20-60 ohms. If the resistance shown is greater or there is no reading at all (infinity) between the 2 terminals, the pulse generator has a short or open and must be replaced.

Remove the 2 Phillips head screws (A, **Figure 33**) and remove the unit. Replace with a unit having the same letter designation stamped on it (B, **Figure 33**). Route the electrical harness through the crankcase half and out the rubber grommet as shown in **Figure 33**.

> *NOTE*
> *If the ignition pulser is replaced, the new one must have the same letter designation stamped on it. Refer to B, **Figure 33**. Failure to do so will result in poor engine performance.*

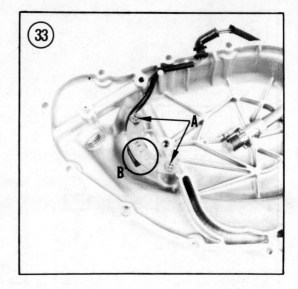

CDI Testing

To test the CDI unit, remove the unit from the frame as described in this chapter.

> *CAUTION*
> *Tests may be performed on the CDI unit but a good one may be damaged by someone unfamiliar with the test equipment. If you feel unqualified to perform the test, have the test made by a Honda dealer or substitute a good unit for a suspected one.*

> *NOTE*
> *Tests must be made with a quality ohmmeter or the test readings may be false.*

Make the test measurements using a quality ohmmeter. Refer to **Table 5** for ohmmeter positive (+) and negative (-) test lead placement, wire color code and specified resistance values.

On XL250R, XR350R, 1983 XR500R and XL600R models, the electrical wire harness connector disconnects from the CDI unit. After removal there are no electrical wires attached to the CDI unit; therefore the tests are made directly to the terminals within the CDI unit. Refer to the following figures for terminal color designation for the various models:

a. XL250R—**Figure 34**.
b. XR350R—**Figure 35**.
c. 1983 XR500R, XL600R—**Figure 36**.

On all other models, there are electrical wires attached to the CDI unit after it has been disconnected from the wire harness. Perform the tests at each individual wire connector.

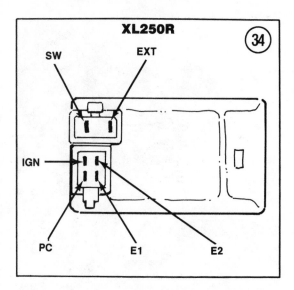

XL250R

SW   EXT

IGN

PC   E1   E2

③④

③⑦

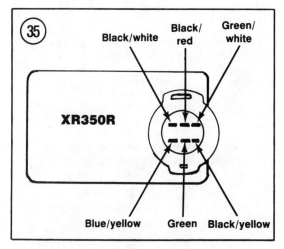

③⑤

Black/white   Black/red   Green/white

XR350R

Blue/yellow   Green   Black/yellow

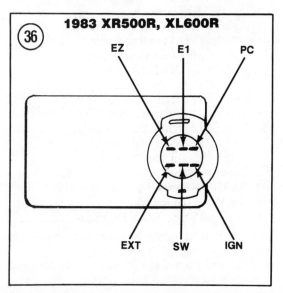

③⑥

1983 XR500R, XL600R

EZ   E1   PC

EXT   SW   IGN

If the CDI unit fails *any one* of the tests, the unit is faulty and must be replaced.

CDI Unit Replacement

1. Remove the side covers, seat and the fuel tank.
2. On XL series models, disconnect the battery negative lead or disconnect the main fuse (**Figure 28**).
3A. On XR350R, XR500R and XL600R models, perform the following:
  a. Disconnect the electrical wires going from the CDI unit to the electrical harness (A, **Figure 37**).
  b. Remove the CDI unit from the rubber vibrator isolator on the frame (B, **Figure 37**).
  c. Remove the CDI unit.
3B. On all other models, perform the following:
  a. Disconnect the electrical wires going from the CDI unit to the electrical harness.
  b. Remove the bolt and nut securing the CDI unit to the frame.
  c. Remove the CDI unit.
4. Install a new CDI unit and attach the electrical wires to it. Make sure all electrical connections are tight.
5. Install the fuel tank, seat and side covers.

SPARK PLUG

The spark plug recommended by the factory is usually the most suitable for your machine. If riding conditions are mild, it may be advisable to go to a spark plug one step hotter than normal. Unusually severe riding conditions may require a slightly colder plug. See Chapter Three for details.

8

LIGHTING SYSTEM

The lighting system on XL series models consists of a headlight, taillight/brakelight combination, directional signals, 3 indicator lights and speedometer illumination light.

Table 6 lists replacement bulbs for these components.

Headlight Replacement (XL Series)

1. Remove the 2 screws (**Figure 38**), one on each side of the headlight housing.
2. Pull the trim bezel and headlight unit up and out of the housing. Disconnect the electrical connector from the backside of the headlight unit.
3. Remove the retainer securing the sealed beam unit and remove it and the sealed beam.
4. Install by reversing these removal steps.
5. Adjust the headlight as described in this chapter.

Headlight Replacement (XR200 and 500 Series)

1. Remove the 3 bolts (**Figure 39**) securing headlight holder.

2. Pivot the holder down and disconnect the electrical connector (**Figure 40**) from the backside.
3. Remove the headlight mounting and adjusting screws and remove the headlight unit.
4. Install by reversing these removal steps.
5. Adjust the headlight as described in this chapter.

Headlight Replacement (XR350R)

1. Unhook the headlight rubber mounting bands (**Figure 41**) securing number plate/headlight shroud to the front forks.
2. Disconnect the electrical wires (**Figure 42**) going to the headlight.

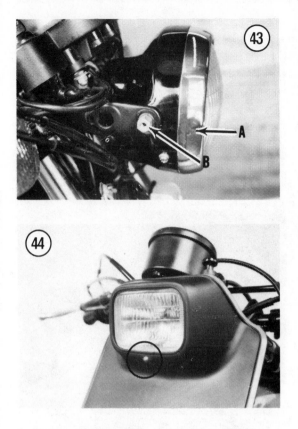

3. Remove the headlight and shroud assembly.
4. Pull the rubber cover off the back of the headlight lens assembly.
5. Unhook the metal clip securing the headlight bulb socket.
6. Remove the headight bulb and replace with a new bulb.
7. Install by reversing these removal steps.

Headlight Replacement (XL600R)

1. Remove the bolts securing the number plate/headlight shroud to the front forks. Remove the shroud.
2. Remove the upper and lower bolt securing the headlight assembly to the headlight bracket.
3. Remove the socket holder from the backside of the lens.
4. Push down and rotate the socket, then remove the socket from the headlight lens unit.
5. Remove the headight bulb from the backside of the headlight lens unit.
6. Install the new bulb. Align the lugs on the bulb with the cutouts in the lens unit.
7. Place the bulb socket over the bulb. Align the lugs of the bulb with the grooves in the socket, then push down and turn the socket until it stops.

8. Install the socket holder with the "TOP" mark and arrow to the top of the lens unit.
9. Install the headlight assembly into the headlight bracket and install the bolts. Tighten the bolts securely.
10. Install the number plate/headlight shroud to the front forks. Tighten the screws securely.
11. Adjust the headlight as described in this chapter.

Headlight Adjustment (XL250S and XL500S)

Adjust the headlight horizontally and vertically according to Department of Motor Vehicle regulations in your area.

To adjust headlight horizontally, turn the screw (A, **Figure 43**). Screwing it in turns the light to the right and loosening it will turn the light to the left. For vertical adjustment, unscrew the front amber reflex reflectors, loosen the mounting bolts (B, **Figure 43**) and tilt the headlight assembly. Tighten the bolts and reinstall the reflectors.

Headlight Adjustment (XL600R)

Adjust the headlight horizontally and vertically according to Department of Motor Vehicle regulations in your area.

To adjust headlight horizontally, turn the screw on the lower right-hand side of the number plate/headlight shroud.

To adjust the headlight vertically, loosen the number plate/headlight shroud mounting bolts and tilt the headlight assembly. Tighten the bolts.

Headlight Adjustment (XR Series Models)

Adjustment is limited to vertical only. Adjust to your own personal preference. Turn the adjust screw (**Figure 44**) at the base of the headlight holder. There are no regulations on headlight adjustment for off-road use yet.

Taillight/Brakelight Replacement

Remove the screws (**Figure 45** shows the XL series and **Figure 46** shows the XR series) securing the lens and remove it. Wash out the inside and outside with mild detergent and wipe dry. Wipe off the reflective base surrounding the bulb with a soft cloth. Replace the bulb and install the lens; do not overtighten the screws or the lens may crack.

8

Directional Signal Light Replacement
(XL Series Models)

Remove the screws securing the lens and remove it. Wash out the inside and outside with a mild detergent and wipe dry. Replace the bulb and install the lens; do not overtighten the screws as that will crack the lens.

Speedometer Illumination Light Replacement
(1978-1980 XL250S, XL500S and XL500R)

1. Remove the headlight (A, **Figure 47**) as described in this chapter.
2. Disconnect the speedometer drive cable (B, **Figure 47**).
3. Remove the acorn nuts and washers (C, **Figure 47**). Pull the instrument cluster forward and turn it upside down.
4. Pull the defective lamp holder/electrical wire assembly up and out of the housing.
5. Remove and replace the defective bulb.

> *NOTE*
> *If a new good bulb will not work, check the wire connections for loose or broken wires. Also check the bulb socket for corrosion. Replace as necessary.*

6. Install by reversing these removal steps.

Speedometer Illumination Light Replacement
(Models XR250, XR350R, XR500 and XR500R)

1. Remove the headlight holder as described in this chapter.
2. Pull the bulb holder/electrical wire assembly (**Figure 48**) down and out of the housing.
3. Remove and replace the defective bulb.

> *NOTE*
> *If a new good bulb will not work, check the wire connections for loose or broken wires. Also check the bulb socket for corrosion. Replace as necessary.*

4. Install by reversing these removal steps.

Speedometer Illumination Light Replacement
(1981 XL250S and XL500S, XL250R)

1. Carefully pull the bulb socket/electrical wire assembly from the backside of the speedometer housing.
2. Remove and replace the defective bulb.
3. Push the bulb socket/electrical wire assembly back into the speedometer housing. Make sure it is completely seated to prevent the entry of water and moisture.

NOTE
If a new good bulb will not work, check the wire connections for loose or broken wires. Also check the bulb socket for corrosion. Replace as necessary.

Speedometer Illumination Light Replacement (1981-1982 XR250R and XR500R)

The speedometer on these models is not illuminated.

Speedometer Illumination Light Replacement (1983 XL600R)

1. Remove the headlight as described in this chapter.
2. Remove the acorn nuts and washers. Pull the instrument cluster up and off of the mounting bracket.
3. Pull the defective lamp holder/electrical wire assembly out of the housing.
4. Remove and replace the defective bulb.

NOTE
If a new good bulb will not work, check the wire connections for loose or broken wires. Also check the bulb socket for corrosion. Replace as necessary.

5. Install by reversing these removal steps, noting the following.

6. Make sure the rubber cushion is in place between the speedometer housing and the mounting plate.

Neutral, High Beam and Turn Signal Indicator Light Replacement (1978-1980)

Follow the procedure for replacement of the speedometer illumination light in this chapter.

Neutral, High Beam and Turn Signal Indicator Light Replacement (1981-on)

1. On 1983 XL600R models, remove the headlight assembly as described in this chatper.
2. Carefully pull the bulb socket/electrical wire assembly from the backside of the instrument cluster housing.
3. Remove and replace the defective bulb.
4. Push the bulb socket/electrical wire assembly back into the instrument cluster housing. Make sure it is completely seated to prevent the entry of water and moisture.

NOTE
If a new good bulb will not work, check the wire connections for loose or broken wires. Also check the bulb socket for corrosion. Replace as necessary.

5. On 1983 XL600R models, install the headlight assembly as described in this chapter.

SWITCHES (XL SERIES MODELS)

Front Brake Light Replacement (Drum Brake Models)

Pull back the rubber protective boot on the brake hand lever. Pull the small rubber boot (**Figure 49**) away from the switch and remove the switch. Disconnect the electrical wires and replace with a new switch.

Front Brake Light Replacement (Disc Brake Models)

Remove the screw and washer securing the brake switch to the bottom of the master cylinder. Disconnect the electrical wires and replace with a new switch. Install the switch and tighten the screw securely.

Rear Brakelight Switch Replacement

1. Unhook spring from brake arm (A, **Figure 50**).
2. Unscrew the switch housing and locknut from bracket (B, **Figure 50**).

8

3. Pull up the rubber boot and remove the electrical wires (C, **Figure 50**).

4. Replace the switch; reinstall and adjust as described in this chapter.

Rear Brakelight Switch Adjustment

1. Turn the ignition switch to the ON position.

2. Depress the brake pedal. Light should come on just as the brake begins to work.

3. To make the light come on earlier, hold the switch body and turn adjusting locknut *clockwise* as viewed from the top. Turn *counterclockwise* to delay the light.

> *NOTE*
> *Some riders prefer the light to come on a little early. This way, they can tap the pedal without braking to warn drivers who follow too closely.*

ELECTRICAL COMPONENTS

Horn (XL Series Models)

Removal/installation

1. Disconnect horn connector from electrical harness (A, **Figure 51**).

2. Remove the bolt securing horn to bracket (B, **Figure 51**).

3. Installation is the reverse of these steps.

Testing

1. Disconnect horn wires from harness.

2. Connect horn wire to the positive terminal of the battery. Connect horn flange to negative terminal. If it is good, it will sound.

Instrument Cluster
Removal/Installation
(XL250S and XL500S)

1. Disconnect the main fuse at the battery (**Figure 52**).

2. Remove the headlight (A, **Figure 53**) as described in this chapter.

3. Disconnect the speedometer drive cable (B, **Figure 53**).

4. Remove the 2 acorn nuts and washers (C, **Figure 53**), pull the instrument cluster forward and turn upside down.

5. Pull out all 6 lamp holder/electrical wire assemblies.

6. Disconnect the ignition switch 4 pin electrical connector located within the headlight housing.

7. Pull the ignition switch (D, **Figure 53**) and electrical harness out from the cluster and remove the switch.

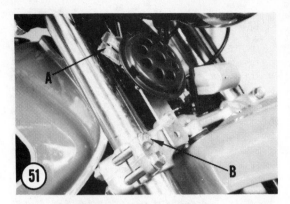

8. Remove the instrument cluster assembly.

9. Install by reversing these removal steps. Be sure the rubber insulators are in place on the mounting studs (C, **Figure 53**).

Speedometer Housing
Removal/Installation
(All Other Models)

1. Remove the 3 bolts (**Figure 54**) securing the headlight holder and pivot it down. Disconnect the electrical connector from the headlight unit.

2. Pull the lamp holder/electrical wire assembly (A, **Figure 55**) down and out of the housing.

3. Disconnect the speedometer drive cable (**B, Figure 55**).

4. Remove the 2 acorn nuts, washers and rubber insulators (C, **Figure 55**). Pull the speedometer up and remove it.

5. Install by reversing these removal steps; be sure to reinstall the rubber insulators (C, **Figure 55**).

FUSES (XL SERIES MODELS)

There is only one fuse on XL series models and it is located under the right-hand side cover. It is a 10A main fuse.

The fuse is attached, in a fuse holder, to the battery hold-down strap (**Figure 52**).

NOTE
Always carry a spare fuse.

Whenever a fuse blows, find out the reason for failure before replacing the fuse. Usually, the trouble is a short circuit in the wiring. This may caused by worn-through insulation or a disconnected wire shorting to the ground.

CAUTION
Never substitute metal foil or wire for a fuse. Never use a higher amperage fuse than specified. An overload could result in fire and complete loss of the bike.

NOTE
The XR series is not equipped with a fuse.

WIRING DIAGRAMS

Full color wiring diagrams for all models are included at the end of this manual.

8

Tables are on the following pages.

Table 1 CHARGING CURRENT

XL250S: Disconnect black wire @ voltage regulator	
Light switch OFF	
5,000 rpm	4.0A/8.9V
8,000 rpm	5.5A/8.0V
Light switch ON (high beam)	
5,000 rpm	2.6A/7.5V
8,000 rpm	4.0A/8.0V
XL250R: Disconnect black wire @ voltage regulator	
2,500 rpm	2.5A/16.8V
8,000 rpm	5.5A/18.4V
XL500S: Disconnect black wire @ voltage regulator	
Light switch OFF	
5,000 rpm	3.2A/8.0V
8,000 rpm	5.5A/8.9V
Light switch ON (high beam)	
5,000 rpm	1.8A/7.5V
8,000 rpm	4.0A/8.0V
XL500R: Disconnect black wire @ voltage regulator;	
disconnect headlight, taillight, running lights	
2,500 rpm	2.7A/16.8V
8,000 rpm	5.5A/18.4V
XL600R: Disconnect black wire @ voltage regulator;	
disconnect headlight, taillight, running lights	
2,500 rpm	3.0A/16.8V
8,000 rpm	6.5A/18.4V

Table 2 ALTERNATOR ROTOR BOLT TORQUE SPECIFICATIONS

Model	ft.-lb.	N•m
XL250S	61-69	85-105
XL250R	72-87	100-120
XR250, XR250R	69-76	95-105
All 350-600 cc engines	72-87	100-120

Table 3 IGNITION COIL RESISTANCE SPECIFICATIONS (OHMS)

Model	Primary	Secondary
XL250S, XL250R, XR250, XR250R	0.2-0.8	8-15 K
XR350R	0.2-.03	3.2-4.2 K
XL500S, XR500	0.2-0.8	8-15 K
XL500R	0.2-0.8	3.4-4.2 K
1981-1982 XR500R	0.2-0.8	2-6 K
1983 XR500R, XL600R	0.8	4.1 K

Table 4 CDI TROUBLESHOOTING

Symptoms	Probable Cause
Weak spark	Low battery
	Poor connections (clean and tighten)
	High voltage leakage (replace defective wire)
	Defective coil
No spark	Discharged battery
	Fuse burned out
	Wiring broken
	Defective coil
	Defective signal generating coil (replace)

Table 5 CDI TEST POINTS

Test Probe		Value (ohms)
Positive (+)	Negative (−)	
XR250R		
Black/red	green	1-30
Black/red	black/white[1]	infinity
Black/red	blue/yellow	2-50
Black/red	black/white[2]	infinity
Green	black/red	infinity
Green	black/white[1]	infinity
Green	blue/yellow	2-50
Green	black/white[2]	infinity
Black/white[1]	black/red	0.3-20
Black/white[1]	green	10-100
Black/white[1]	blue/yellow	10-150
Black/white[1]	black/white[2]	infinity
Blue/yellow	black/red	infinity
Blue/yellow	green	infinity
Blue/yellow	black white[1]	infinity
Blue/yellow	black/white[2]	infinity
Black/white[2]	black/red	infinity
Black/white[2]	green	infinity
Black/white[2]	black/white[1]	infinity
Black/white[2]	blue/yellow	infinity
XL250S, XR250, XR500, XL500S		
Black/red	green	0.5-10
Black/red	black/white[1]	infinity
Black/red	blue/yellow	2-50
Black/red	black/white[2]	infinity
Green	black/red	infinity
Green	black/white[1]	infinity
Green	blue/yellow	0.5-10
Green	black/white[2]	infinity
Black/white[1]	black/red	0.5-10
Black/white[1]	green	2-50
(continued)		

8

Table 5 CDI TEST POINTS (continued)

Positive (+)	Test Probe Negative (−)	Value (ohms)
XL250S, XR250, XR500, XL500S (continued)		
Black/white[1]	blue/yellow	2-50
Black/white[1]	black/white[2]	infinity
Blue/yellow	black/red	infinity
Blue/yellow	green	infinity
Blue/yellow	black white[1]	infinity
Blue/yellow	black/white[2]	infinity
Black/white[2]	black/red	infinity
Black/white[2]	green	infinity
Black/white[2]	black/white[1]	infinity
Black/white[2]	blue/yellow	infinity
XL500R		
SW	EXT	0.1-20
SW	PC	10-100
SW	E1/E2	1-50
SW	IGN	infinity
EXT	SW	infinity
EXT	PC	5-50
EXT	E1/E2	0.1-20
EXT	IGN	infinity
PC	SW	infinity
PC	EXT	infinity[3]
PC	E1/E2	1-50
PC	IGN	infinity
E1/E2	SW	infinity
E1/E2	EXT	infinity[3]
E1/E2	PC	1-50
E1/E2	IGN	infinity
IGN	SW	infinity
IGN	EXT	infinity
IGN	PC	infinity
IGN	E1/E2	infinity
XR250, XR500R		
Black/red	green	1-30
Black/red	black/white[1]	infinity
Black/red	blue/yellow	2-50
Black/red	black/white[2]	infinity
Green	black/red	infinity
Green	black/white[1]	infinity
Green	blue/yellow	2-50
Green	black/white[2]	infinity
Black/white[1]	black/red	0.3-20
Black/white[1]	green	10-100
Black/white[1]	blue/yellow	10-150
Black/white[1]	black/white[2]	infinity
Blue/yellow	black/red	infinity
Blue/yellow	green	infinity
Blue/yellow	black white[1]	infinity
Blue/yellow	black/white[2]	infinity
Black/white[2]	black/red	infinity
Black/white[2]	green	infinity
Black/white[2]	black/white[1]	infinity
Black/white[2]	blue/yellow	infinity

Table 5 CDI TEST POINTS (continued)

Test Probe Positive (+)	Test Probe Negative (−)	Value (ohms)
XL250R, XR350R		
SW	EXT	0.1-20
SW	PC	30-300
SW	E1/E2	1-50
SW	IGN	infinity
EXT	SW	infinity
EXT	PC	10-200
EXT	E1/E2	infinity
EXT	IGN	infinity
PC	SW	infinity
PC	EXT	infinity
PC	E1/E2	1-100
PC	IGN	infinity
E1/E2	SW	infinity
E1/E2	EXT	infinity
E1/E2	PC	1-100
E1/E2	IGN	infinity
IGN	SW	infinity
IGN	EXT	infinity
IGN	PC	infinity
IGN	E1/E2	infinity
XR500R, XL600R		
SW	EXT	0.1-20
SW	PC	30-300
SW	E1/E2	1-50
SW	IGN	infinity
EXT	SW	infinity
EXT	PC	10-200
EXT	E1/E2	0.1-20
EXT	IGN	infinity
PC	SW	infinity
PC	EXT	infinity[3]
PC	E1/E2	1-100
PC	IGN	infinity
E1/E2	SW	infinity
E1/E2	EXT	infinity[3]
E1/E2	PC	1-100
E1/E2	IGN	infinity
IGN	SW	infinity
IGN	EXT	infinity
IGN	PC	infinity
IGN	E1/E2	infinity

1. Engine stop switch.
2. Primary coil
3. Needle swings and returns to infinity.

8

Table 6 REPLACEMENT BULBS*

Model	Headlight	Taillight/ brakelight	Turn signal
XL250S	6V 35/36.5W	6V/32W	6V/18W
XL250R	12V 35/36.5W	12V/32W	12V/23W
XR250	6V 25/25W	6V/6/3	–
XR250R	6V 25/25W	6V/3W	–
XR350R			
Standard	6V/35W	6V/3W	–
Optional	12V/55W	12V/3.4W	–
XL500S	6V 35/36.5W	6V/32W	6V/17W
XL500R	12V 35/36.5W	12V/32W	12V/23W
XR500	6V 25/25W	6V/6/3	–
XR500R			
1981-1982	6V 25/25W	6V/3W	–
1983	12V 25/25W	12V/3W	–
XL600R	H4JA 12V/60/55W	12V/32W	12V/23

*All indicator and illumination bulbs 6V or 12V and 1.7W or 3W.

FRONT SUSPENSION AND STEERING

This chapter describes repair and maintenance on the front wheel, forks and steering components.

Refer to **Table 1** for torque specifications. **Tables 1-4** are located at the end of this chapter.

FRONT WHEEL
(DRUM BRAKE)

Removal
(1981-1982 XR250R and XR500R)

1. Place a wood block(s) under the skid plate to support the bike securely with the front wheel off the ground.
2. Slacken the brake cable at the hand lever.
3. Unscrew the speedometer cable set screw (A,

Figure 1). Pull the speedometer cable free from the speedometer gear box.
4. At the brake panel, loosen the locknut (A, **Figure 2**) and remove the cable end from the brake arm (B, **Figure 2**). Remove the brake cable from the bracket on the brake panel.
5. Loosen the axle holder nuts (B, **Figure 1**) and loosen the axle holder. It is not necessary to remove the axle holder, just loosen it enough to clear the front axle.
6. Unscrew the axle (C, **Figure 1**) from the left-hand fork leg.
7. Pull the wheel down and forward. This allows the brake panel to disengage from the boss on the left-hand fork slider.
8. Remove the wheel.

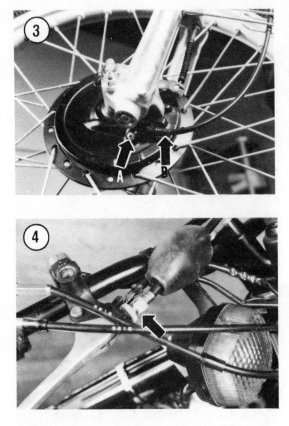

Removal (All Other Models)

1. Place a wood block(s) under the skid plate to support the bike securely with the front wheel off the ground.

2. Loosen the screw (A, **Figure 3**) securing the speedometer cable (B, **Figure 3**). Withdraw the cable from the hub.

3. Slacken the brake cable at the hand lever (**Figure 4**).

4. Slacken the brake cable at the fork leg (A, **Figure 5**). Remove the cable end (B, **Figure 5**) from the brake arm.

5A. On XL250S models, remove the cotter pin, then remove the axle nut.

5B. On all other models, remove the axle nut (**Figure 6**).

6A. On XL250S models, loosen the axle pinch bolt (**Figure 7**).

6B. On all other models, loosen the axle holder nuts (**Figure 8**) in a crisscross pattern. Remove the nuts and the axle holder.

7. Remove the front axle from the right-hand side.

8. Pull the wheel down and forward. This allows the brake panel to disengage from the boss on the left-hand fork slider.

9. Remove the wheel.

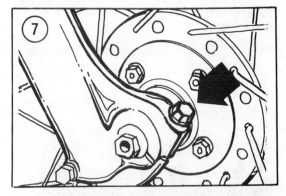

**Installation
(1981-1982 XR250R and XR500R)**

1. Make sure the axle bearing surfaces of the fork sliders and axle holder are free from burrs and nicks.
2. Clean the axle in solvent and thoroughly dry. Make sure all surfaces that the axle comes in contact with are clean and free from road dirt and old grease prior to installation.
3. Position the wheel into place, carefully inserting the groove in the brake panel into the groove in the left-hand fork slider. This is necessary for proper brake operation.
4. Position the tang on the speedometer gear box under the lip on the fork slider.
5. Install the axle from the right-hand side through the axle holder, the speedometer gear box and the wheel hub. Screw it into the left-hand slider and temporarily tighten the axle.
6. If removed, install the axle holder with the "UP" mark facing upward. Install the nuts and tighten lightly.
7. Tighten the front axle to the torque specification listed in **Table 1**.
8. Tighten the axle holder nuts a little tighter.
9. Install the front brake cable.
10. Slowly rotate the wheel and install the speedometer cable into the speedometer gear box. Install and tighten the cable set screw.
11. Remove the wood blocks from under the skid plate.
12. With the front brake applied, push down hard on the handlebars and pump the forks several times to seat the front axle.
13. Retighten the front axle holder nuts. Tighten the upper nuts first then the lower nuts. Tighten the nuts to the torque specification listed in **Table 1**.

WARNING
The axle holder nuts must be tightened in this manner and to this torque value. After installation is complete, there will be a slight gap at the bottom, with no gap at the top. If done incorrectly the studs may fail, resulting in loss of control of the bike when riding.

14. After the wheel is completely installed, rotate it several times and apply the brakes a couple of times to make sure that it rotates freely and that the brake is operating correctly.
15. Adjust the front brake as described in Chapter Three.

**Installation
(All Other Models)**

1. Make sure the axle bearing surfaces of the fork sliders and axle holder are free from burrs and nicks.
2. Clean the axle and axle holder in solvent and thoroughly dry. Make sure all surfaces that the axle comes in contact with are clean and free from road dirt and old grease prior to installation.
3. Install the axle holder with the "UP" mark facing upward (**Figure 8**). Install the axle holder nuts only finger-tight at this time.
4. Position the wheel into place, carefully inserting the groove in the brake panel into the groove in the left-hand fork slider (**Figure 9**). This is necessary for proper brake operation.
5. Install the axle from the right-hand side through the axle holder, the speedometer gear box and the wheel hub.
6A. On XL250S models, slide the axle into position and install the axle nut.
6B. On all other models, screw the axle into the left-hand slider.
7A. On XL250S models, tighten the axle nut to the torque specification listed in **Table 1**.
7B. On all other models, tighten the front axle to the torque specification listed in **Table 1**.
8. Tighten the axle holder nuts a little tighter.
9. Install the front brake cable.
10. Slowly rotate the wheel and install the speedometer cable into the speedometer gear box. Install and tighten the cable set screw.
11. Remove the wood blocks from under the skid plate.
12. With the front brake applied, push down hard on the handlebars and pump the forks several times to seat the front axle.
13. Retighten the front axle holder nuts. Tighten the upper nuts first then the lower nuts. Tighten the nuts to the torque specification listed in **Table 1**.

9

WARNING
The axle holder nuts must be tightened in this manner and to this torque value. After installation is complete, there will be a slight gap at the bottom, with no gap at the top. If done incorrectly the studs may fail, resulting in loss of control of the bike when riding.

14. On XL250S models, tighten the axle pinch bolt to the torque specifications listed in **Table 1**.

15. After the wheel is completely installed, rotate it several times and apply the brakes a couple of times to make sure that it rotates freely and that the brake is operating correctly.

16. Adjust the front brake as described in Chapter Three.

FRONT WHEEL (DISC BRAKE)

Removal

1. Place a wood block(s) under the skid plate to support the bike securely with the front wheel off the ground.

2. Unscrew the speedometer cable set screw (**Figure 10**). Pull the speedometer cable free from the speedometer gear box.

3. Loosen the axle holder nuts (A, **Figure 11**) and loosen the axle holder. It is not necessary to remove the axle holder, just loosen it enough to clear the front axle.

4. Unscrew the axle (B, **Figure 11**) from the left-hand fork leg.

5. Pull the wheel down and forward. This allows the brake disc to slide out of the caliper assembly.

NOTE
Insert a piece of wood or vinyl tubing in the caliper in place of the disc. That way, if the brake lever is inadvertently squeezed, the pistons will not be forced out of the cylinder. If this does happen, the caliper might have to be disassembled to reseat the pistons and the system will have to be bled. By using the wood, bleeding the brake is not necessary when installing the wheel.

6. Remove the wheel.

CAUTION
Do not set the wheel down on the disc surface as it may get scratched or warped. Set the wheel on 2 blocks of wood.

Installation

1. Make sure the axle bearing surfaces of the fork sliders and axle holder are free from burrs and nicks.

2. Clean the axle in solvent and thoroughly dry. Make sure all surfaces that the axle comes in contact with are clean and free from road dirt and old grease prior to installation.

3. Remove the vinyl tubing or wood pieces from the caiper.

4. Position the wheel in place, carefully inserting the disc between the pads.

5. Position the groove on the speedometer gear box onto the tab on the fork slider (**Figure 12**).

6. Install the axle from the right-hand side through the axle holder, the speedometer gear box and the

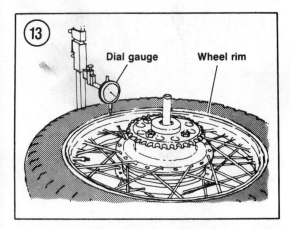

Dial gauge   Wheel rim

⑬

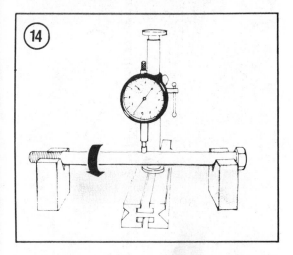

⑭

wheel hub. Screw it into the left-hand slider and temporarily tighten the axle.

7. If removed, install the axle holder with the "UP" mark facing upward. Install the nuts and tighten lightly.

8. Tighten the front axle to the torque specification listed in **Table 1**.

9. Tighten the axle holder nuts a little tighter.

10. Slowly rotate the wheel and install the speedometer cable into the speedometer gear box. Install and tighten the cable set screw.

11. Remove the wood blocks from under the skid plate.

12. With the front brake applied, push down hard on the handlebars and pump the forks several times to seat the front axle.

13. Retighten the front axle holder nuts. Tighten the upper nuts first then the lower nuts. Tighten the nuts to the torque specification listed in **Table 1**.

> *WARNING*
> *The axle holder nuts must be tightened in this manner and to this torque value.*

> *After installation is complete, there will be a slight gap at the bottom, with no gap at the top. If done incorrectly the studs may fail, resulting in loss of control of the bike when riding.*

14. After the wheel is completely installed, rotate it several times and apply the brakes a couple of times to make sure that it rotates freely and that the brake pads are against the disc.

WHEEL INSPECTION (ALL MODELS)

Measure the axial and radial runout of the wheel with a dial indicator as shown in **Figure 13**. The maximum axial and radial runout is 2.0 mm (0.08 in.). If the runout exceeds this dimension, check the wheel bearing condition.

Tighten or replace any bent or loose spokes as described in this chapter.

Check axle runout as described under *Front Hub* in this chapter.

FRONT HUB

Inspection

Inspect each wheel bearing prior to removing it from the wheel hub.

> *CAUTION*
> *Do not remove the wheel bearings for inspection purposes as they will be damaged during the removal process. Remove the wheel bearings only if they are to be replaced.*

1. Perform Steps 1-7 of *Disassembly* in this chapter.

2. Turn each bearing by hand. Make sure each bearing turns smoothly.

3. On non-sealed bearings, check the balls for evidence of wear, pitting or excessive heat (bluish tint). Replace the bearings if necessary; always replace as a complete set. When replacing the bearings, be sure to take your old bearings along to ensure a perfect matchup.

> *NOTE*
> *Fully sealed bearings are available from many bearing specialty shops. Fully sealed bearings provide better protection from dirt and moisture that may get into the hub.*

4. Check the axle for wear and straightness. Use V-blocks and a dial indicator as shown in **Figure 14**. If the axle runout is 0.01 in. (0.2 mm) or greater, the axle must be replaced.

9

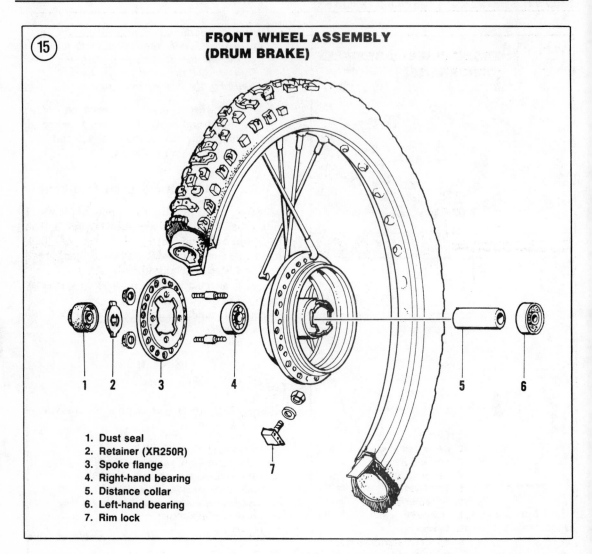

FRONT WHEEL ASSEMBLY
(DRUM BRAKE)

1. Dust seal
2. Retainer (XR250R)
3. Spoke flange
4. Right-hand bearing
5. Distance collar
6. Left-hand bearing
7. Rim lock

Disassembly

Refer to **Figure 15** for drum brake models or **Figure 16** for disc brake models during this procedure.

1. Remove the front wheel as described in this chapter.

2. On drum brake models, from the left-hand side, pull the brake assembly straight up and out of the brake drum.

3. On disc brake models, remove the speedometer gear box.

4. From the right-hand side, remove the dust seal (**Figure 17**).

5. On models so equipped, remove the retainer.

6. Remove the speedometer drive dog (A, **Figure 18**) and grease seal (B, **Figure 18**).

7. On disc brake models, perform the following:

a. Remove the nuts (A, **Figure 19**) securing the brake disc and remove the disc.

b. Remove the grease seal (B, **Figure 19**).

8. Before proceeding further, inspect the wheel bearings as described in this chapter.

9. To remove the left- and right-hand bearings and distance collar, insert a soft aluminum or brass drift into one side of the hub. Push the distance collar over to one side and place the drift on the inner race of the lower bearing. Tap the bearing out of the hub with a hammer, working around the perimeter of the inner race.

10. Remove the distance collar.

11. Remove the other bearing in the same manner.

Asssembly

1. Pack the bearings thoroughly with a good quality bearing grease. Work the grease in between

(16) **FRONT WHEEL ASSEMBLY (DISC BRAKE)**

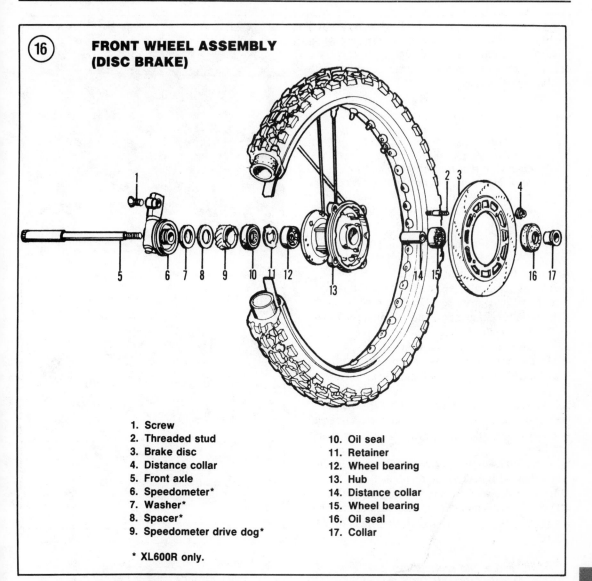

1. Screw
2. Threaded stud
3. Brake disc
4. Distance collar
5. Front axle
6. Speedometer*
7. Washer*
8. Spacer*
9. Speedometer drive dog*

10. Oil seal
11. Retainer
12. Wheel bearing
13. Hub
14. Distance collar
15. Wheel bearing
16. Oil seal
17. Collar

   * XL600R only.

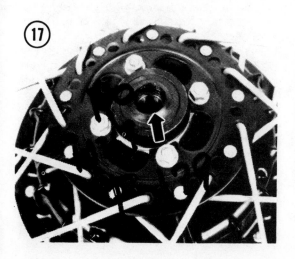

(17)

(18)

9

the balls thoroughly. Turn the bearing by hand a couple of times to make sure the grease is distributed evenly inside the bearing.

2. Pack the wheel hub and distance collar with multipurpose grease.

> *CAUTION*
> *Install non-sealed bearings with the single sealed side facing outward. Tap the bearings squarely into place and tap on the outer race only. Use a socket (Figure 20) that matches the outer race diameter. Do not tap on the inner race or the bearing might be damaged. Be sure that the bearings are completely seated.*

3. Install the left-hand bearing and the distance collar.

4. Install the right-hand bearing.

5. On disc brake models, perform the following:
   a. Install the grease seal (B, **Figure 19**).
   b. Install the brake disc and the nuts (A, **Figure 19**). Tighten the nuts to the torque specification listed in **Table 1**.

6. Install grease seal (B, **Figure 18**) and the speedometer drive dog (A, **Figure 18**).

7. On models so equipped, on the right-hand side, align the tangs of the retainer with the slots in the hub and install the retainer. Push the retainer all the way down onto the surface of the bearing and the hub.

8. Apply grease to the dust seal and install the dust seal (**Figure 17**) next to the retainer.

9A. On disc brake models, align the tangs (**Figure 21**) of the speedometer drive gear with the notches in the front hub and install the speedometer gearbox.

> *NOTE*
> *Make sure the speedometer gear box seats completely. If the speedometer components do not mesh properly the wheel will be too wide for installation.*

9B. On drum brake models, make sure the speedometer drive dog (**Figure 22**) is in place in the brake assembly. Align the tangs of the drive gear with the notches in the front hub and install the assembly into the brake drum.

> *NOTE*
> *Make sure the assembly seats completely. If the speedometer components do not mesh properly, the brake assembly will not seat correctly in the hub.*

10. Install the front wheel as described in this chapter.

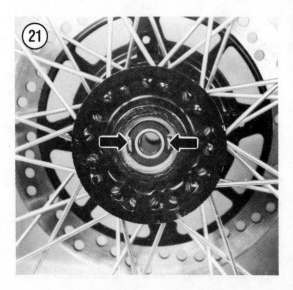

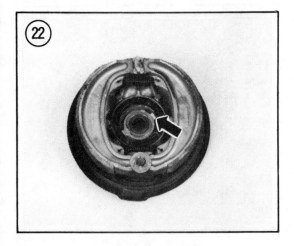

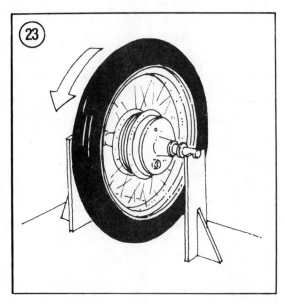

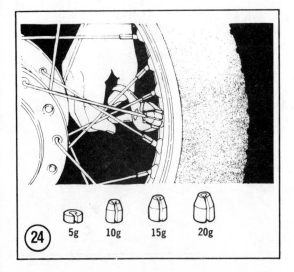

WHEELS

Wheel Balance

An unbalanced wheel is unsafe. Depending on the degree of unbalance and the speed of the motorcycle, the rider may experience anything form a mild vibration to a violent shimmy which may even result in loss of control.

The balance weights are applied to the spokes on the light side of the wheel to correct this condition.

Before you attempt to balance the wheel, check to be sure that the wheel bearings are in good condition and properly lubricated and that the brakes do not drag. The wheel must rotate freely.

1. Remove the wheel as described in this chapter.
2. Mount the wheel on a fixture such as the one shown in **Figure 23** so it can rotate freely.
3. Give the wheel a spin and let it coast to a stop. Mark the tire at the lowest point.
4. Spin the wheel several more times. If the wheel keeps coming to rest at the same point, it is out of balance.
5. On spoke type wheels, attach a weight to the upper (or light) side of the wheel at the spoke (**Figure 24**). Weights are crimped onto the spoke with ordinary gas pliers.
6. Experiment with different weights until the wheel, when spun, comes to rest at a different position each time.

Spoke Adjustment

Spokes loosen with use and should be checked periodically. If all appear loose, tighten all spokes on one side of the hub, then tighten all the spokes on the other side. One-half to one turn should be sufficient; do not overtighten. If you have a torque spoke wrench, tighten the spokes to 23-52 in.-lb. (2.0-4.5 N•m).

After tightening spokes, check rim runout to be sure you haven't pulled the rum out of shape.

One way to check rim runout is to mount a dial indicator on the front fork so that it bears on the rim.

If you don't have a dial indicator, improvise as shown in **Figure 25**. Adjust position of bolt until it just clears rim. Rotate rim and note whether clearance increases or decreases. Mark the tire with chalk or crayon at areas that produce significantly large or small clearance. Clearance must not change by more than 0.08 in. (2 mm).

To pull rim out, tighten spokes which terminate on opposite side of hub. See **Figure 26**. In most cases, only a slight amount of adjustment is necessary to true a rim. After adjustment, rotate

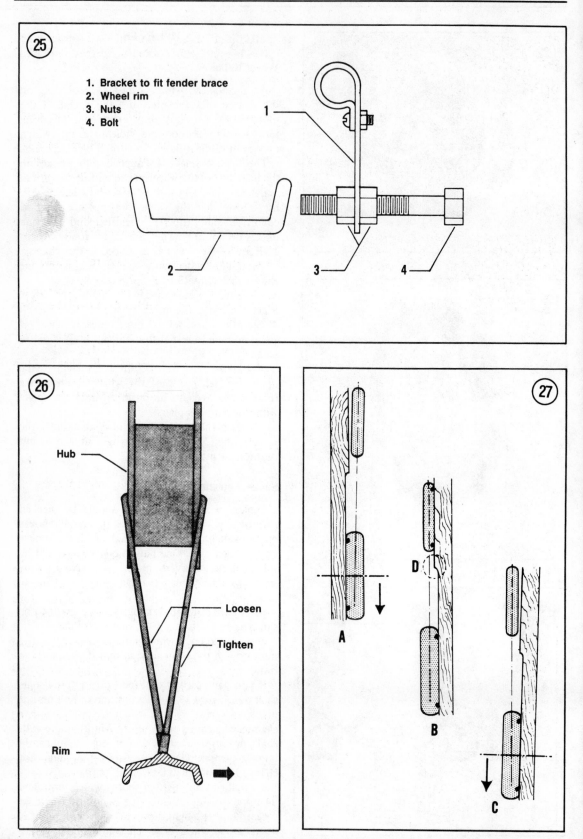

25

1. Bracket to fit fender brace
2. Wheel rim
3. Nuts
4. Bolt

26

Hub

Loosen

Tighten

Rim

27

A

D

B

C

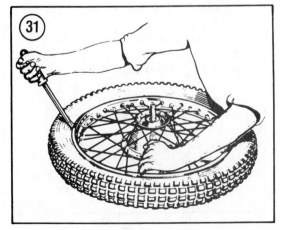

pulled out of true. Continue adjustment and checking until runout does not exceed 0.08 in. (2 mm).

Wheel Alignment

1. Measure the width of the 2 tires at their widest points.
2. Subtract the smaller dimension from the larger.
3. Make an alignment tool out of wood, approximately 7 feet long, with an offset equal to one half of the dimension obtained in Step 2. See D in **Figure 27**.
4. If the wheels are not aligned as in A and C, **Figure 27**, the rear wheel must be shifted to correct the situation.
5A. On dual-shock models, perform the following:
   a. Loosen the rear axle nut.
   b. Loosen the drive chain adjuster locknut and turn the adjuster (**Figure 28**) until the wheels align.
5B. On Pro-Link models, perform the following:
   a. Loosen the rear axle nut (A, **Figure 29**).
   b. Turn both snail adjusters (B, **Figure 29**) in either direction until the wheels align.
6. Adjust the drive chain as described in Chapter Three.

TIRE CHANGING

Removal

1. Remove the valve core to deflate the tire. On models so equipped, loosen the rim locknuts (**Figure 30**) fully, but do not remove them.
2. Press the entire bead on both sides of the tire into the center of the rim.
3. Lubricate the beads with soapy water.
4. Insert the tire iron under the bead next to the valve. Force the bead on the opposite side of the tire into the center of the tire into the center of the rim and pry the bead over the rim with the tire iron.
5. Insert a second tire iron next to the first to hold the bead over the rim.. Then work around the tire with the first tire iron, prying the bead over the rim (**Figure 31**). Be careful not to pinch the inner tube with the tire irons.
6. Remove the valve from the hole in the rim and remove the tube from the tire. Lift out and lay aside.
7. Stand the tire upright. Insert a tire iron between the second bead and the side of the rim that the first bead was pried over (**Figure 32**). Force the bead on the opposite side from the tire iron into the center of the rim. Pry the second bead off the rim, working around as with the first.

9

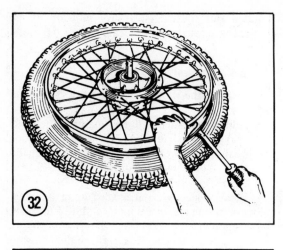

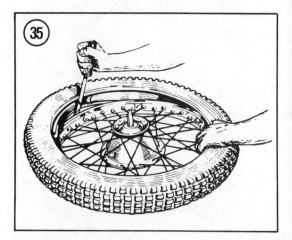

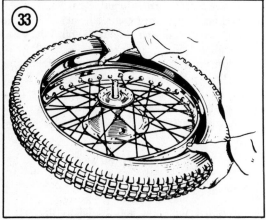

Installation

1. Carefully check the tire for any damage, especially inside.

2. A new tire may have balancing rubbers inside. These are not patches and should not be disturbed. A colored spot near the bead indicates a lighter point on the tire. This should be placed next to the valve or midway between the 2 rim locks if they are installed.

3. Check that the spoke ends do not protrude through the nipples into the center of the rim to puncture the tube. File off any protruding spoke ends.

4. Be sure the rim rubber tape is in place with the rough side toward the rim.

5. Put the core in the tube valve. Put the tube in the tire and inflate just enough to round it out. Too much air will make installing the tire difficult and too little will increase the chances of pinching the tube with the tire irons.

6. Lubricate the tire beads and rim with soapy water. Pull the tube partly out of the tire at the valve. Squeeze the beads together to hold the tube and insert the valve into the hole in the rim (**Figure 33**). The lower bead should go into the center of the rim with the upper bead outside it.

7. Press the lower bead into the rim center on each side of the valve, working around the tire in both directions (**Figure 34**). Use a tire iron for the last few inches of bead (**Figure 35**).

8. Press the upper bead into the rim opposite the valve. Pry the bead into the rim on both sides of the initial point with a tire iron, working around the rim to the valve (**Figure 36**).

9. Wiggle the valve to be sure the tube is not trapped under the bead. Set the valve squarely in its hole before screwing on the valve nut to hold it against the rim.

10. Check the bead on both sides of the tire for even fit around the rim. Inflate the tire slowly to seat the beads in the rim. It may be necessary to bounce the tire to complete the seating. Inflate to the required pressure. Balance the wheel as described in this chapter.

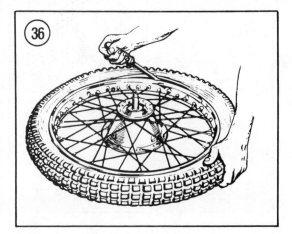

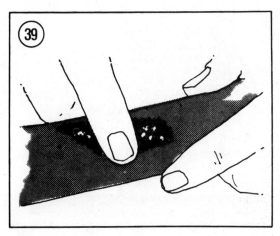

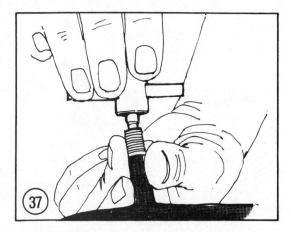

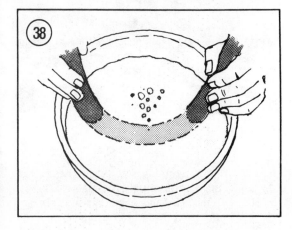

TIRE REPAIRS

Every rider eventually experiences trouble with a tire or tube. Repairs and replacement are fairly simple and every rider should know the techniques.

Patching a motorcycle tube is only a temporary fix. A motorcycle tire flexes too much and could rub a patch right off. However, a patched tire will get you far enough to buy a new tube.

Tire Repair Kits

Tire repair kits can be purchased from motorcycle dealers and some auto supply stores. When buying, specify that the kit you want is for motorcycles.

There are two types of tire repair kits:
a. Hot patch.
b. Cold patch.

Hot patches are stronger because they actually vulcanize to the tube, becoming part of it. However, they are far too bulky too carry for roadside repairs and the strength is unnecessary for a temporary repair.

Cold patches are not vulcanized to the tubes; they are simply glued to it. Though not as strong as hot patches, cold patches are still very durable. Cold patch kits are less bulky than hot and more easily applied under adverse conditions. A cold patch kit containing everything necessary tucks in easily with your emergency tool kit.

Tube Inspection

1. Install the valve core into the valve stem (**Figure 37**) and inflate the tube slightly. Do not overinflate.
2. Immerse the tube in water a section at a time. See **Figure 38**. Look carefully for bubbles indicating a hole. Mark each hole and continue checking until you are certain that all holes are discovered and marked. Also make sure that the valve core is not leaking; tighten it if necessary.

NOTE
If you do not have enough water to immerse sections of the tube, try running your hand over the tube slowly

and very close to the surface. If your hand is damp, it works even better. If you suspect a hole anywhere, apply some saliva to the area to verify it (Figure 39).

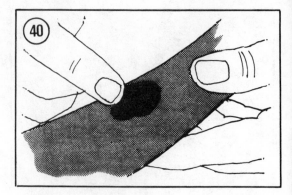

3. Apply a cold patch as described in this chapter.

4. Dust the patch area with talcum powder to prevent it from sticking to the tire.

5. Carefully check inside the tire casing for glass particles, nails or other objects which may have damaged the tube. If inside of tire is split, apply a patch to the area to prevent it from pinching and damaging the tube again.

6. Check the inside of the rim. Make sure the rim bank is in place, with no spoke ends protruding which could puncture the tube.

7. Deflate tube prior to installation in the tire.

Cold Patch Repair

1. Remove the tube from tire as described in this chapter.

2. Roughen the area around the hole slightly larger than the patch; use the cap from tire repair kit or a pocket knife. Do not scrape too vigorously or you may cause additional damage.

3. Apply a small quantity of special cement to the puncture and spread it evenly with a finger (**Figure 40**).

4. Allow cement to dry until tacky—usually 30 seconds or so is sufficient.

5. Remove the backing from the patch.

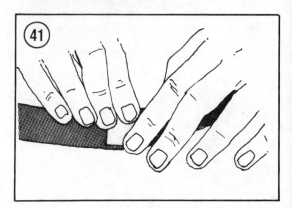

> *CAUTION*
> *Do not touch the newly exposed rubber with your fingers or the patch will not stick firmly.*

6. Center patch over hole. Hold patch firmly in place for about 30 seconds to allow the cement to set (**Figure 41**).

7. Dust the patched area with talcum powder to prevent sticking.

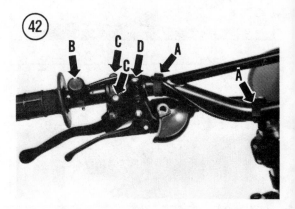

HANDLEBAR (WITH DISC BRAKE)

1. Remove the headlight as described in Chapter Eight.

2. Remove the fuel tank as described in Chapter Seven.

3. Remove the right- and left-hand wire harness bands (A, **Figure 42**).

4. On XR500R models, remove the bolt and nut securing the engine kill switch (B, **Figure 42**) and remove the switch.

5. Remove the screws clamping the clutch lever assembly (C, **Figure 42**) and remove the assembly.

6. Loosen the clamping screws on the manual decompressor lever assembly (D, **Figure 42**).

7. Remove the left-hand hand grip and slide off the manual decompressor lever assembly.

8. Remove the clamping screws on the throttle housing (**Figure 43**) and slide off the assembly.

9. On XL600R models, remove the screws securing the engine kill switch and remove the switch assembly.

> *CAUTION*
> *Cover the frame with a heavy cloth or plastic tarp to protect it from the*

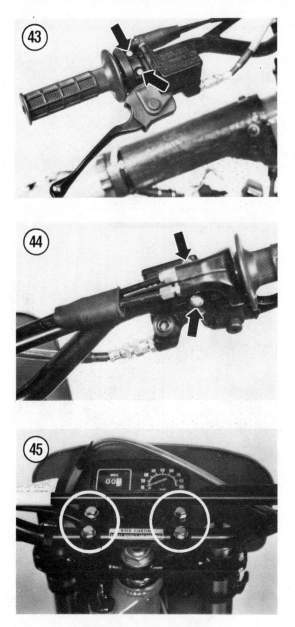

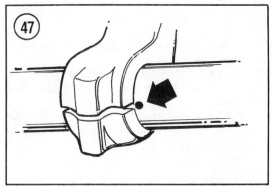

accidental spilling of brake fluid. Wash any spilled brake fluid off any painted or plated surface immediately, as it will destroy the finish. Use soapy water and rinse thoroughly.

10. Remove the clamping screws on the brake master cylinder (**Figure 44**) and slide off the assembly.

11. Tie the master cylinder up to the frame keeping the reservoir upright to minimize the loss of brake fluid and to keep air from entering into the brake system. It is not necessary to remove the hydraulic brake line from the master cylinder.

12. On XL600R models, remove the clamping screws on the turn signal assemblies on both sides and remove both assemblies.

13. Remove the bolts (**Figure 45**) securing the handlebar upper holders and remove the holders.

14. Remove the handlebar assembly.

15. Install by reversing these removal steps, noting the following.

16. Align the punch mark on the handlebar with the top surface of the handlebar lower holder (**Figure 46**).

17. When installing all assemblies, align the punch mark on the handlebar with the split line on the mounting bracket (**Figure 47**).

18. Tighten all bolts and nuts to the torque specifications listed in **Table 1**.

19. Adjust the clutch as described in Chapter Three.

HANDLEBAR (WITH DRUM BRAKE)

Removal/Installation

1. Remove the rear view mirrors.

2. Remove the right- and left-hand wire harness bands.

3. Remove the screws (A, **Figure 48**) clamping the throttle grip assembly and slide it off.

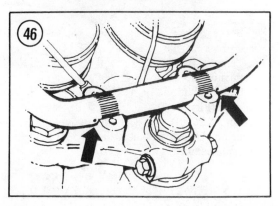

9

4. Disconnect the from brakelight switch electrical wire (B, **Figure 48**).

5. Slacken the front brake cable at the hand lever (C, **Figure 48**).

6. Loosen the clamping screw (**Figure 49**) on the engine kill switch/front brake lever bracket. Slide the assembly off.

7. On XL series models, loosen the clamping screws on the right-hand turn signal (D, **Figure 48**) and slide it off.

8. Slacken the clutch cable at the hand lever (A, **Figure 50**).

9. Loosen the screws securing the left-hand grip/light switch assembly (B, **Figure 50**) and slide it off.

10. Loosen the clamping screw securing the clutch lever assembly (C, **Figure 50**) and slide it off.

11. On XL series models, loosen the clamping screws on the left-hand turn signal and slide it off.

12. Remove the fuel fill cap vent tube (A, **Figure 51**) from the steering head receptacle.

13. Remove the bolts (B, **Figure 51**) securing the handlebar upper holders and remove them and the holders.

14. Remove the handlebar.

15. Install by reversing these removal steps, noting the following.

16. Tighten the bolts securing the handlebar upper holder to the torque specification listed in **Table 1**.

NOTE
*Align the punch marks on the handlebar with the top of the handlebar lower holder (**Figure 46**).*

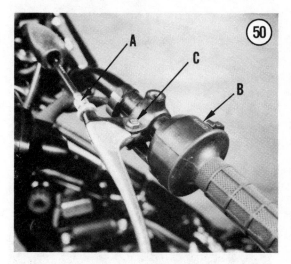

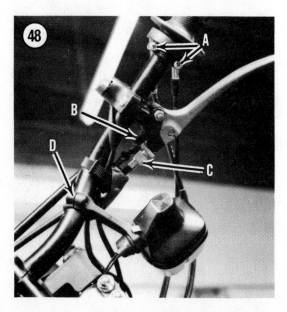

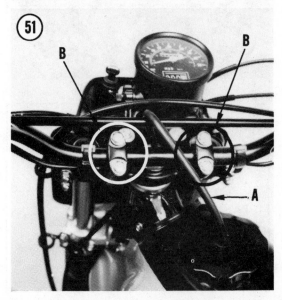

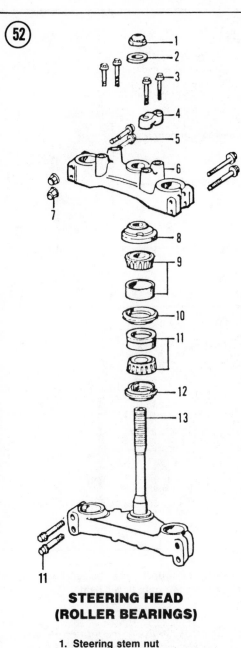

(52)

1. Steering stem nut
2. Washer
3. Bolt
4. Handlebar holder
5. Bolt
6. Upper fork bridge
7. Nut

STEERING HEAD (ROLLER BEARINGS)

1. Steering stem nut
2. Washer
3. Bolt
4. Handlebar holder
5. Bolt
6. Upper fork bridge
7. Nut
8. Steering head adjust nut
9. Upper roller bearing and race
10. Grease plate
11. Lower roller bearing and race
12. Dust seal
13. Steering stem

17. When installing all assemblies, align the punch mark on the handlebar with the split on the mounting bracket (**Figure 47**).

> *NOTE*
> *Apply a light coat of multipurpose grease to the throttle grip area on the handlebar prior to installation.*

> *WARNING*
> *After installation is complete make sure the brake lever does **not** come in contact with the throttle grip assembly when it is pulled on fully.*

18. Adjust the front brake and clutch as described in Chapter Three.

STEERING HEAD (ROLLER BEARINGS)

Disassembly

Refer to **Figure 52** for this procedure.

1. Remove the front wheel as described in this chapter.
2. Remove the fuel tank as described in Chapter Seven.
3. Remove the handlebar as described in this chapter.
4. Remove the bolts securing the front fender and remove the fender.
5. Remove the front forks as described in this chapter.
6. Remove the number plate/headlight as described in Chapter Seven.
7. Remove the steering stem nut and washer (A, **Figure 53**).
8. Remove the upper fork bridge assembly (B, **Figure 53**).

(53)

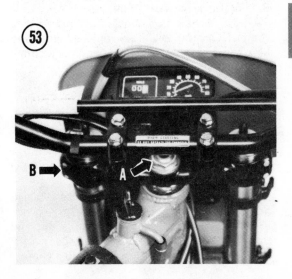

9

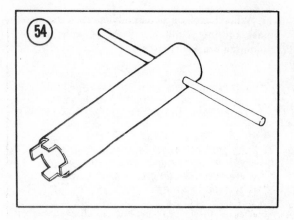

9. Remove the steering head adjusting nut. Use a large drift and hammer or use the easily improvised tool shown in **Figure 54**.

10. Lower the steering stem assembly down and out of the steering head.

11. Remove the upper bearing from the top of the headset.

Inspection

1. Clean the bearing races in the steering head, the steering stem races and the bearings with solvent.

2. Check the welds around the steering head for cracks and fractures. If any are found, have them repaired by a competent frame shop or welding service.

3. Check the rollers for pitting, scratches or discoloration indicating wear or corrosion. Replace them in sets if any are bad.

4. Check the races for pitting, galling and corrosion. If any of these conditions exist, replace the races as described in this chapter.

5. Check the steering stem for cracks and check its race for damage or wear. If this race or any race is damaged, the bearings should be replaced as a complete bearing set. Take the old races and bearings to your dealer to ensure accurate replacement.

Assembly

Refer to **Figure 52** for this procedure.

1. Make sure the steering head and stem races are properly seated.

2. Install the upper roller bearing assembly into the steering head.

3. Install the steering stem into the head tube and hold it firmly in place.

4. Install the steering stem adjusting nut and tighten it to 4-5 ft.-lb. (5.5-6.5 N•m). Loosen the adjust nut and retighten it to 5 ft.-lb. (6.5 N•m).

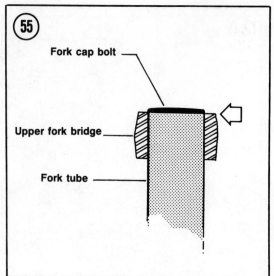

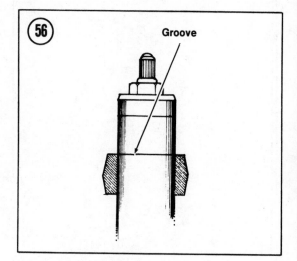

5. Install the upper fork bridge, washer and steering stem nut only finger-tight.

NOTE
Steps 5-9 must be performed in this order to assure proper upper and lower fork bridge to fork alignment.

6A. On 1982 XR250R, 1982-1983 XL250R and 1983 XL600R models, slide the fork tubes into position so that the top surface of the fork tube aligns with the top surface of the upper fork bridge (**Figure 55**).

6B. On 1983 XR350R and XR500R models, slide the fork tubes into position so that the lower groove on the fork tube aligns with the top surface of the upper fork bridge (**Figure 56**).

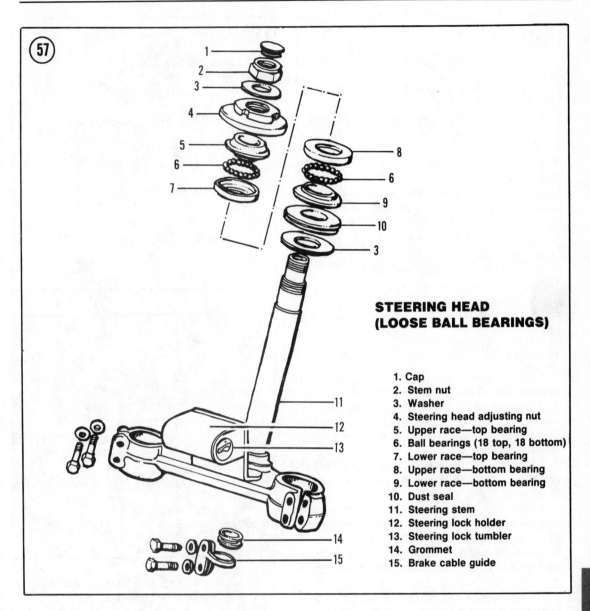

**STEERING HEAD
(LOOSE BALL BEARINGS)**

1. Cap
2. Stem nut
3. Washer
4. Steering head adjusting nut
5. Upper race—top bearing
6. Ball bearings (18 top, 18 bottom)
7. Lower race—top bearing
8. Upper race—bottom bearing
9. Lower race—bottom bearing
10. Dust seal
11. Steering stem
12. Steering lock holder
13. Steering lock tumbler
14. Grommet
15. Brake cable guide

9

7. Tighten the lower fork bridge bolts to the torque specification listed in **Table 1**.

8. Tighten the steering stem nut to the torque specification listed in **Table 1**.

9. Tighten the upper fork bridge bolts to the torque specification listed in **Table 1**.

10. Install the front fender, handlebar, number plate/headlight assembly, fuel tank and the front wheel as described in their related chapters.

Steering Stem Adjustment

If play develops in the steering system, it may only require adjustment. However, don't take a chance on it. Disassemble the stem and look for

possible damage. Then reassemble and adjust as described in Step 4 of the *Steering Head Assembly* procedure.

**STEERING HEAD
(LOOSE BALL BEARINGS)**

Disassembly

Refer to **Figure 57** for this procedure.

1. Remove the front wheel as described in this chapter.

2. Remove the handlebar as described in this chapter.

3. On XL series models, disconnect the battery negative lead or disconnect the main fuse.

4. Remove the headlight assembly as described in Chapter Eight.

5. Remove the instrument cluster assembly as described in Chapter Eight.

6. Remove the bolts (**Figure 58**) securing the front fender and remove the fender.

7. Loosen the pinch bolts on the upper and lower fork bridge (**Figure 59**) and slide out both fork tubes.

8. Remove the steering stem nut and washer (**Figure 60**). Remove the upper fork bridge.

9. Remove the steering head adjusting nut with the pin spanner, provided in the factory tool kit, or use an easily improvised unit (**Figure 54**).

10. Have an assistant hold a large pan under the steering stem to catch the loose ball bearings and carefully lower the steering stem (**Figure 61**).

NOTE
There are 36 balls total—18 on the top and 18 on the bottom.

11. Remove the upper 18 ball bearings.

Inspection

1. Clean the bearing races in the steering head, the steering stem races and all the ball bearings with solvent.

2. Check for broken welds on the frame around the steering head.

3. Check each of the balls for pitting, scratches or discoloration indicating wear or corrosion. Replace them in set if any are bad.

4. Check upper and lower races in the steering head. See *Bearing Race Replacement* if races are pitted, scratched or badly worn.

5. Check steering stem for cracks. Check bearing race on stem for pitting, scratches or excessive wear.

6. Check inside of steering head adjuster (top ball race) for pitting, scratches or excessive wear.

Assembly

Refer to **Figure 57** for this procedure.

1. Make sure the steering head races are properly seated.

2. Install the washer, dust seal and lower race onto the steering stem.

3. Apply a coat of cold grease to the upper bearing race cone and fit 18 balls into it (**Figure 62**).

4. Apply a coat of cold grease to the lower bearing race and fit 18 balls around it (**Figure 63**). The grease will hold them in place.

5. Insert the steering stem into the head tube and hold it firmly in place.

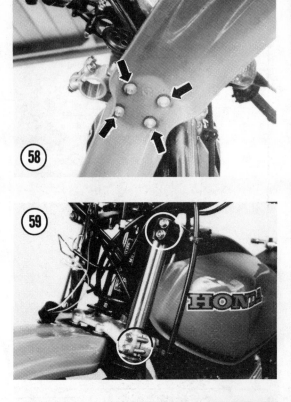

6. Install the steering head adjusting nut (**Figure 64**) and tighten it until it is snug against the upper race, then back it off 1/8 turn.

NOTE
The adjusting nut should be just tight enough to remove play, both horizontal and vertical, yet loose enough so that the assembly will turn to both lock positions under its own weight after an initial assist.

7. Install the top fork bridge and steering stem nut only finger-tight at this time (**Figure 65**).

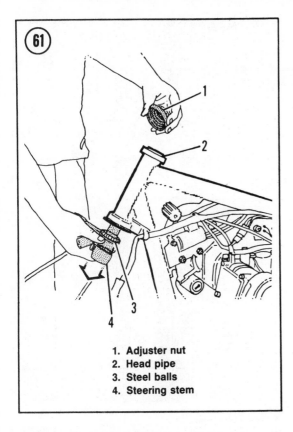

1. Adjuster nut
2. Head pipe
3. Steel balls
4. Steering stem

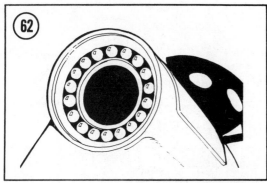

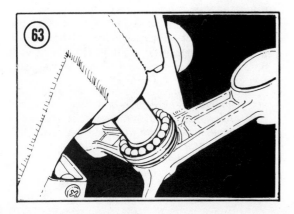

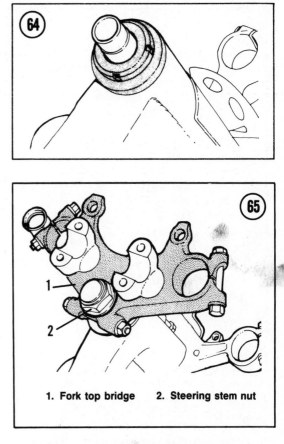

1. Fork top bridge   2. Steering stem nut

NOTE
Steps 7-10 must be performed in this order to assure proper upper and lower fork bridge to fork alignment.

8. Slide the fork tubes into position and tighten the upper fork bridge bolt(s) to the torque specifications listed in **Table 1**.

NOTE
*The top of the fork tube must be flush with the top of the upper fork bridge surface (**Figure 55**).*

9. Tighten the steering stem nut to the torque specifications listed in **Table 1**.

10. Tighten the lower fork bridge clamping bolts to the torque specifications listed in **Table 1**.

11. Continue assembly by reversing Steps 1-6, *Steering Stem Disassembly*.

Steering Stem Adjustment

If play develops in the steering system, it may only require adjustment. However, don't take a chance on it. Disassembly the stem and look for possible damage. Then reassemble and adjust as

9

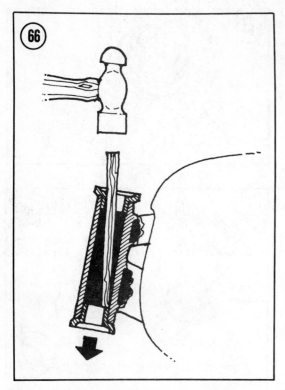

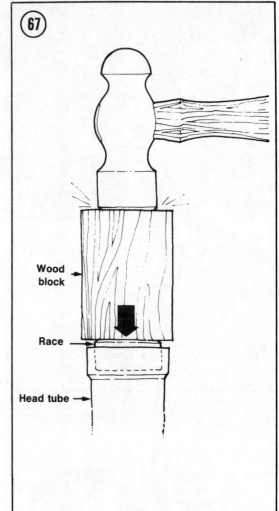

described in Step 6, *Steering Head Assembly* in this chapter.

STEERING HEAD BEARING RACES (ALL MODELS)

The headset and steering stem bearing races are pressed into place. Because they are easily bent, do not remove them unless they are worn and require replacement.

Headset Bearing Race Removal/Installation

On models with loose ball bearings, the upper and lower bearing races are not the same size. The lower one is the slightly larger of the two. Be sure that you install them at the proper ends of the head tube.

To remove the headset race, insert a hardwood stick or soft punch into the head tube (**Figure 66**) and carefully tap the race out from the inside. After it is started, tap around the race so that neither the race nor the head tube is damaged.

To install the headset race, tap it in slowly with a block of wood, a suitable size socket or piece of pipe (**Figure 67**). Make sure that the race is squarely seated in the headset race bore before tapping it into place. Tap the race in until it is flush with the steering head surface.

Steering Stem Bearing Race and Grease Seal Removal/Installation

1. To remove the steering stem race (lower bearing or inner race on roller bearing models), try twisting and pulling it up by hand. If it will not come off, carefully pry it up with a screwdriver; work around in a circle, prying a little at a time. On models with loose ball bearings, remove the lower bearing race, dust seal and dust seal spacer.

CAUTION
On models with roller bearings, do not attempt to remove the lower bearing, inner race and dust seal from the steering stem. Removal of these components requires the use of a hydraulic press and should be entrusted to a dealer or machine shop.

2A. On models with loose ball bearings, install the dust seal spacer and dust seal. Slide the lower race over the steering stem with the bearing surface pointing up.

2B. On models with roller bearings, have the dealer or machine shop install the dust seal and lower roller bearing and internal race.

3. Tap the race or roller bearing down with a piece of hardwood; work around in a circle so the race (or bearing) will not be bent. Make sure it is seated squarely and is all the way down.

FRONT FORKS
(XL250S, XR250, XL500S, XR500)

The Honda front suspension consists of a spring-controlled, hydraulically dampened telescopic fork. Before suspecting major trouble, drain the fork oil and refill with the proper type and quantity; refer to Chapter Three. If you still have trouble, such as poor dampening, tendency to bottom out or top out or leakage round rubber seals, then follow the service procedures in this section.

To simplify forks service and to prevent the mixing of parts, the legs should be removed, serviced and reinstalled individually.

Removal/Installation

1. Remove the front wheel as described in this chapter.
2. On XR models, remove the speedometer cable from the clamp on the left-hand fork slider (**Figure 68**). Loosen the clamp screw (**Figure 69**) on the protective boot and slide the boot down.
3. Loosen the clamping bolts on the upper and lower fork bridges (A, **Figure 70**).
4. Remove the fork tubes (B, **Figure 70**). It may be necessary to slightly rotate a fork tube while pulling it down and out.
5. Install by reversing these removal steps.
6. The top of the fork tube must be flush with the top of the upper fork bridge surface (**Figure 55**).
7. Tighten the top fork bridge bolts to the torque specifications listed in **Table 1**.
8. Tighten the lower fork bridge bolts to the torque specifications listed in **Table 1**.

Disassembly

Refer to **Figure 71** for this procedure.
1. Hold the upper fork tube in a vise with soft jaws. Remove the top bolt and spring seat. Use the 17 mm male box wrench in the factory tool kit.
2. Remove the fork spring(s) and washer.
3. Remove the fork from the vise. Pour the oil out and discard it. Pump the fork several times by hand to expel most of the remaining oil.
4. Remove the rubber boot out of the notch in the slider and slide it off of the fork tube.

9

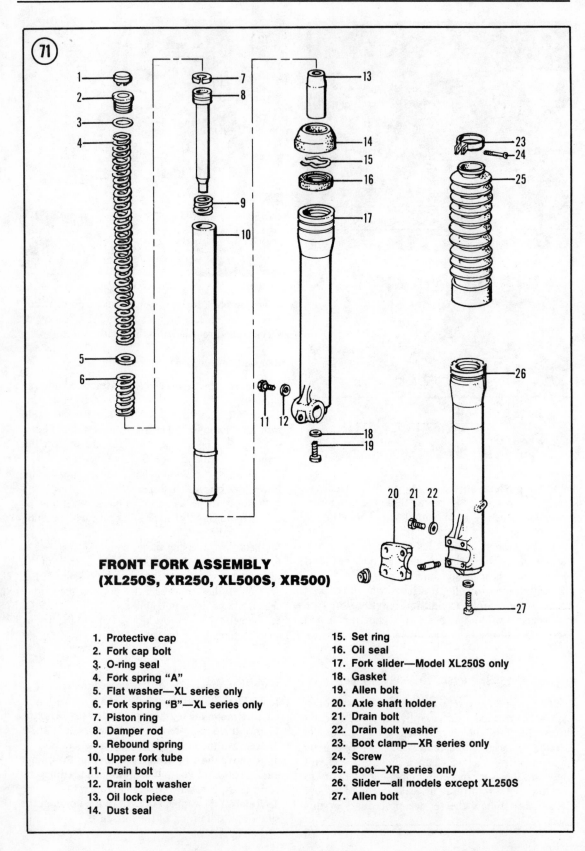

**FRONT FORK ASSEMBLY
(XL250S, XR250, XL500S, XR500)**

1. Protective cap
2. Fork cap bolt
3. O-ring seal
4. Fork spring "A"
5. Flat washer—XL series only
6. Fork spring "B"—XL series only
7. Piston ring
8. Damper rod
9. Rebound spring
10. Upper fork tube
11. Drain bolt
12. Drain bolt washer
13. Oil lock piece
14. Dust seal

15. Set ring
16. Oil seal
17. Fork slider—Model XL250S only
18. Gasket
19. Allen bolt
20. Axle shaft holder
21. Drain bolt
22. Drain bolt washer
23. Boot clamp—XR series only
24. Screw
25. Boot—XR series only
26. Slider—all models except XL250S
27. Allen bolt

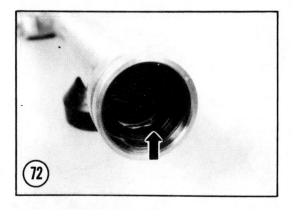

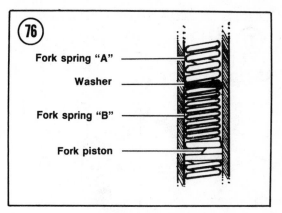

Fork spring "A"

Washer

Fork spring "B"

Fork piston

Drive weight
Drive guide
Oil seal

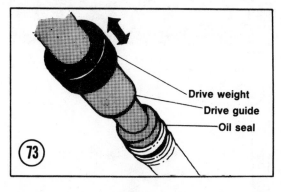

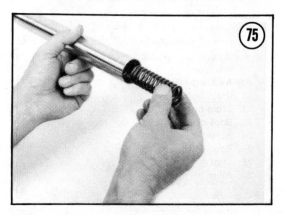

5. Clamp the slider in a vise with soft jaws.

6. Remove the 6 mm Allen bolt and gasket from the bottom of the slider.

7. Pull the fork tube out of the slider.

8. Remove the oil lockpiece, the damper rod and rebound spring.

9. If oil has been leaking from the top of the slider, remove the set ring from the top of the slider. Remove the oil seal and backup ring.

NOTE
It may be necessary to slightly heat the area on the slider around the oil seal prior to removal.

10. Inspect components as described in this chapter.

Assembly

1. Install the backup ring, oil seal and set ring (**Figure 72**). Coat all parts with fresh fork oil prior to installation. Drive the seal into the slider (**Figure 73**) with Honda special tool No. 07744-0010000 or a suitable size socket. Drive the seal in until the set ring groove appears.

2. Install the rebound spring onto the damper and insert them both into the fork tube (**Figure 74**).

3. On XL models, install the short spring "B" (**Figure 75**), flat washer and long spring "A."

NOTE
Make sure these springs are installed in this sequence. Refer to ***Figure 76***.

4. On XR models, install the long spring (**Figure 77**).

5. Temporarily install the top bolt.

6. Install the oil lockpiece (**Figure 78**) and install upper fork tube assembly into the slider (**Figure 79**).

7. Make sure the gasket (**Figure 80**) is on the Allen bolt.

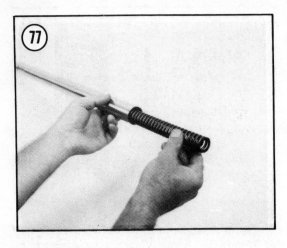

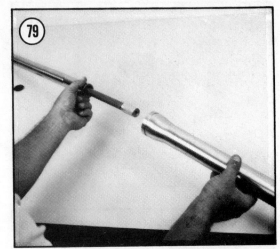

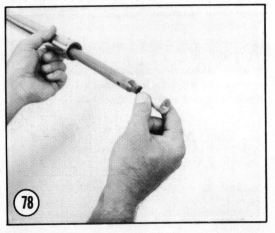

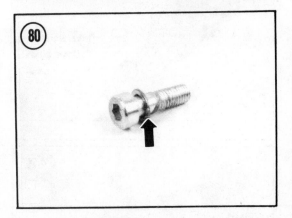

8. Apply liquid gasket sealer to the gasket and apply Loctite Lock N' Seal to the threads of the Allen bolt prior to installation. Tighten the Allen bolt (**Figure 81**) to the torque specifications listed in **Table 1**.

9. Install the rubber boot on the slider (**Figure 82**).

10. Remove the top bolt and fill each fork tube with fresh fork oil or automatic transmission fluid. Capacity after disassembly is listed in **Table 2**.

> *NOTE*
> *In order to measure the correct amount of fluid, use a plasic baby bottle. These have measurements in fluid ounces (oz.) and cubic centimeters (cc) on the side.*

11. Install the top bolt (A, **Figure 83**). Make sure the O-ring seal (B, **Figure 83**) is in place and in good condition.

12. Install the fork as described in this chapter.

FRONT FORKS
(XR250R AND 1981-1982 XR500R)

Removal/Installation

1. Remove the front wheel as described in this chapter.

2. Disconnect the speedometer and brake cables from the clamps on the fork slider (**Figure 84**).

3. Remove the air valve cap and *bleed off all air pressure* by depressing the valve stem (**Figure 85**). Repeat for both fork assemblies.

> *WARNING*
> *Always bleed off all air pressure; failure to do so may cause personal injury when disassembling the fork.*

> *NOTE*
> *Release the air pressure gradually. If released too fast, fork oil will spurt out with the air. Protect your eyes and clothing accordingly.*

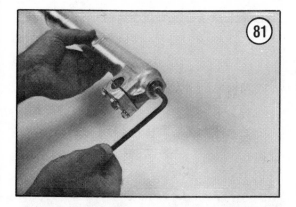

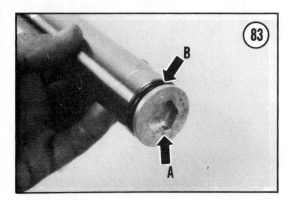

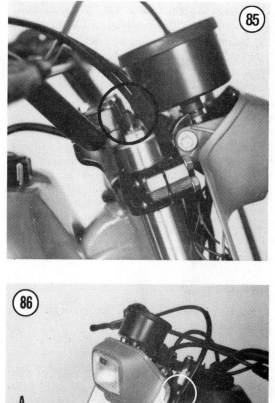

4. Remove the bolts securing the front fender and remove the fender (A, **Figure 86**).

5. Loosen the upper clamping band and slide the rubber boot (B, **Figure 86**) from the lower fork bridge down onto the slider.

6. Loosen the upper and lower fork bridge bolts (C, **Figure 86**).

7. Remove the fork tube. It may be necessary to slightly rotate the fork tube while pulling it down and out.

8. Install by reversing these removal steps, noting the following.

9. Be sure to install any clamps onto the fork tube during installation.

10. Install the fork tubes so that the lower groove on the fork tube aligns with the top surface of the upper fork bridge (**Figure 56**).

9

11. Tighten the upper and lower fork bridge bolts to the torque specification listed in **Table 1**.

12. Inflate the forks to the standard air pressure listed in **Table 3**. Do not use compressed air, only use a small hand-operated air pump as shown in **Figure 87** or equivalent.

> *WARNING*
> *Never use any type of compressed gas as an explosion may be lethal. Never heat the fork assembly with a torch or place it near an open flame or extreme heat as this will also result in an explosion.*

> *CAUTION*
> *Never exceed an air pressure of 14 psi (1.0 kg/cm²) as damage may occur to internal components of the fork assembly.*

Disassembly

Refer to **Figure 88** during the disassembly and assembly procedures.

1. Remove the rubber boot from the slider.
2. Clamp the slider in a vise with soft jaws.
3. Remove the Allen head screw and gasket from the bottom of the slider.

> *NOTE*
> *This screw has been secured with Loctite and is often very difficult to remove because the damper rod will turn inside the slider. It sometimes can be removed with an air impact driver. If you are unable to remove it, take the fork tubes to a dealer and have the screws removed.*

4. Hold the upper fork tube in a vise with soft jaws and loosen the top cap bolt/air valve assembly.

> *WARNING*
> *Be careful when removing the top cap bolt as the spring is under pressure.*

5. Remove the top cap bolt from the fork.
6. On 1982-on models, remove the collar and spring seat.
7. Remove the fork spring.
8. Remove the fork from the vise. Pour the fork oil out and discard it. Pump the fork several times by hand to expel most of the remaining oil.
9. Remove the dust seal from the slider. Remove the circlip (**Figure 89**) and the backup plate from the slider.

> *NOTE*
> *On this type of fork, force is needed to remove the fork tube from the slider.*

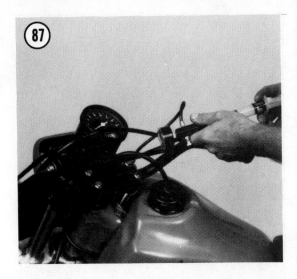

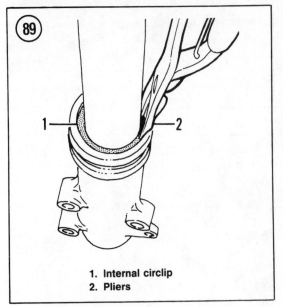

1. Internal circlip
2. Pliers

10. Install the fork slider in a vise with soft jaws.
11. There is an interference fit between the bushing in the fork slider and the bushing on the fork tube. In order to remove the fork tube from the slider, pull hard on the fork tube using quick in and out strokes. Doing this will withdraw the bushing, backup ring and oil seal from the slider.

> *NOTE*
> *It may be necessary to slightly heat the area on the slider around the oil seal prior to removal. Use a rag soaked in hot water; do not apply a flame directly to the fork slider.*

12. Withdraw the fork tube from the slider.

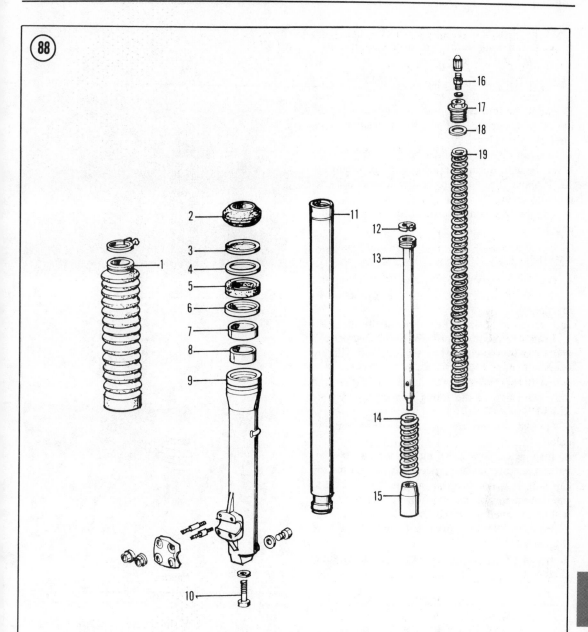

**FRONT FORK ASSEMBLY
(XR250R, 1981-1982 XR500R)**

1. Rubber boot
2. Dust seal
3. Circlip
4. Backup plate
5. Oil seal
6. Backup ring
7. Fork slider bushing
8. Fork tube bushing
9. Fork slider
10. Allen bolt and washer
11. Fork tube
12. Piston ring
13. Damper rod
14. Rebound spring
15. Oil lock piece
16. Air valve assembly
17. Top cap bolt
18. O-ring seal
19. Fork spring

9

CAUTION
Do not remove the fork tube bushing unless it is going to be replaced. Inspect it as described under **Fork Inspection (All Models)** *in this chapter.*

13. Turn the fork tube upside down and slide off the oil seal, backup ring and slider bushing from the fork tube (**Figure 90**).

14. Do not discard the slider bushing at this time. It will be used during the installation procedure.

15. Remove the oil lock piece, the damper rod and rebound spring.

16. Inspect the components as described in this chapter.

Assembly

1. Coat all parts with fresh DEXRON automatic transmission fluid (ATF) or fork oil prior to installation.

2. If removed, install a new fork tube bushing.

3. Install the rebound spring onto the damper rod and insert this assembly into the fork tube (**Figure 91**).

4. Install the spring into the fork tube. Either end may go in first as the spring is not progressively wound.

5. On 1982-on models, install the spring seat and collar.

6. Inspect the O-ring seal on the top cap bolt/air valve assembly; replace if necessary. Install the top cap bolt. It is not necessary to tighten the bolt to the correct torque specification at this time as it will be removed when the fork oil is added.

7. Install the oil lock piece onto the damper rod (**Figure 92**).

8. Install the upper fork assembly into the slider (**Figure 93**).

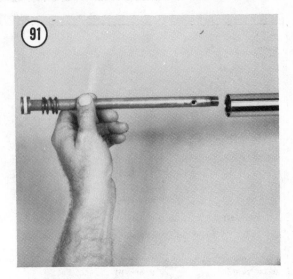

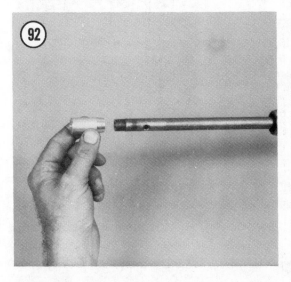

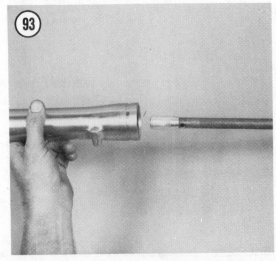

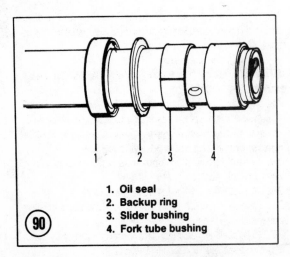

1. Oil seal
2. Backup ring
3. Slider bushing
4. Fork tube bushing

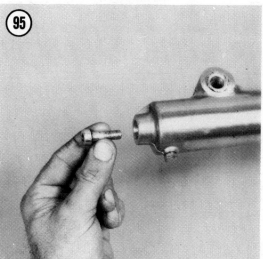

94

Fork seal driver body

Fork seal driver attachment

Oil seal

9. Slide the fork slider bushing down the fork tube and rest it on the slider.

10. Slide the fork slider backup ring (flange side up) down the fork tube and rest it on top of the fork slider bushing.

11. Place the old slider bushing on top of the backup ring. Drive the bushing into the fork slider with Honda special tool Fork Seal Driver Body (part No. 07747-0010100) and Fork Seal Driver Attachment (part No. 07947-3710101). Drive the bushing into place until it seats completely in the recess in the slider. Remove the old slider bushing.

12. Install the backup ring.

13. To prevent damage to the inside of the new fork seal during installation, wrap the groove in the top of the fork tube with clear tape (something smooth and non-abrasive—do not use duct or masking tape).

14. Coat the new seal with DEXRON automatic transmission fluid. Position the seal with the marking facing upward and slide it down onto the fork tube. Drive the seal into the slider (**Figure 94**) with Honda special tool Fork Seal Driver Body (part No. 07747-0010100) and Fork Seal Driver Attachment (part No. 07947-3710101). Drive the oil seal in until the groove in the slider can be seen above the top surface of the oil seal. Remove the tape from the top of the fork tube.

NOTE
If the seal must be driven further down, remove the special tools and insert the backup plate on top of the seal. Repeat Step 14 until the seal is correctly seated.

95

15. Install the backup plate and circlip. Make sure the circlip is completely seated in the groove in the fork slider.

16. Install the dust seal.

17. Make sure the gasket is on the Allen head screw.

18. Apply Loctite Lock N' Seal to the threads of the Allen head screw prior to installation. Install it in the fork slider (**Figure 95**) and tighten to the torque specification listed in **Table 1**.

19. Install the rubber boot and snap it into place on the fork slider.

20. Repeat for the other fork assembly.

21. Install the fork assemblies as described in this chapter.

22. Fill the forks with the correct quantity and type of fork oil. Refer to **Table 2**.

9

FRONT FORKS
(1982-1983 XL250R, XR350R, XL500R, 1983 XR500R AND XL600R)

Removal/Installation

1. On disc brake models, perform the following:
   a. Remove the bolts (**Figure 96**) securing the caliper assembly to the left-hand fork slider.
   b. Remove the bolts (**Figure 97**) securing the brake hose to the left-hand fork slider.
   c. Tie the caliper assembly up to the frame to take the strain off the brake hose.

2. On XR500R and XL600R models, remove the speedometer cable clamp (**Figure 98**) on the right-hand fork leg.

3. Remove the front wheel as described in this chapter.

4. Remove the air valve cap (**Figure 99**) and *bleed off all air pressure* by depressing the valve stem. Repeat for both fork assemblies.

> *WARNING*
> *Always bleed off all air pressure; failure to do so may cause personal injury when disassembling the fork.*

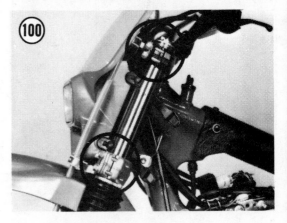

> *CAUTION*
> *Release the air pressure gradually. If released too fast, fork oil will spurt out with the air. Protect your eyes and clothing accordingly.*

5. Loosen the upper and lower fork bridge bolts (**Figure 100**).

6. Loosen the clamping screws on the rubber boot bands. Slide off both rubber boots (**Figure 101**).

7. Remove the fork tube. It may be necessary to slightly rotate the fork tube while pulling it down and out.

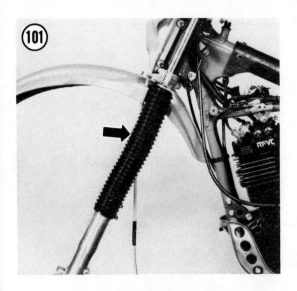

8. Install by reversing these removal steps, noting the following.

9A. On XL series models, install the fork tubes so that the top of the fork tube aligns with the top surface of the upper fork bridge.

9B. On XR series models, install the fork tubes so that the lower groove of the fork tube aligns with the top surface of the upper fork bridge.

10. Tighten the upper and lower fork bridge bolts to the torque specifications listed in **Table 1**.

11. Position the rubber boots with the greater number of breather holes toward the rear of the bike.

12. Inflate the forks to the standard air pressure listed in **Table 3**. Do not use compressed air, use only a small hand-operated air pump (**Figure 87**) or equivalent.

WARNING
Never use any type of compressed gas as an explosion may be lethal. Never heat the fork assembly with a torch or place it near an open flame or extreme heat as this will also result in an explosion.

CAUTION
Never exceed an air pressure of 100 kPa (14.2 psi) as damage may occur to internal components of the fork assembly.

Disassembly

Refer to **Figure 102** for 1983 XR350R or **Figure 103** for all other models during the disassembly and assembly procedures.

1. Clamp the slider in a vise with soft jaws.

2. Remove the Allen head screw and gasket from the bottom of the slider.

NOTE
This screw has been secured with Loctite and is often very difficult to remove because the damper rod will turn inside the slider. It sometimes can be removed with an air impact driver. If you are unable to remove it, take the fork tubes to a dealer and have the screws removed.

3. Hold the upper fork tube in a vise with soft jaws and remove the top bolt.

WARNING
Be careful when removing the top bolt as the spring is under pressure.

4. Remove the fork top bolt from the fork.

5. Remove the spacer, the spring seat and the fork spring.

6. Remove the fork from the vise, pour the fork oil out and discard it. Pump the fork several times by hand to expel most of the remaining oil.

7. Pull the fork tube out of the slider.

8. Remove the oil lock piece, the damper rod and the rebound spring.

9. If oil has been leaking from the top of the slider, remove the dust seal, the circlip (**Figure 104**), the oil seal and the backup plate.

10. It may be necessary to slightly heat the area on the slider around the oil seal prior to removal. Use a rag soaked in hot water; do not apply a flame directly to the fork slider.

CAUTION
Use a dull screwdriver blade to remove the oil seal (Figure 105). Do not damage the outer edge or inner surface of the slider.

11. Inspect the components as described in this chapter.

Assembly

1. Coat all parts with fresh DEXRON automatic transmission fluid or SAE 10W fork oil prior to installation.

2. Install the rebound spring onto the damper rod (**Figure 106**) and insert this assembly into the fork tube (**Figure 107**).

3. Temporarily install the fork spring, spacer and top bolt to hold the damper rod in place.

4. Install the oil lock piece onto the damper rod (**Figure 108**).

5. Install the upper fork assembly into the slider (**Figure 109**).

9

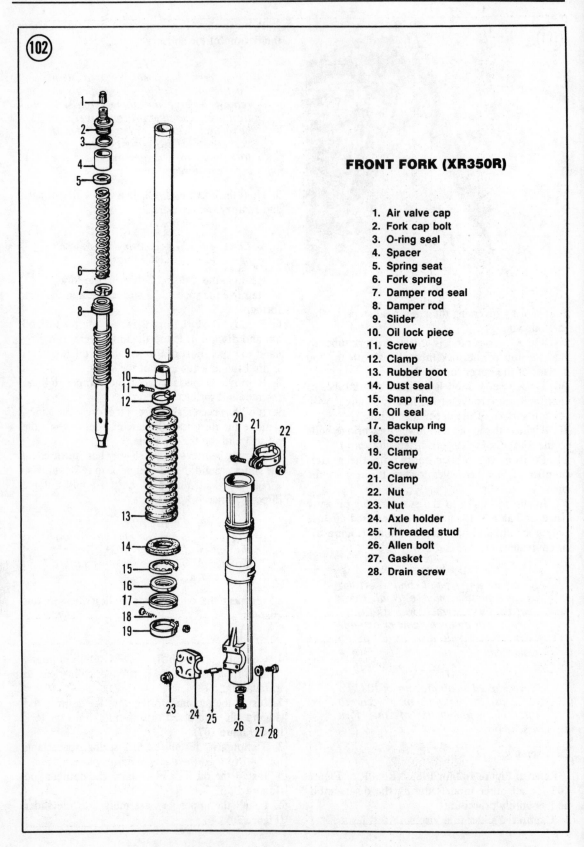

(102)

FRONT FORK (XR350R)

1. Air valve cap
2. Fork cap bolt
3. O-ring seal
4. Spacer
5. Spring seat
6. Fork spring
7. Damper rod seal
8. Damper rod
9. Slider
10. Oil lock piece
11. Screw
12. Clamp
13. Rubber boot
14. Dust seal
15. Snap ring
16. Oil seal
17. Backup ring
18. Screw
19. Clamp
20. Screw
21. Clamp
22. Nut
23. Nut
24. Axle holder
25. Threaded stud
26. Allen bolt
27. Gasket
28. Drain screw

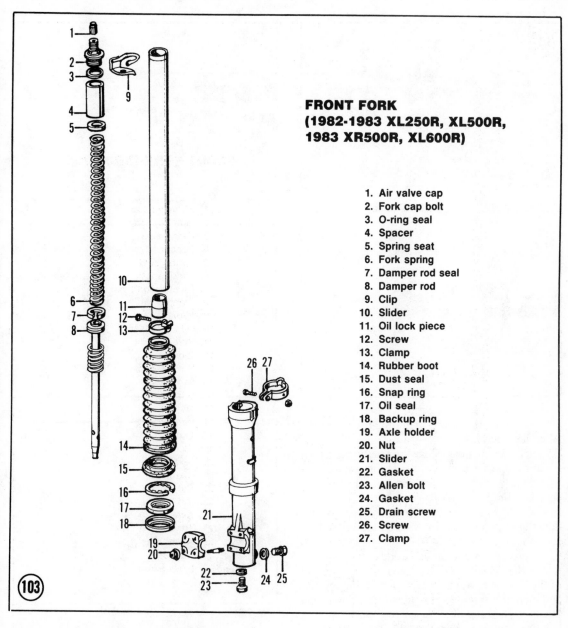

FRONT FORK
(1982-1983 XL250R, XL500R,
1983 XR500R, XL600R)

1. Air valve cap
2. Fork cap bolt
3. O-ring seal
4. Spacer
5. Spring seat
6. Fork spring
7. Damper rod seal
8. Damper rod
9. Clip
10. Slider
11. Oil lock piece
12. Screw
13. Clamp
14. Rubber boot
15. Dust seal
16. Snap ring
17. Oil seal
18. Backup ring
19. Axle holder
20. Nut
21. Slider
22. Gasket
23. Allen bolt
24. Gasket
25. Drain screw
26. Screw
27. Clamp

(103)

9

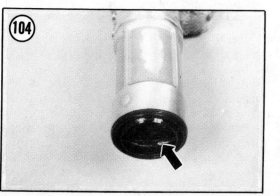

(104)

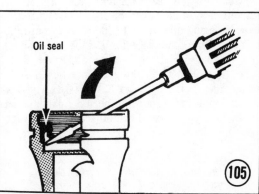

Oil seal

(105)

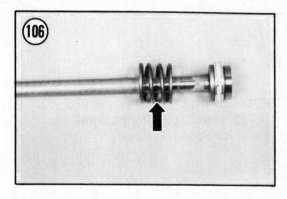

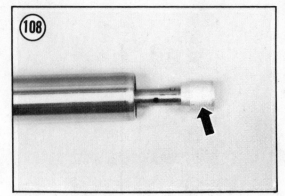

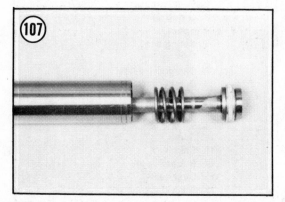

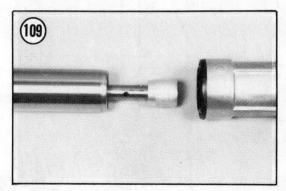

6. Make sure the gasket (**Figure 110**) is on the Allen head screw.

7. Apply Loctite Lock N' Seal to the threads of the Allen head screw prior to installation. Install it in the fork slider and tighten to the torque specification listed in **Table 1**.

8. Slide the fork slider backup ring (flange side up) down the fork tube until it rests on top of the fork slider bushing.

9. To prevent damage to the inside of the new fork seal during installation, wrap the groove in the top of the fork tube with clear tape (something smooth and non-abrasive—do not use duct or masking tape).

10. Coat the new seal with DEXRON automatic transmission fluid. Position the seal with the marking facing upward and slide it down onto the fork tube. Drive the seal into the slider (**Figure 94**) with Honda special tool Fork Seal Driver Body (part No. 07947-KA50100) and Fork Seal Driver Attachment (part No. 07947-KA40200). Drive the oil seal in until the groove in the slider can be seen above the top surface of the oil seal. Remove the tape from the top of the fork tube.

NOTE
If the seal must be driven further down, remove the special tools and insert the

backup plate on top of the seal. Repeat Step 10 until the seal is correctly seated.

11. Install the circlip. Make sure the circlip is completely seated in the groove in the fork slider.

12. Install the dust seal.

13. Refer to **Figure 111** and make sure that all the components installed in Steps 8-11 are in their correct position.

14. Remove the top bolt, spacer and the spring installed in Step 4. Fill the fork tube with DEXRON automatic transmission fluid or SAE 10W fork oil. The correct quantity is listed in **Table 2**.

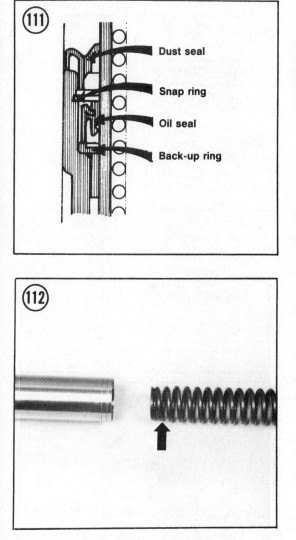

Dust seal

Snap ring

Oil seal

Back-up ring

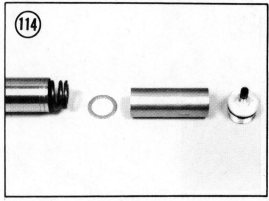

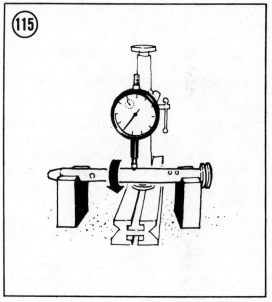

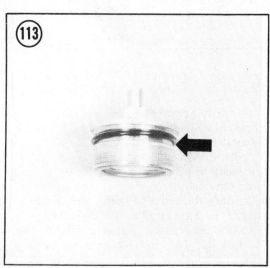

NOTE
In order to measure the correct amount of fluid, use a plastic baby bottle. These have graduations in fluid ounces (oz.) and cubic centimeters (cc) on the side.

15. Install the spring with the tapered end in first (**Figure 112**).

16. Inspect the condition of the O-ring seal on the fork top bolt (**Figure 113**); replace if necessary.

17. Install the spring seat, spacer and fork top bolt (**Figure 114**).

18. Install the fork top bolt and tighten to the torque specification listed in **Table 1**.

19. Repeat for the other fork assembly.

20. Install the fork assemblies as described in this chapter.

9

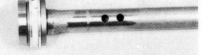

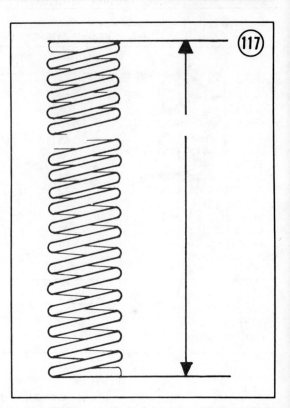

FORK INSPECTION (ALL MODELS)

1. Thoroughly clean all parts in solvent and dry them. Check the fork tube for signs of wear or scratches.

2. Check the damper rod for straightness. **Figure 115** shows one method. The rod should be replaced if the runout is 0.2 mm (0.008 in.) or greater.

3. Carefully check the damper rod and piston rings (**Figure 116**) for wear or damage; replace if necessary.

4. Inspect the oil seals for scoring, nicks and loss of resiliency. Replace if their condition is questionable.

5. Check the upper fork tube for straightness. If bent or severely scratched, it should be replaced.

6. Check the lower slider for dents or exterior damage that may cause the upper fork tube to hang up during riding. Replace if necessary.

7. Measure the uncompressed length of the fork springs (not rebound spring) as shown in **Figure 117**.

8. If the springs have sagged to the service limit listed in **Table 4** they must be replaced.

9. On 1981-1982 XR250R and XR500R models, inspect the slider and fork tube bushings. If either is scratched or scored they must be replaced. If the Teflon coating is worn off so that the copper base material is showing in approximately 3/4 of the total surface, the bushing must be replaced. Also check for distortion on the check points of the backup ring; replace as necessary (**Figure 118**).

10. Any parts that are worn or damaged should be replaced. Simply cleaning and reinstalling unserviceable components will not improve performance of the front suspension.

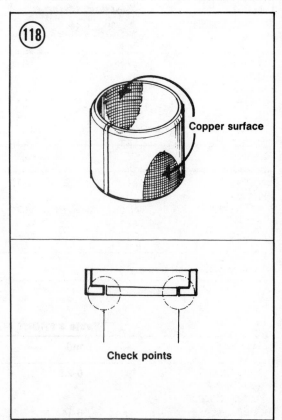

Copper surface

Check points

Table 1 FRONT SUSPENSION TORQUE SPECIFICATIONS

Item	ft.-lb.	N•m
Front axle	36-58	50-58
Front axle nut	36-58	50-85
Front axle holder nuts	7-10	10-14
Front axle pinch bolt (XL250)	17-20	23-28
Handlebar holder bolts	13-22	18-30
Upper fork bridge bolts		
XL250S, XR250	6-7	8-10
XL500S, XR250R, XL250R	13-18	18-25
XR350R, XR500, XL500R,	13-22	18-30
XR500R, XL600R		
Lower fork bridge bolts		
XR350R, XR500R	22-25	30-35
All other models	13-22	18-30
Steering stem nut		
XR350R, 1983 XR500R	69-101	95-140
XL600R	58-87	80-120
All other models	51-72	70-100
Front fork Allen bolt		
XL250S	.6-9	8-12
All other models	11-22	15-30

Table 2 FRONT FORK OIL CAPACITY*

Model	Standard capacity		Standard distance from top of fork	
	cc	fl. oz.	mm	in.
XL250S	190	6.4	–	–
XL250R	300	10.14	173	6.81
XR250R				
1981	368	12.4	152	6
1982	395	13.4	156	6.125
XR250	202	6.8	–	–
XR350R	553	18.7	132	5.2
XR500	202	6.8	–	–
XL500S	190	6.4	–	–
XL500R	379	12.75	163	6.42
XR500R				
1981-1982	345	11.7	181	7.1
1983	651	22	141	5.5
XL600R	455	15.4	150	5.9

* Capacity for each fork leg.

Table 3 FRONT FORK AIR PRESSURE

Model	psi	kg/cm²
1982 XL250R	0-2.8	0-0.2
1982 XL500R,		
XL600R, XR350R	0	0
1983 XR500R	0-14	0.98

9

Table 4 FRONT FORK SPRING FREE LENGTH*

Model	Standard		Service length	
	mm	in.	mm	in.
XL250S	501.9	19.76	483.5	19.04
XL250R	579.9	22.83	568.3	22.37
XR250R				
1981	562.4	22.1	551	21.7
1982	NA	NA	NA	NA
XR250, XR500	562.4	22.1	551	21.7
XR350R	559.9	22.4	554.3	21.82
XL500S	481.9	18.97	477.7	18.81
XL500R	580.4	22.85	568.8	22.38
XR500R				
1981	617.5	24.31	605.1	24
1982	NA	NA	NA	NA
1983	568.9	22.40	563	22.2
XL600R	563.5	22.18	557	21.93

*NA = Information not available.

CHAPTER TEN

REAR SUSPENSION

This chapter contains repair and replacement procedures for the rear wheel and rear suspension components. Tire changing and wheel balancing are covered in Chapter Nine.

Refer to **Table 1** for rear suspension torque specifications. **Tables 1-3** are located at the end of this chapter.

REAR WHEEL (DUAL-SHOCK)
Removal/Installation

1. Place wood block(s) under the skid plate to support the bike securely so that the rear wheel is off the ground.

2. Loosen the rear brake cable adjustment nut and pull the cable retainer and cable out of the brake arm (**Figure 1**).

3. Loosen the locknut and axle adjusting bolt (**Figure 2**) on each side.

4. Remove the cotter pin and loosen the rear axle nut (**Figure 3**).

5. Remove the screws (**Figure 4**) securing the drive sprocket cover and remove the cover.

6. Remove the bolts (**Figure 5**) securing the drive sprocket. Remove the sprocket retainer, the sprocket and the drive chain. Let the drive chain rest on the chain slider on the swing arm.

10

7. Remove the axle nut and withdraw the axle from the right-hand side.

8A. On 1981 XL250S and all XL500S and XR500 models, pivot the brake set plate down (**Figure 6**) and slide it off the brake torque link. Remove the brake torque link from the brake panel (**Figure 7**). Let the torque link pivot down and rest on the floor.

8B. On 1978-1980 XL250S models, pull the wheel to the rear to disengage the brake panel from the swing arm.

9. Remove the drive chain from the wheel sprocket and remove the wheel.

10. Install by reversing these removal steps, noting the following.

11A. On 1978-1980 XL250S models, be sure to align the groove in the brake panel onto the boss on the swing arm.

11B. On 1981 XL250S and all XL500S and XR500 models, be sure to install the brake set plate onto the brake panel and torque link (**Figure 6**).

12. If the drive chain master link was removed, install a new clip on the master link. Install it so the closed end of the clip is facing the direction of travel (**Figure 8**).

13. Install the axle from the right-hand side.

14. Adjust the drive chain tension as described in Chapter Three.

15. Tighten the axle nut to the torque specification listed in **Table 1**. Install a new cotter pin and bend the ends over completely.

16. After the wheel is completely installed, rotate it several times to make sure it rotates smoothly. Apply the brake several times to make sure it operates correctly.

17. Adjust the rear brake as described in Chapter Three.

REAR WHEEL (PRO-LINK)

Removal/Installation

1. Place wood block(s) under the engine to support the bike securely so that the rear wheel is off the ground.

2. Pull the rear brake cable holder plate (**Figure 9**) toward the rear and disconnect it from the brake arm.

3. Loosen the rear axle nut (A, **Figure 10**).

4. Rotate both drive chain snail adjusters (B, **Figure 10**) toward the front so the wheel can be moved forward for maximum chain slack.

5. Move the wheel forward and position the notch in the snail adjusters onto the stopper pin on the swing arm.

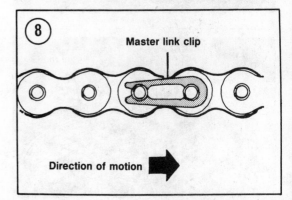

Master link clip

Direction of motion

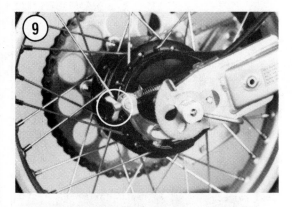

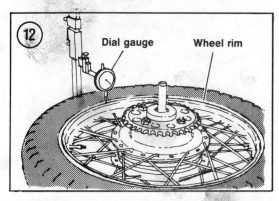

Dial gauge   Wheel rim

6. Rotate the rear wheel to derail the drive chain.

7. On the right-hand side, pull the stopper plate (**Figure 11**) off of the stopper pin on the swing arm.

8. Slide the wheel and axle assembly to the rear and remove it.

9. Install by reversing these removal steps, noting the following.

10. Make sure the groove in the brake panel is properly meshed with the tang on the swing arm. This is necessary for proper brake operation.

11. Adjust the drive chain tension as described in Chapter Three.

12. Tighten the axle nut to the torque specification listed in **Table 1**.

13. After the wheel is completely installed, rotate it several times to make sure it rotates smoothly. Apply the brake several times to make sure it operates correctly.

14. Adjust the rear brake as described in Chapter Three.

REAR WHEEL INSPECTION (ALL MODELS)

Measure the radial and axial runout of the wheel rim with a dial indicator as shown in **Figure 12**. The standard value for both radial and axial runout is 0.02 in. (0.5 mm). The maximum permissible limit is 0.08 in. (2.0 mm).

Tighten or replace any bent or loose spokes. Refer to *Spoke Adjustment* in Chapter Nine.

Check axle runout as described under *Rear Hub Inspection* in this chapter.

REAR HUB

Disassembly

Refer to **Figure 13** for this procedure.

1. Remove the rear wheel as described in this chapter.

2. Pull the brake assembly straight up and out of the brake drum.

3. Remove the axle spacer (**Figure 14**).

4. Unscrew the bearing retainer (**Figure 15**) and remove it.

5. Remove the dust seal.

6. Remove the right-hand (**Figure 16**) and left-hand bearings and distance collar. Tap the bearings out with a soft aluminum or brass drift.

Inspection

1. Clean bearings thoroughly in solvent and dry with compressed air. Do not let the bearing spin while drying.

2. Clean the inside and outside of the hub with solvent. Dry with compressed air.

10

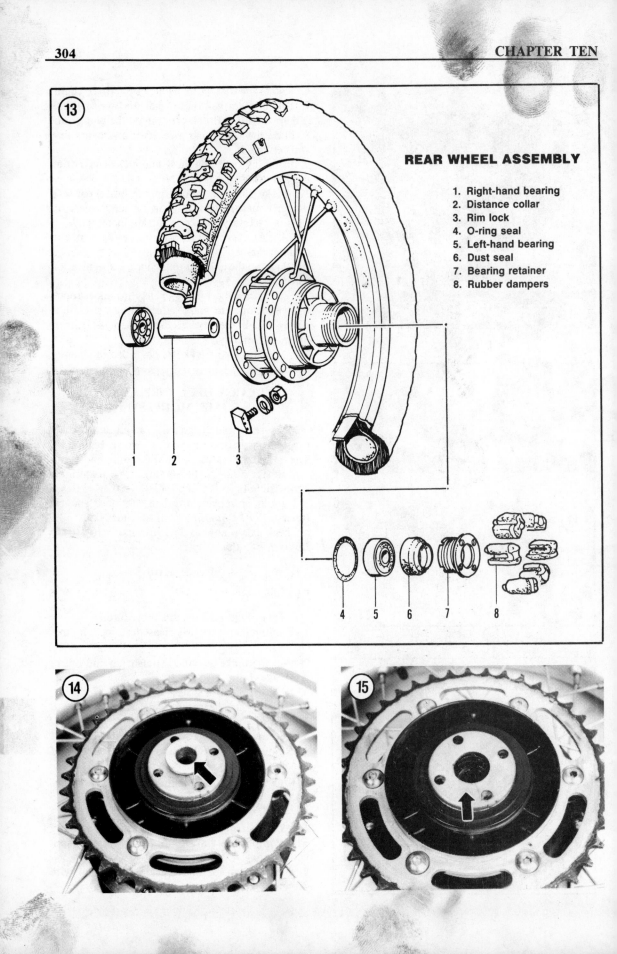

REAR WHEEL ASSEMBLY

1. Right-hand bearing
2. Distance collar
3. Rim lock
4. O-ring seal
5. Left-hand bearing
6. Dust seal
7. Bearing retainer
8. Rubber dampers

3. Turn each bearing by hand. Make sure bearings turn smoothly. Check the balls for evidence of wear, pitting or excessive heat (bluish tint). Replace bearings if necessary; always replace as a complete set.

4. Check the axle for wear and straightness. Use V-blocks and a dial indicator as shown in **Figure 17**. If the runout is 0.008 in. (0.2 mm) or greater, the axle should be replaced.

Assembly

1. Pack the bearings thoroughly with a good quality bearing grease. Work the grease in between the balls thoroughly; turn the bearing by hand a couple of times to make sure the grease is distributed evenly inside the bearing.

2. Blow any dirt or foreign matter out of the hub prior to installing the bearings.

3. Install the right-hand bearing.

4. Install the distance collar and the left-hand bearing.

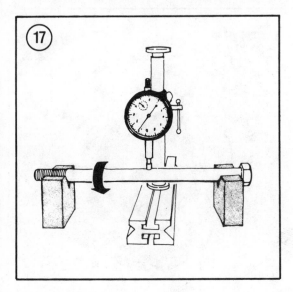

> *NOTE*
> *Install both bearings with the sealed side facing toward the outside.*

> *CAUTION*
> *Tap the bearing squarely into place and tap only on the outer race. Use a socket (Figure 18) that matches the outer race diameter. Do not tap on the inner race or the bearing will be damaged. Be sure to tap the bearings until they seawl completely.*

5. Install the brake assembly into the hub.

6. Install the rear wheel as described in this chapter.

FINAL DRIVE SPROCKET

> *NOTE*
> *There is no separate final drive sprocket assembly on the XR500R.*

Disassembly/Assembly

Refer to **Figure 19** for this procedure.

1. Remove the rear wheel as described in this chapter.

2. On XR500R models, remove the Allen bolts, washers and nuts securing the driven sprocket to the wheel hub.

3. Remove the dust cover (A, **Figure 20**).

4. Remove the circlip and thrust washer.

5. Remove the final drive sprocket assembly.

6. If necessary, remove the Allen bolts (B, **Figure 20**) securing the sprocket to the drive flange.

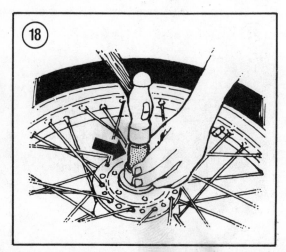

10

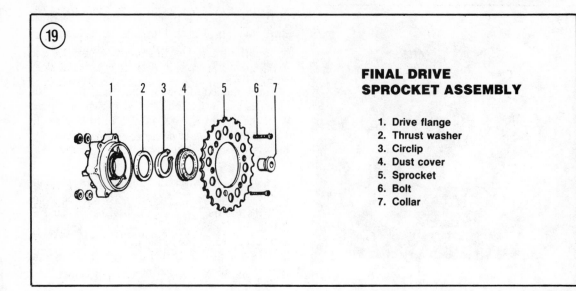

**FINAL DRIVE
SPROCKET ASSEMBLY**

1. Drive flange
2. Thrust washer
3. Circlip
4. Dust cover
5. Sprocket
6. Bolt
7. Collar

7. Assemble by reversing these disassembly steps, noting the following.

8. The snap ring and dust cover must be installed as shown in **Figure 21**.

9. On XR500R models, tighten the Allen bolts to the torque specification listed in **Table 1**.

Inspection

1. Visually inspect the rubber dampers for signs of damage or deterioration. Replace all if any are damaged.

2. Inspect the teeth (C, **Figure 20**) of the sprocket. If the teeth are visibly worn (**Figure 22**), replace sprocket with a new one.

3. If the sprocket requires replacing, the drive chain is probably worn also. Refer to Chapter Three.

SWING ARM (DUAL-SHOCK)

Under normal use and with correct periodic lubrication, the swing arm bushings or needle bearings have a long service life. However, in time they will wear and must be replaced. Indications of excessive wear are imprecise steering and a tendency for the motorcycle to pull to one side or other during acceleration and braking.

Removal/Installation

1. Remove the right- and left-hand side covers.

2. Remove the rear wheel as described in this chapter.

3. Remove both lower shock absorber bolts.

NOTE
It is not necessary to completely remove the shocks.

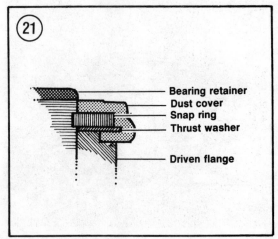

Bearing retainer
Dust cover
Snap ring
Thrust washer

Driven flange

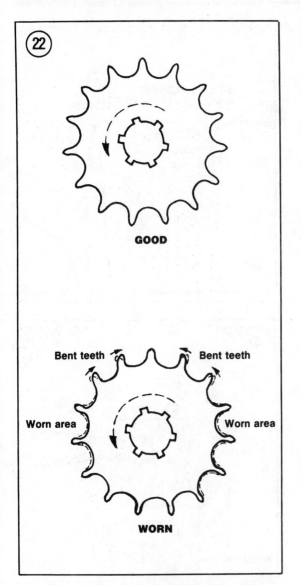

GOOD

Bent teeth   Bent teeth

Worn area   Worn area

WORN

4. Remove the bolts securing the chain cover (A, **Figure 23**).
5. On XL series models, remove the chain guide.
6. Remove the self-locking nut (B, **Figure 23**) and withdraw the pivot bolt from the right-hand side.
7. Pull back on the swing arm and remove it from the frame.

> *NOTE*
> *Don't lose the dust caps on each side of the pivot points; they may fall off during removal.*

8. Install by reversing these removal steps. Tighten the self-locking nut to the torque specifications listed in **Table 1**.
9. Adjust the drive chain and rear brake as described in Chapter Three.

Disassembly/Inspection/Assembly (XL500S)

The swing arm is equipped with needle bearings at each end. The bearing will be damaged when removed, so don't remove it unless absolutely necessary.

The bearing can be removed either with a long drift and hammer or with the use of special tools that are available from a Honda dealer.

1. Remove the swing arm as described in this chapter.
2. Secure the swing arm in a vise with soft jaws.
3A. If special tools are not available, carefully tap out the needle bearing and collar. Use a suitable size drift or socket and extension and carefully drive them out from the opposite end (**Figure 24**).

> *CAUTION*
> *Do not remove the bearings just for inspection as they are damaged during removal and new bearings must be installed.*

3B. If special tools are used, install the Swing Arm Bearing Remover (Honda part No. M967X-038-XXXXX) into one side of the swing arm. Insert a drift or punch behind the bearing remover and tap out the bearing and thrust washer.
4. Repeat Step 3A or 3B for the other end.
5. Wash all parts, including the inside of the swing arm pivot area, in solvent and thoroughly dry.
6. Apply a light coat of waterproof grease to all parts prior to installation.

10

> *NOTE*
> *Install the new bearings with the manufacturer's marks facing toward the outside.*

7A. If the special tools are not available, tap new bearings into place slowly and squarely with a block of wood and hammer (**Figure 25**). Tap the bearing in until it is slightly below the surface of the swing arm. Make sure that they are not cocked and that they are completely seated. Set the collar in place and install it in the same manner until completely seated against the swing arm surface.

7B. If special tools are used, tap new bearings into place slowly and squarely with Needle Bearing Driver Attachment (Honda part No. 07749-0010000), Bearing Driver Handle (Honda part No. 07946-3710300) and a hammer. Tap the bearing in until it is slightly below the surface of the swing arm. Make sure that they are not cocked and that they are completely seated. Set the collar in place and install it in the same manner until completely seated against the swing arm surface.

> *CAUTION*
> *Never reinstall a bearing that has been removed. Removal slightly damages it so that it is no longer true to alignment. If installed, it will damage the pivot collar and create an unsafe riding condition.*

8. Repeat Step 7A or 7B for the other side.
9. Install the swing arm as described in this chapter.

Disassembly/Inspection/Assembly (All Other Models)

Refer to **Figure 26** for this procedure.
1. Remove the rubber dust covers.
2. Remove the chain slider from the left-hand side.
3. Secure the swing arm in a vise with soft jaws.
4. Tap the bushing out of one end of the swing arm and remove the collar. Remove the other bushing.
5. Wash all parts in solvent and dry with compressed air.
6. Measure the outside diameter of the collar at both ends. If the diameter is 0.841 in. (21.35 mm) or less at either end, the collar must be replaced.
7. Measure the inside diameter of both bushings. If the diameter is 0.853 in. (21. 67 mm) or less on either bushing, replace both as a set.

> *NOTE*
> *Always replace both bushings even though only one may be worn.*

8. The maximum clearance between the collar and the bushing is 0.013 in. (0.32 mm). Replace one or all parts if this dimension is exceeded.
9. Apply oil to the inside and outside of the bushings prior to installation.

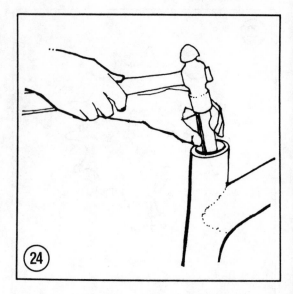

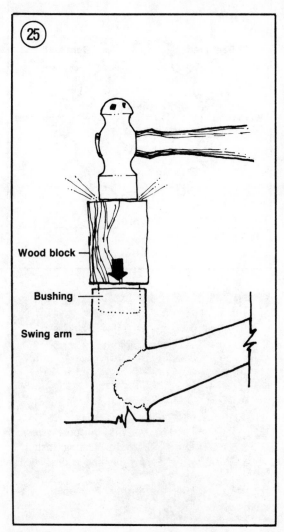

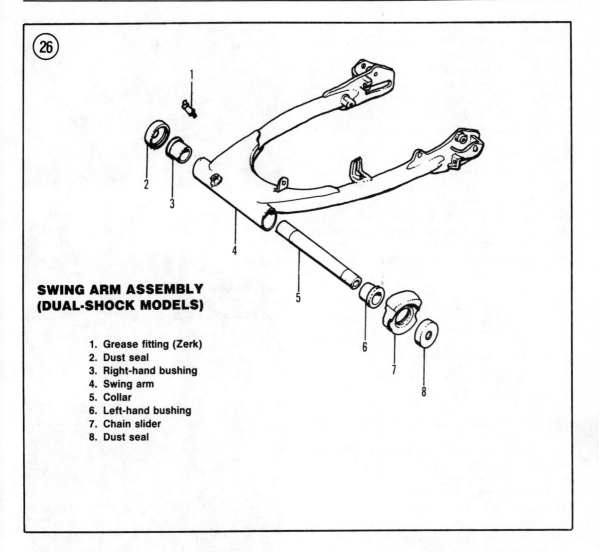

**SWING ARM ASSEMBLY
(DUAL-SHOCK MODELS)**

1. Grease fitting (Zerk)
2. Dust seal
3. Right-hand bushing
4. Swing arm
5. Collar
6. Left-hand bushing
7. Chain slider
8. Dust seal

10. Tap one bushing into place slowly and squarely with a block of wood (**Figure 25**). Make sure it seats completely and is not cocked in place.

CAUTION
Never reinstall a bushing that has been removed. During removal it becomes slightly damaged and is no longer true to alignment. If reinstalled, it will damage the collar and create an unsafe riding condition.

11. Apply a good coat of multipurpose grease to the collar and the inside of the bushing. Install the collar and install the other bushing as described in Step 10.
12. Inspect the condition of the chain slider and replace if necessary.
13. Install new grease seals.

SWING ARM (PRO-LINK)

In time, the needle bearings or the pivot collar will wear beyond the service limits and will have to be replaced. The condition of the needle bearings can greatly affect handling performance and if worn parts are not replaced they can produce erratic and dangerous handling. Common symptoms are wheel hop, pulling to one side during acceleration and pulling to the other side during braking.

Removal

1. Place wood block(s) under the engine to support the bike securely with the rear wheel off of the ground.
2. Remove both side covers and the seat.
3. Remove the fuel tank as described in Chapter Seven.

10

4. Remove the air cleaner case.

5. Remove the shock absorber unit (**Figure 27**) as described in this chapter.

6. Grasp the rear end of the swing arm and try to move it from side to side to side in a horizontal arc. There should be no noticeable side play. If play is evident and the pivot bolt is tightened correctly, the bushings or pivot collar should be replaced.

7. Remove the bolt and nut (**Figure 28**) securing the shock arm to the shock link.

8. Remove the rear wheel (A, **Figure 29**) as described in this chapter.

9. Remove the self-locking nut (B, **Figure 29**) and withdraw the pivot bolt from the left-hand side.

10. Pull back on the swing arm, free it from the drive chain and remove the swing arm from the frame.

> *NOTE*
> *Don't lose the dust seal caps on each side of the pivot points; they will usually fall off when the swing arm is removed.*

Disassembly/Inspection/Assembly

Refer to **Figure 30** for this procedure.

1. Remove the swing arm as described in this chapter.

2. Remove the chain guard and the mud guard from the swing arm.

3. Remove the drive chain slider from the left-hand side of the swing arm.

4. If necessary, remove the bolt and nut securing the shock arm from the swing arm. It does not have to be removed for this procedure.

5. Remove both dust seal caps if they have not already fallen off during the removal sequence.

6. Withdraw the pivot collar, clean in solvent and dry it.

7. Inspect the pivot collar for abnormal wear, scratches or score marks. Replace as necessary.

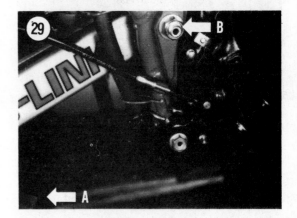

> *NOTE*
> *There are no factory specifications for the outside diameter of the pivot collar.*

> *NOTE*
> *If the pivot collar is replaced, the needle bearings at each end must be replaced at the same time.*

8. Wipe off any excess grease from the needle bearings at each end of the swing arm. The needle bearings wear very slowly and wear is very difficult to measure. Turn each bearing with your fingers; make sure they rotate smoothly. Check the rollers for evidence of wear, pitting or color change (bluish tint) indicating heat from lack of lubrication.

> *NOTE*
> *Always replace both needle bearings even though only one may be worn. Needle bearing replacement is described in this chapter.*

9. Prior to installing the pivot collar, coat the collar and both needle bearings with molybdenum disulfide grease. Insert the pivot collar and install the drive chain slider, the chain guard and the mud guard.

10. Coat the inside of both dust seal caps with molybdenum disulfide grease and install them onto the swing arm.

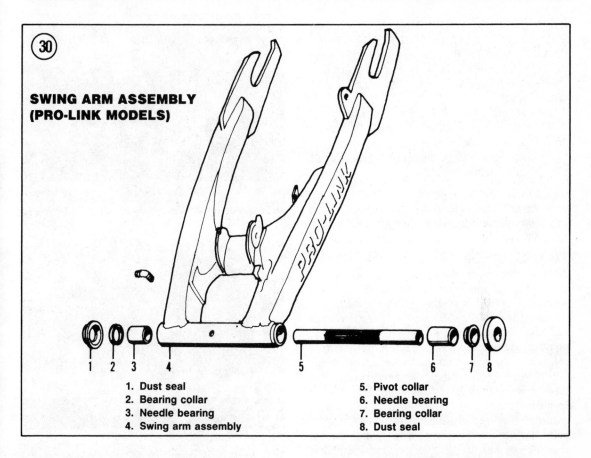

**SWING ARM ASSEMBLY
(PRO-LINK MODELS)**

1. Dust seal
2. Bearing collar
3. Needle bearing
4. Swing arm assembly
5. Pivot collar
6. Needle bearing
7. Bearing collar
8. Dust seal

11. Install the swing arm as described in this chapter.

Installation

1. Position the swing arm into the mounting area. Align the holes in the swing arm with the holes in the frame. To help align the holes, insert a drift in from the right-hand side.
2. Apply a light coat of grease to the pivot bolt. After all holes are aligned, insert the pivot bolt from the left-hand side and install the self-locking nut. Tighten the self-locking nut to the torque specification listed in **Table 1**.
3. Connect the shock arm to the shock link and install the bolt and nut. Tighten the bolt to the torque specification listed in **Table 1**.
4. Install the rear wheel as described in Chapter Ten.
5. Install the shock absorber as described in this chapter.
6. Install the air cleaner case.
7. Install the fuel tank, the seat and the side covers.
8. Lubricate swing arm pivot bolt and shock linkage as described in Chapter Three.

Swing Arm Needle Bearing Replacement

The swing arm is equipped with needle bearings at each end. The bearing will be damaged when removed, so don't remove it unless absolutely necessary.

The bearing can be removed either with a long drift and hammer or with the use of special tools that are available from a Honda dealer.

1. Remove the swing arm as described in this chapter.
2. Secure the swing arm in a vise with soft jaws.
3A. If special tools are not available, carefully tap out the needle bearing and collar. Use a suitable size drift or socket and extension and carefully drive them out from the opposite end (**Figure 26**).

CAUTION
Do not remove the bearings just for inspection as they are damaged during removal and new bearings must be installed.

3B. If special tools are used, install the Needle Bearing Remover (Honda part No. 07936-3710000) into one side of the swing arm. Push it past the end of the needle bearing and pull

10

it up against the backside of the bearing. Install the Slide Weight and Handle (Honda part No. 07936-3710000) into the bearing remover. Remove the needle bearing and collar by pulling it out with the slide weight and handle (similar to a body shop slide hammer).

4. Repeat Step 3A or 3B for the other end.

5. Wash all parts, including the inside of the swing arm pivot area, in solvent and thoroughly dry.

6. Apply a light coat of waterproof grease to all parts prior to installation.

NOTE
Install the new bearings with the manufacturer's marks facing toward the outside.

7A. If special tools are not available, tap new bearings into place slowly and squarely with a block of wood and hammer (**Figure 25**). Tap the bearing in until it is slightly below the surface of the swing arm. Make sure that they are not cocked and that they are completely seated. Set the collar in place and install it in the same manner until completely seated against the swing arm surface.

7B. If special tools are used, tap new bearings into place slowly and squarely with Swing Arm Bearing Installer (Honda part No. 07946-KA50000) and a hammer. Tap the bearing in until it is slightly below the surface of the swing arm. Make sure that they are not cocked and that they are completely seated. Set the collar in place and install it in the same manner until completely seated against the swing arm surface.

CAUTION
Never reinstall a bearing that has been removed. Removal slightly damages it so that it is no longer true to alignment. If installed, it will damage the pivot collar and create an unsafe riding condition.

8. Repeat Step 7A or 7B for the other side.

9. Install the swing arm as described in this chapter.

DUAL SHOCK ABSORBERS

The rear shocks are spring controlled and gas charged. Spring preload can be adjusted on all models. The shock damper unit is sealed and cannot be serviced. Service is limited to removal and replacement of the damper unit and/or spring.

WARNING
Do not try to dismantle the gas filled damper unit or apply any form of heat

to it. If the unit is heated in any way it will result in an extremely dangerous explosion.

Spring Preload Adjustment

XL models

1. Remove the right- and left-hand side covers.

2. Rotate the cam ring (**Figure 31**) at the upper end of the shock to one of the 5 positions—counterclockwise to increase preload or clockwise to decrease preload.

NOTE
Use the spanner wrench furnished in the factory tool kit for this adjustment.

3. Both cams must be indexed on the same detent.

XR models

1. Remove the right- and left-hand side covers.

2. Pull down on the spring coils (A, **Figure 32**).

3. Make sure the adjusting collar (B, **Figure 32**) slides down the spring.

4. Reposition the set ring on the damper units—down to increase spring preload and up to decrease preload to any of the three settings.

NOTE
Make sure the set ring is correctly seated in the groove in the damper unit.

5. The set ring on both shocks must be positioned in the same groove.

NOTE
After resetting, push down on the rear end of the bike several times to ensure the set rings have been properly seated.

Removal/Installation

Removal and installation of the rear shocks are easier if they are done separately. The remaining unit will support the rear of the bike and maintain the correct relationship between the top and bottom shock mounts.
1. Remove the right- and left-hand side covers.
2. Adjust the shocks to their softest settings.
3. Remove the upper and lower mounting bolts (**Figure 33**).
4. Install by reversing these removal steps.
5. Repeat Steps 3 and 4 for the other unit.
6. Tighten the upper and lower bolts to the torque specifications listed in **Table 1**.

Disassembly/Inspection/Assembly

Refer to **Figure 34** for XL models and **Figure 35** for XR models.

WARNING
Without the proper tool, this procedure can be dangerous. The spring can fly loose, causing injury. For a small bench fee, a dealer can do the job for you.

1. Install the compression tool as shown in **Figure 36**. This is a special tool and is available from a Honda dealer. It is Shock Absorber Compressor tool, No. 07959-3290001.
2. Compress the spring and remove the lower spring seat.
3. Loosen the lower locknut and unscrew the lower joint.
4. Release the spring compression and remove the shock from the compression tool.
5. Slide off the spring and measure the spring free length (**Figure 37**). The spring must be replaced if it has sagged to the service limit dimension or less (**Table 2**).
6. Check the damper unit for leakage and make sure the damper rod is straight.

NOTE
The damper unit cannot be rebuilt; it must be replaced as a unit. See WARNING at the beginning of this procedure regarding the gas filled unit.

7. Assembly is the reverse of these disassembly steps. Note the order of the parts shown in **Figure 34** and **Figure 35**.

NOTE
Apply Loctite Lock N' Seal to the threads prior to installation of the lower joint. Tighten locknut securely.

PRO-LINK SUSPENSION SYSTEM

The single shock absorber and linkage of the Pro-Link rear suspension system (**Figure 38**) are attached to the swing arm just to the rear of the swing arm pivot point and to the lower rear portion of the frame. All of these items are located forward of the rear wheel.

The shock link and shock arm working together with the matched spring rate and damping rates of the shock absorber combine to achieve a "progressive rising rate" rear suspension. This system provides the rider with the best of two worlds—greater rider comfort and better transfer of power to the ground.

As the rear suspension is moved upward by bumps, the shock absorber is compressed by the movement of the shock arm. As rear suspension travel increases, the portion of the shock arm where the shock absorber is attached rises above the swing arm thus increasing shock absorber travel (compression). This provides a progressive rise rate in which the shock eventually moves at a faster rate than the wheel. At about half way through the wheel travel the shock begins to move at a faster rate than it did in the beginning.

10

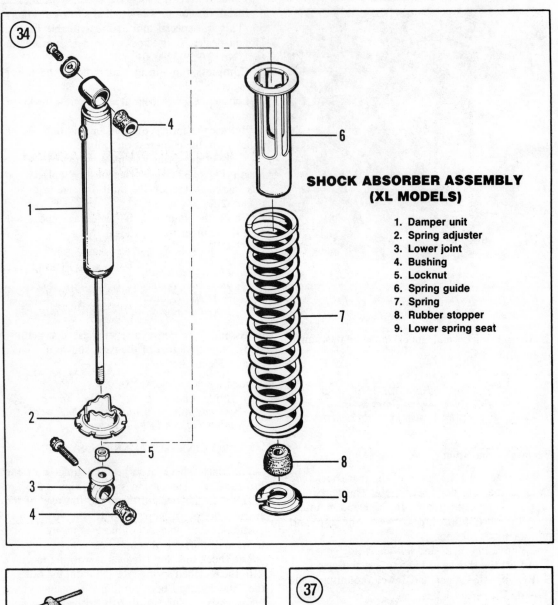

**SHOCK ABSORBER ASSEMBLY
(XL MODELS)**

1. Damper unit
2. Spring adjuster
3. Lower joint
4. Bushing
5. Locknut
6. Spring guide
7. Spring
8. Rubber stopper
9. Lower spring seat

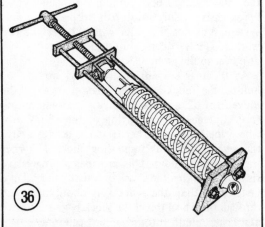

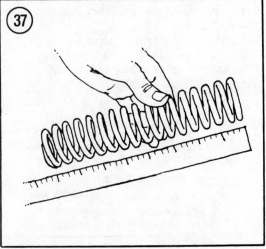

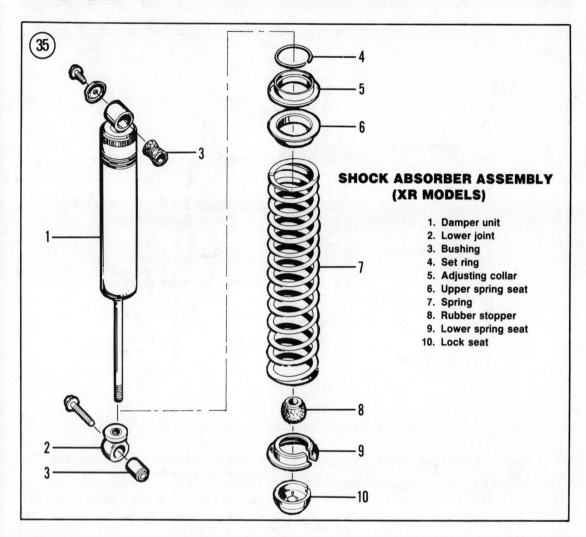

㉟

**SHOCK ABSORBER ASSEMBLY
(XR MODELS)**

1. Damper unit
2. Lower joint
3. Bushing
4. Set ring
5. Adjusting collar
6. Upper spring seat
7. Spring
8. Rubber stopper
9. Lower spring seat
10. Lock seat

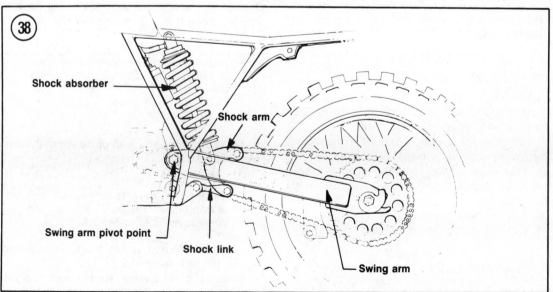

㊳

Shock absorber

Shock arm

Swing arm pivot point

Shock link

Swing arm

10

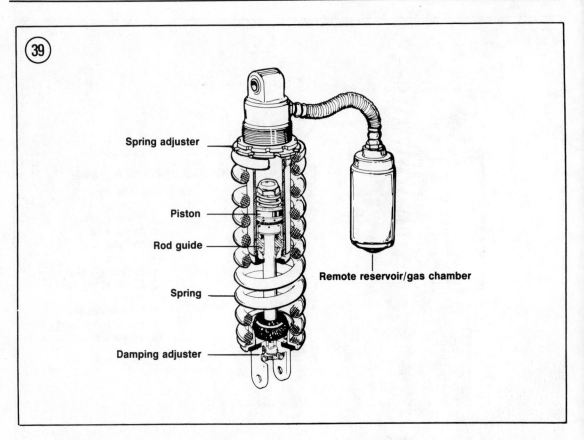

(39)

Spring adjuster

Piston

Rod guide

Spring

Damping adjuster

Remote reservoir/gas chamber

SHOCK ABSORBER (PRO-LINK)

The single shock absorber (**Figure 39**) used in the Pro-Link suspension system has a remote oil/nitrogen reservoir on all models except the XL600R. The remote reservoir allows more rapid oil cooling and helps prevent the oil from frothing. The shock is adjustable for both shock rate and damping action.

Spring Pre-load Adjustment

There must be pre-load on the spring at all times. Never ride the bike without spring pre-load as possible loss of control will result.

The spring length (pre-load) must be maintained within the dimensions listed in **Table 3**.

1. Place wood block(s) under the engine to support the bike securely with the rear wheel off of the ground.
2. Remove both side covers.
3. Remove the air cleaner air box.

CAUTION
After the air cleaner air box is removed the carburetor throat is exposed. Cover the opening with a clean shop cloth so

that dirt or foreign matter will not enter into the carburetor.

4. Measure the existing spring length (**Figure 40**).
5. To adjust, loosen the locknut and turn the adjuster (**Figure 41**) in the desired direction. Tightening the adjuster increases spring pre-load and loosening it will decrease pre-load.

NOTE
Special tools are required for the locknut and the adjuster. These are pin spanners, Honda part No. 89201-KA4-810 and part No. 89202-KA4-810.

6. One complete turn (360°) of the adjuster moves the spring 0.006 in. (1.5 mm).

NOTE
*Remember the spring length (pre-load) must be maintained within the dimensions listed in **Table 3**.*

7. After the desired spring length is achieved, tighten the locknut securely.
8. Install the air cleaner air box and the side covers.

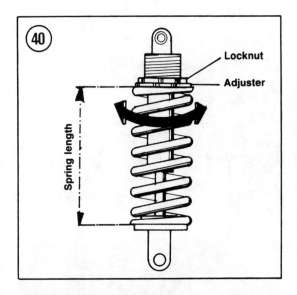

Locknut

Adjuster

Spring length

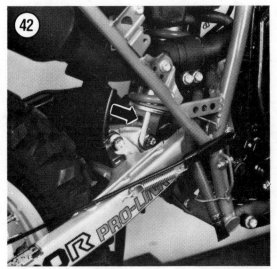

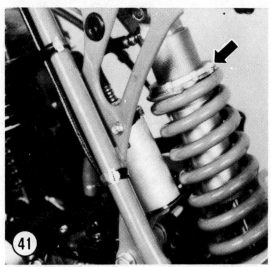

Rebound Damping Adjustment

Rebound damping can be adjusted to 4 different settings. The adjuster knob is located at the base of the shock absorber (**Figure 42**) between the legs of the lower mounting bracket.

The rebound setting should be adjusted to personal preference to accomodate rider weight and riding conditons.

Make sure that the adjuster is located into one of the detents and not in between any 2 settings.

Removal

1. Place wood block(s) under the engine to support the bike securely with the rear wheel off of the ground.
2. Remove both side covers and the seat.

3. Remove the fuel tank as described in Chapter Seven.
4. Remove the muffler as described in Chapter Seven.
5. On XR350R models, disconnect the electrical connector to the rear brake light switch and move the wires out of the way.
6. On 1983 XR500R and XL600R models, perform the following:
  a. Disconnect the electrical connector to the regulator.
  b. Remove the bolt (**Figure 43**) securing the regulator to the air box and remove the regulator.
  c. Unhook the cable clamp and move the electrical wires out of the way from the top of the air box.

10

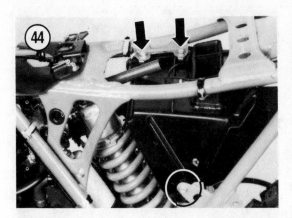

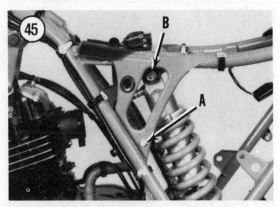

7. Remove the top bolts and the side bolt (**Figure 44**) securing the air cleaner air box to the frame. Loosen the clamping band on the portion going to the carburetor(s) and remove the air box from the frame.

8. Cover the inlet to the carburetor(s) with a clean shop cloth or plastic to prevent the entry of foreign matter.

9A. On 1983 XR350R and XR500R models, remove the bolts securing the remote reservoir to the frame.

9B. On all other models, remove the bolt (A, **Figure 45**) securing the remote reservoir to the frame.

> *WARNING*
> *Do not attempt to disconnect the reservoir hose from the shock absorber body. The compressed nitrogen within the shock absorber body and remote reservoir is pressurized to 285 psi (20 kg/cm²).*

10. Remove the shock absorber upper mounting bolt and nut (B, **Figure 45**).

11. Loosen the lower mounting bolt (**Figure 46**). There is no nut as the bolt is screwed into the other side of the shock absorber lower mounting bracket.

12. Move the upper portion of the shock absorber toward the rear.

> *NOTE*
> *The next step requires the aid of a helper. While raising the rear wheel, make sure the upper portion of the shock absorber clears the air box mounting brackets on the frame.*

13. Raise the rear wheel up as far as possible and have the helper install blocks of wood under the wheel.

14. Remove the shock absorber lower mounting bolt and remove the shock absorber out through the top of the frame.

15. Keep the rear wheel in the raised position (**Figure 47**).

Disassembly/Assembly
(XR250R, XR350R and XR500R)

Refer to the following illustrations for this procedure:
 a. **Figure 48**—XR250R and 1981-1982 XR500R.
 b. **Figure 49**—XR350R and 1983 XR500R.

Service by the home mechanic is limited to removal and installation of the spring. Under no

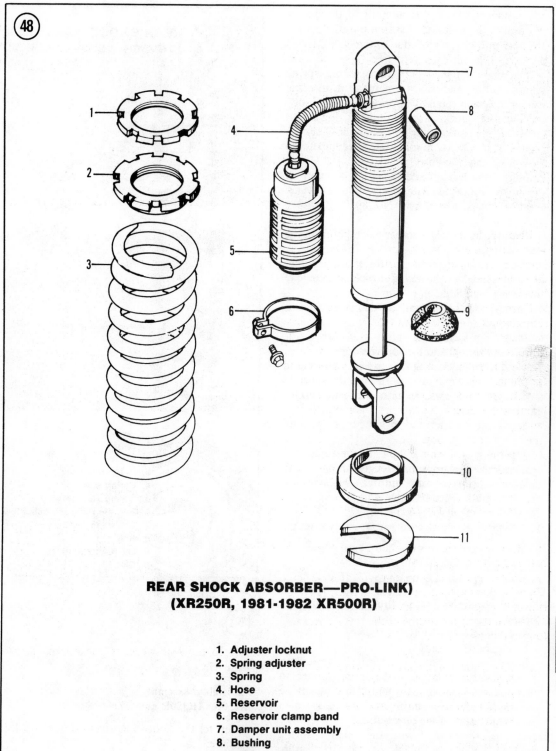

**REAR SHOCK ABSORBER—PRO-LINK)
(XR250R, 1981-1982 XR500R)**

1. Adjuster locknut
2. Spring adjuster
3. Spring
4. Hose
5. Reservoir
6. Reservoir clamp band
7. Damper unit assembly
8. Bushing
9. Rubber stopper
10. Spring seat
11. Spring stopper

10

circumstances should you attempt to disconnect the reservoir hose or disassemble the shock absorber unit or reservoir due to the high internal pressure of the nitrogen.

If you are satisfied with the existing spring pre-load setting and want to maintain it, measure the spring length (**Figure 50**) prior to disassembly.

1. Hold the shock absorber upside down and secure the upper mounting portion of the shock (A, **Figure 51**) in a vise with soft jaws. Be careful not to kink or damage the hose.

2. Loosen the locknut and the spring adjuster all the way (B, **Figure 51**) with special tools. These are 2 pin spanners, Honda part No. 89201-KA4-810 and No. 89202-KA4-810.

3. Remove the shock absorber assembly from the vise.

4. From the lower portion of the shock absorber assembly, slide out the spring stopper and remove the spring seat. Slide off the spring.

5. Inspect all components as described in this chapter.

6. Install the spring, the spring seat (flange side toward the spring) and the spring stopper.

7. Hold the shock absorber upside down and secure the upper mounting portion of the shock in a vise with soft jaws. Be careful not to kink or damage the hose.

8. Screw the adjuster and locknut by hand until they contact the spring.

9. Use the special tools and tighten the adjuster to achieve the standard spring length or the length measured prior to disassembly. The standard spring length is listed in **Table 3**.

10. Tighten the locknut securely.

11. Remove the shock absorber assembly from the vise.

Disassembly/Assembly (XL250R, XL500R and XL600R)

Refer to the following illustrations for this procedure:

   a. **Figure 52**—XL250R, XL500R.

   b. **Figure 53**—XL600R.

Service by the home mechanic is limited to removal and installation of the spring. Under no circumstances should you attempt to disassemble the shock absorber damper unit due to the high internal pressure of the nitrogen.

If you are satisfied with the existing spring pre-load setting and want to maintain it, measure the spring length (**Figure 50**) prior to disassembly.

1. Hold the shock absorber upside down and secure the upper mounting portion of the shock in a vise with soft jaws.

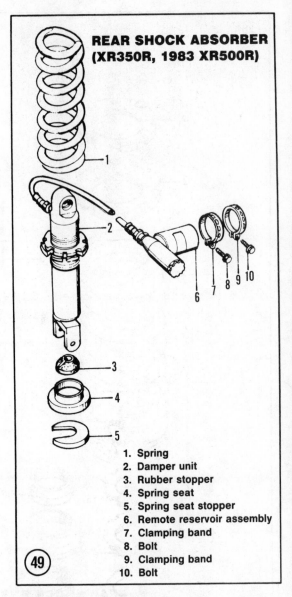

REAR SHOCK ABSORBER (XR350R, 1983 XR500R)

1. Spring
2. Damper unit
3. Rubber stopper
4. Spring seat
5. Spring seat stopper
6. Remote reservoir assembly
7. Clamping band
8. Bolt
9. Clamping band
10. Bolt

(49)

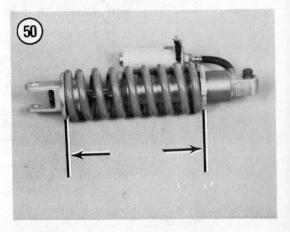

(50)

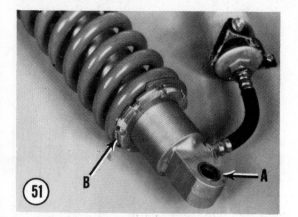

(51)

2. Loosen the locknut and the spring adjuster with special tools. These are 2 pin spanners, Honda part No. 89201-KA4-810 and No. 89202-KA4-810.
3. Remove the shock absorber assembly from the vise.
4. Completely unscrew the locknut and the adjust nut.
5. Slide the spring off of the damper unit.

NOTE
On XL600R models, no further disassembly is possible.

6. On XL250R and XL500R models, perform the following:

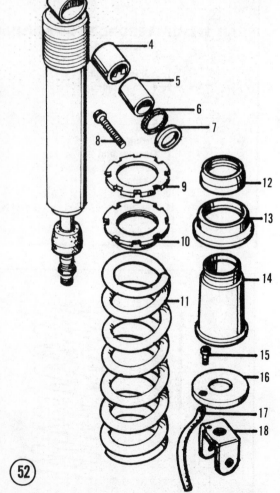

(52)

REAR SHOCK ABSORBER—PRO-LINK (XL250R, XL500R)

 1. Seal
 2. Seal
 3. Damper unit
 4. Outer bushing
 5. Inner bushing
 6. Seal
 7. Seal
 8. Bolt
 9. Adjuster locknut
10. Spring adjuster
11. Spring
12. Dust seal
13. Spring seat
14. Spring guide
15. Fitting
16. Seat stop
17. Drain tube
18. Lower mount

10

a. Secure the lower mounting portion of the shock in a vise with soft jaws.

b. Loosen the locknut on the damper rod.

c. Remove the shock from the vise.

d. Completely unscrew the lower mount from the damper rod.

e. Slide off the seat stop, spring guide, spring seat and dust seal.

7. Inspect all components as described in this chapter.

8. On XL250R and XL500R models, perform the following:

a. Slide on the dust seal, spring seat (flange side on toward the spring), spring guide (flange end on last) and seat stop.

b. Apply Loctite Lock N' Seal to the threads on the damper rod.

c. Screw on the lower mount; align the locating pin on the seat stop with the notch on the lower mount.

d. Secure the lower mounting portion of the shock in a vise with soft jaws.

e. Tighten the locknut on the damper rod to the torque specifications listed in **Table 1**.

9. Install the spring and screw on the adjusting nut and the locknut.

10. Hold the shock absorber upside down and secure the upper mounting portion of the shock in a vise with soft jaws.

11. Screw the adjuster and locknut by hand until they contact the spring.

12. Use the special tools and tighten the adjuster to achieve the standard spring length or the length measured prior to disassembly. The standard spring length is listed in **Table 3**.

13. Tighten the locknut securely.

14. Remove the shock absorber assembly from the vise.

Inspection

1. Measure the free length of the spring (**Figure 54**). Replace the spring if it has sagged to the service limit listed in **Table 2**.

2. Inspect the upper mounting bushing (**Figure 55**); replace if necessary.

3. Check the damper unit for dents, oil leakage or other damage. Make sure the damper rod is straight.

> *WARNING*
> *The shock absorber body and remote reservoir contain highly compressed nitrogen gas. Do not tamper with or attempt to open the damper unit or disconnect the reservoir hose from either unit. Do not place it near an open*

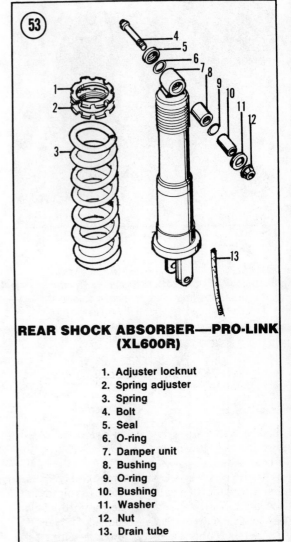

REAR SHOCK ABSORBER—PRO-LINK (XL600R)

1. Adjuster locknut
2. Spring adjuster
3. Spring
4. Bolt
5. Seal
6. O-ring
7. Damper unit
8. Bushing
9. O-ring
10. Bushing
11. Washer
12. Nut
13. Drain tube

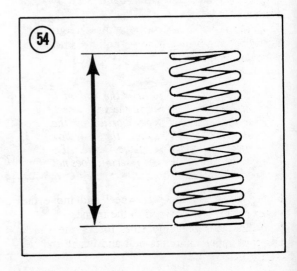

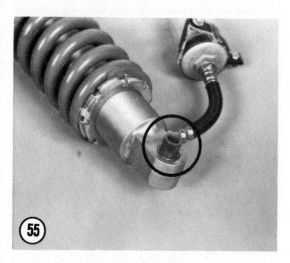

flame or other extreme heat. Do not dispose of the damper assembly yourself. Take it to a dealer where it can be deactivated and disposed of properly. Never attempt to remove the valve core in the base of the reservoir.

NOTE
The damper unit cannot be rebuilt; it must be replaced as a unit.

Installation

1. The rear wheel must be in the same raised position as it was in Step 15 of *Removal*. Refer to **Figure 47**.
2. Position the shock absorber assembly in the frame with the hose to the remote reservoir toward the front. This will position the threaded side of the lower mount on the left-hand side.
3. Install the shock absorber lower mounting bolt (**Figure 46**) from the right-hand side. Do not tighten at this time.
4. Apply a coat of molybdenum disulfide grease to the upper mounting bushing and the mounting yoke on the frame.

NOTE
The next step requires the aid of a helper. While lowering the rear wheel, make sure the upper portion of the shock absorber clears the air box mounting brackets of the frame. Also make sure the remote reservoir does not get damaged.

5. Slowely lower the rear wheel and move the upper mount into position in the frame.
6. From the right-hand side, install the shock absorber upper mounting bolt and install the nut (B, **Figure 45**).

7. Tighten the upper mounting bolt and nut and the lower mounting bolt to the torque specifications listed in **Table 1**.

WARNING
*All bolts and nuts used on the Pro-Link suspension must be replaced with parts of the same type. Do **not** use a replacement part of lesser quality or substitute design, as this may affect the performance of the system or result in failure of the part which will lead to loss of control of the bike. Torque values listed must be used during installation to assure proper retention of these parts.*

8. Position the remote reservoir in the frame and install the bolt (A, **Figure 45**) securing the remote reservoir to the frame. Tighten the bolt securely.
9. Remove the wood block(s) from under the engine. Push down on the rear of the bike and make sure the rear suspension is operating properly.
10. Rest the bike on the side stand.
11. From the left-hand side, install the air cleaner air box into the frame. Install the top bolts and the bolt on the right-hand side (**Figure 44**). Make sure the clamping band on the portion going to the carburetor(s) is tight.
12. On XR350R models, connect the electrical connector to the rear brake light switch and move the wires back into position.
13. On 1983 XR500R and XL600R models, perform the following:
   a. Move the electrical wires back into position and secure them with the cable clamp.
   b. Install the regulator to the air box and secure with the bolt (**Figure 43**).
   c. Connect the electrical connector to the regulator.
14. Install the muffler, fuel tank, seat and both side covers.

PIVOT ARM ASSEMBLY (PRO-LINK)

Removal/Inspection/Installation

Refer to **Figure 56** for this procedure.
1. Remove the shock absorber as described in this chapter.
2. Remove the shock arm pivot bolt (A, **Figure 57**).
3. From the lower portion of the frame, remove the bolt and nut securing the shock link to the frame (B, **Figure 57**).

10

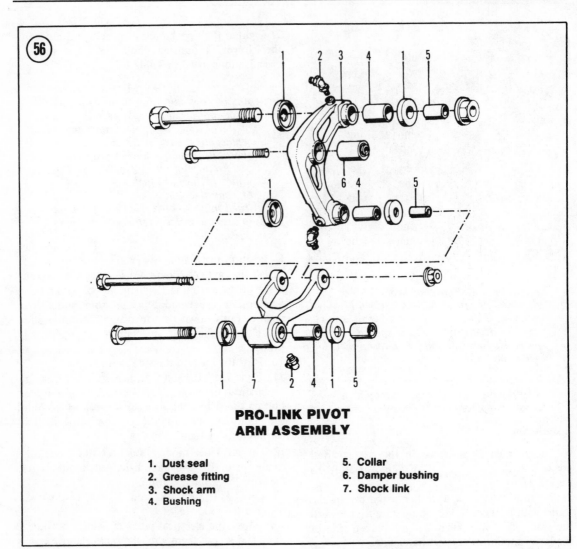

**PRO-LINK PIVOT
ARM ASSEMBLY**

1. Dust seal
2. Grease fitting
3. Shock arm
4. Bushing
5. Collar
6. Damper bushing
7. Shock link

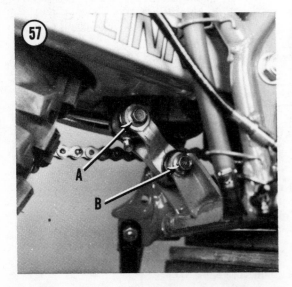

4. Remove the bolt (**Figure 58**) securing the shock arm to the swing arm.

5. Remove the pivot arm assembly.

6. Inspect both arms for cracks or damage; replace as necessary.

7. Remove the dust seals at all pivot points and push out the bushings.

8. Clean all parts in solvent and thoroughly dry with compressed air.

9. Inspect the bushings and the area in both arms where the bushings ride. The sintered metal bushings should last for a long time but should be inspected periodically for wear. There are no factory specifications for dimensions for the bushings nor the bushing receptacles in the arms.

10. Inspect the dust seals. Replace all of them as a set if any are worn or starting to deteriorate. If the dust seals are in poor condition they will allow dirt to enter into the pivot areas and cause the bushings to wear.

11. Coat all surfaces of the pivot receptacles, the bushings and the inside of the dust seals with molybdenum disulfide grease. Insert the bushings into the shock link and shock arm and install the dust seals.

12. Install the shock arm onto the swing arm and install the bolt from the right-hand side (**Figure 58**). Tighten the bolt to the torque specification listed in **Table 1**.

13. Install the shock link onto the frame and install the pivot bolt (B, **Figure 57**) in from the right-hand side. Install the nut and tighten to the torque specification listed in **Table 1**.

14. Make sure the dust seals are installed on the shock arm. Move the shock link up into position with the shock arm and install the shock arm pivot bolt (A, **Figure 57**) from the right-hand side. Install the nut and tighten to the torque specifications listed in **Table 1**.

15. Install the shock absorber as described in this chapter.

Table 1 REAR SUSPENSION TORQUE SPECIFICATIONS

Item	ft.-lb.	N•m
Rear axle nut		
Dual shock.	51-80	70-110
Pro-Link		
1981	51-80	70-110
1982-1983	58-80	80-110
Rear swing arm	51-72	70-100
Shock absorber		
Dual shock		
Upper	6-10	8-14
Lower	22-36	30-50
Pro-Link		
Upper	43-54	60-75
Lower	27-35	38-48
Pro-Link linkage		
XR350R, 1983 XR500R, XL600R		
Shock arm to swing arm pivot bolt	65-87	90-120
Shock link to frame pivot bolt	29-36	40-50
Shock arm to shock link pivot bolt	29-36	40-50
All other models		
Shock arm to swing arm pivot bolt	65-87	90-120
Shock link to frame pivot bolt	43-54	60-75
Shock arm to shock link pivot bolt	43-54	60-75

10

Table 2 REAR SHOCK SPRING FREE LENGTH

Model	Service limit	
	mm	in.
XL250S	320.5	12.61
XL250R	244.0	9.56
XR250R	219	8.62
XR250	339	13.3
XR350R	264.8	10.43
XR500	332	13.1
XL500S	321.8	12.7
XL500R	248.5	9.78
XR500R		
1981-1982	219	8.6
1983	264.5	10.41
XL600R	273	10.75

Table 3 REAR SHOCK SPRING PRE-LOAD STANDARD DIMENSION

Model	mm	in.
XL250R	241	9.5
XR250R	212.6	8.4
XR350R	255.1	10.04
XL500R	241	9.49
XR500R		
1981-1982	212.6	8.4
1983	255	10.1
XL600R	265	10.43

CHAPTER ELEVEN

BRAKES

The front brake on the 1983 XR500R and XL600R is a disc type. The front brake on all other models as well as the rear brake on all models is a drum type.

Table 1 contains specifications for both the drum and disc brakes. **Table 1** and **Table 2** are located at the end of this chapter.

DRUM BRAKES

The front brake on the XR250R and 1981-1982 XR500R models is a double leading shoe type. All other models are of the single leading shoe type.

Figure 1 illustrates the major parts of the brake assembly. Activating the brake lever or pedal pulls the lever which in turn rotates the camshaft. This forces the brake shoes out into contact with the brake drum.

Lever and pedal free play must be maintained on both brakes to minimize premature brake wear and maximize braking effectiveness. Refer to Chapter Three for complete adjustment procedures.

Each drum brake assembly is equipped with wear indicators (**Figure 2**). These should be inspected frequently, especially if riding in competition. When the two arrows align it is time to replace the brake linings.

The brake cables must be inspected and replaced periodically as they stretch with use and can no longer be properly adjusted.

FRONT DRUM BRAKE

Disassembly

1. Remove the front wheel as described in Chapter Nine.

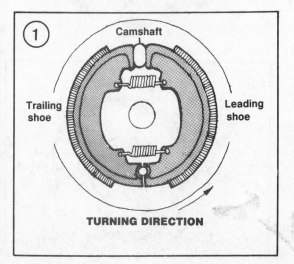

(1)

Camshaft

Trailing shoe

Leading shoe

TURNING DIRECTION

(2)

11

2. Pull the brake assembly straight up and out of the brake drum.

> *NOTE*
> *Prior to removing the brake shoes from the backing plate, measure them as described under **Inspection** in this chapter.*

3A. On double leading shoe models, remove the cotter pins and flat washers on both brake camshafts.
3B. On single leading shoe models, remove the cotter pin and flat washer (**Figure 3**).
4. Place a clean shop cloth on the linings to protect them from oil and grease during removal.
5. Remove the brake shoes from the backing plate by pulling up on the center of each shoe as shown in **Figure 4**.
6. Remove the return springs and separate the brake shoes.
7. Loosen the clamp bolt on the brake lever. Remove the cam lever, lining wear indicator, return spring, dust seal and camshaft.

Inspection

1. Thoroughly clean and dry all parts except the linings.
2. Check the contact surface of the brake drum (**Figure 5**) for scoring or grooves. If there are goooves deep enough to snag a fingernail, the drum should be reground and new shoes fitted. This type of wear can be avoided to a great extent if the brakes are disassembled and thoroughly cleaned after riding in the water, mud or deep sand.

> *NOTE*
> *If oil or grease is on the drum surface, clean it off with a clean rag soaked in lacquer thinner—do not use a solvent that will leave an oil residue.*

3. Use vernier calipers and check the inside diameter of the drum for out-of-round or excessive wear (**Figure 6**). Replace the drum if it is worn to the service limit listed in **Table 1**.
4. If the drum is turned, the linings will have to be replaced and the new linings arced to conform to the new drum contour.
5. Inspect the linings for imbedded foreign material. Dirt can be removed with a stiff wire brush. Check for traces of oil or grease. If they are contaminated, they must be replaced.
6. Measure the brake linings with vernier calipers (**Figure 7**). They should be replaced if worn to within 0.08 in. (2 mm) of the metal backing plate.

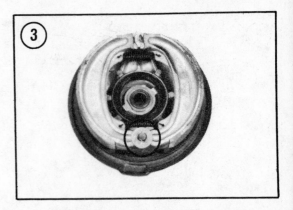

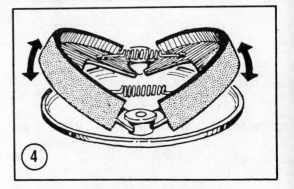

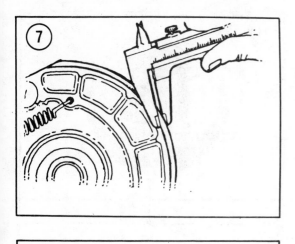

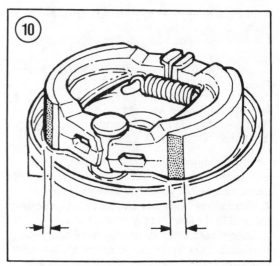

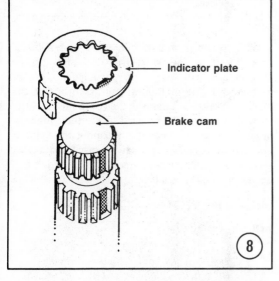

Indicator plate

Brake cam

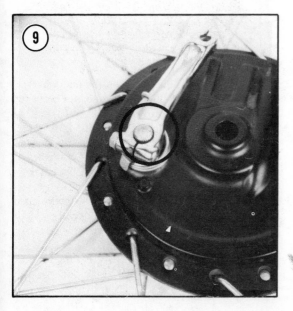

7. Inspect the cam lobe(s) for wear and corrosion. Minor roughness can be removed with fine emery cloth.

8. Inspect the bearing surface for the camshaft(s) in the backing plate. If it is worn or damaged the backing plate must be replaced. The camshaft(s) should also be replaced at the same time.

9. Inspect the brake shoe return springs for wear. If they are stretched, they will not fully retract the brake shoes from the drum, resulting in a power-robbing drag on the drums and premature wear of the linings. Replace as necessary and always replace as a pair.

Assembly

1. Assemble the brake by reversing the disassembly steps, noting the following.

2. Grease the camshaft(s) with a light coat of molybdenum disulfide grease. Avoid getting any grease on the brake plate where the linings come in contact with it.

3. Install the return spring and wear indicator. Be sure to install the wear indicator correctly onto the camshaft as shown in **Figure 8**.

4. When installing the brake lever(s) onto the brake camshaft(s), be sure to align the 2 parts with the punch marks (**Figure 9**).

5. Hold the brake shoes in a "V" formation with the return springs attached and snap them in place on the brake backing plate. Make sure they are firmly seated on it.

NOTE
If new linings are being installed, file off the leading edge of each shoe a little (Figure 10) so that the brake will not grab when applied.

11

6. Install the brake panel assembly into the brake drum.

7. Install the front wheel as described in Chapter Nine.

8. Adjust the front brake as described in Chapter Three.

Brake Arm, Brake Cam and Connecting Rod Replacement (1981-1982 XR250R and XR500R)

Refer to **Figure 11** for this procedure.

1. Remove the front brake assembly and remove the brake shoes as described in this chapter.

2. Remove the bolts and nuts securing brake arm "A" and "B" to each brake cam.

3. Loosen both locknuts on the connecting rod.

4. Remove both brake arms and connecting rod.

5. Unscrew the brake arms from the connecting rod.

6. Assemble by reversing these disassembly steps, noting the following.

7. Align the punch marks on the brake cams and the brake arms and tighten the bolts and nuts to 6-9 ft.-lb. (8-12 N•m).

> *NOTE*
> *After the brake arms and connecting rod have been removed or replaced they have to be adjusted as follows.*

8. Loosen both other connecting rod locknuts.

9. Place a clean shop cloth on the brake shoes. With your hands, push both brake shoes together until they are tight against both brake camshafts, with no free play.

10. Turn the connecting rod as indicated by direction "C" until there is free play between the connecting rod and the brake arm.

11. Now turn the connecting rod as indicated by direction "D" to just the point where the free play disappears (not any further).

12. Tighten the locknuts securely and recheck the free play. Readjust if necessary.

13. Remove the shop coth and make sure that both brake cams are parallel to each other. If not, repeat this procedure until correct.

14. Move the brake lever and make sure that both brake arm "A" and "B" start to move at the same time.

FRONT DISC BRAKE

The front disc brake is actuated by hydraulic fluid and is controlled by a hand lever on the master cylinder. As the brake pads wear, the brake fluid level drops in the reservoir and automatically adjusts for wear.

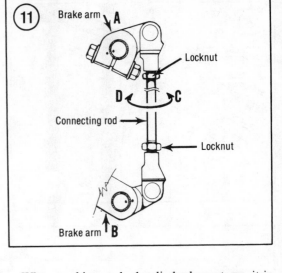

When working on hydraulic brake systems, it is necessary that the work area and all tools be absolutely clean. Any tiny particles of foreign matter and grit in the caliper assembly or the master cylinder can damage the components. Also, sharp tools must not be used inside the caliper or on the piston. If there is any doubt about your ability to correctly and safely carry out major service on the brake components, take the job to a dealer or brake specialist.

FRONT MASTER CYLINDER

Removal/Installation

> *CAUTION*
> *Cover the fuel tank and front fender with a heavy cloth or plastic tarp to protect them from accidental brake fluid spills. Wash brake fluid off any painted or plated surfaces immediately, as it will destroy the finish. Use soapy water and rinse completely.*

1. Slide back the rubber boot on the hand lever.

2. Remove the bolt (**Figure 12**) and nut securing the hand lever and remove the lever.

3A. On XR500R models, unscrew the brake hose (A, **Figure 13**) from the fitting on the master cylinder and remove the brake hose. Tie the brake hose up and cover the end to prevent the entry of foreign matter.

3B. On XR600L models, unscrew the brake hose from the master cylinder and remove the brake hose. Tie the brake hose up and cover the end to prevent the entry of foreign matter.

4. Remove the clamping bolts (B, **Figure 13**) and clamp securing the master cylinder to the handlebar and remove the master cylinder.

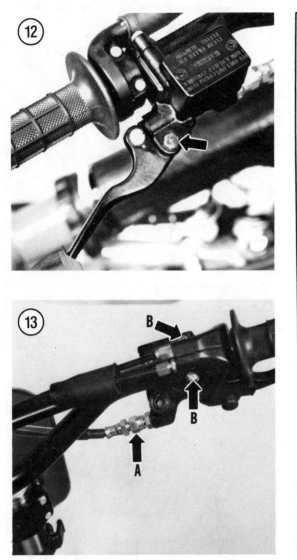

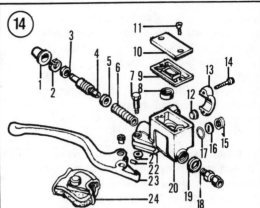

FRONT MASTER CYLINDER

1. Rubber boot	13. Clamp
2. Circlip	14. Bolt
3. Secondary cup	15. Viewing port
4. Piston	16. Window
5. Primary cup	17. O-ring
6. Spring	18. Fitting
7. Bolt	19. Sealing washer
8. Separator	20. Body
9. Diaphagm	21. Nut
10. Cover	22. Pin
11. Screw	23. Hand lever
12. Plug	24. Rubber boot

5. Install by reversing these removal steps, noting the following.

6. On XL600R models, install the clamp with the "UP" mark facing up.

7. Tighten the upper clamping bolt first then the lower. Tighten the bolts securely.

8A. On XR500R models, install the brake hose onto the fitting on the master cylinder. Tighten the hose securely.

NOTE
If the fitting was removed from the master cylinder, install a new sealing washer between the fitting and the master cylinder.

8B. On XL600R models, install the sealing washer and brake hose onto the master cylinder. Tighten the hose securely.

9. Refill the master cylinder with DOT 4 brake fluid from a sealed can. Bleed the brake system as described in this chapter.

Disassembly

Refer to **Figure 14** for this procedure.

1. Remove the master cylinder as described in this chapter.

2. Remove the screws securing the cover and remove the cover and diaphragm; pour out the brake fluid and discard it. *Never reuse brake fluid.*

11

3. Remove the rubber boot from the area where the hand lever actuates the internal piston.

4. Using circlip pliers, remove the internal circlip from the body.

5. Remove the piston assembly.

6. Remove the spring.

7. On XR500R models, remove the fitting and sealing washer from the body.

Inspection

1. Clean all parts in denatured alcohol or fresh brake fluid. Inspect the cylinder bore and piston contact surfaces for signs of wear and damage. If either part is less than perfect, replace it.

2. Check the end of the piston for wear caused by the hand lever. Replace the piston assembly if either cup is worn or damaged.

3. Inspect the pivot hole in the master cylinder body. If worn or elongated the master cylinder body must be replaced.

4. Make sure the passages in the bottom of the brake fluid reservoir are clear. Check the reservoir cap and diaphragm for damage and deterioration and replace as necessary.

5. Inspect the threads in the bore for the fitting.

6. Check the hand lever pivot lug for cracks or excessive wear to the pivot bore.

7. Measure the cylinder bore (**Figure 15**). Replace the master cylinder if the bore exceeds the service limit listed in **Table 1**.

8. Measure the outside diameter of the piston assembly as shown in **Figure 16** with a micrometer. Replace the piston assembly if it is less than the service limit listed in **Table 1**.

Assembly

1. Soak the new piston assembly in fresh brake fluid for at least 15 minutes to make the cups pliable. Coat the inside of the cylinder with fresh brake fluid prior to the assembly of parts.

2. Install the spring with the tapered end facing toward the piston assembly.

> *CAUTION*
> *When installing the piston assembly, do not allow the cups to turn inside out as they will be damaged and allow brake fluid leakage within the cylinder bore.*

3. Install the piston assembly into the master cylinder.

4. Install the circlip and make sure it is seated properly in the groove. Slide in the rubber boot.

5. Install a new sealing washer and the fitting. Tighten the fitting securely.

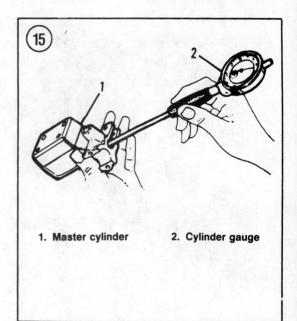

1. Master cylinder   2. Cylinder gauge

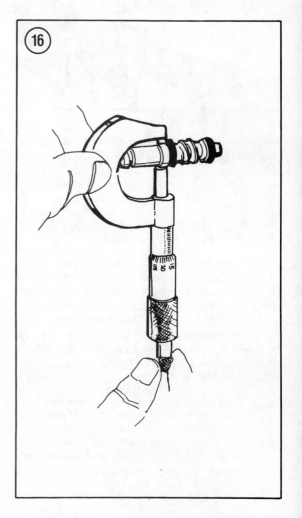

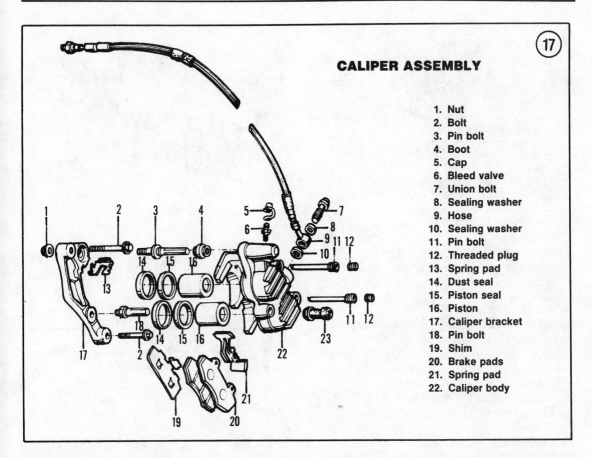

CALIPER ASSEMBLY

1. Nut
2. Bolt
3. Pin bolt
4. Boot
5. Cap
6. Bleed valve
7. Union bolt
8. Sealing washer
9. Hose
10. Sealing washer
11. Pin bolt
12. Threaded plug
13. Spring pad
14. Dust seal
15. Piston seal
16. Piston
17. Caliper bracket
18. Pin bolt
19. Shim
20. Brake pads
21. Spring pad
22. Caliper body

6. Install the diaphragm and cover. Do not tighten the cover screws at this time as fluid will have to be added later.

7. Install the master cylinder as described in this chapter.

FRONT DISC BRAKE PAD REPLACEMENT

There is no recommended mileage interval for changing the friction pads in the disc brake. Pad wear depends greatly on riding habits and conditions. The pads should be checked for wear every 6 months and replaced when the wear indicator reaches the edge of the brake disc. To maintain an even brake pressure on the disc always replace both pads in the caliper at the same time.

CAUTION
Watch the pads more closely when the pads wear close to the wear line. If pad wear happens to be uneven for some reason the backing plate may come in contact with the disc and cause damage.

Refer to **Figure 17** for this procedure.

1. Place wood blocks under the skid plate to support the bike securely with the front wheel off the ground.

2. Remove the threaded plugs (**Figure 18**) from the caliper body.

3. Loosen the pin bolts (A, **Figure 19**) but do not remove them at this time.

4. Remove the bolts (B, **Figure 19**) securing the caliper assembly to the front fork. Remove the caliper assembly from the disc.

5. Completely unscrew the pin bolts.

6. Remove both brake pads and shims.

7. Clean the pad recess and the end of the pistons with a soft brush. Do not use solvent, a wire brush or any hard tool which would damage the cylinders or the pistons.

8. Carefully remove any rust or corrosion from the disc.

9. Lightly coat the end of the pistons, the pin bolts and the backs of the new pads (*not the friction material*) with disc brake lubricant.

NOTE
When purchasing new pads, check with your dealer to make sure the friction compound of the new pad is compatible

11

with the disc material. Remove any roughness from the backs of the new pads with a fine-cut file; blow them clean with compressed air.

10. When new pads are installed in the caliper the master cylinder brake fluid level will rise as the caliper pistons are repositioned. Clean the top of the master cylinder of all dirt and foreign matter. Remove the cap and diaphragm from the master cylinder and slowly push the caliper pistons into the caliper. Constantly check the reservoir to make sure brake fluid does not overflow. Remove fluid, if necessary, prior to it overflowing. The caliper pistons should move freely. If they don't, and there is evidence of them sticking in the cylinders, the caliper should be removed and serviced as described under *Caliper Rebuilding* in this chapter.

11. Push the caliper pistons in all the way to allow room for the new pads.

12. Install the anti-rattle spring (A, **Figure 20**).

14. Install the shim into the caliper (B, **Figure 20**).

15. Install the outboard pad into the caliper (**Figure 21**).

16. Install the inboard pad into the caliper (**Figure 22**).

17. Push both pads against the anti-rattle spring, then insert one of the pin bolts (**Figure 23**).

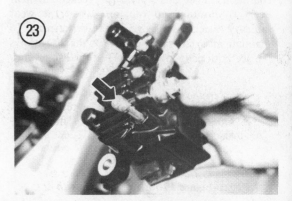

18. Install the other pin bolt (**Figure 24**).
19. Tighten the pin bolts hand-tight at this time.
20. Carefully install the caliper assembly onto the disc. Be careful not to damage the leading edge of the pads during installation.
21. Install the caliper mounting bolts and tighten to the torque specification listed in **Table 2**.
22. Tighten the pin bolts securely and install the threaded plugs. Tighten the threaded plugs securely.
23. Spin the front wheel and activate the brake lever as many times as it takes to refill the cylinder in the caliper and correctly locate the pads.

WARNING
Use brake fluid clearly marked DOT 4 from a sealed container. Other types may vaporize and cause brake failure. Always use the same brand name; do not intermix as many brands are not compatible.

24. Refill the master cylinder reservoir, if necessary, to maintain the correct fluid level. Install the diaphragm and top cap.

WARNING
Do not ride the bike until you are sure the brake is operating correctly with full

hydraulic advantage. If necessary, bleed the brake as described in this chapter.

25. Bed the pads in gradually for the first 10 days of riding by using only light pressure as much as possible. Immediate hard application will glaze the new friction pads and greatly reduce the effectiveness of the brake.

FRONT DISC BRAKE CALIPER

Removal/Installation

Refer to **Figure 17** for this procedure.

CAUTION
Do not spill any brake fluid on the painted portion of the fork or wheel. Wash any spilled brake fluid immediately, as it will destroy the finish. Use soapy water and rinse completely.

1. Place wood block(s) under the skid plate to support the bike with the front wheel off the ground.
2. Clean the top of the master cylinder of all dirt and foreign matter. Loosen the cap on the master cylinder. This will allow the brake fluid to drain out more quickly in the next step.
3. Place a container under the brake line at the caliper. Remove the union bolt and sealing washers (A, **Figure 25**) securing the brake hose (XR500R) or metal brake line (XL600R) to the caliper assembly. Remove the brake hose or brake line and let the brake fluid drain out into the container. Dispose of this brake fluid—never reuse brake fluid. To prevent the entry of moisture and dirt, cap the end of the brake line and tie the loose end up to the front fork.
4. Remove the bolts securing the caliper assembly to the front fork (B, **Figure 25**). Push on the caliper while loosening the bolts to push the pistons back into the caliper.
5. Remove the caliper assembly.
6. Install by reversing these removal steps, noting the following.
7. Carefully install the caliper assembly onto the disc. Be careful not to damage the leading edge of the pads during installation.
8. Tighten the caliper mounting bolts to the torque specification listed in **Table 2**.
9. Install the brake hose or brake line, with a sealing washer on each side of the fitting, onto the caliper. Install the union bolt and tighten to the torque specification listed in **Table 2**.
10. Spin the front wheel and activate the brake lever as many times as it takes to refill the cylinder in the caliper and correctly locate the pads.

11

WARNING
Use brake fluid clearly marked DOT 4
from a sealed container. Other types
may vaporize and cause brake failure.
Always use the same brand name; do
not intermix as many brands are not
compatible.

11. Refill the master cylinder reservoir, if necessary, to maintain the correct fluid level. Install the diaphragm and cap.

WARNING
Do not ride the bike until you are sure
the brake is operating correctly with full
hydraulic advantage.

12. Bleed the brake as described in this chapter.

Caliper Rebuilding

If the caliper leaks, the caliper should be rebuilt. If the pistons stick in the cylinders, indicating severe wear or galling, the entire unit should be replaced. Rebuilding a leaky caliper requires special tools and experience.

Caliper service should be entrusted to a dealer, motorcycle repair shop or brake specialist. Considerable money can be saved by removing the caliper yourself and taking it in for repair.

FRONT DISC BRAKE HOSE REPLACEMENT

There is no factory-recommended replacement interval but it is a good idea to replace the flexible brake hose(s) every 4 years or when it shows signs of cracking or damage.

The hose routing and type vary among the various models. This procedure is shown in a XR500R. Where differences occur they are identified.

CAUTION
Cover the front wheel, fender and fuel
tank with a heavy cloth or plastic tarp
to protect it from accidental spilling of
brake fluid. Wash brake fluid off of any
painted or plated surface immediately,
as it will destroy the finish. Use soapy
water and rinse completely.

1. Place wood block(s) under the skid plate to support the bike with the front wheel off the ground.
2. Clean the top of the master cylinder of all dirt and foreign matter. Loosen the cap on the master cylinder. This will allow the brake fluid to drain out more quickly in the next step.

3A. On XR500R models, place a container under the brake hose at the caliper. Remove the union bolt and sealing washers (A, **Figure 25**) securing the brake hose to the caliper assembly. Remove the brake hose and let the brake fluid drain out into the container.
3B. On XL600R models, place a container where the lower flexible brake hose attaches to the metal brake line. Unscrew the lower flexible brake hose from the metal brake line. Remove the lower flexible brake hose and let the brake fluid drain out into the container.
4. To prevent the entry of moisture and dirt, cap the end of the brake line and tie the loose end up to the front fork.

WARNING
Dispose of this brake fluid—never reuse
brake fluid. Contaminated brake fluid
can cause brake failure.

5. Remove the clamping bolts securing the brake hose to the fork slider (**Figure 26**).

NOTE
On XL600R models, the brake hose is
attached to the backside of the front
fork slider.

6A. On XR500R models, perform the following:
   a. Disconnect the brake hose from the fitting on the master cylinder (**Figure 27**).
   b. Pull the hose up and out of the retaining loops on the left-hand fork leg and remove the hose.
6B. On XL600R models, perform the following:
   a. Remove the screw securing the upper metal brake line to the lower fork bridge.

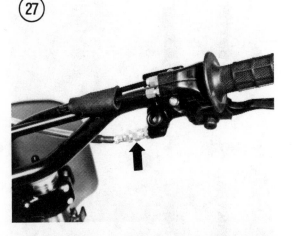

b. Pull the upper metal brake line out to the left a little and unscrew the lower flexible brake hose from the upper metal brake line.

c. Disconnect the upper flexible brake hose from the master cylinder.

d. Disconnect the upper flexible brake hose from the upper metal brake line.

7. Install a new hose(s), sealing washers and union bolts in the reverse order of removal. Be sure to install new sealing washers in the correct positions.

8. Tighten all union bolts to the torque specifications listed in **Table 2**.

9. Refill the master cylinder with fresh brake fluid clearly marked DOT 4 only. Bleed the brake as described in this chapter.

WARNING
Do not ride the bike until you are sure that the brakes are operating properly.

FRONT BRAKE DISC

Removal/Installation

1. Remove the front wheel as described in Chapter Nine.

NOTE
Place a piece of wood or vinyl tube in the caliper in place of the disc. This way, if the brake lever is inadvertently squeezed the pistons will not be forced out of the cylinders. If this does happen, the caliper might have to be disassembled to reseat the pistons and the system will have to be bled. By using the wood, bleeding the system is not necessary when installing the wheel.

2. Remove the nuts (**Figure 28**) securing the brake disc to the hub assembly.

3. Install by reversing these removal steps, noting the following.

4. Install and tighten the disc mounting nuts to the torque specification listed in **Table 2**.

Brake Disc Inspection

It is not necessary to remove the disc from the wheel to inspect it. Small marks on the disc are not important, but radial scratches deep enough to snag a fingernail reduce braking effectiveness and increase brake pad wear. If these grooves are found, the disc should be replaced.

1. Measure the thickness of the disc at several locations around the disc with vernier calipers or micrometer (**Figure 29**). The disc must be replaced if the thickness, in any area, is less than the service limit listed in **Table 1**.

11

2. Clean the disc of any rust or corrosion and wipe clean with lacquer thinner. Never use an oil based solvent that may leave an oil residue on the disc.

BLEEDING THE SYSTEM

This procedure is not necessary unless the brakes feel spongy, there has been a leak in the system, a component has been replaced or the brake fluid has been replaced.

1. Remove the dust cap from the bleed valve on the caliper.
2. Connect a length of clear tubing to the bleed valve on the caliper (**Figure 30**). Place the other end of the tube into a clean container. Fill the container with enough fresh brake fluid to keep the end submerged. The tube should be long enough so that a loop can be made higher than the bleed valve to prevent air from being drawn into the caliper during bleeding.

> *CAUTION*
> *Cover the front rim with a heavy cloth or plastic tarp to protect it from the accidental spilling of brake fluid. Wash brake fluid off of any painted or plated surface immediately, as it will destroy the finish. Use soapy water and rinse completely.*

3. Clean the cap of the master cylinder of all dirt and foreign matter. Remove the cap and diaphragm. Fill the reservoir almost to the top lip; insert the diaphragm and gasket and the cap loosely. Leave the cap in place during this procedure to prevent the entry of dirt.

> *NOTE*
> *Use brake fluid clearly marked DOT 4 only. Others may vaporize and cause brake failure. Always use the same brand name; do not intermix as many brands are not compatible.*

4. Slowly apply the brake lever several times. Pull the lever in and hold it in the applied position. Open the bleed valve about one-half turn. Allow the lever to travel to its limit. When this limit is reached, tighten the bleed screw.
5. As the fluid enters the system, the level will drop in the reservoir. Maintain the level at about 3/8 inch from the top of the reservoir to prevent air from being drawn into the system.
6. Continue to pump the lever and fill the reservoir until the fluid emerging from the hose is completely free of bubbles.

> *NOTE*
> *Do not allow the reservoir to empty during the bleeding operation or more air will enter the system. If this occurs, the entire procedure must be repeated.*

7. Hold the lever in and tighten the bleed valve securely. Remove the bleed tube and install the bleed valve dust cap.
8. If necessary, add fluid to correct the level in the reservoir. It should be to the upper level line.
9. Install the reservoir top and tighten securely.
10. Test the feel of the brake lever. It should be firm and should offer the same resistance each time it's operated. If it feels spongy, it is likely that there is still air in the system and it must be bled again. When all air has been bled from the system and the fluid level is correct in the reservoir, double-check for leaks and tighten all fittings and connections.

> *WARNING*
> *Before riding the bike, make certain that the brake is operating correctly by operating the lever several times.*

11. Test ride the bike slowly at first to make sure that the brakes are operating properly.

REAR BRAKE

Disassembly

1. Remove the rear wheel as described in Chapter Ten.
2. Pull the brake assembly straight up and out of the brake drum.
3. Remove the brake shoes from the backing plate by pulling up on the center of each shoe as shown in **Figure 4**.

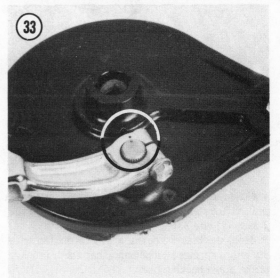

NOTE
Place a clean shop rag on the linings to protect them from oil and grease during removal.

4. Remove the return springs and separate the shoes.

5. Loosen the clamp bolt on the cam lever. Remove the cam lever, lining wear indicator, dust seal and camshaft.

Inspection

1. Thoroughly clean and dry all the parts except the linings.

2. Check the contact surface of the drum (**Figure 31**) for scoring. If there are grooves deep enough to snag a fingernail, the drum should be reground.

3. Measure the inside diameter of the brake drum with vernier calipers (**Figure 32**). Service limits are listed in **Table 1**.

4. If the drum is turned, the linings will have to be replaced and the new ones arced to the new drum contour.

5. Inspect the brake linings. The dimension for new linings, on all models, is 0.16 in. (4.0 mm). They should be replaced if worn within 0.08 in. (2.0 mm) of the metal shoe table (**Figure 7**).

6. Inspect the linings for imbedded foreign material. Dirt can be removed with a stiff wire brush. Check for any traces of oil or grease. If they are contaminated, they must be replaced.

7. Inspect the cam lobe and the pivot pin area of the shaft for wear and corrosion. Minor roughness can be removed with fine emery cloth.

8. Inspect the brake shoe return springs for wear. If they are stretched, they will not fully retrace the brake shoes and they will drag and wear out prematurely. Replace if necessary.

Assembly

1. Assemble the brake by reversing the disassembly steps.

2. Grease the shafts, cams and pivot posts with a light coat of molybdenum disulfide grease; avoid getting any grease on the brake plate where the linings may come in contact with it.

3. Install the wear indicator onto the camshaft as shown in **Figure 8**.

11

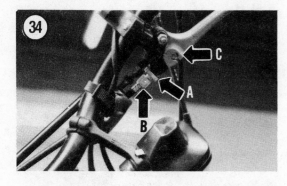

4. When installing the brake lever onto the brake camshaft, be sure to align the punch marks on the 2 parts (**Figure 33**).

5. Hold the brake shoes in a "V" formation with the return springs attached and snap them in place in the brake backing plate.

> *NOTE*
> *If new linings are being installed, file off the leading edge of each shoe a little (**Figure 10**) so that the brake will not grab when applied.*

6. Install the rear wheel as described in Chapter Ten.

7. Adjust the rear brake as described in Chapter Three.

BRAKE CABLE

Brake cable adjustment should be checked periodically as the cables stretch out with use and increase brake lever free play. Free play is the distance that the brake lever or pedal travels between the released position and the point when the brake shoes come in contact with the drum.

If brake adjustment as described in Chapter Three can no longer be achieved, the cable(s) must be replaced.

Front Cable Replacement (Drum Brake Only)

1. At the hand lever, loosen the locknut (A, **Figure 34**) and turn the adjuster barrel (B, **Figure 34**) all the way toward the cable sheath.

2. At the brake assembly, loosen the locknut (A, **Figure 35**) and back off the adjuster (B, **Figure 35**) all the way toward the cable sheath.

3. Push up on the brake arm and slip the end of the cable out (C, **Figure 34**).

4. Pull the hand lever all the way back to the grip, remove the cable nipple holder and remove the cable from the lever.

5. Remove the cable from the cable retainer on the front fork and the cable guides (**Figure 36**).

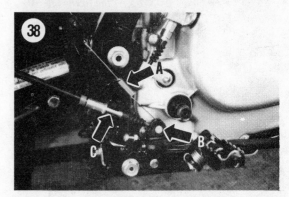

NOTE
Prior to removal of the cable, make a drawing of the routing of the cable through the frame. It is very easy to forget how it was once it has been removed. Replace it exactly as it was, avoiding any sharp turns.

6. Install by reversing these removal steps.
7. Adjust the brake as described in Chapter Three.

Rear Cable Replacement

1. At the brake assembly, remove the adjusting nut and cable retainer (A, **Figure 37**) from the brake arm.
2. At the brake pedal, remove the brakelight switch spring (A, **Figure 38**) from the cable end.

3. Remove the cable and retainer (B, **Figure 38**) from the brake pedal.
4. Pull the rear end of the cable out from the guide on the swing arm (B, **Figure 37**) and frame guide (C, **Figure 38**).

NOTE
Prior to removal of the cable, make a drawing of the routing of the cable through the frame. It is very easy to forget how it was once it has been removed. Replace it exactly as it was, avoiding any sharp turns.

5. Install by reversing these removal steps.
6. Adjust the brake as described in Chapter Three.

Tables are on the following page.

11

Table 1 BRAKE SPECIFICATIONS

	Standard	Service Limit
DRUM BRAKES		
Front brake drum ID		
XL250S, XR250R, XR250, XR500, XL500S	140.1 mm (5.15 in.)	141.0 mm (5.55 in.)
XL250R, XR350R, XL500R, XR500R	130.0 mm (5.12 in.)	131.0 mm (5.16 in.)
Rear brake drum ID		
XL250S, XL250R, XR250, XR350R	110.0 mm (4.33 in.)	111.0 mm (4.37 in.)
XR250R, XR500, XL500S, XL500R, XR500R, XR500R, XL600R	130.0 mm (5.21 in.)	131.0 mm (5.20 in.)
Brake shoe thickness	4.0 mm (0.16 in.)	2.0 mm (0.08 in.)
FRONT DISC BRAKE		
Master cylinder		
1983 XR500R		
ID	12.7-12.743 mm (0.5000-0.5017 in.)	12.755 mm (0.5022 in.)
Piston OD	12.657-12.684 mm (0.4983-0.4994 in.)	12.640 mm (0.4976 in.)
XL600R		
ID	12.7-12.743 mm (0.5000-0.5017 in.)	12.755 mm (0.5022 in.)
Piston OD	12.716-12.743 mm (0.5006-0.5017 in.)	12.640 mm (0.4976 in.)
Caliper		
1983 XR500R		
ID	25.400-25.405 mm (1.000-1.0002 in.)	25.45 mm (1.002 in.)
Piston OD	25.318-25.368 mm (0.9968-0.9987 in.)	25.30 mm (0.9996 in.)
XR600R		
ID	25.40-25.45 mm (1.000-1.002 in.)	25.30 mm (0.9661 in.)
Piston OD	25.3-25.40 mm (0.999-1.000 in.)	25.45 mm (1.002 in.)
Brake disc		
Thickness	3.5 mm (0.14 in.)	3.0 mm (0.12 in.)
Runout	–	0.30 mm (0.012 in.)

Table 2 DISC BRAKE TORQUE SPECIFICATIONS

Item	ft.-lb.	N•m
Caliper mounting bolts	15-22	20-30
Pin bolts	11-15	15-20
Union bolts	22-29	30-40

INDEX

12

NOTES

NOTES

NOTES

1978-1980 XR250 & XR500

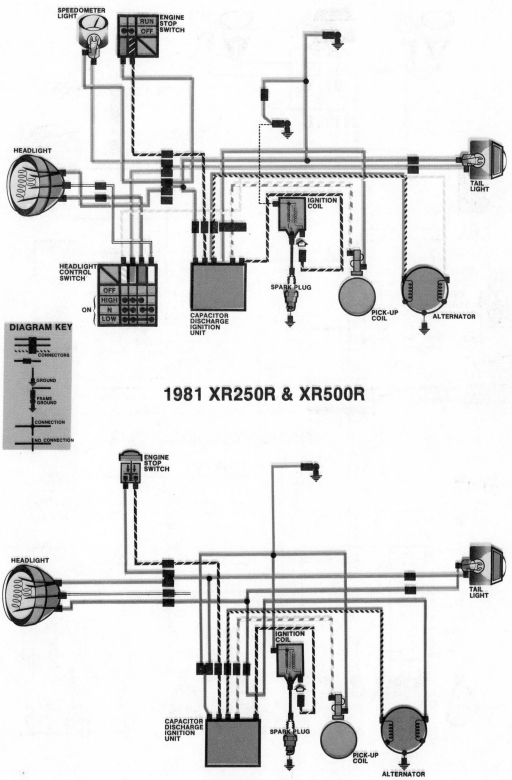

1981 XR250R & XR500R

1978-1981 XL250S & XL500S

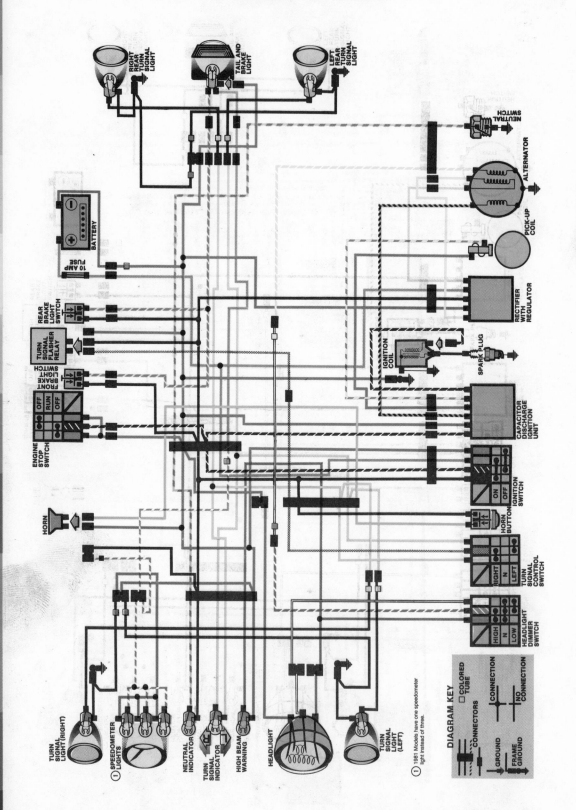

1982-1983 XL250R & 1982 XL500R

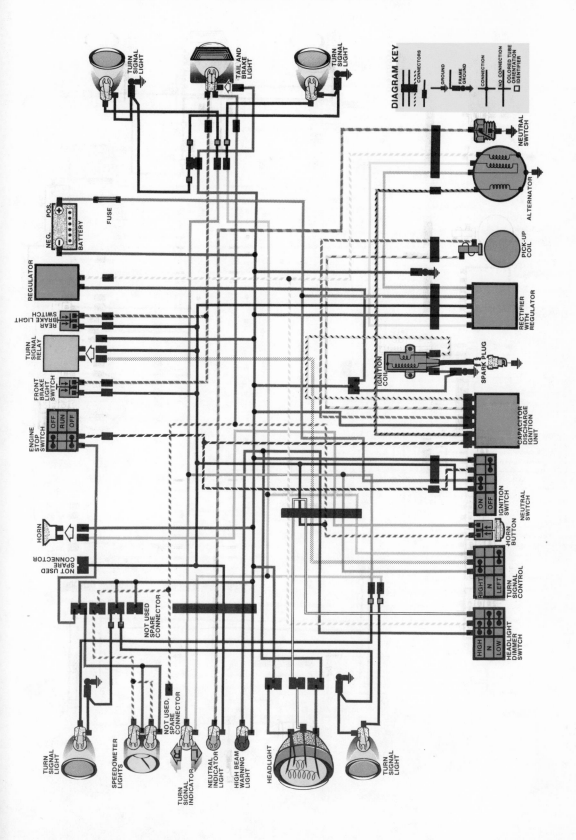

1983 XL600R

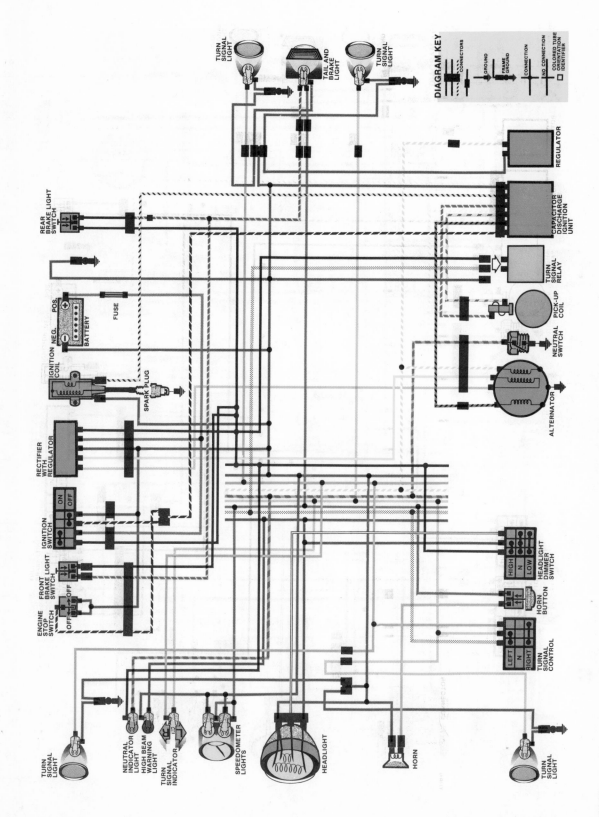

1983 XR350R

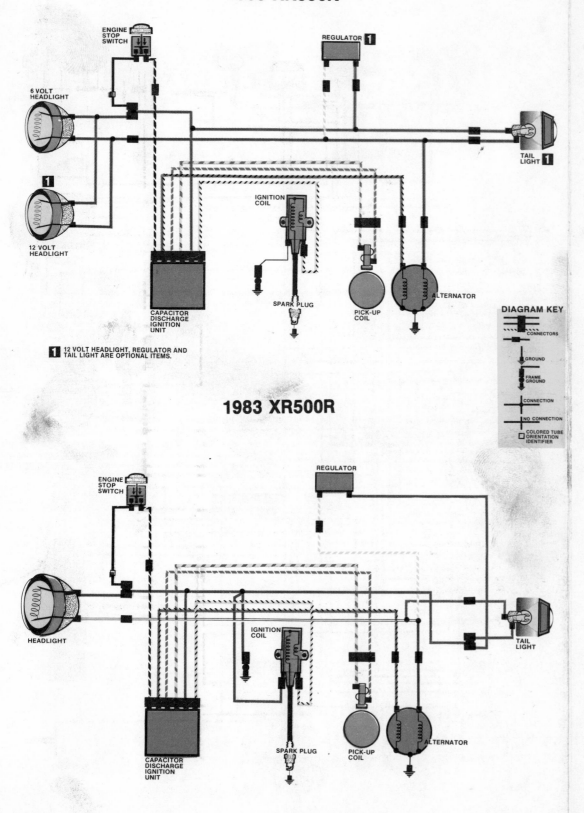

ENGINE
STOP
SWITCH

REGULATOR 1

6 VOLT
HEADLIGHT

1

12 VOLT
HEADLIGHT

IGNITION
COIL

TAIL
LIGHT 1

SPARK PLUG

PICK-UP
COIL

ALTERNATOR

CAPACITOR
DISCHARGE
IGNITION
UNIT

1 12 VOLT HEADLIGHT, REGULATOR AND
TAIL LIGHT ARE OPTIONAL ITEMS.

1983 XR500R

DIAGRAM KEY

CONNECTORS

GROUND

FRAME
GROUND

CONNECTION

NO CONNECTION

COLORED TUBE
ORIENTATION
IDENTIFIER

ENGINE
STOP
SWITCH

REGULATOR

HEADLIGHT

IGNITION
COIL

TAIL
LIGHT

SPARK PLUG

PICK-UP
COIL

ALTERNATOR

CAPACITOR
DISCHARGE
IGNITION
UNIT